Bargaining for Supremacy

James R. Leutze is associate professor of
history and acting director of the Curriculum of
Peace, War, and Defense at The University of
North Carolina at Chapel Hill.

FOR THE WOMEN IN MY LIFE:

*my Mother, Kathy, Leigh,
and Miss Mary Jane*

LEUTZE, James R. **Bargaining for supremacy: Anglo-American naval collaboration, 1937–1941.** North Carolina, 1977. 328p bibl index 77-669. 17.95 ISBN 0-8078-1305-2. C.I.P.

CHOICE   FEB. '78
History, Geography &
Travel

The story of the Anglo-American struggle for leadership during the period that preceded the American entry into World War II. Leutze (University of North Carolina) contends that long-standing naval rivalry had impeded diplomatic cooperation between the two major English-speaking nations, despite the camaraderie of World War I and decades of shared heritage. At once both a history of naval and diplomatic affairs, additional dimensions of national leadership from Roosevelt and Churchill are interwoven into this fascinating Clausewitzian drama. Although lacking illustrations or operational maps, the study includes adequate index and bibliography and highly informative footnotes, evidencing research in both American and British archives. The discussion is very important for present as well as past studies of allied cooperation and inter-operability in peace and war. Leutze's conclusion reinforces the theory that the U.S. was well into active wartime participation long before Pearl Harbor. Graduate and upper-division undergraduate level.

Bargaining for Supremacy

*Anglo-American
Naval Collaboration,
1937–1941*

by James R. Leutze

The University of North Carolina Press
Chapel Hill

Copyright © 1977 by
The University of North Carolina Press
All rights reserved
Manufactured in the United States of America
Library of Congress Catalog Card Number 77–669
ISBN 0–8078–1305–2

Library of Congress Cataloging in Publication Data

Leutze, James R   1935–
  Bargaining for Supremacy.

  Bibliography: p.
  Includes index.
  1. World War, 1939–1945—Diplomatic history.
  2. Great Britain—History, Naval—20th century.
  3. United States—History, Naval—20th century.
  4. Naval strategy.   I. Title.
  D750.L47   940.53'22.   77–669
  ISBN 0–8078–1305–2

Contents

Acknowledgments

So many people have helped me on this project that it is impossible to note them all. What I shall do, therefore, is make a deep bow toward the many colleagues, teachers, and friends who have sustained me over the years and list only those who have provided special assistance or inspiration. So to William E. Scott, Theodore Ropp, Sir B. H. Liddell Hart, Captain A. W. Clarke (RN), Vice Admiral Bernard L. Austin, Vice Admiral Brian Schofield (RN), Lieutenant General Sir Ian Jacob, William Franklin, John Semonche, Sam Williamson, Robert M. Miller, Richard Watson, George Autry, Dianne and Michael Craft, Mrs. Alfreda Kaplan, and Dean Allard and the entire staff at the Naval Archives goes my sincere and heartfelt appreciation.

I would also like to thank The University of North Carolina Research Council for its generous support.

Portions of this book have been previously published in somewhat different form under the following titles: "The Secret of the Churchill-Roosevelt Correspondence," *Journal of Contemporary History* (July 1975), and "Anglo-American Technological Cooperation, 1937–1945," *U.S. Naval Institute Proceedings* (June 1977).

Bargaining for Supremacy

I.

Introduction

This is the story of Anglo-American naval strategy and its development between 1937 and 1941. The Clausewitzean principle that war is a continuation of state policy by other means, whether accepted or not, is usually applied only to periods of actual hostilities and then only to relations between the combatants. My intention is to show that periods of strain begin before war and relations between friendly powers, especially when only one is engaged in hostilities, provide the best example of Clausewitz's principle. Naval relations between England and America ideally exemplify this thesis, for wrapped within the convoluted folds of those relations one can discern the clear outlines of England's and America's broader policies.

For England those policies were animated by a desire to survive and while doing so to maintain as much of her vigor and influence as possible. America's policies were directed toward assisting the British defeat the aggressors, but assisting in such a fashion that America would emerge from the conflict as the leading power in the Western world.

Much valuable work has already been done on the interwar period. In his authoritative two-volume work *Naval Policy between the Wars*, Captain Stephen Roskill characterizes the 1920s as "The Period of Anglo-American Antagonism" and suggests that during the pre-World War II period antagonism was overtaken by cooperation.[1] While demonstrating that naval affairs provide a study in microcosm of how wars and rumors of war can give nominally friendly powers fertile grounds for interest seeking, it is also the purpose here to examine carefully this popularly held concept of cooperation. Rather than disappearing, antagonism and rivalry seem to have continued during the entire pre-1942 period; though expressions of hostility and suspicion were muted, competition remained the dominant theme. It was a simple matter of growing interdependence. As conditions made independence less possible, a guarded alliance became more practical—a result that came only with the exchange of many assurances and much maneuvering. During the course of that maneuvering the strident rhetoric of competition was drowned out by the more disarming rhetoric of bargaining.

The most significant change in the relationship came in the spring of 1941, when the British allowed the Americans theoretical supremacy in any wartime alliance that might be established between the two countries. The military situation had deteriorated so badly by March 1941 that the British government was willing to pay that high price to get America into war, a development some expected within weeks.[2] That situation alone accounts for British willingness to allow the U.S. Navy a major role in the Atlantic/European area with a concomitant increase in America's influence in directing the war. Although they were suspicious of Britain's motives, American military strategists were eager by that time to accept the challenge. The stakes were high: leadership in the wartime coalition, with all that it implied in terms of political, diplomatic, and economic opportunity when peace came.

There is no question that the tone of naval relations between Britain and the United States became less strident, but those relations had been so acrimonious during the first eighteen years after World War I that any increase in trust would have been an improvement. Although the two navies had worked closely in 1917–1918, there was considerable anti-British sentiment in Washington among U.S. naval officers who bridled at living in the shadow of the Royal Navy and continued to dream of that much-ballyhooed "Navy second to none." At the Admiralty there was so much suspicion of America's ambition that a new naval race seemed imminent. The Washington Conference (1921–22), hailed by some as a first step toward a disarmed world, was viewed by the Admiralty as an attempt by the Americans to win by treaty (the Naval Limitation Treaty) what they had failed to win in the shipyards.[3]

Ironically, U.S. naval enthusiasts were also generally disappointed with the treaties that resulted from the conference because the treaties (1) established parity in capital ships and carriers rather than superiority as a national goal, and (2) the competition now shifted to auxiliaries, especially cruisers, which were ideally suited to Britain's and Japan's needs and for which Congress was dis-tinctly unwilling to provide funds.[4]

Most significantly, the treaties left the two major naval powers in a quandary regarding the Pacific, an ocean both considered of secondary importance. Strategically they had three options: they could grant Japan supremacy in the Pacific, accept independent responsibility for that ocean, or they could cooperate in its defense. Since true cooperation seemed unlikely, U.S. war plans called for concentrating her naval power in the Pacific, thus granting Britain supremacy in the primary theater, the Atlantic. And although these plans were tacitly accepted in the 1930s when the U.S. Navy's Scouting Force was transferred to the Pacific, they were not considered practical by all American strategists. But from 1922 to 1932 the pursuit of a "Navy second to none" became a distinctly hopeless preoccupation anyway in view of congressional parsimony.

The election of Franklin D. Roosevelt, an enthusiastic navy man, initially did little to improve Anglo-American naval relations. Because of his efforts in 1940 and 1941 to aid the British and because of his celebrated relationship with Winston Churchill, Roosevelt was popularly characterized as an uncritical friend of Great Britain. Not so. Appropriately enough, Roosevelt's role in Anglo-American naval affairs was one measure of his real attitude. When J. M. Blum suggested that Roosevelt was "always uneasy about British colonialism, always afraid of losing a round in negotiation to London, always conscious that British and American interests were not identical," he was not talking about naval affairs but the description would have been distinctly applicable.[5] That judgment remains accurate despite the fact that relations between the two countries became less strained during the mid-thirties and even more amicable during the 1937–41 period. The Vinson-Trammel Act (1934), which provided that the United States "must build and maintain a Navy of modern, under-age warships second to none, on a true and reasonable parity with the navies of rival maritime powers,"[6] was passed under Roosevelt's guidance.

Four years later in 1938 Roosevelt received authorization to increase the navy's building program by 20 percent, and in 1940 two more increments totaling 92 percent were approved. When, years later, these programs were completed the United States would have a navy superior to all. The congressional hearings on these various acts make it clear that although Japan provided much of the impetus, it was the Royal Navy that provided the standard by which America measured herself. It is also clear that some U.S. naval officers and some congressmen still questioned the wisdom of ever accepting as a national goal parity with, rather than superiority over, Great Britain.[7]

Roosevelt's ambitions for the Navy were not aimed solely at Great Britain. On the contrary, they were stimulated by the action of Japan as well as of Germany. Still, it would take an extremely shortsighted individual not to see that a concomitant effect of U.S. policy was to challenge Great Britain's long-standing naval supremacy. Roosevelt has seldom been accused of myopia regarding his country's self-interest. Indeed, although he does not emerge from this story as a totally candid, admirably courageous individual willing to take full responsibility for his actions, he does demonstrate a shrewd and tenacious pursuit of the main chance.

It is not my intent to suggest that America logically and carefully pursued a course that resulted in naval supremacy in the Atlantic area. Indeed, the American policymaking machinery was so haphazardly constructed, so improvisationally administered that predicting or pursuing any predetermined goal was extremely difficult. Although bureaucratized at the beginning of the twentieth century, the U.S. Navy was still an unwieldy organization for planning and fighting a modern war. In theory, the Office of Chief of Naval Operations (CNO) and committees, such as the General Board of the Navy, were supposed to systematize decision making and streamline execution. In actuality, bureau chiefs and fleet commanders retained considerable autonomy, and the success of a chief of naval operations depended largely on the personal support he could win from his subordinates. This gave the president considerable power if he was inclined to use it. Roosevelt was so inclined. Improvisation, sometimes brilliant, sometimes disastrous, was his hallmark, and he impressed it indelibly upon the navy in which he took a proprietary interest.

By 1937, Roosevelt had determined, over the objections of

some naval advisers, to work with the British in containing Japanese expansion. Prior to 1935, Japan had expanded to treaty limits, thus insuring that the Imperial Navy could present either Britain or the United States with a creditable challenge. But in 1936 Japan renounced all naval limitations and began to express in words and in the shipyards increasingly bellicose ambitions. In Roosevelt's view the only practical way to limit those ambitions was by Anglo-American naval collaboration.

Collaboration in the Pacific was fine in theory, but how could it be done? For British strategists one solution was to avoid conflict with Japan or, if conflict came, to have the United States protect British interests while guarding its own. But could the United States, regarded by many as the "reluctant Achilles" and the "uncertain ally" be depended upon to fulfill the role assigned by Whitehall?[8] For American strategists the issue was more clear-cut: do not get involved in hostilities with the Japanese unless the British are inextricably committed to cooperate.[9] But in view of what many Americans regarded as a record of appeasement in China and clearer obligations in European waters, could Britain be so committed?[10] Furthermore, did the United States want any role, no matter how temporary, in helping to protect the anachronistic "Empire"?

Ironically, these questions and doubts, which continued to impede planning right up to 7 December 1941, contributed to the major Anglo-American naval agreement of the century. If agreement could not be reached regarding the Pacific, which provided the original raison d'être for naval collaboration, perhaps some bargain could be struck regarding the Atlantic. On that issue both sides were flexible. The war and its disastrous early course provided an additional catalyst.

When appeasement ultimately failed in September 1939, American military assistance seemed desirable, but not essential, to British policymakers. In fact, there was a strong sentiment for keeping America out of the war so that her material resources would be available for allies and not diverted to her own use. The situation changed dramatically in June 1940, when France fell and England faced the aggressors alone. Churchill's goal then became full-fledged American involvement in the war no matter what the cost. Now he needed a way to balance Britain's need with American ambition.

And what was America's price? Although never precisely stated, it was predominance in any partnership. That was the result, and that it was also the intent can be discerned from a variety of actions. In the field of naval affairs, the desire for supremacy is evident in the Atlantic First agreement reached in March 1941, when this study concludes. The decision was made and accepted by the British that "if and when" America entered the war, her primary effort would be expended in the Atlantic area; that if attacked by Japan, American efforts in the Pacific would be conducted so as not to detract from the war against Germany. At the same time, Great Britain would move portions of her navy from the Atlantic to the Pacific.

As long as America had been willing to play a major role in a minor theater, her ambitions had been circumscribed. Now new worlds opened. Such distinguished historians as Samuel Eliot Morison see the Germany First agreement (Atlantic First, in naval terms) as setting the "major overall strategy of the war" as well as being the principal Anglo-American cooperative agreement.[11] The decision was equally important for establishing the United States as the ascendant power in the Atlantic community, where it was replacing Great Britain.

Attention recently has been focused on the degree of collaboration, or cooperation, or calculation evident in the relations between the United States and the Soviet Union during World War II. Some historians have written detailed studies in which they propose that self-interest, in the form of anticommunism, was never far from American minds. The evidence developed in the course of this study would suggest that Americans pursued their self-interest in relations with friend and foe alike. There is no doubt that the world after the war was on American minds; the issue is perspective. In the postwar world, relations between the United States and Communist countries assumed a new importance and no doubt some prescient individuals anticipated this in the 1940–41 period. But the majority of U.S. policymakers measured their country and defined America's postwar political and economic aims in relation to Great Britain. Given that situation, the question of where and how the United States would exert its naval power was pivotal.

2.

Prelude and Paradox

July 1937–January 1938

It is impossible to consider naval affairs in a vacuum. Politics, economics, and diplomacy all have their impact on the navy, and as the first line of national defense, the navy has an effect on these other elements of national life. Events in 1937–38 provide a prime example of the interaction of these various elements. At the same time these events illustrate how cooperation and suspicion were intermingled in British-American naval relations. Both countries considered cooperation in the Pacific* during the summer of 1937, but it took a strong push by Franklin D. Roosevelt to overcome the doubts that stood in the way of action. Roosevelt proposed a dramatic break with traditional American policy and a bold use of Anglo-American naval forces. What the president proposed was dangerous, but it was welcomed in London—if the United States would back tough talk with resolute action. Neither power wished to allow Japanese aggression to go unchallenged; however, neither cared to take on the task of challenging that aggression unilaterally.

*There is potential for confusion in references to this area of the world, for the British and Americans had fundamentally different views and even used different terms when referring to it. In this manuscript we will use "Pacific" when talking about the area as a whole; "South West Pacific" when referring to ocean areas from the South China Sea as far north as 20° latitude, the waters surrounding the Netherlands East Indies, Australia, and New Guinea, and extending to 159° east longitude; "Far East" when referring to land and ocean areas within the same coordinates; and "Central Pacific" when referring to the ocean areas that extend in a broad band (between 42° north latitude and the equator) from the Americas to Asia, but excluding the Philippines.

Cooperation seemed desirable, but only if each partner had equal determination. Willingness to extend naval power became the test; results of that test would have wide-ranging implications.

* * *

On 7 July 1937 the long-simmering Sino-Japanese conflict exploded with the invasion of Chinese territory. The "China Incident" between Japanese soldiers and a Chinese border garrison at the Marco Polo bridge was a clear signal that the Japanese army was now ready to back tough talk with action. American sympathies were generally with the Chinese, and many expressed sentiments that were intended to give moral support to China and forestall further Japanese expansion. In those days of isolationism, however, there were few in the United States willing to take action. The Neutrality Acts of 1935–36 were one indication of public sentiment, but many, like Congressman Louis Ludlow (Democrat, Indiana), would not feel secure until his constitutional amendment calling for a national referendum on any declaration of war was accepted.[1]

President Roosevelt had to move cautiously in this atmosphere of actual and intended restraint on his authority, but caution did not stop him from considering dramatic moves. Feeling that a demonstration of resolve was needed, Roosevelt suggested to Sumner Welles, U.S. undersecretary of state, a "trade embargo" in the Pacific, enforced by British and American naval units, to cut Japanese trade until she came to her senses. For unknown reasons, but presumably on the advice of "ranking admirals" who warned that such an embargo might result in war "for which the American Navy was unprepared," the president temporarily abandoned the plan.[2]

London was also interested in ending the fighting in China, although Prime Minister Neville Chamberlain and Foreign Secretary Anthony Eden were no more enthusiastic than the American admirals when they heard of the embargo plan. Joint mediation seemed a more reasonable approach, but two proposals in this regard were rebuffed by the U.S. Department of State, where British Ambassador Sir Ronald Lindsay was told that America wanted cooperation on parallel but independent lines.[3] Independent but parallel action might be sufficient for diplomacy, but if force were to be applied neither side cared to operate unilaterally.

The reason can be found by surveying Anglo-American war plans as well as the relative strength of the navies that would be involved if any move resulted in war.

For the British, only the security of the home islands themselves ranked above the security of the Commonwealth. The governments of Australia and New Zealand had been assured repeatedly that in the event of war in the Pacific a strong force of capital ships would be dispatched to Singapore.[4] This would keep the Japanese from moving south of the Malaya Barrier or cutting the vital lines of communication that ran across the South West Pacific, into the Indian Ocean, and beyond. This was good strategy as well as good politics. Commonwealth support in men and material would be essential in any full-scale war; such support would hardly be forthcoming unless London could guarantee defense of the Commonwealth. Unfortunately there were problems with these assurances. For one thing, Singapore was not fully prepared to be a base for capital ships in 1937. For another, moving a large force to Singapore was only possible if Great Britain faced antagonists seriatim; if there were a coalition of aggressors, a contingency that grew more likely every day, protecting the Far East would mean uncovering some other area. For instance, what if a choice were required between the Middle East and the Far East? The strategists consistently came down in favor of defending the Far East. The choice was not easy, though, and a better solution would be to avoid confrontation in the Pacific, or, if it came, to seek the support of the United States.

Any conflict in the Pacific posed problems for the Americans as well. Since 1904 the Army-Navy Joint Board had been making plans for a possible war with Japan.[5] American war plans were color-coded, with the appropriate plan for American-Japanese hostilities labeled ORANGE. The basic ORANGE plan anticipated that Japan's initial move would be to attack the Philippines. America's response would be a naval offensive across the Pacific aimed at gaining control of the sea-lanes and ultimately striking at Japan's economic base. A primary object and a strategic necessity in sustaining the naval offensive were relief and retention of the Philippines.

As the British found when examining their plan, there were several conundrums evident to American planners. Foremost among them was interservice debate over the possibilities of successfully defending the Philippines. In 1933 this debate broke into the open. Army officers stationed in the Philippines argued that the islands could not be defended unless funds were appropriated for their fortification. Since the country was in the midst of a depression, and sentiment was building for Philippine independence, the possibility of Congress appropriating the required funds seemed remote. Army commanders on the spot, therefore, wanted ORANGE revised to reflect these new realities. In Washington, the Joint Board ducked the issue. After reviewing ORANGE the board members reported in 1934 that retention of the Philippines was essential to the exercise of American diplomatic, economic, and military influence in the Far East. That report was not entirely responsive to the army's objections, but there the matter stood until 1936. When the plan was reviewed in that year it became extremely clear that the navy was irreconcilably opposed to dropping the concept of a Pacific offensive. The result was a compromise. The navy retained its plan for an ORANGE offensive built in part around a base in the Philippines, and the army retained its plan for defending those islands, but, significantly, made no provision for their relief.[6]

This kind of basic strategy dispute was entirely understandable considering the level of U.S. interservice cooperation. For one thing, there was no national defense coordinating group. There was a Joint Board made up of the army chief of staff, the chief of naval operations, their deputies, and the chiefs of the War Plans Division of each service that could make policy recommendations. These recommendations, however, had no binding effect unless the services chose to be bound by them. The navy, and presumably the army as well, was run in a similarly loose manner. Heading the United States Navy was a civilian secretary who was responsible to the president if the president chose to make him responsible or consult him. There was also a civilian assistant secretary and later an undersecretary. Then came a naval officer, the chief of naval operations (a post created in 1915), and he theoretically reported directly to the secretary. Under the chief of naval operations came the bureau chiefs—the chief of navigation, the chief of ordnance, and the chief of plans, for example—and the commanders of the various fleets, i.e., the U.S., the Asiatic, and, after 1941, the Atlantic. If these officers were senior to, or more assertive than, the chief of naval operations, they could make it very difficult for him effectively to put policy into practice. The General Board of the Navy, made up of senior admirals, acted as an advisory body for the Navy Department and though it had no executive responsibility its influence was considerable. The result of all this organization, or lack thereof, was that interservice and even intraservice disputes could go unresolved for years, while whimsy and personality were given considerable reign.

This state of affairs may help explain why the Royal Navy considered its American counterpart amateurish, since the British undoubtedly recognized at least the potential for, if not the details of, U.S. disputes. The British policymaking system was far more formalized. The prime minister was responsible to the king for naval policy. Assisting the prime minister was the Board of Admiralty, which was headed by a civilian first lord. Operating under the first lord were two other political appointees (a civil lord and the parliamentary and financial secretary), and a civil servant (the permanent secretary). The Royal Navy was represented by four or five sea lords, one of whom, the first sea lord, would correspond to the chief of naval operations. The Board of Admiralty, responsible to the government in all naval matters, formulated and executed policy. National defense policy was coordinated by the Committee on Imperial Defense (CID), which was made up of the secretaries of state for foreign affairs, home affairs, the colonies, and war; the first lord of the Admiralty; the chancellor of the Exchequer; the professional heads of the services; and anyone else whom the prime minister thought it useful to include. There also was a small permanent secretariat made up of civil servants who insured continuity. The CID was purely advisory, in theory, but had considerable authority and served to insure at least interservice cooperation. Despite this high degree of organization, the British system was not free from the influence of strong personalities and could create and perpetuate confusion, particularly in areas such as the Far East, where multiple interests clashed.

Essential to understanding the difficulties that Britain and America had in planning for a Pacific war is consideration of Japanese naval power. In the view of British and American professional navalists, the Washington treaty not only made Japan the foremost naval power in the Pacific but it also gave her additional advantages by denying Britain and America the right to fortify new bases in the Western Pacific. The Japanese government had gladly accepted these opportunities, building and remodeling her fleet up to treaty limits. With the expiration of the treaty in 1936, Japan had embarked on a new shipbuilding program. Since neither Britain nor America had built to treaty limits, it should come as no surprise to find that the Japanese navy was considered a formidable adversary. Between 1922 and 1936 Japanese capital ship tonnage had increased by 45 percent, while comparable American tonnage had declined by 5 percent and British tonnage by 12 percent. Moreover, Japan was in the process of laying down some of the world's largest battleships and in several significant areas of ship design and material led the world.[7] And while the United States Navy operated its ships at approximately 80 percent of complement, the Japanese had resorted to conscription to fill the Imperial Navy's ranks, thus allowing her to man her ships with full crews.[8] Consequently, although each was larger than the Imperial Navy, neither the U.S. Navy nor the Royal Navy could be complacent when contemplating war with Japan. To the United States Navy, Japanese naval expansion had one advantage—it offered justification for U.S. expansion. The navy was not simply being contentious in its debate with the army over the ORANGE plan; a potential offensive in the Pacific was essential to rationalizing requests for congressional appropriations.[9]

Their relative advantage may have convinced the Japanese that they could act with impunity; in any case they turned a deaf ear to American and British attempts at mediation. By October 1937 tempers were wearing thin, and Sino-Japanese tensions were clearly in Roosevelt's mind on 5 October when he called for an international "quarantine" of the aggressors. What he interpreted as an adverse public response to this call for action ostensibly caused the president to back away from the positive moves his speech seemed to portend.[10]

Even before the president hesitated, the British reaction was to view the "quarantine" with suspicion. Neville Chamberlain summed up his sentiment by observing that "it is always best and safest to count on nothing from the Americans but words."[11] But given a bit more time to reflect, Chamberlain reacted with some alarm. As he told the Cabinet on 6 October, he hoped nothing would come of Roosevelt's idea since it was the most unfortunate time to force Japan's hand. An economic embargo was a very serious move and might well bring on a war in the Far East. That development would be not at all in Britain's interest. At the same time he warned that his government should avoid being maneuvered into a position by the Americans in which the United States could claim that Britain was impeding a settlement in China. The bitterness resulting from any such claims would make future cooperation unlikely.[12]

Chamberlain need hardly have feared precipitous American action because it seemed to many in the Roosevelt administration that London had more at stake in the Far East than America did. This led to the conclusion that the British should bear the brunt of any offensive, or the administration would be accused of "pulling her [Britain's] chestnuts out of the fire."[13] Even if the British did put up the bulk of the forces, there were still risks in any cooperative venture. The British were regarded by the Americans as extremely devious, and there was virtually no limit to the chicanery their policies might conceal. One American diplomat guessed that the British foreign secretary, Anthony Eden, wished to see Britain and America fighting side by side in the Far East since "in such a contingency Germany and Italy would be immobilized, as an extension of the conflict would involve them in hostilities with the United States; if, on the other hand, they should move, then England could count on us as a co-belligerent."[14]

The possibility of moves in the Far East having European repercussions was increased when, on 6 November 1937, Japan joined Germany and Italy in the Anti-Comintern Pact, thus raising the specter of a two-ocean war. In the event of such a development, cooperation between Britain and America, at least to the extent of learning the war plans of each nation, would be very useful. Cooperation even to that extent might have long-range implications, but there were those who felt that binding commitments might be necessary. Rear Admiral J. O. Richardson, assistant chief of naval operations (1937–38), for instance, repeatedly urged his superior, Admiral William Leahy (chief of naval operations, 1937–39) to convince the president not to become involved in any Pacific war "unless we have others so bound to us that they cannot leave us in the lurch."[15] This was an obvious reference to the British, who for their part became increasingly willing to consider cooperation in the Pacific if they could be assured that the United States would fulfill its obligations. Or, as Anthony Eden put it, any cooperative action in the Far East must be taken "with our eyes open and with a willingness to share the risks . . . right through to the end."[16]

Though not devoid of innuendo and suspicion, these comments indicated a mutual willingness to consider some form of joint action. Finding the form would not be easy. When the Anti-Comintern Pact was announced Norman Davis was in Brussels representing the United States at the Nine-Power Conference. In conversation with the British delegates, Davis suggested that Roosevelt's idea of a joint naval blockade might again merit discussion. But when Sir Ronald Lindsay explored that possibility with Sumner Welles on 13 November, the undersecretary of state said that such joint fleet action in the Pacific seemed a "remote" possibility and not worthy of consideration.[17] Although they were not eager to implement a blockade, this negative response and the unwillingness of the Americans to go forward with any other joint *démarche* was discouraging to the British.[18] It also did little to increase confidence in American reliability.

Norman Davis's proposal had piqued British interest, though, and when the Japanese seized the British customs vessels in Tientsin and Shanghai, Eden decided to approach the United States again. On 27 November, Ambassador Lindsay told Welles that the British government was considering an "overwhelming display of naval force." He wondered whether the United States would enter staff conversations "to consider appropriate and adequate combined steps."[19]

Welles replied that he had been advised by reliable British authorities that because of other commitments Britain was in no position to employ her naval forces in Far Eastern waters. Indeed he had been told that the whole policy of the British government was not to be drawn into a Far Eastern commitment because of possible European repercussions. Therefore, it appeared to him that in any joint move the British were counting on the Americans to provide the "overwhelming display of naval force." Lindsay denied this allegation, contending that the purpose of the staff conferences was to allocate resources in a mutually agreeable way. Welles was not convinced but promised to comment further on staff conversations when he received specific instructions.[20]

Welles was prudent to seek further instructions, for if staff conversations were to be held it would be a significant move toward cooperation as well as a break with American tradition. As far as is known, the United States had never engaged in formal staff planning and coordination with another country before the advent of hostilities. The only prior military alliance had been concluded with France in 1778; and even in World War I the United States had preserved her independence by fighting as an "associate" rather than as an "ally." Staff conversations, though not binding in themselves, implied cooperative intent. Unless allied action were being considered, such close collaboration ran, at the least, the risk of serious miscalculation. The talks held between Britain and France prior to World War I, though specified as noncommitting, had been interpreted as constituting "moral obligation[s] of honour," implying British intervention when war broke out in 1914.[21] Moreover, war planning, even by her own military, was a comparatively recent development for the United States; Woodrow Wilson had not allowed it even after hostilities in Europe had begun.[22] Thus not only would cooperative war planning be a dramatic break with tradition but it could also be a dangerous political move should Franklin Roosevelt's isolationist constituents learn of it.

In the meantime, other actions were being taken that would complement the move toward naval cooperation. In view of the worsening situation in the Far East, the U.S. Joint Board directed the planners to reexamine the ORANGE plan with explicit attention to the possibility of a two-ocean war. The services again found agreement impossible. The navy favored an offensive policy, the army a defensive one. Inherent in the navy's plan was the concept that if the European Axis gave aid to Japan, America's potential allies would give sufficient assistance to allow the United States Navy to fulfill its mission. The naval planners, however, noted that the "character, amount and location of allied assistance [could] not be predicted."[23] Obviously, predictions of the size and nature of any assistance could be more readily made if staff conversations were held with the British, the most likely ally. The British, with their naval base at Singapore, thousands of miles closer to the Philippines than Pearl Harbor, could give legitimacy to the navy's offensive plans. Anglo-American cooperation, or at least a semblance of it, could provide a way out of the United States Navy's Pacific dilemma. Admiral Leahy therefore recommended staff conversations with the Royal Navy.[24]

Despite the navy's enthusiasm, on 30 November Welles rejected Lindsay's suggestion. Displaying remarkable persistence, on 6 December Anthony Eden directed that Lindsay make a more specific request. Expressing the opinion that joint action might be beneficial, Eden backed up the British suggestion in a very specific way. The Royal Navy would send eight or nine capital ships, he said, "if the United States would make at least an equivalent effort." If the Americans would not go this far, Eden suggested consideration of a less drastic step, such as making a show of preparing the fleet for action. The British government was ready to call up reservists, and if the United States would take similar action and agree to staff talks, Eden thought the prestige of the democracies might be restored.[25]

Lindsay did not act immediately and on 12 December 1937 the Japanese seized the initiative. On that date, planes of the Imperial Air Force attacked and sank the U.S.S. *Panay*, which was on patrol in the Yangtze River. Several British vessels were fired upon at the same time and Lindsay immediately approached the Americans with the proposal for "secret and confidential staff discussions between Great Britain and the United States." Welles was still not ready to make a positive response.[26] Though discouraged, the British yet hoped at least for agreement to act in tandem when protesting the Japanese attacks.[27]

In Washington the *Panay* incident caused considerable protest, and some talked excitedly of war. Admiral Leahy felt that the time had come to "get the fleet ready for sea, to make an agreement with the British Navy for joint action and to inform the Japanese that we expect to protect our nationals."[28] But for others the increase in tensions and the talk of war provided the impetus for moving the Ludlow Resolution out of committee and onto the House floor. Ludlow got the required number of signatures on his discharge petition, so after Christmas recess Congress would decide whether to allow debate on the war referendum.

Ignoring the British request for a mutual response, the United States government sent an independent protest to Tokyo on 13 December. The Ludlow Resolution may have provided the caution signal, but even without it there were those within the administration who opposed acting jointly with the British. Jay Pierrepont Moffat, chief of the European Division in the Department of State, for instance, was very reluctant to see the United States "become the junior partner of Great Britain in policing the world."[29] As disappointing as American official reaction was, on 14 December the British ambassador again proposed cooperative action—this time to Cordell Hull, the secretary of state. As a result of this conversation, a meeting was arranged between Lindsay, the president, and Hull.

Lindsay was a guest at a White House diplomatic reception on the evening of 16 December.[30] After the festivities the president, the secretary of state, and the British ambassador went to Roosevelt's study for a private conversation. Although only three days before, the president had restrained those, like Leahy, who called for forceful joint action, now he responded fully—and enthusiastically—to the British requests for a coordinated response. He suggested that the United States and Great Britain join their naval forces to establish a "peaceful blockade" of the Japanese home islands. It was Roosevelt's opinion that this blockade could be established covertly and would be denied as official policy if questioned. The plan was something of a shock. The British had not been thinking in terms of anything that bellicose; Eden wanted merely a show of force in an attempt to avert hostilities, not an act of war.[31]

The ambassador told the president that in his view a blockade would constitute a *causus belli* between Japan and the English-speaking democracies. Roosevelt denied this inference. What he wanted was a "quarantine" of Japan. Many wondered what the president meant when he used that term in his Chicago speech; he spelled it out for Lindsay. He wanted a cruiser blockade thrown across the Pacific, from the Aleutian Islands through the Central Pacific to the Philippines and on to Hong Kong. The United States would assume responsibility for the area east of the Philippines and Great Britain would look after the western sector. The purpose of the joint move was to cut Japan off from raw materials and to starve "by military measures" any Japanese mandated islands within the blockaded area. Lindsay again suggested that such a blockade would be an act of war. Roosevelt again said no; it was clearly within the powers of the executive. Furthermore, there was "new doctrine and technique" regarding war, and the United States had waged undeclared war before. Lindsay offered what he later described as "horrified criticisms" but felt that they made little impact on the president, who seemed "wedded to this scheme for preventing war (but not 'hostilities')."

In an effort to divert the president from the blockade scheme Lindsay referred to Eden's suggestion for a joint "naval demonstration." Surprisingly, Roosevelt replied that the Royal Navy should keep its heavy ships in the European theater; he thought that some cruisers, destroyers, and long-range submarines would be sufficient. Lindsay then tried to arouse some interest in a decisive act such as naval mobilization by the United States. Roosevelt thought that that suggestion was useless, but he did think it might be possible to advance the date of naval maneuvers in the Pacific. Lindsay quickly agreed and suggested a visit by U.S. ships to Singapore. Roosevelt said he could send no battleships, but the more he thought about it the more enthusiastic he became about sending a squadron of cruisers to visit the British base.

Any action would require planning, and the president agreed to the British suggestion for staff conversations. Roosevelt's use of an analogy from World War I suggests that he may have intended these conversations to go beyond mere blockade planning. He said that between 1915 and 1917, while he had been assistant secretary of the navy, there had been a mechanism arranged for the "systematic exchange of secret information." Commodore Guy Gaunt, the British naval attaché, and Captain W. V. Pratt, of the United States Navy, had been the mediums for this exchange. By the president's account, the process had evolved so far that when war came in April 1917 "complete war plans had been elaborated and Admiral Sims's well-known mission was really of minor importance." Not only war plans but all kinds of "intelligence" had been exchanged. According to Roosevelt, he had been deeply involved in these earlier exchanges and now hoped to foster a similar liaison. He had not given much thought to the practicalities of his scheme—like a meeting place, for example—but he seemed open to suggestions.

Lindsay reported his conversation with the president to his superiors in London. Since the president had been in his "worst 'inspirational' mood," it was difficult to give a report that was "consistent and sensible," especially concerning the blockade. Obviously Roosevelt was proposing moves that might cause a dramatic and historic turn in Anglo-American naval relations. And even though Lindsay thought Roosevelt's suggestions might seem like the "utterances of a harebrained statesman or an amateur strategist . . . ," the ambassador could see value in pursuing the issue.

As far as the staff conversations were concerned, Lindsay thought they had great potential value as well. He interpreted the president's comments to mean that he was anxious to bring America over to the allied side before it was "too late." Conversations to make allied cooperation possible would have to be wide-ranging and, regardless of the value or wisdom of the specific plan that resulted, the talks themselves would have merit insofar as they implied an American commitment to work closely with Great Britain.

It is clear from the Admiralty files that the British were confused by Roosevelt's reference to extensive Gaunt-Pratt exchanges. Their records showed that Roosevelt had been extremely helpful once the United States had entered the war, but there was no other indication of clandestine cooperation. The Royal Navy, nevertheless, was pleased that the United States had now agreed to some form of staff contact. Reaction to the blockade was not as enthusiastic, but preparation for tactical cooperation was the first priority in the British lexicon anyhow. It would be impossible in any emergency to face Japan with overwhelming force without an interchange of information on signaling, maneuvering, cruising formations, and night fleet actions. These preliminaries were critical, for it was recalled at the Admiralty that twice in the eighteenth century France and Spain had tried to combine their naval forces to threaten England. However, "they spent weeks trying to agree on and learn new methods and then made a muddle," and thus the opportune moment passed. That should not be allowed to happen again.[32]

With interest on both sides, preliminaries were soon completed. Since secrecy was essential for both foreign and domestic reasons, a cloak-and-dagger atmosphere surrounded American preparations. On 23 December, Captain Royal E. Ingersoll received a mysterious summons to come to the White House.[33] Ingersoll was director of plans for the United States Navy and had been the American technical representative at the 1935–36 London Naval Conference.

A quick, perceptive officer, Ingersoll was outwardly unimpressive. Of medium height and medium build, with sandy hair and blue eyes, the soft-spoken Midwesterner was no head-turner. However, he had an unparalleled knowledge of American war plans and a mind that quickly grasped technical details and understood delicate international relationships. These qualities led the president to choose him for the mission he had in mind and the same qualities would carry Ingersoll to the post of assistant chief of naval operations during World War II. But Ingersoll was still surprised to find himself sitting in the Oval Office in the presence of the president; the secretary of state, Cordell Hull; the secretary of the treasury, Henry Morgenthau, Jr.; and Admiral William Leahy, the chief of naval operations. He was still more surprised when he learned the president's plan. Roosevelt wanted Ingersoll to leave for England immediately to consult with Admiralty officials on the means for implementing his scheme for blockading Japan. The president detailed his plan for two lines of ships to patrol the Pacific, thus severing Japanese trade links. When Ingersoll pointed out that such a blockade would require a large fleet, Roosevelt countered by proposing that private yachts could easily supplement the naval vessels. The important thing was to interrupt Japanese trade, and the president did not much care how it was done. The British had responded favorably to his overture and the president wanted immediate talks "off the record and informally."[34] After making some hurried preparations, Ingersoll boarded a ship for England on 26 December 1937.

Ingersoll arrived in London on 31 December 1937 and went first to the Embassy and then to the Foreign Office. Anthony Eden told Ingersoll that the United States could count on "full cooperation" from the British.[35] Despite his reassuring statements, Ingersoll felt that the foreign secretary was much more interested in action than in planning.[36] Ingersoll said that he was actually on an information-gathering mission, but had he been pressed he might have admitted that his vague instructions left him with only uncertain indications about what kind of information Washington wanted. He was willing to provide information on American plans in certain contingencies (presumably War Plan ORANGE) and he would have been glad to learn of Britain's corresponding plans. He could, however, make no commitments.

There was an air of improvisation about the whole project, and Sir Alexander Cadogan, the permanent undersecretary of state for foreign affairs, who was also present, noted that Ingersoll seemed unsure of his mission's "*objective*."[37] Therefore, Sir Alexander drafted a dispatch to the British ambassador in an effort to "draw out" the Americans. London was willing to go along with the president's wishes, wrote Cadogan, but the Foreign Office was uncertain about the scope and purpose of the staff conversations the president had proposed. Furthermore, the British wanted to know something more definite about that visit to Singapore by U.S. ships. Such a movement would be a fine demonstration of cooperative resolve and would confirm American resolve to back up words with action.[38]

The ambassador cautioned London about proceeding too fast or pushing too hard for a Singapore visit. It was his impression that the Roosevelt administration was a "horse that [would] run best when the spur [was] not used." The president was very sensitive to public opinion and wished to avoid "any appearance of collusion or joint action."[39] This sensitivity might explain Roosevelt's vagueness concerning staff talks—a subject on which Lindsay also had only "uncertain indications." In his late night conversation, however, Roosevelt had said that before World War I complete war plans had been elaborated. Lindsay interpreted these comments to mean that the president wanted extensive conversations, and while his lack of specific guidelines might be bizarre, his intent appeared obvious. To the ambassador it also seemed advantageous to leave the scope of the conversations vague; thus they could become as "vast as possible" or as desirable.

It was in this uncertain atmosphere that Ingersoll held his first formal conference, on 3 January 1938. To his pleasure, he found that his British counterpart was Captain T. S. V. Phillips, whom he had met at the 1935–36 London Naval Conference. Ingersoll immediately explained to Phillips that he had no "specific instructions" but had been sent to "exchange general information." He did say that Admiral Leahy was anxious to have a British naval officer conversant with British war plans against Japan stationed at the Embassy in Washington. Phillips agreed to this and suggested that recognition signals and other operational code information could be exchanged as well. The British officer then told Ingersoll that, as a demonstration of resolve, a large fleet was already being prepared for dispatch to the Far East. Ingersoll said his navy was not ready to take such a drastic step. Plans were to bring the fleet to readiness only after a Declaration of National Emergency, but at the moment the United States wished to avoid precipitous action.[40]

The two officers next turned to the president's proposed

blockade. There was considerable discussion concerning possible bases and areas of responsibility for the blockading units. Obviously it would not be easy to blockade the entire Pacific Ocean, and neither Phillips nor Ingersoll was enthusiastic about the prospect. However, they came up with an outline of a plan whereby the blockade would be anchored on North America, Australia, and China, and stretched, rather thinly, across the Pacific.

When the two planning officers met on 5 January they continued their discussion of the blockade. The British were willing to accept responsibility for interdicting Japanese trade south of the Philippines; the United States would take responsibility for waters from the Philippines to the North American continent. In addition, the United States Navy would patrol the west coast of South America.[41] That plan was obviously impractical, but discussing it provided an opportunity for Ingersoll and Phillips to consider general cooperative strategy in the Pacific, including the number of ships the British could send to Singapore, the units the United States could send to Hawaii, possible joint use of facilities, the exchange of codes, cyphers, intelligence, and other methods for concerting action. After discussing these matters in a general way they concluded their second day of conversations.

As Phillips had indicated, British naval preparations were in advance of America's; in fact, the British had gone about as far as they could without announcing mobilization. When the Foreign Office received a report on 7 January of another "outrage" in Shanghai, Eden and Cadogan agreed that the time had come to do "*something*." Ingersoll had said that without a Declaration of National Emergency, American forces could not be brought to a full condition of readiness. Therefore, before taking further action Eden asked Lindsay to determine whether Roosevelt would "parallel" their next move with such a declaration. Again the intent was to draw the Americans out and determine how far they would go.[42]

Lindsay immediately went to see Sumner Welles. The ambassador told the undersecretary that the British government was considering an "announcement of the completion of naval preparations." What was the significance of such an announcement, Welles asked. It should be regarded, Lindsay replied, as meaning that England was only one step away from mobilization and that the Royal Navy was on a virtual war footing. Lindsay then inquired whether the United States would make some "similar gesture." As an example of what he thought would be appropriate, he suggested announcing that ships of the United States Navy were "proceeding towards Hawaii in the course of Naval maneuvers, or that certain units of the United States Navy were being moved from the Atlantic to the Pacific." Welles said that he would require instructions before replying.[43] According to Welles's memorandum of the conversation there was no mention of a Declaration of National Emergency or any similarly decisive move.

The pending vote in the House of Representatives on the Ludlow Resolution may well have caused Lindsay to hedge his proposal and Welles to delay his answer. The administration had summoned its forces to defeat the move to debate the resolution and both the president and Secretary Hull wrote strong letters of opposition. Roosevelt, writing to the Speaker of the House, stated that passage would "cripple any President in his conduct of our foreign relations" while encouraging others to violate American rights.[44] Despite these efforts, when the vote came on 10 January 1938 it was uncomfortably close—209 to 188—a very strong indication that the country was not ready for an interventionist policy or provocative action.[45] The vote was not enough, however, to deter Roosevelt from taking some positive action. On the same day the House voted, Roosevelt ordered the transfer of major units of the fleet from the Atlantic to the Pacific, an advance in the date of maneuvers, and the dispatch of three cruisers to Singapore.[46]

The Americans had thus done almost precisely what the British ambassador had requested. The reaction in London, however, was not joy but gloom. After discussions with the British leadership, Sir Alexander Cadogan recorded in his diary on 11 January: "We have a telegram from Washington that Americans, *if* we declare our preparedness, will (1) 'Scrape their bottoms' (i.e., dock their battleships) and (2) advance date of maneuvers." He went on to note that the first sea lord was quite uneasy about the situation and that he, Cadogan, agreed that if Britain were to be in negotiations with Italy in a couple of weeks it was not a good time "to send our fleet away." The editor of Cadogan's *Diaries* interprets the general reaction as follows: "Here the British Government found themselves in the familiar dilemma," for the moves Roosevelt proposed would not commit the United States to war with

Japan "even if the British should be so embroiled."[47] It is difficult to explain why the British reacted in such a contradictory fashion after Roosevelt had virtually acceded to their requests. Did they misinterpret Roosevelt's intent or mistrust his will to follow through? Or had the Foreign Office hoped that Lindsay would feel justified in pushing harder?

Whatever the reason, the British government obviously had hoped for more, but Roosevelt's move was quite courageous, considering American public opinion. A clear commitment to war in the Far East was politically unfeasible at this time. In any case, Cadogan took America's response to be conditional: they would take action only if Britain acted. Eden, on the other hand, called the action "not decisive" but "encouraging." It was not encouraging enough, however, to prompt Britain to announce completion of naval preparations or to take further action in the Far East. Nor were further requests made of the Americans. Most important, it is difficult to avoid the conclusion that the disappointing American reaction played a role in the dramatic rebuff about to take place.

Without waiting for British reaction to his naval moves, the president, who was hyperactive during this period, decided to call for an international conference on arms reduction, international law, and some form of economic agreement.[48] At Secretary Hull's insistence, Roosevelt sought England's approval before announcing the conference. Roosevelt's message was transmitted to London on 12 January and he requested a response within five days. Sir Alexander Cadogan, who received the president's request, was not enthusiastic about the conference proposal, but at the same time he was reluctant to snub the president by dismissing the suggestion out of hand. When he was informed, Prime Minister Chamberlain showed less concern for Roosevelt's feelings. The British statesman thought that the American initiative would undermine his efforts to negotiate privately with the Italians over Ethiopia, and he found "hateful" the idea of a conference with only vague, general objectives. Chamberlain, therefore, asked Roosevelt to hold off for a short while since his suggestion "cut across efforts to negotiate on immediate issues with the dictators."[49] That response, which Sumner Welles described as being like a "douche of cold water," effectively ended all planning for the conference and aroused deep resentment in Washington.[50]

On the same day that Chamberlain drafted his response to

Roosevelt, Ingersoll and Phillips signed an agreed-upon record of their conversations. Their talks and the exchanges that resulted from them were to be the only positive product of British-American efforts at cooperation during the hectic winter of 1937–38. The "record" suggested a division of responsibilities for the proposed blockade, an outline of forces available for dispatch to the Far East, and a tentative agreement on interchange of communications data. Ingersoll also provided details on the degree of readiness of various American naval units and agreed to the exchange of intelligence concerning Japanese military moves. At the same time the American officer insisted on tight security measures to keep any hint of the conversations from appearing in the press; therefore, the "record" was circulated only to the prime minister, who signed a copy, the foreign secretary, and the first lord of the Admiralty.[51]

Ingersoll returned to the United States on 29 January 1938 and reported to the president. Roosevelt was pleased with the discussions and the exchanges arranged by his emissary, although he did not sign a "record" as the British prime minister had. Admiral Leahy also seemed satisfied with Ingersoll's accomplishments and advised the American fleet commanders of possible Anglo-American cooperative action in the Pacific. The orders stated that if the two governments did act in cooperation—and if only one of the two were provoked to war they might not—the British would operate out of Singapore and the United States would move west from Hawaii, with Truk the possible first objective. If the British sent the large number of ships they proposed to Singapore, the two fleets would operate in widely separated locations and cooperation would be strategic. If there were trouble in European waters, however, the Royal Navy might not be able to send the anticipated forces; if that were the case, close tactical cooperation would be instituted between U.S. forces and the ships the British had available. In either instance, Leahy advised, joint communications would have to be agreed upon; therefore, commanders should be prepared to exchange communications officers with the British.[52]

Ingersoll had tried to keep his activities secret, but stories suggesting that Britain and America were planning a blockade of Japan soon leaked to the press.[53] Even in view of the adverse comment and administration efforts to deny the existence of any agreement, Roosevelt still considered joint action in the Pacific possible. However, the resignation on 20 February 1938 of Anthony Eden, considered a strong friend of America and an opponent of appeasement, effectively ended discussion at the highest level of Pacific cooperation.[54]

* * *

The diplomatic and personal interchanges had really solved little. Chamberlain, and other British statesmen as well, still doubted Roosevelt's willingness or ability to act. They may have been right, but when they killed Roosevelt's conference scheme they set in motion events that some saw as decisive. Critics of Chamberlain and of appeasement were particularly harsh. In Sumner Welles's view, rejection of Roosevelt's plan made World War II virtually inevitable. Anthony Eden agreed that a comparable opportunity to avert catastrophe had "never occurred nor been created," while Winston Churchill characterized Roosevelt's initiative the "last frail chance" for peace.[55]

These are probably exaggerations. It is more likely that both sides share responsibility for failing to evince decisive cooperative resolve. After years of competition and suspicion the collective peril was insufficient to enforce trust. The British were not content to let Roosevelt go forward step by step as he felt able; the Americans, conversely, resented evidence of British mistrust, especially when it followed on the heels of what, to Roosevelt, must have appeared a courageous action. At the same time it should be recognized that the president's proposals did bear the stamp of impetuous improvisation. These qualities not unnaturally concerned the British, who reasoned that careful preparations to meet consequences should precede strong moves. Considered in this light, Chamberlain's rejection of Roosevelt's international conference scheme, "cold douche" or not, is, if not justifiable, at least understandable. In the prime minister's opinion, Roosevelt had just retreated from what the British had hoped would be an advance position. That they may have misinterpreted his response to their overture is of little moment. What mattered was that Roosevelt reinforced the impression of influential members of the Chamberlain government that he was erratic, vacillating, and undependable. The Ingersoll mission had surely advanced the cause of cooperation, yet the two countries were still far from agreement—or trust. The first moves in the alliance game revealed familiar strains that did not augur well for the future.

3.

Attempting Practical Adjustments

February 1938–June 1939

Despite the evidence of mistrust at the highest levels of government, the Ingersoll mission would have a continuing influence on Anglo-American relations. For one thing, logic suggested following up the general, strategic agreements with exchanges of tactical information. Strenuous efforts were made in this regard; yet even at this practical level détente ran into difficulty. At the same time it is obvious that while nothing binding was accomplished, the mission did provide the momentum for further strategic discussions. Once the two nations learned something about each other's naval plans the mutual knowledge itself became a persuasive argument for keeping abreast of changes. In the months leading up to World War II those changes would be significant. The situation seemed to make cooperation a necessity, but maneuver and advantage seeking were still much in evidence.

* * *

The 1938 version of ORANGE, developed after the Ingersoll conversations, was essentially a continuation of the compromise between U.S. Army and U.S. Navy planners. Each service got some of what it wanted. The army insisted that care be taken during the initial period of a Pacific war to insure protection of the mainland coasts and the strategic triangle formed by Alaska, Panama, and Oahu. Only after these defensive steps were taken would the navy begin its progressive advance across the Pacific. It was tacitly accepted that the Philippines could not be held, since no provision was made for reinforcement of the garrison nor was there any timetable given for the fleet's arrival off Manila. Despite this gloomy note, the planners were confident that Japan could be defeated and American national interests safeguarded.[1]

To give substance to this optimism, on 3 January 1938 President Roosevelt had introduced to congressional leaders the second Vinson-Trammel naval shipbuilding program. Presumably this program would equip the navy to defend both the Atlantic and the Pacific coasts should the United States find itself imperiled from two directions. In actuality, the bill would increase the size of the navy 20 percent above treaty limits at a time when Japan was also known to be increasing the size of her fleet. There is no doubt that the additional ships provided by the Vinson Act would increase the navy's fighting capability, but even as it became law in May 1938 it was apparent that more would be needed before the United States would be secure even on one coast.[2]

In neither the ORANGE plan nor in the debate over the Vinson Act was there reference to possible Anglo-American naval cooperation. Any such reference would only have made the Vinson Act harder to pass. However, the hope of such cooperation obviously made the U.S. Navy's arguments for its kind of ORANGE war more practical.

Ingersoll's talks in London, general as they were, did provide some grounds for confidence. In view of those talks, Admiral Leahy had ordered his commanders to be prepared for either strategic or tactical cooperation with Great Britain.[3] To give substance to these orders exchanges of technical information were essential so that ships of the two navies could coordinate operations.

But exchanging detailed technical information to make combined operations possible would mean trusting each other with secrets vital to naval supremacy. Strategic cooperation and agreement on general objectives in the Far East seemed possible; tactical cooperation was another matter. To merge the two navies into one fleet—as Leahy had said might be necessary if the British sent only a small force—would require mastering two different signaling systems, as well as overcoming significant differences in screening methods, attack formations, and other aspects of ship handling. In other words, merger meant giving substance to the discussions on possible joint action. On the issue of substance, particularly where it involved their most cherished secrets, the Royal Navy balked.

The U.S. naval attaché, Captain Russell Willson, had been urging the British for months to be more forthcoming and, after Ingersoll's visit, he intensified his efforts. The Admiralty contended that Britain already gave Americans preferential access, but Willson's requests for detailed information on tactics and secret devices were blocked by elements within the Royal Navy. In essence it came down to this: the policy divisions (Naval Intelligence and Naval Plans) favored a liberalized exchange procedure; the technical divisions (Ordnance, Anti-Submarine Warfare, et al.) opposed extensive exchanges. The technicians felt that England had much more than the Americans could provide in exchange and that American security procedures were so poor that they could not be trusted with secrets. The policy divisions, on the other hand, believed that Britain would gain so much by fostering cooperation that it would "outweigh anything we can lose in exchange of technical information."[4]

The higher command in the Admiralty tended to agree with the policy divisions. As Lord Chatfield, the first sea lord, wrote: "I consider that the closer we can get to the U.S. Navy the better. If we have to expand our fleet, opposition from the U.S. Navy is always possible and politically difficult. If we had a very friendly understanding it might make a vast difference." Chatfield, however, agreed that England would lose rather than gain in technical information and that, once started, exchanges would be difficult to control. In a larger sense he saw the question as being primarily political rather than military and wanted the Board of Admiralty to decide it.[5] There were ambiguous feelings at the political level that Duff Cooper, the first lord, characterized as an attitude "in favor of exchanging information with the Americans, but against giving anything away."[6] In May 1938 the Board of Admiralty decided that the United States should receive exceptional treatment. More specifically, when the Americans requested something it should be provided on a quid pro quo basis.[7]

Shortly after this decision Captain Willson came forward

with a test case. He called upon the director of naval intelligence, reminded him of Ingersoll's visit, and said that a situation might arise in which the two fleets would have to cooperate. He wanted to exchange information on fleet tactics, formations on leaving port, battle formations, and destroyer attack procedures.[8] The lines were drawn again: the technical departments opposed the exchange, the policy departments favored it. The director of plans thought that in the present world situation Anglo-American cooperation was so vital that "no proposal which may lead to closer relations between the two navies should be rejected without consideration."[9]

The deputy chief of naval staff, however, saw no reason for giving Willson the information he sought. In his view, if there were cooperation it would be strategic, with each fleet operating independently; therefore, it was unwise and unnecessary to provide the U.S. Navy with tactical information. On the more general point he wrote, "Director of Plans takes the line that we want to be friends and so we should give the Americans what they want. But though the U.S.A. officers are very friendly and the U.S.A. naval authorities would doubtless like to go far in arranging for cooperation in war, the indications today are that the U.S.A. government and people are just as far away from anything approaching an Anglo-American pact or treaty as they have ever been." He felt "caution was imposed" and favored denying the request.[10]

Chatfield, the first sea lord, again came down on the side of cooperation. He recalled that the initiative toward cooperation during the recent crisis had come from the Americans and that the president had sent Ingersoll over to "get matters on a practical footing," something he considered "an international factor of very great importance." Therefore, he thought that if the British could work more closely with the U.S. Navy "they were more likely to influence the American Administration towards international cooperation in time of trouble." To enjoy the best of both worlds he suggested discussing "principles" and not particulars of "tactics, battle formations, and so on."[11]

The first sea lord's position was accepted and the exchange proceeded—not completely freely, but in a manner that boded well for the future. Then an unfortunate incident occurred. Captain Willson requested information on the defenses of Singapore. The

British agreed but requested in return some data on the highly secret, and highly prized, Norden bombsight. Willson relayed the Royal Navy's request to the Navy Department, where it was immediately rejected. Willson returned to the charge, asking for details on British harbor defenses, i.e., booms and submarine nets. Again the Royal Navy agreed, saying in return they would like details on the aircraft arresting gear on U.S. carriers. Again the Navy Department refused to provide the *quo* for the British *quid*.[12] Obviously, the desire to "exchange information yet not give anything away" was not limited to Whitehall. The fact that both sides were being intransigent did little to relieve the disappointment of those who favored a liberalized exchange policy.

Despite setbacks, the bargaining over technical secrets went on and in March 1939 Admiral Sir Roger Backhouse, who had replaced Chatfield as first sea lord, summed up the situation: "It is not that I wish to be 'sticky' with the Americans, but hitherto they have been very much the reverse of helpful in this matter of exchanges. Therefore, I consider we should proceed with great caution."[13] And proceed with caution they did.

* * *

When Hitler threatened war over the issue of the Sudeten Germans in the fall of 1938, there was a brief resumption of high-level Anglo-American cooperation. Roosevelt called in Lindsay and talked of a possible world conference on peace and avowed his willingness to support the Allies in any way. At the same time he admitted that it would be difficult to convince the American people that they should go to war if only British possessions in the Far East were attacked.[14] It was all rather tentative and with the Munich settlement Roosevelt dispatched a short telegram to Neville Chamberlain. "Good man!" it read.[15]

Despite the reduced tensions in Europe, prior to his departure for Washington in January 1939, Captain Russell Willson suggested bringing the Ingersoll-Phillips conversations up to date. The new first sea lord, Admiral Sir Dudley Pound, was not enthusiastic. "The American Government," he wrote, "have proved to be extremely reluctant to make any sort of engagement which might commit them to warlike action," and he doubted that they would soon change their attitude.[16] But despite Pound's reservations, meetings were held with Willson and the agreements somewhat modified.

British plans had changed and it now appeared unlikely that they could contribute more than seven or eight battleships, two aircraft carriers, twenty cruisers, several destroyers, and twenty submarines to any Far Eastern force.[17] This was less than they had originally hoped to send, and it meant that the American and British fleets would have to be combined, as Leahy had anticipated. Furthermore, the Royal Navy did not intend taking offensive action north of Singapore at all unless they could be supported by a major detachment from the U.S. Pacific Fleet.[18] In any case, the two navies should be prepared to cooperate tactically. Willson's reaction to this point is not included in the record, although he legitimately could have commented that his efforts to learn British procedures to make tactical cooperation possible had met a mixed response. It is certain, however, that he undertook no commitment: the letter advising the Foreign Office of the conversations stated that "since there was no change in policy or principle" it seemed unnecessary to draw up a new accord.[19]

Events soon intervened to force policy changes. In November 1938 the Japanese Foreign Office had announced a "new order" in Asia, following this up three months later by seizing Hainan Island off the South China coast. These extensions of Japanese power southward toward French Indochina, Singapore, and the Philippine Islands were a clear indication that Japan might soon become more than a hypothetical foe.

On 15 March 1939 Hitler added to the anxiety by breaking the promise he had made at Munich and absorbing the rest of Czechoslovakia. While the British government was reconsidering appeasement and preparing to guarantee Polish territorial integrity, they also made overtures toward the United States. Sir Ronald Lindsay was asked on 19 March to ascertain whether the Americans were ready to "resume [the] naval exchange of views" initiated the previous year. In making this approach he was to emphasize that should Britain become involved in a European war, it might be impossible to reinforce their fleet in the Far East.[20] This was the pronouncement many Americans had always feared and had used in arguing against commitment to the British.

Several nights later, on 21 March, Sumner Welles called secretly at the British Embassy to give Roosevelt's reaction. On the general subject of further meetings, the president was enthusiastic. However, security would have to be tighter than it had been in

1938, when there had been the unfortunate press leak about the Ingersoll mission. A more secret method of consultation was needed and all papers relating to the meetings must be destroyed. Perhaps, the president suggested, a new British naval attaché could be sent to Washington with authority to conduct conversations. As far as the content of those conversations was concerned, Roosevelt recommended that they be similar to those "conducted in 1915 by Gaunt."[21] In view of Roosevelt's previous comments about the Gaunt-Pratt talks, Lindsay inferred from the reference to Gaunt that President Roosevelt intended "something of wide scope."[22]

The director of British plans, Victor Danckwerts, on the other hand, understood the reference to 1915 to mean that the president wanted to establish a procedure for exchanging intelligence information rather than holding staff conversations on "joint action." While it was extremely important that "no sort of rebuff should be offered to any advances from the U.S.A.," Danckwerts could see the potential for grave misunderstanding unless it were determined in advance which form of contact was desired. Since the British government had made the first overture, Danckwerts recommended determining what the foreign secretary or the prime minister had in mind. Then he proceeded to observe that establishing close liaison would carry constant risk of leaks, any one of which could have important ramifications and "even possibly deprive us of our power to choose our own political course." He further noted that the Ingersoll-Phillips conversations had recently been updated and already contained a general plan for strategic cooperation in the Pacific. What was now desirable was an assurance from the United States that they would move, or would prepare to move, in a manner "calculated to deter Japan either from entering the war, or operating in strength to the Southward." It obviously was his opinion that a strategic commitment would be more likely to result from talks on the 1938 model. The awkward part was that such a commitment was a "political rather than a naval question" and Danckwerts strongly implied that the political departments should decide what they wanted.[23]

The director of naval intelligence also saw the question as essentially political. In his view there was slight value in discussing naval plans unless the British government was certain of American intervention in the Pacific. Britain could not send major units to the Far East, but the American navy could, if they chose to, insure the safety of British possessions as well as guarantee the security of Australia and New Zealand. American acceptance of responsibility in the Pacific would free British units for action in the Atlantic and the Mediterranean with results "impossible to exaggerate." For this reason he urged that the British ministers arrive at a political decision; once a political course was charted, naval adjustments could be made.[24]

At this point there is a break in the record of almost a month. During this period the United States took the action, presumably without prompting, that the director of plans had wanted it to take: that is, it moved more major fleet units to the west coast. Obviously, this move was aimed at Japan, and it elicited the first comment in almost four weeks from the Admiralty concerning staff talks. In one sense, the American action reduced the need for discussions. But, since it might also prompt a Japanese response, talks were still desirable.[25]

It was all a little awkward. No one at the Admiralty expected much to come from talks, yet the Royal Navy did not want the Americans to think that they put a low value on cooperation. At the same time they feared that appearing too eager might make the Americans suspicious. Finally, there was the embarrassing fact that the initiative for conversations had come from London and now London was being dilatory. The first lord suggested that the Admiralty planners renew the proposal by prodding the Foreign Office to find out what they had in mind when the talks were proposed.[26]

What the planners found was that no one, not even Sir Alexander Cadogan, who had drafted the original telegrams, could remember what the intention had been or who had instructed him to make the overture.[27] The "political" departments in the Foreign Office were certain, though, that they still wanted to hold some kind of conversations. Lindsay, finding these delays and uncertainties rather tiresome, inquired on 2 May why nothing had been done to follow through with the exchange that the president had agreed to in March.[28] His inquiry stimulated renewed action on the project.

In light of the worsening international situation, American military planners had been independently reviewing the strategic possibilities. In April, the Joint Planners had completed a comprehensive evaluation of current war plans. This review was intended to help design a course of action should the United States become embroiled in a two-ocean war. Ironically, in view of the then-present world situation, the most applicable previous study was one that hypothesized a RED-ORANGE alliance in which the United States would wage a two-ocean war against Britain and Japan.[29] The RED-ORANGE plan had proposed that in fighting an enemy in the Atlantic and in the Pacific, priority be given to confronting the Atlantic foe. In the spring of 1939 the planners came to the same general conclusion: Pacific activities should be assigned secondary importance. Indeed, the thrust of the planners' conclusions was that a defensive posture in the Pacific was to be preferred. Obviously, this ran counter to the long-standing orientation toward an ORANGE war and reflected the army's lack of enthusiasm for the offensive features of the ORANGE plan. As soon would become clear, the navy was not ready to accept this orientation. It was prepared, however, to talk with the British.

Considerable discussion ensued in London over how the exchange could most secretly and conveniently be conducted, with the Admiralty clearly preferring the 1938-style conversations to intelligence exchanges on the 1915 model. It finally was decided that on 26 May 1939 Commander T. C. Hampton would travel first to Canada and then to Washington, where he would hold secret staff conversations with American officials. His principal objective was to explain England's inability to send a large fleet to the Pacific if Japan entered a war in which England was fighting Germany and Italy. The initiative for proposing any "combined strategy" must be left to the Americans. If they opened the question, Commander Hampton should point out that (1) the British would prefer that America's main naval concentration be in the Pacific and that Singapore be made available for its use if desired, and (2) the British would welcome such assistance from cruiser forces in the Western Atlantic as America could afford.[30]

Commander Hampton arrived in Washington on 12 June and was advised by the British ambassador not to visit the Embassy nor contact any of the staff. Instead he should proceed to the home of Admiral Leahy, where he and the British naval attaché, Captain L. C. A. Curzon-Howe, would meet with Leahy and Rear Admiral Robert L. Ghormley, the director of plans.

The first meeting was held the day he arrived and Hampton opened the session by describing the changes in British strategic dispositions. If England were engaged in a war with Germany, Italy, and Japan, it was impossible, he said, to determine what ships could be spared for the Far East or when they might be dispatched. Admiral Leahy said he was interested to learn this, but even in discussion the United States would have to be assumed to be neutral. With the United States neutral, he thought that when war broke out the president would send the fleet to Hawaii. From Pearl Harbor the fleet could threaten any Japanese move to the south. As for the Atlantic, Leahy said that the president intended to establish some form of naval patrol in the Caribbean and along the east coast of South America. This patrol was designed to protect neutral shipping, but it was possible that information obtained on German activities could be passed to the Royal Navy.

Leahy was unwilling to say anything more about a possible naval alliance and Hampton thought it was best to "refrain from pressing him too closely on this point." Furthermore, Leahy displayed great security consciousness, requesting that no written record be kept of the meeting. Hampton acceded since he thought Leahy more likely to be "forthcoming verbally than he would be if asked to commit his views to paper." Leahy's cautiousness made it difficult to understand why the Americans had been so willing to hold talks, and Hampton and Curzon-Howe agreed to try once more to lead him into discussing "cooperation in war." Another meeting, consequently, was arranged for 14 June.

The first matter discussed at the second meeting was the distribution of codes, signal books, and cyphers. It was quickly agreed that a method should be devised for distributing copies to all units of the U.S. and British navies so that at the very least communication would be possible. Then the crucial question was put forward. What were Leahy's views about cooperation between the two fleets (British and American) in a war with Germany, Italy, and Japan? Leahy emphasized that his comments would be personal and not part of any "settled war plan." With that caveat accepted, he said the United States would look out for the Pacific while the allied navies took care of the Mediterranean and the Atlantic. Any American forces in the Atlantic would remain there and would cooperate with the British. He thought that the U.S. Fleet "should move to Singapore in sufficient force to be able to engage and defeat any Japanese Fleet it met with on passage." He was opposed to sending any weak force to Singapore and he implied that a minimum of ten capital ships would be required. The United States, however, would not send ships to Singapore unless the British sent an "adequate token force" to cooperate with them. He did not define just how large "adequate" was but said that some capital ships would be required. Planning for a move to Singapore had not been completed, but if relief of the fortress were predicated on the arrival of U.S. forces, defenses should be prepared for at least 120 days. But Leahy made it clear that he was not prepared to engage in a detailed discussion of Pacific cooperation. The same was generally true concerning the Atlantic, although he did say that if the United States entered the war, it would cooperate in the organization and support of convoys as in 1917–18. The second and last session concluded with a brief comment on the Philippines, which Leahy admitted would be difficult to relieve and hence an unsatisfactory base, and some talk about technical exchanges.

Hampton quietly left Washington on 16 June and arrived home ten days later. He realized that in some ways his mission had been disappointing. The extreme secrecy surrounding his mission had been a hindrance. It made detailed discussion with experts impossible and the talks had remained general. "The number of Americans who can be trusted with secrets," Hampton reported, "is apparently strictly limited." For instance, Leahy had said that "on no account" should the U.S. director of naval intelligence be informed of Hampton's visit. Whether this was because he might oppose the talks or might prove unreliable was never made clear. Nevertheless, despite the emphasis on security, Hampton thought that Leahy was very appreciative of British efforts to keep him informed. Leahy was "extremely pro-British," Hampton had found, as was Admiral Harold Stark, who would soon take over the CNO. Furthermore, despite the lack of specific American plans for cooperation in the event of war, Hampton felt that broad strategic concepts were already agreed upon. That, plus the cooperative bent of the president and the naval staff, boded well for the future.

The director of plans at the Admiralty, Captain Victor Danckwerts, was happy with the results of the Hampton mission despite the lack of written accord. Admiral Tom Phillips, now deputy chief of the naval staff, was also pleased. As he noted, American willingness even to consider going to Singapore was a "great advance." On balance, it seemed a successful visit and Commander Hampton was commended for his good work.[31]

After the talks with Hampton the U.S. Navy felt better prepared to face the uncertain future. Back in April 1939, the Joint Planners had suggested an Atlantic orientation in a two-ocean war; but on 30 June 1939 the Joint Board directed that instead a series of plans be prepared. Five different contingencies were envisaged and defined as follows:

RAINBOW 1 assumed the United States to be at war without major allies. United States forces would act jointly to prevent the violation of the Monroe Doctrine by protecting the territory of the Western Hemisphere north of latitude 10° south, from which the vital tasks of the United States might be threatened. The joint tasks of the Army and Navy included protection of the United States, its possessions and its seaborne trade. A strategic defensive was to be maintained in the Pacific, from behind the line Alaska-Hawaii-Panama, until developments for offensive action against Japan.

RAINBOW 2 assumed that the United States, Great Britain, and France would be acting in concert, with limited participation of U.S. forces in continental Europe and in the Atlantic. The United States could, therefore, undertake offensive operations across the Pacific to sustain the interests of democratic powers by the defeat of enemy forces.

RAINBOW 3 assumed the United States to be at war without major allies. Hemisphere defense was to be assured, as in RAINBOW 1, but with early projection of U.S. forces from Hawaii into the western Pacific.

RAINBOW 4 assumed the United States to be at war without major allies, employing its forces in defense of the whole of the Western Hemisphere, but also with provision for United States Army forces to be sent to the Southern part of South America, and to be used in joint operations in eastern Atlantic areas. A strategic defensive, as in RAINBOW 1, was to be maintained in the Pacific until the situation in the Atlantic permitted transfer of major naval forces for an offensive against Japan.

RAINBOW 5 assumed the United States, Great Britain, and France to be acting in concert; hemisphere defense was to be assured as in RAINBOW 1, with early projection of U.S. forces to the eastern Atlantic, and to either or both the African and European continents; offensive operations were to be conducted, in concert with British and allied forces, to effect the defeat of Germany and Italy. A strategic defensive was to be maintained in the Pacific until success against European Axis Powers permitted transfer of major forces to the Pacific for an offensive against Japan.[32]

Of these five plans RAINBOW 1 and RAINBOW 4 were clearly the least ambitious, but some members of the Joint Board, probably naval members, rejected the idea that America was unable to protect the hemisphere and launch a Pacific offensive simultaneously. RAINBOW 3 was inherently a restatement of the old ORANGE plan, while RAINBOW 5, under conditions existing in 1939, would put United States forces in a subordinate position to those of Britain and France. From the navy's perspective, RAINBOW 2 was the most desirable plan. To ambitious navalists, it held out the prospect of maintaining a position in the Far East rather than fighting to regain harbors and islands. With allies, and the navy now knew it would likely have at least one ally, the old objection about relieving the Philippines could be countered. An immediate offensive could be launched south and west from Hawaii by way of the Fijis through the Moluccas into the Java Sea. Once in that tropic sea they could be joined by units from Singapore and Subic Bay and prepare to shut the Japanese off north of the Malay Barrier. These moves, even if they did not quickly climax in a classic naval victory, like Tsushima, in reverse, would surely deny the Japanese their most strategic requirement—oil. Therefore the navy concentrated on RAINBOW 2 as not only a good prospective scenario but as the scenario most likely to insure the navy's major participation.[33] Whether this rationale, or even the degree and extent of Anglo-American contact, was ever explained to the army is not clear. It seems not unlikely that part of the penchant for secrecy observed by Leahy and others was intended to keep certain developments from their interservice colleagues.

Though unaware of the contingency planning, the British were pleased with developments vis-à-vis the U.S. Navy. Although no commitments had been made, the Americans seemed willing to consider a move to Singapore. That they also wanted a substantial British force dispatched was somewhat troublesome, but perhaps that was not an insuperable problem. Obviously, neither side was yet ready to accept verbal agreements as commitments, but out of mutual deficiencies might grow mutual dependence. Most encouraging of all was Roosevelt's tendency to come up with unexpected and unconventional proposals. The president's idea for an Atlantic patrol, for instance, might have many desirable repercussions. If given enough leeway, it must have seemed at least possible that Roosevelt would blunder into war.

4.

Origins of the "Naval Person" Correspondence

June 1939–May 1940

President Franklin Roosevelt had played a major role in all the Anglo-American contacts up to this point. Genius of the unexpected, maestro of the improvisational, artist of the dramatic, his mind danced across the scene where his legs would not carry him. Since his taste in concepts was catholic, it should come as no surprise that some of his schemes were imprudent and unwise and that most were unconventional. Had he expended the same effort convincing the public to do what he felt was right that he spent dreaming up ways to advance clandestine projects, it probably would have been more productive. There would be a number of such projects in the 1939–41 period, but perhaps none more dramatic, or of more questionable propriety, than the one he began to concoct in June 1939.

* * *

As far as the public was concerned, the greatest single example of British-American friendship during the tense summer of 1939 was the visit to the United States of King George VI and Queen Mary. They were toured and feted, applauded and cheered. They did all the conventional things expected of celebrities while radiating charm and dignity. From their point of view, the highlight of the trip was a homey gathering at the Roosevelts' Hyde Park estate. Squeezed in between hot-dog roasts and drives around the grounds were several informal strategy sessions held by the king and the president.

During the first meeting, which went on until very late on the night of 10 June 1939, Roosevelt expounded on a slowly maturing naval plan. Since 1936, he said, he had been thinking of establishing bases on Newfoundland, Bermuda, Jamaica, St. Lucia, Antigua, and Trinidad, the better to protect the American continent and to keep those islands from falling to a European enemy. He did not mention whether he had considered how to convince the British and Dutch governments to grant the bases, preferring instead to dwell on the naval aspects of the plan. Naval maneuvers in 1938–39 had determined that a Western Atlantic patrol could deny the coastal waters of the Americas to belligerent submarines and commerce raiders. Roosevelt, recorded the king, who had kept careful notes of the meetings, was "terribly keen" about the patrol and returned to the subject the next evening. If a submarine were sighted the U.S. Navy would "sink it at once and wait for the consequences." Sighting submarines was a reasonably certain prospect since the proposed Trinidad patrol could range out a thousand miles, while the Bermuda patrol could protect convoys from attack. As Leahy had hinted in his meetings with Hampton, the object was to relieve the Royal Navy of "these responsibilities." Helpful as the patrol might be, there were numerous problems, including sovereignty at the required bases and neutrality. The issue of neutrality would be the most difficult to surmount, for, as the king wrote, "can it be done without [a] declaration of war?"[1] Obviously not—if what was being done should become public knowledge.

When the king returned to England he took the notes of his conversations with him, but the president was not depending on the king to carry the plan forward. On 30 June 1939, Roosevelt called in Ambassador Lindsay for another secret conference. By this time the president was prepared to be quite specific. In case of war he wanted the U.S. Navy to establish a neutrality patrol to keep the waters of the Western Hemisphere clear of all belligerents. The patrol, the president said, would free British ships for more important duties closer to home. Not surprisingly, this benefit could not be gained without paying a price. The price was that Britain should grant base rights to the United States in Trinidad, St. Lucia, and Bermuda. If these rights were not granted until war broke out, suspicions and awkward questions about unneutral conduct might be raised. Therefore the president wanted the rights granted during peacetime—in other words, right away.[2]

The British government moved swiftly to accept the president's proposal, though some points concerning the extent and nature of the patrol needed clarification. The Admiralty made the reason for their positive response explicit. In their view "the permission to use our bases now will lead to greater collaboration to [with?] the U.S.A. and the development of the plan in time of war would be bound sooner or later to involve the U.S.A. in hostilities on our side." At the same time they had some specific questions about precisely how well the president would keep the Admiralty informed of enemy ship movements and where the patrol would operate.[3]

Using the same method of communication sometimes employed before, Lindsay conveyed these questions through Undersecretary Welles, who in turn brought Roosevelt's reply. The president was not pleased by the British attempt to pin him down. The matter of how and where the patrol would be put into effect could await developments, but the British questions seemed to imply doubt about his resolution and "misapprehension of his intentions." Especially irritating apparently was the question about passing on information about enemy ship movements. According to Welles, the president had responded with a "rough colloquial expression" that meant, "This is a delicate question to which you ought not to expect an answer." The undersecretary suggested, however, that Commander Hampton should have indications of the U.S. Navy's views. That Welles considered the indications positive and highly sensitive is suggested by his request that Lindsay burn all notes on the conversation.[4]

Despite Roosevelt's unwillingness to be more precise, which some attributed to his failure to think very deeply about his patrol, the British government proceeded to grant the United States the requested base facilities, with the short-range goal of bettering relations and with the hope of eventually involving the United States in the war.[5] There was some disappointment that the president would not be more explicit in his intentions or open in his sympathies, but, then, Roosevelt usually sounded most brave when he confined himself to generalities. The subject, however, was not closed and the president's patrol, which he did institute when war broke out, would be the subject of some most unusual communications during the coming months.

* * *

The German army crossed the Polish border on 31 August 1939 and two days later, for the second time in twenty-five years, the Allies declared war on Germany. President Roosevelt immediately proclaimed American neutrality, and put the arms embargo into effect, while at the same time calling for revision of the Neutrality Act. Simultaneously he announced the creation of a buffer zone in the Western Hemisphere. To see that it was observed, he instituted the incongruously titled "Neutrality Patrol." With something of the same disingenuousness, he began campaigning for repeal of the cash-and-carry provisions of the Neutrality Act, contending that revision would insure actual neutrality and help keep the United States out of war.[6] Apparently it was felt that the American public was not yet prepared for candor.

Roosevelt was obviously feeling his way in a new situation and he had a number of concerns. For one thing it seemed essential to keep in close touch with the Royal Navy. Therefore, on 11 September 1939, Roosevelt sent a personal message to the new first lord of the Admiralty, Winston Churchill. The president wrote:

It is because you and I occupied similar positions in the World War that I want you to know how glad I am that you are back again in the Admiralty. Your problems are, I realize, complicated by new factors, but the essential is not very different. What I want you and the Prime Minister to know is that I shall at all times welcome it, if you will keep me in touch personally with anything you want me to know about. You can always send sealed letters through your pouch or my pouch.[7]

This was the first of the famous messages that were to pass between Roosevelt and Churchill, the latter styling himself as "Naval Person" until events in May 1940 transformed him to "Former Naval Person." How natural it seemed, how convenient the naval link between the two men and the two countries, but how unusual for the president of a neutral nation to communicate personally with the head of a warring government's naval establishment![8]

Whether the British thought it was unusual we do not know, but we now know that Churchill and the foreign secretary, Lord Halifax, sensed immediately the value of this personal contact. The first lord thought, and the foreign secretary agreed, that it would be a "good thing to 'feed' Mr. Roosevelt at intervals."[9] "Feed" him Churchill did, clearing the messages with the Cabinet as he did so.

The clearance procedure worked swiftly. Roosevelt's first message traveled to England via the diplomatic pouch and on 3 October Ambassador Kennedy forwarded it to Mr. Churchill. Two days later the first lord sent the president two messages.[10] The first was a cryptic note concerning an apparent German plot to blow up the American passenger liner S.S. *Iroquois*. According to Admiral Erich Raeder, the commander of the German Reichsmarine, a bomb had been planted before the ship left Ireland, to simulate a submarine attack "for the apparent purpose of arousing anti-German feeling."[11] Captain Alan Kirk, the new American naval attaché in London, had been asked to query the British, and Churchill replied in a personal cable to Roosevelt.

Iroquois is probably 1000 miles West of Ireland. Presume you could not meet her before 50th meridian. There remains about 1000 miles in which outrage might be committed. U-boat danger inconceivable in these broad waters. Only method can be time-bomb planted at Queenstown. Stop. We think this not impossible. Stop.

Am convinced full exposure of all facts known to U.S. Government, including sources of information, especially if official, only way of frustrating plot. Stop. Action seems urgent. Stop. Presume you have warned *Iroquois* to search ship. Stop.[12]

There were hurried consultations within the administration. It was decided to avoid publicity, but to escort the ship into port. She was joined by U.S. warships and on 11 October, while still six hundred miles from New York, was given air cover as well.[13] Apparently there was no bomb or it had been disarmed, for the *Iroquois* completed her journey safely and no more was heard of the incident.

The second message, sent on 5 October, dealt with the Security

Zone that had been drawn around the continents of North and South America and which the United States had persuaded the Western Hemisphere Foreign Ministers' meeting in Panama to sanction.[14] Churchill cabled: "We do not mind how far south the prohibited zone goes provided that it is effectively maintained. We shall have great difficulty in accepting a zone which was only policed by some weak neutral. But of course if the American Navy takes care of it, that is all right." Despite this helpful tone, the burden of this portion of Churchill's message was that Britain would have to pursue German warships inside the Security Zone unless the United States could make German ships respect it.[15]

At the same time Churchill made it clear that he anticipated reports on any German ships that did not comply. "The more American ships cruising along the South American coast the better," he wrote, "as you, sir, would no doubt hear what they saw or did not see. Raider [the German commerce raider] might then find American waters rather crowded, or anyhow prefer to go on to sort of trade route, where we are preparing." Included with this message was an interpretive memorandum by Admiral Phillips that reiterated the point made when the president first broached his patrol idea. "We should hope," Phillips commented, "to obtain any information concerning the movements of enemy Forces within the area since otherwise the operation of the scheme [the Patrol] would greatly reduce the possibilities on [of?] obtaining such information for ourselves."[16] It was reporting on the German ships that the British had hoped would "sooner or later . . . involve the U.S.A. in hostilities on [the British] side."

Washington's failure to respond to these communiqués prompted Churchill, who was eager to continue the correspondence, to write Lord Halifax. "I think I ought to send something to our American friend," Churchill wrote, "in order to keep him interested in our affairs." In anticipation that the foreign minister would agree, he had prepared a message that he proposed clearing through the prime minister. As Churchill noted, he felt that the British must not let "the liaison lapse."[17]

The message he had prepared was filled with tidbits of naval news. Its general tone was optimistic. The German pocket battleship *Scheer* had disappeared, but the Royal Navy was looking hard for her. German submarines were being located, and sunk, with satisfying regularity. Hitler's oil supply was limited and he was hesitating; but if he attacked, the British were ready. Furthermore, the British were ready to help America be more prepared, as the first lord made clear when he referred to an important piece of naval hardware. "We should be quite ready to tell you about our ASDIC [the British underwater detection device similar to the U.S. Navy's SONAR] methods whenever you feel they would be of use to the United States Navy and are sure the secret will go no further."[18] It was all rather chummy and light. However, complications were not long in developing.

Despite Halifax's agreement and Cabinet approval, no one had bothered to inform the American Division of the Foreign Office or the new British ambassador, Lord Lothian, of the correspondence. The ambassador was therefore embarrassed and shocked when Sumner Welles questioned him about Churchill's 5 October message. For one thing, Lothian had never seen the message, and for another there was the danger that the first lord's views on the Neutrality Zone might be taken as the official British position, which only the ambassador was charged with interpreting. Lothian protested to the American Division of the Foreign Office, but they knew nothing of any Churchill messages and sent to the Admiralty for copies. These were duly received and dispatched to Lord Lothian, but there was concern within the department that if the correspondence continued, more confusion would inevitably result. Sir David Scott, chief of the American division, observed that he had scant hopes of stopping or even clearing the messages; however, he found it "very awkward" since the line between what is "purely naval and what is partly naval and partly political is not one which can in war time be drawn with any exactitude."[19]

This was a logical attitude, but it is hard to escape the feeling that the Foreign Office objected not only to the subjects being discussed but also to the person discussing them. Winston Churchill was not everyone's model of propriety or stability. His methods of operation were at least unorthodox and to some seemed irrational; furthermore, he was impossible to contain within a bureaucratic mold.[20]

The Foreign Office did see, however, that one subject touched on in Churchill's 16 October message might be turned to British advantage. They knew, and probably Mr. Churchill did too, that in August 1939 Prime Minister Chamberlain had written President Roosevelt for information on the top-secret Norden bombsight.

Roosevelt had turned the request down, but now that Churchill had offered ASDIC perhaps some trade could be arranged.[21] This suggestion was passed to the Admiralty but Roosevelt had not answered Churchill's message and the first lord was reluctant to push him.[22] Lord Lothian showed no such sensitivity and went to the president with the outline of a quid pro quo arrangement whereby the British would provide ASDIC in return for the Norden bombsight. The president said he would look into the matter but he took no action.[23]

At approximately this time, mid-November 1939, Lord Lothian learned that the U.S. Department of State was interpreting Churchill's comments on the Neutrality Zone as British official policy. Unfortunately, Lord Lothian had yet to receive his copies of the messages in question and did not even know what the first lord's comments were. This situation confirmed the fears of the Foreign Office and Lord Halifax addressed a personal letter to Churchill. "I fully appreciate the value of using the opportunity for direct personal contact with the President," he wrote, but went on to request that the Foreign Office be sent copies of future messages so that Lothian could be kept informed and positions "squared."[24]

In response to this request, on 25 December Churchill sent the Foreign Office a copy of a message he had just given to Joseph Kennedy for transmission to the president. According to Churchill's later recollection, the president had "reluctantly complained" about British violations of the Neutrality Zone in pursuit of the German battleship *Admiral Graf Spee*. In response, Churchill pointed out the advantages wrought for the South American republics by the British action and implied that it was the Royal Navy that actually made the Security Zone secure.[25] The president apparently did not reply to this somewhat supercilious message.

Despite Churchill's attempt to comply with the wishes of Lord Halifax, this 25 December message also caused complications. Although the Foreign Office was provided with a copy at approximately the same time the American Embassy was, Lord Lothian was again put in the embarrassing position of being informed of an important communication by someone other than his own government. In this case the Argentine ambassador, who had been advised by the Americans of the message, was the medium through which Lothian was first informed.[26] Tempers in the Foreign Office, and one would assume in the British Embassy, were becoming a trifle strained. For one thing, the American Division of the Foreign Office had already come to distrust the defeatist views of Joseph Kennedy, whose telegrams they appeared to have been reading, and heartily wished that his office would not be used as the channel for such a highly sensitive correspondence.[27] There is the possibility that from Churchill's perspective Kennedy's presumed unreliability provided an extra dividend. Would it not be advantageous to have the Germans learn that Churchill and Roosevelt were maintaining such close personal contact?

Such subtleties were either not involved or not grasped by the Foreign Office, where Sir David Scott noted on the file: "I fancy that the channel of the U.S. Embassy was used as the result of a suggestion by Mr. Kennedy and with the idea of making the messages seem more personal and 'exclusive.'"[28] But aside from the channel used, as Halifax wrote to Churchill, "it will always be embarrassing to Lothian not to know about these messages beforehand," and there was the very real possibility of getting at "cross purposes" if statements were coming from two different quarters.[29] Therefore, the foreign secretary asked that Churchill in the future send his messages by way of the Foreign Office.[30]

Churchill agreed that confusion should be avoided, but also suggested that it would be a "great pity" to close down the "private line" of communication through the American Embassy and the State Department. He suggested that Lothian be sent future messages simultaneously. This would keep the British ambassador fully informed while "giving the President the feeling that he [had] a special line of information."[31] Halifax agreed to this procedure, and admitted that it was "most valuable" to keep in direct touch with the president. The American Division, on the other hand, would not agree that it was wise to go through the American Embassy, where Kennedy could pry.[32]

Foreign Office sensitivities did not deter the first sea lord from pursuing his correspondence with the president. In early 1940 the "Naval Person" sent two more messages on neutrality matters to Roosevelt. The manner in which the Royal Navy was conducting its blockade had stirred the ire of American shippers and members of the administration, including the president. The British government believed that it was lawfully exercising its belligerent rights, but to the Americans the British actions smacked of harassment.

The issue had become heated when the Royal Navy brought the U.S. flagship *Mooremacsun* into a British port in early January and refused to release the ship or its cargo without navicerts or destination guarantees. Pressure was brought from various quarters and on 29 January Churchill informed the president of a change in official policy. "I gave orders last night," Churchill's message read, "that no American ship should in any circumstances be diverted into the combat zone round the British Isles declared by you. I trust this will be satisfactory."[33]

Churchill sent another message on 30 January, asking the president not to publicize the assurance of nondiversion in order to avoid the appearance of discrimination. Furthermore, he advised the president that in "exceptional cases" it might be necessary to bring American ships in for inspection if there were definite grounds for suspicion about their cargoes.[34] According to one authoritative source, the messages were "some balm for these wounds" to American feelings, but other irritations soon followed.[35] On 1 February the president replied:

My dear Churchill:

Ever so many thanks for that tremendously interesting account of the extraordinarily well fought action of your three cruisers. I am inclined to think that when we know more about the facts, it will turn out that the damage to the ADMIRAL GRAF SPEE was greater than reported.

At the time of dictating this, I think our conversation in regard to search and detention of American ships is working out satisfactorily—but I would not be frank unless I told you that there had been much public criticism here. The general feeling is that the net benefit to your people and to France is hardly worth the definite annoyance caused to us. That is always found to be so in a nation which is 3,000 miles away from the fact of war.[36]

I wish much that I could talk things over with you in person—but I am grateful to you for keeping me in touch as you do.[37]

The *Graf Spee* incident was interesting and exciting, but there had indeed been repercussions. There was public criticism in the United States of British actions, and the Department of State made official representations. Churchill describes it as a time in which the United States was "cooler than in any other period." However, he persevered in his correspondence with the president, "but with little response."[38] The 1 February message was a response, but although it was sympathetic, the president's letter was more concerned with problems than with pleasantries.[39]

But there were rewards as well. Although there is no evidence that the U.S. Navy had been of assistance in tracking down the *Graf Spee*, it had been providing the British with valuable assistance. This became clear during the continuing debate within the Admiralty concerning technological cooperation with the U.S. Navy. The director of naval intelligence, Rear Admiral John Godfrey, was in favor of such cooperation, saying that "their patrols in the Gulf of Mexico gave us information, and recently they have been thoroughly unneutral in reporting the position of the S.S. *Columbus*." Godfrey went on to note that the Americans passed on all information they had on the Japanese navy, as well as other intelligence "tidbits" picked up in Berlin and Tokyo. In Godfrey's opinion, senior U.S. naval officers were "almost unanimously pro ally," and the president had often shown himself "anxious to meet us half way."[40]

The *Columbus* was a German flag vessel that had been tracked down by the British and eventually scuttled just outside American territorial waters, so the U.S. Navy was clearly following through with Roosevelt's concept of a neutrality patrol.

Churchill was obviously aware of these benefits, and on 28 February warmly answered the president's letter:

> Very warm thanks for your most kind letter of February 1. Since on January 29 I gave orders to the Fleet not to bring any American ships into the zone you have drawn around our shores, many of the other Departments have become much concerned about the efficiency of the blockade and the difficulties of discriminating between various countries. The neutrals are all on them and they are all on me. Nevertheless the order still stands and no American ship has been brought by the Navy into the danger zone.
>
> . . . .
>
> I do hope that I may be helped to hold the position I have adopted by the American shipping lines availing themselves to the great convenience of navicerts which was an American invention and thus enable American trade to proceed without hindrance.
>
> It is a great pleasure to me to keep you informed about Naval matters, although alas I cannot have the honour of a talk with you in person.[41]

The last message in the series came within the week. An American shipping company was still having difficulties with some of its European routes and a 5 March 1940 cable from Roosevelt referred to this matter. The president's cable simply reads: "I deeply appreciate your efforts. I am having the situation thoroughly studied and will communicate with you further as soon as possible."[42] If the president ever communicated further with Churchill on this subject or on any other the record does not reveal it. The next message the president sent to Churchill is dated 16 May 1940 and by that time the "Naval Person" had become prime minister and "Former Naval Person."

The "Naval Person" correspondence would probably have remained a secret much longer if the sensitivities of the American Division had been heeded. Ironically, Ambassador Kennedy was not the weak link, but using the American Embassy for transmission was. The problem came from within the code room of the Embassy, where a young clerk by the name of Tyler Kent worked on coding and decoding diplomatic messages. He followed the Churchill-Roosevelt correspondence from its inception and it seemed to him that the messages compromised the neutrality of the United States. He even theorized that they might be part of a plot to involve America in the more vigorous war that Churchill, as prime minister, might wage. The assumption, of course, that Churchill would take over as prime minister was highly speculative when Kent started collecting messages. In any case, he felt that it was his higher duty as an American citizen to collect the messages and other incriminating data. He later stated that he hoped to turn the evidence over to responsible American officials, possibly to Congress, in order to prove how misguided was public confidence in Mr. Roosevelt's credibility.

Kent was not to get a chance to put his case to the Congress or the press. On 20 May 1940 British security agents burst into his room, where they discovered 1,500 classified documents, many of which Kent later claimed were Churchill-Roosevelt messages. Kent clearly had no right to remove the copies of the messages from the Embassy files and there was even evidence indicating that he had passed some classified data on to enemy agents. Since some of the messages related to British policy and Kent was in London, prosecution by American authorities was waived and he was tried and convicted of spying by the British government.[43] He was confined in England until 1945, when he returned to America. After the war, when the case was brought to public attention in the United States, Kent's charges were seized upon by the anti-Roosevelt forces and the suspicion began to grow that there had been a vast clandestine exchange of messages. The matter was mentioned in the newspapers, on the floor of Congress, during the Pearl Harbor hearings, and has been referred to from time to time since.[44]

Since the case had legal and partisan overtones, and since some of the participants, most notably Kent, are still alive, the United States government has been reluctant to release data on the matter. However, a list of documents found in Kent's possession has now been made available and by putting it together with documents in the public domain it is possible to form a good picture of the Churchill-Roosevelt correspondence during the period September 1939 to May 1940. The picture revealed tends to bear out the explanation that Roosevelt provided to Secretary of State Cordell Hull. After describing the contacts as being few in number, the president said that all the messages "obviously were related to naval matters." He further described the exchanges as "wholly consonant to the policy of this Government to give all possible legal aid to the preservation of British defense."[45] This description seems to be accurate, if one realizes how broadly Roosevelt interpreted that policy.

By experience and predilection Roosevelt was a navalist. His service as assistant secretary of the navy in World War I also had taught him the value of personal contacts. As he had told an audience, which included Winston Churchill, at Grey's Inn in London in 1918, he recognized the "necessity for more of this intimate personal relationship."[46] Therefore, it was logical and consistent for him to form such a relationship with the first lord of the Admiralty, whoever he happened to be. Although Roosevelt suggested that it might prove very helpful for both parties to have a special understanding, his motivation was probably primarily self-serving. Thus, from Roosevelt's perspective the correspondence, although of questionable propriety, was practical and potentially useful. The president himself provided evidence that the contact was not as unusual or as personal a gesture as it might initially seem. On 11 September 1939, the same day he wrote Churchill, he also wrote Chamberlain. In this letter he said: "I need not tell you that you have been much in my thoughts during these difficult days and further that I hope you will at all times feel free to write me personally and outside of diplomatic procedure about any problems as they may arise."[47] The president enjoyed special relationships and it was not necessarily a sign of particular favoritism for him to urge people to bypass the diplomats and eliminate formality.

The "neutrality patrol" as practiced, not as advertised, is one of the most blatant examples of Roosevelt's disingenuousness. The chance that Kent's rash actions would reveal the president's duplicity sent shock waves through the Department of State. Breckinridge Long, assistant secretary of state, was badly shaken, noting in his diary that Kent's actions were "almost a major catastrophe"[48] and that further revelations might "implicate the chief [Roosevelt],"[49] which they surely would have. Kent was silenced, though, and the secret behind the secret correspondence was kept.

From the British perspective, Kent's actions were not particularly threatening, although the case could do nothing to increase respect for U.S. security procedures. The patrol had not yet involved the United States in the war, but the inside line to the White House should prove valuable. The patrol had already provided some direct benefits and the base-leasing arrangement would ultimately provide a vital precedent. All in all, by 10 May 1940, when he became prime minister, Churchill could feel rather pleased with himself and with his collaborationist in Washington.

5.

Technology and Bargaining

July 1939–10 May 1940

While Churchill and Roosevelt had been establishing their line of communications, relationships had been developing at the working level. Shortly after the Ingersoll-Phillips conversations there had been a flurry of interest in the exchange of technological information. There had been little practical result, but between June 1939 and May 1940 interest revived. The discussions and actual exchanges that took place comprised the primary form of contact between the two navies during this eleven-month period, and the manner in which the negotiations were handled provides a measure of Anglo-American naval relations.

When on 3 September 1939 Britain declared war on Germany, relations between the two friendly powers changed dramatically. One measure of that change can be found in the technological area. For one thing, the Americans became increasingly eager to learn from British practical experience; for another, war-damaged ships could tell a lot about the reliability of armor and the effects of bombs and guns. Moreover, since this was going to be a highly technological war, there was a lot to learn about new weapons and techniques for defense against them.

With so much at stake it is not surprising, yet it is still sad, to find that once again the search for advantage retarded the search for mutual progress. Some American officers believed, wrongly, that their country was ahead on devices like radar (RDF to the British) and on bombsights, and although eager to learn British techniques, they were hesitant to share information unless assured of a worthwhile return. The British were hobbled by similar concerns. They wanted good relations with the United States, but they judged themselves to be well advanced beyond their American cousins and worried lest they give away too much. There were varying reasons for this reluctance. One was the fear that the U.S. Navy's security system was dangerously inefficient. Another was hesitancy to share, with a vocally insistent neutral, secrets learned with blood and sweat. The Americans were being helpful in some ways to be sure, but every step the president took was publicly presented in terms of keeping the country out of war. Finally, there were those, like Winston Churchill, who wished to consider technical exchanges only in conjunction with broader cooperative arrangements. Evident on both sides were the familiar issues of pride and competitiveness.

* * *

Some of the burden of dealing with the drastically revised plans that events necessitated fell upon the new American naval attaché, Captain Alan G. Kirk, who arrived in England in June 1939. For the next eighteen months Kirk played a significant role in Anglo-American naval relations. As attaché he was essentially an intelligence operative accredited by a friendly country. His orders were to work as closely as possible with the Royal Navy and to keep Washington apprised of the methods and matériel that were being developed in Britain. At the same time Kirk was supposed to be a military diplomat, the chief representative of the U.S. Navy in London and the channel for naval liaison. During the fall of 1939 and the spring of 1940 his primary duties were to stimulate exchanges of technical data and to report on Britain's military chances.

He ran into the same difficulties in his attempt to exchange technical information that had frustrated previous efforts by others. Each side wanted certain information; on the other hand, neither gave up secrets readily, at least not to the other. Consequently, Kirk found himself in the position of at one time requesting information from the British and explaining why his Navy Department had not complied with British requests, and shortly thereafter interpreting British intransigence to Washington as he recommended that his country not display the same trait. His other area of primary concern, gauging Britain's chances, influenced his relations in London and his impact on opinion in Washington.

Making the task more difficult was the general course of the war. Attachés are subject to accusations of bias toward their hosts. If Washington were to suspect that his reports were not objective, Kirk's usefulness would be substantially reduced. Kirk was undoubtedly aware of this potential problem and sometimes may have leavened his assessments with a pinch of pessimism. On the other hand, he was not swept off his feet by British military prowess and there were times when he was acutely depressed about British prospects. In this regard he very probably reflected the general attitude of his superiors toward the Royal Navy. Friendship was tinged with just a little jealousy and a certain lack of respect for Britain's traditional muddling through. Also likely to affect Kirk was Ambassador Kennedy's less than total confidence in the prospects for British arms. At the same time Kirk had to be cautious that the British did not get the idea that he was a defeatist or they might conclude that he was not worth influencing. If that idea took hold they might stop trying to ingratiate themselves by honoring his requests. All in all it was a difficult post.

Fifty-year-old Alan G. Kirk was equal to the challenge. Seeing him in London, where prior to September 1939 he seldom wore his uniform, one might mistake him for a prosperous member of the sporting set. Tall and spare, with thick, graying hair and a handsome face, Kirk cut quite a figure. With his wife, an attractive woman of great charm, he was a frequent visitor in some of England's finer homes. He soon won the friendship and professional esteem of military and civilian officials alike, who marked him as an officer with a bright future. His own Navy Department considered his reports thorough, authoritative estimates of the situation, as were his frequent personal letters to his immediate superior, Rear Admiral Walter Anderson, chief of naval intelligence. And for special situations, Kirk claimed to have a special line into the White House.

It took Kirk only a short time after arriving in London to realize that his naval hosts were being exceptionally friendly. They gave a definite impression of willingness to be just as cooperative as the United States would let them be.[1] Kirk did not immediately suspect that they wanted something in return, but tried to do nothing to impede the growth of a close liaison. When war broke out in September 1939, Kirk's duties and his desire to learn from the Royal Navy's experience increased considerably.

One of the most logical ways to learn about the Royal Navy was to send observers to bases and on fleet maneuvers, or to go himself. Initially the process worked quite smoothly and Kirk's observers brought back valuable information on a number of subjects, including harbor defenses, which was duly relayed to Washington.[2] The British quickly discovered a way to make these visits mutually beneficial. The German press was prominently claiming that the carrier *Ark Royal* had been sunk in harbor. It occurred to Winston Churchill that a convenient way to contradict these reports would be for an American naval officer to find the ship riding safe at anchor. The first lord relayed this suggestion to Ambassador Kennedy at lunch, and the next day Kirk was on his way toward the Royal Navy's anchorage at Scapa Flow. When he returned to London, his discovery of the *Ark Royal* received a degree of publicity as pleasing to the British as it was galling to the Nazis.[3]

Despite these hopeful beginnings, cautious bargaining continued. Some of Kirk's superiors in Washington were worried lest British agreement to visits by American observers presaged requests for the same privilege. Consequently, when Kirk requested clearance to expand the observer program and to send American officers on special maneuvers with the Home Fleet, he was advised that before agreeing, he should receive "definite assurances" that the observers could go without any promise of "reciprocity."[4] The British gave the assurance, and several assistant naval attachés were dispatched to perform the observer duty. As would become clear, the ready agreement on this issue did not mean that the British wanted nothing in return. Nor did it mean that exchanging secrets would immediately become easy.

In November 1939 Kirk incorporated his general philosophy on exchanges in a letter to Admiral Walter S. Anderson. As the British navy gained in war experience Kirk thought it would "gradually outdistance" the United States in many technical subjects. Therefore, America's best interest would be served by "liberalizing" the policies of exchange set down in Washington. "The way the opposing forces line up," he wrote, "ought to make it pretty safe for us to swap with the British."[5] As long as reciprocity provided more than it relinquished, he could not see why the Navy Department should be reluctant to share.

American reluctance made pressuring the British difficult, and there were many items he wished to pressure the British about. High on his list was their underwater listening device called ASDIC. It was ASDIC that Churchill had offered to Roosevelt in his third missive, but apparently the first lord had not assayed the sensitivities of his own service, which was unwilling to provide even a general description of the secret device. Roosevelt never followed up on Churchill's offer and when Lothian next broached the subject it was in terms of a trade: ASDIC for the Norden bombsight. Roosevelt simply ignored the ambassador's suggestion.[6]

Kirk could get no offer on ASDIC from his contacts even though there were people at the Admiralty who saw the exchange situation as he did. This "generous" position was aptly summed up in a memorandum written by the director of naval intelligence, Admiral John Godfrey, in December 1939. In Godfrey's view a balance had to be struck between political gains and technical losses. For his part, he wished nothing done to inhibit Anglo-American friendship. For, as he put it, "the more the Americans have the feeling of being 'in' with us—without necessarily getting the impression that we are under an obligation to them—the more easily and fluently will the countries merge, if need be, as allies." He then discussed one of the barriers to frank exchanges—security, or, more precisely, American lack of security, since, as we have seen, it was a widely accepted truth in London that the Americans were incredibly inefficient about keeping secrets. Especially disturbing were the ubiquitous newspaper reporters and their close relationship with the Navy Department. It was Godfrey's conclusion that leaks in the United States were practically inevitable, but that they were usually leaks on general developments rather than on specific plans. Neither was desirable, but that was the way things were, and it was a liability that would just have to be accepted.[7] Acceptance did not mean that Godfrey liked having British secrets leaked, and Kirk would hear more on this subject.

It was somewhat awkward, for whether Kirk realized it or not, past events and comments by high American officials tended to undermine any defense he might make of Navy Department reliability. News of the Ingersoll mission had promptly appeared in the American press, Roosevelt had emphasized to the Admiralty the need for secrecy during the Hampton visit, and Hampton had been cautioned by the chief of naval operations about revealing his presence even to the director of naval intelligence.

It was part of Admiral Godfrey's job to be concerned about security, but he had already decided what his personal position vis-à-vis the Americans should be. Regardless of leaks or sensitivities, his job was to "cultivate" Kirk and his staff and to "look after their interests" by providing information and arranging visits by observers wherever possible. He hoped that America might soon be an ally and sought to hasten that happy eventuality.

John Godfrey was a good man for the delicate job of "tactful, secretive, assiduous, and above all, personal wooing and salesmanship" that such "cultivation" required.[8] The new director of naval intelligence was not the average sailor; most especially, he was not the average desk-bound sailor. He had seen considerable sea duty, most recently commanding the modernized battle cruiser *Repulse*. Despite his active life, Godfrey had a "touch of the academic manqué" about him although he would vehemently deny any suggestion that he was an "intellectual." He enjoyed the company of scholars, artists, journalists, and men of affairs and brought many of these people into his department. It had been difficult for Godfrey to leave the *Repulse*, but with war threatening he could see the opportunity and the challenge of taking over as director of naval intelligence. He was very conscious of the work done in World War I by the legendary Vice Admiral Reginald "Blinker" Hall and his team of cryptanalysts. Godfrey studied Hall's operations, put together an equally brilliant group, which included the young Ian Fleming, and set out to accomplish from Room 39 what Hall had done in Room 40. So when Kirk came to bargain or to be bargained with, the big man with the round face and leonine head who met him at the door of Room 39 was a worthy competitor.[9]

In December, when he had been in England for six months, Kirk wrote a survey of the situation; this report provides insight on his not totally optimistic impressions. The Allies were standing on the defensive, he wrote, putting no pressure on the Germans, and absorbing some heavy losses. "Mr. Churchill makes his case publicly, but the picture is less rosy than he paints," Kirk reported.

He went on to suggest that the blockade of Germany would not have the impact that it had had in World War I, since no matter how effective Britain was at sea, there was "no pressure on Germany for any of her land frontiers." It also seemed questionable to him whether military pressure could be put on Germany via "the old western front" while in the air "England and France are definitely on the defensive." Kirk was also worried about an "undercurrent of apathy and distaste for the whole war" in England. It was his impression that the country had been lulled into a "false sense of security, and that there is not the strong, confident, inspiring leadership the seriousness of the situation demands."[10]

There was no immediate change in the military situation as the new year began and Kirk continued his visits to the Admiralty. Early in January someone told him the reason for some of the delays in meeting his requests. British distrust of the Navy Department's security system had been reinforced by an article in the 16 December 1939 issue of *Army and Navy Register* that discussed navy appropriation requests. Included in the article was the notation that the U.S. Navy was buying submarine nets and net material "of British design."[11] German agents now knew that if they could penetrate plant security in the United States, a nation not at war, they could learn the secret of British harbor defense. Those observers Kirk had sent to British bases were learning things that might aid the enemy.

Kirk quickly advised his superiors of the situation and asked for help. Anderson did not respond to Kirk's embarrassing revelation, perhaps because he already knew the appalling state of naval security. For one thing, the definition of authority between the B-3 branch, which was to make investigations of all kinds, and the B-4 branch, which was to handle "security problems," was quite imprecise. As issues arose, new sections were set up as offshoots of old sections, but with some authority left with the original sections. Moreover, all branches were undermanned. B-4, for instance, which was responsible for plant and base security, as well as for personnel checks, was staffed by only three officers and two clerks. It is little wonder that B-4 was not very effective in another area of its responsibility—press leaks.[12]

Despite the friction, Kirk's personal associations continued to improve. Admiral Godfrey had always been friendly but somewhat formal and always very reserved. Therefore, Kirk was surprised to find himself cordially invited into Admiral Godfrey's office one day early in February. Godfrey was expansive, actually inviting Kirk to talk about any problems he was encountering. First they discussed what Kirk called the "legalistic" approach of the British toward the exchange of information, with Kirk noting that apparently the United States was less popular than it had been at the outbreak of the war and that the "honeymoon period" seemed to be over. He suggested that this was very unfortunate since "the best interests of the British Empire ran parallel to the interests of the United States" and it was unwise to "let the long-range objectives of the two nations be obscured by irritations."

The British were misguided, Kirk argued, in not freely giving the United States all the information they had on German operations and equipment. It seemed "self-evident," the American attaché said, "that while no one could or should count on the United States entering the war on the Allied side, it would certainly be most difficult to visualize our being in the war as an enemy." Godfrey replied that he personally agreed, as did other members of the policy divisions. However, there were others, presumably in the technical divisions, who were "very loath" to tell the United States anything. Kirk deduced that part of the reason was sensitivity about U.S. security measures, so he bluntly asked Godfrey if any of the leaks of confidential information had been traced to the Navy Department. Godfrey at once replied emphatically, "No!" That seemed to clear the air of that nagging problem and the men concluded their conversation on a friendly note.

In reporting this conversation to Washington, Kirk emphasized that Godfrey had said that anything the United States could freely provide the British would strengthen the hands of those who wanted to see better cooperation. Kirk added a personal plea: "Anything that could be done would undoubtedly help loosen up the bonds of uncommunicativeness, now much more tightly drawn than formerly."[13]

Godfrey's reaction, at this point, was in many ways similar to Kirk's. Using his conversation with the attaché as introduction, he proposed to his superiors that the Admiralty should be "more magnanimous" in granting American requests. Godfrey realized that the United States had little to offer in exchange and that they had been "sticky" in the past about meeting quid pro quo requests. But he shrewdly guessed that in some instances "stickiness" resulted from embarrassment at being behind in technological developments.[14] Moreover, the Americans were being extremely helpful with things like the "neutrality patrol," which naturally could not be publicized. He thought that it was to British advantage to aid the U.S. Navy in becoming as efficient as possible "in case they come into the war."[15]

As Godfrey had said, there was some dissent within the Admiralty. The deputy chief of the staff, now Rear Admiral Tom Phillips, usually quite friendly toward the United States, agreed in general with the director of naval intelligence, but he wanted a distinction drawn between short-term developments like ASDIC, countermeasures against mines and submarines, and long-term developments like ship designs. The short-term measures he thought could be exchanged with the United States on a quid pro quo basis even if what Britain got in return was less than equivalent. On long-term design matters he balked at telling the Americans much. His reason was that after the war Britain would depend on those improvements "made as a result of hard-won experience" for keeping her position "in the van of naval shipbuilding."[16] On the other hand, Rear Admiral John Burrough, the assistant chief of the naval staff, felt that since it was unthinkable that Britain and the United States would fight against each other, a "deliberate pooling of all our knowledge with that of the U.S." was in order. The fact that Britain had more to give and was being generous "might initiate a liaison between the two countries which would encourage mutual trust and form in time very strong bonds."[17] Everyone did not agree, though, with that broad and possibly very wise suggestion. As one officer put it: "[T]he things we have learnt or are learning by bitter experience should be given only to those who are fighting for us."[18] In the face of such divergent opinions, even though further discussions were held within the Admiralty, little action was taken.

In Washington, Admiral Anderson could not offer Kirk much hope of better cooperation since the Navy Department was wracked by doubts and sensitivities similar to the Admiralty's. According to Anderson, the difficulties arose from a complex process of bargaining and reciprocity. The U.S. Navy had requested that they be allowed to send more observers with British units, and the British had refused. That refusal, he believed, resulted from U.S. unwillingness to allow British officers to sail on U.S. ships. Furthermore, he did not see much chance of offering reciprocity in the future because "one technical bureau" (which he did not identify) was obstructing the agreement. Anderson did wonder if the British might be mollified if their observers could see everything but "code books and other items you will think of."[19]

Since Anderson did not spell out what he meant, it is impossible to be precise about American sensitivities. However, several logical suppositions can be made. In the first place, the reference to code books implies a lack of willingness to share or discuss cryptographic information. As early as October 1939 the Royal Navy had suggested exchanging cryptographic secrets concerning Japanese codes. The U.S. Navy had refused "for the time being" on the grounds that "equitable exchange" was impossible "at the present."[20] We now know that the United States was actually working hard on breaking Japanese codes and would eventually achieve significant success. Whether they ever shared this breakthrough with the British is still unknown; what we do know is that in the spring of 1940 cryptography was one subject the navy did not wish to discuss with the British.[21]

The "other items" Anderson referred to require a little more supposition. Both countries had been experimenting with locating aircraft by use of radio waves. By early 1940 the U.S. Navy had already installed some rudimentary radar sets on ships in the fleet and the technicians were inordinately proud of their achievement. Many officers, Kirk included, believed the American system to be superior to the British system. Therefore, although they were very eager to learn about RDF (British radar), there may well have been sensitivity again lest British observers gain more than they could provide.[22]

Whatever his reasons, Anderson's reaction was not very helpful, but Alan Kirk kept up his search for British information. Sometimes it was possible to pick up valuable data from the most informal kinds of visits. In February, for instance, he went with his friends Lord and Lady Astor to tour the damaged British cruiser *Exeter*. The party was taken aboard, shown the shell holes, but told little about the battle itself. As soon as Kirk boarded the train for London he wrote an analysis of what each hit indicated about the action. His account was amazingly accurate—and he later learned that he had failed to record only one shell hole. He immediately sent his report to Washington, where it was enthusiastically received. The highest compliment, however, came from the British. Months later they learned of the report and were so impressed by its accuracy and perceptiveness that they asked for a copy.[23]

It would not be long before there would be many damaged ships to examine, for what Kirk said many were calling "Der kalte Krieg" began to heat up in the early spring. The Finns had sued for peace in March 1940 and one month later the British and the Germans clashed in Norway. The British had long been disturbed by German shipments of Swedish iron ore down the Norwegian coastline but they had done nothing other than shadow the German convoys. Then, on 16 February, the Royal Navy seized the German prison ship *Altmark* in Josing fjord, well within Norwegian territorial waters. That act triggered German plans for an invasion of Norway. Actually, the British had also prepared an invasion of Norway and the two forces locked in a vicious slugging match on 9 April 1940. Winston Churchill, who had been pressing for action in northern waters, was overjoyed, anticipating an easy victory. Despite the Admiralty's optimistic view—"they really are almost jubilant"—Kirk feared the Norway offensive might run into serious trouble.[24]

Some British officers, Kirk reported, shared his worries about the Norwegian adventure, especially in view of the uncertain state of affairs in the Far East. To these individuals it seemed that the Royal Navy was overcommitted in Europe and could not divert any forces to fight the Japanese. If the Japanese moved against the Dutch East Indies it would pose a "dire threat to British interests in the Far East, her Indian Empire, and her communication with Australia and New Zealand."[25] British fears of not having ships to divert to the Far East, expressed to the Americans in June 1939, were coming true in April 1940.

Despite their obvious need for American support and the early moves toward cooperation, the British seemed to become less helpful as the situation became more serious. On 24 April 1940, Captain Kirk called on Admiral Godfrey again. The American officer repeated his comment that some of his requests were running into what he thought were unnecessary delays. This time Godfrey was not in a receptive mood. He did not agree that the delays were unnecessary and warned Kirk that some British officers were asking why they should do anything for the Americans. Their argument remained that the United States was not in the war and, to make things worse, kept insisting that she was not coming in. His colleagues, therefore, were asking why they should bother to give information to the American navy when they had gathered that information "with their own blood and sweat." Godfrey indicated his disagreement with that argument, at the same time observing that if the Royal Navy furnished all the information the Americans requested, "during the long period of peace, say twenty-five years or more," which the British hoped would follow the war, the United States would be "abreast of them throughout." The expertise the British had was their capital, but when it was exhausted, what then?

Kirk empathized, so when he reported this conversation to Washington he noted that "it boils down to this, we cannot go on indefinitely expecting to get something for nothing." The British were making great advances in war techniques, he wrote, and their experience could be helpful to the United States. It seemed so obviously in America's self-interest to "open up with them" that he could not appreciate the "factors which appear to weigh so heavily against such a policy." He advocated discretion and safeguards, but within those limits he thought that much more could be done for the British.[26]

At the Admiralty, Godfrey continued to advocate "an extensive revelation of naval secrets" to the Americans. Giving and receiving such secrets would establish a whole range of contacts, with opportunities for "personal collaboration" that would be "invaluable in war." The process was a delicate one, though, and no "trading" should be allowed to creep in and befoul the relationship. The rule of thumb he had established for his officers was that "those who gave should ask for nothing in return."[27]

Many scientists and diplomats argued the case in similar terms. To them technical exchanges could not be measured simply in terms of information leaked to Germany or reciprocity gained for access to specific items. They saw Britain dealing from a position of technological superiority, and they argued that she could afford to provide information to the Americans without asking anything in return. That would eliminate delays and gain for Britain an intangible yet priceless increase in bargaining leverage because the most ingratiating favors were those offered freely. Viewed in this light, technological exchanges might offer the key to a whole series of American favors.

One man who saw technology as the key to American friend-ship was Sir Henry Tizard, brilliant physicist and chairman of the Scientific Survey of the Air Defense Committee. As early as the fall of 1939, he was talking of "bringing American scientists into the war before their Government."[28] One of the items that Tizard's committee was working on may have contributed to his eagerness. The British had begun in the fall of 1939 to consider the possibility of making a superbomb by harnessing the power emitted when uranium atoms were split. In March 1940, a subgroup, later known as the MAUD Committee, was formed to investigate and report on chances of actually producing atomic bombs.[29] Tizard knew that the Americans were also working on this theoretical subject and he was eager to learn their progress; the work of the MAUD Committee provided one opportunity for contact.

On another device, the British had made more substantial progress. RDF was a dramatic new technique for aircraft detection and, no matter what the Americans liked to think, the British were ahead of all other nations in its development. Professor A. V. Hill, a mathematician and Member of Parliament from Cambridge University, was aware of British experiments in both fields. He had been sent to Washington in January 1940 to stimulate a broad range of scientific contacts but, most important, he was the logical channel for communication with the Americans on RDF and atomic energy.

Hill quickly developed a generous point of view regarding exchanges. His attitude, however, was built on logic, not sympathy. Using the RDF situation as his point of departure, he explained his logic to the new British ambassador, Lord Lothian. The British bargaining position was presently strong, Hill argued, but it would grow progressively weaker. The Americans were behind at the moment but would soon discover the essentials. Wisdom dictated helping them soon, before they could help themselves. Hill per-suaded the ambassador, who wired London accordingly on 24 April 1940. Lothian noted that whereas Hill was motivated by technical concerns, he supported the proposal on the general ground that it would bring the "services of the two countries into closer liaison and sympathy [on?] war preparations."[30]

The civilian scientists were no more unanimous in their co-operativeness than the military. Sir Robert Watson-Watt, for in-stance, considered by some the inventor of RDF, felt that "the

Americans could not teach us anything and we should get much the worst of the bargain."[31] Tizard, of course, agreed with Hill and Lothian that great benefits were to be reaped by an exchange of "all technical information" with the American military. He granted that leaks were a risk, but concluded that the opportunity for working with the American scientists, and thus influencing them, plus access to American industrial potential, outweighed that risk. As he saw it, "RDF is perhaps the best bargaining counter we have." Used properly, it might get the "whole-hearted co-operation of the Americans."[32]

Not waiting for a specific reply to Lothian's telegram, Hill broached the subject of uranium research with American scientists in May 1940 and received a friendly but discouraging reply. The Americans, Hill found, were quite pro-British, and perhaps for this reason they advised that English scientists not put their time in on something that, although interesting, was unpromising. Some American scientists were working on uranium, to be sure, and if anything of war value turned up they would gladly share the information. However, they doubted the applicability of atomic fission to bombs.[33] The American reply, though for practical purposes negative, provided an opportunity that Hill felt should not be missed.

Back in London there had been a meeting on 3 May to discuss the differences of opinion on the less theoretical, yet still esoteric, subject of RDF. Tizard, Watson-Watt, two air marshals, one vice admiral, a major general, and several civilian secretaries drew up a paper concerning making RDF information available to the Americans. There was, they agreed, great political advantage to sharing secrets with the Americans. RDF, though, was a very special and very subtle case. As Hill had noted, the United States was experimenting with its own radar apparatus and if they succeeded in developing it they would be in a position to dispense with British assistance in the field. "Our bargaining position," the paper noted, "is therefore at present high, but may well diminish." There was the added advantage that if the offer were made soon, the British could request in return that the Americans allow them to utilize the resources of the research laboratories "in which America is so rich." Finally, it would be a great advantage to have America producing RDF on the British design in the event Britain should need the reserve productive capacity.

On the other side of the equation, it was known that the Germans were working on RDF and the British had perfected techniques that still had the Germans baffled. If RDF were provided to the United States, the Germans might well learn what they needed to know via a security leak and thus advance their development by as much as a year. They also might learn how advanced the British system was and in any bombing offensive concentrate on the RDF stations.[34] The fear of security leaks in the United States was far from a British supposition. The Americans themselves admitted it—an assistant naval attaché was quoted as saying that he would not send certain secret information home since it was "almost certain" to go straight to Germany. The problem was sufficiently delicate that the issue was referred to higher authority with the recommendation that if it were decided to disclose RDF information to the United States, it should be done by a high-level mission. And even then every effort should be made to sensitize Americans, specifically the president, to the necessity for secrecy.[35]

One member of the "higher authority," Admiral Tom Phillips, reacted predictably. He was not in favor of exchanging RDF information with the United States, he wrote, unless something very valuable was received in exchange. He was still interested in obtaining some Norden bombsights, but he was also certain that any information given to the United States would leak.[36] Winston Churchill, at this point still first lord of the Admiralty, agreed, at least with the advantage-seeking aspect. No RDF information, he advised, "unless we can get some very definite advantage in return." As for the bombsight, he doubted that it was sufficiently novel to justify the sacrifice. If the United States would deliver "some thousands" of sights, however, it might make the exchange worthwhile.[37]

Developments beyond the laboratory and the two naval establishments would soon induce a more cooperative attitude. Up to 10 May 1940, however, the two countries had been remarkably circumspect in their dealings. The British still were not providing the Americans with techniques like RDF—which they had given to the Polish navy—and the Americans were chauvinistically safeguarding their secrets on their version of the same device.[38] The situation smacked of artificiality. The Americans were being thoroughly unneutral in their neutrality patrol and whatever other deficiencies the British may have noted in Alan Kirk, he was clearly pro-British. As far as the British were concerned, although no decision had yet been made on how fully they wanted America in the war, there was no question that they wanted and needed considerable material assistance. Cooperation was now more than ever essential, but the old competitive spirit remained, with some American officers even obstinately insisting that they would rather learn for themselves than accept favors from the British. There is no doubt that the British were ahead in some areas, including experience, and from their point of view the only valid argument against sharing that the skeptics could still promote was that of security.

The Americans were almost as bad about keeping secrets as the British thought they were. Articles had appeared in the press about American radar, for instance, and there were those embarrassing developments like Tyler Kent's activities at the American Embassy that British intelligence had to interrupt. Added to what we know the British knew about American laxity, there are some grounds for suspicion that they knew even more. Their knowledge about Ambassador Kennedy's views was so accurate that it leads to the suspicion that they had broken some U.S. codes. If they had, they might suspect the Germans had also. Since cryptographic secrets are often the last that governments give up, this explanation of British sensitivities must remain speculative, but it would help to explain why they were unwilling to have Kirk send vital information to America over the wires.

Sensitivities and competitiveness would erode slowly, but they were among many other things that would be transformed by the German columns forming on the borders of Western Europe.

6.

"Blackmail—and Not Very Good Blackmail at That"

10 May 1940–21 June 1940

The most significant act of cooperation during 1940 and the situation that provided the greatest opportunity for bargaining were the negotiations over the Destroyer-Bases-Fleet transfer. Formally opened in May 1940, when Winston Churchill requested some overage destroyers from President Roosevelt, the negotiations were not concluded for four months. Technological exchanges and other matters were openly or tacitly drawn in, and the whole issue became suffused with rhetoric, advantage-seeking, and strategic dilemmas. Naval officials were not as active in the negotiations as might be supposed, but the Royal Navy—all of it—was very much at issue. For, although referred to as simply the "Destroyer-Bases" transfer, careful analysis proves that anxiety about the fleet, how it was raised and how it was allayed, was very much part of the story and part of the deal.

Viewed accurately, the Destroyer-Bases-Fleet transfer puts the bargaining that characterized prewar British-American relations into perspective. For, in this deal, various techniques were tested by the British while the Americans sought to balance their fears and self-interest. Which argument will work best and how far can we go with generosity, scare tactics, and blackmail, the British asked themselves. How long can we wait and what can we get, wondered the Americans. At the same time, the deal had an integrity all its own, for if the ships requested by the prime minister in apocalyptic terms could not be furnished, then little hope for partnership remained.

* * *

10 May 1940 broke on the Western world like a thunderclap. Starting on that day and continuing with increasing fury, the German blitzkrieg rolled into Holland, Belgium, and France. Seasoned troops found themselves outflanked; reserve units fled in panic; refugees cowered in terror as Stuka dive-bombers strafed crowded roads. On the same day, Neville Chamberlain lost his prime ministership over his handling of the Norwegian campaign and, ironically, considering the role he had played in that misadventure, Winston Churchill became His Majesty's first minister. Churchill, who had optimum confidence in the French army, watched in horror as what he had described as the finest mechanized force in the world stumbled and staggered backward under the hammerlike blows of the outnumbered Panzers. America would now have to play a larger role and Churchill lost no time in appealing to his mother's country.

Churchill wired Roosevelt on 15 May 1940 to ask whether they might continue their private correspondence now that he had changed jobs. Churchill assumed the friendly contact would continue. That was not his only optimistic assumption, for he opened this new round of correspondence in a very presumptuous manner. "All I ask now," he wrote, "is that you should proclaim nonbelligerency, which would mean that you would help us with everything short of actually engaging armed forces." He went on to list the war matériel he wanted: forty or fifty "older" destroyers, several hundred modern aircraft, antiaircraft guns, ammunition, steel, and other matériel. But, the prime minister noted ominously, American assistance might "count for nothing" unless rendered soon.[1] The rolling German columns and buckling Allied lines made the moment seem critical.

On the same day the prime minister told Ambassador Kennedy that no matter what Germany did, England would never give up as long as Churchill remained "a power in public life." Churchill also said, "Why . . . the Government will move to

Canada and take the fleet and fight on." Kennedy, sensing the significance, added, "I think this is something I should follow up."[2]

Churchill's comment was obviously intended to spur the Americans into generous activity. But if the situation were that desperate, it was equally logical to concentrate on national defense. To Ambassador Kennedy, for instance, British vulnerability meant that "if we had to fight to protect our lives we would do better fighting in our own backyard."[3] However, if Churchill were willing to guarantee that Britain's fleet would come to Canada, that would put things on a more negotiable basis.

When Roosevelt answered Churchill's message, he seemed to reflect some of Kennedy's attitude. The president stated he would gladly continue their private correspondence, but unfortunately the destroyers could not be provided. Congressional authorization would be needed and the time was not propitious. "Furthermore," he wrote, "it seems to me doubtful, from the standpoint of our own defense requirements which inevitably must be linked with the defense requirements of this hemisphere and with our obligations in the Pacific, whether we could dispose even temporarily, of these destroyers." The president referred to the material aid the United States was already providing the Allies, and stated his willingness to consider more of the same. He did not even mention Churchill's provocative suggestion about a declaration of nonbelligerency.[4]

And, on 16 May, as if to emphasize his determination to concentrate on American defense, Roosevelt asked Congress in a special message for increased expenditures for military equipment.[5] The emphasis was on security as he outlined the dangers to the Continental United States should territory within the hemisphere fall into unfriendly hands. The justification for the expenditures was the familiar one: increased security would keep the United States out of the war. Actually, Churchill's message made such a justification very logical. For, as Adolf A. Berle, assistant secretary of state and a Roosevelt intimate, had confided to his diary after reading the prime minister's plea, if the dire predictions were accurate "nothing we could do could get there in time." Therefore, America should collect the "strongest and solidest defense force we can."[6] Fears were already abroad that France and her fleet might be lost; if there was any doubt about the future of Britain and the Royal Navy, self-interest demanded concentration on American security.

Churchill was not deterred. His next message was received on 18 May, and Roosevelt took the occasion to invite Lord Lothian to the White House.[7] The president was worried about the fate of the British fleet and he referred to the suggestion that the fleet should come to bases in Canada or the United States if Britain were about to collapse. Lothian took a hard line; such a move would depend on America's entering the war. It was a straightforward invitation —or bargain: Declare war and you will get the fleet; remain neutral, and take your chances. The president's mental attitude during this discussion can be inferred from the ambassador's indelicate reference to the loss of the fleet as Mr. Roosevelt's "paralyzing illusion."[8] The prime minister had captured Roosevelt's attention, but it was focused on an anticipated tragedy in the last act rather than on the mise en scène.

Strong measures were called for and Churchill rose to the occasion. In his 20 May 1940 message to the president, he again urgently requested the destroyers, expressed disappointment at unfulfilled requests, and noted that although his government "would likely go down" during the close battles that would be fought, "in no conceivable circumstances" would they surrender. Churchill, apparently sensing that further reference to a Canadian redoubt might only confuse the situation, tried a new approach. If his government did go down, he wrote, and "others came in to parley amid the ruins," the president should realize that the only thing left to bargain with would be the fleet. And of course, if America had left England unaided, the Americans would have no grounds for complaint should a new British government make the best possible deal. Churchill knew that he was bluntly stating the alternatives, but, quite obviously, he could not speak for his possible successors "who in utter despair and helplessness might well have to accommodate themselves to the German will."[9] The reference to a new, and more threatening, appeasement policy could hardly be expected to set Roosevelt's fears at rest. It did not.[10]

But while the president worried, others in London considered more subtle ways to get American attention and aid. There had been much talk earlier about winning American cooperation through British generosity. There had once been military objections to this approach, but the German advance seemed to sweep those objections and Belgian defenses aside with equal ease. On 18 May the British Joint Chiefs of Staff met to consider a general technical exchange. Admiral Sir Dudley Pound, the first sea lord, was eager to gain as much information as possible on the American developments in the esoteric science of very short-wave communication; therefore, he favored some form of cooperative program. General Sir Edmund Ironside, chief of the Imperial general staff, commented that he had no objections to freedom of exchange since the army had no secrets to provide, while the air staff as well offered no objection.[11]

The respected civil servant Sir Maurice Hankey, serving in 1940 as minister without portfolio, agreed wholeheartedly with the military recommendations for the exchange of information and on 20 May, Mr. A. V. Alexander, the new first lord of the Admiralty, added his support for the project. Alexander believed that the prime minister should contact the president with the suggestion for a formal agreement on scientific exchanges, leaving bargaining out of the matter. At least there should be "no appearance on our part of attempting to bargain." In this spirit, Alexander was ready to release without restraint information on ASDIC and RDF.[12]

At lower levels, this policy was already being forwarded. Captain Kirk had long been trying to obtain information on warding off German magnetic mines by "degaussing."[13] When he renewed his efforts in mid-May he surprisingly met with success. It had been decided, as a Royal Naval Intelligence Division (NID) memorandum put it, that American involvement in the war would be "late rather than early and will find us in urgent need of destroyers and other warships adequately protected against magnetic mines and torpedos."[14] Therefore, providing them with the data to prepare their ships was in the British interest. Within two days Kirk was given full information on the British techniques, and ten days later he was given an actual magnetic mine to send to the Navy Department laboratories.[15]

With the support of the Chiefs of Staff, the first lord of the Admiralty, Lord Hankey, and with some cooperative action going forward, it might be assumed that Churchill, often thought to be in the forward ranks of scientifically oriented civilians and supposedly possessing the quintessence of acumen when dealing with Americans, would have taken decisive action. But the prime minister continued to stall. On 21 May he replied to Alexander's letter, explaining that although he understood the importance of retaining American goodwill and "extracting from them all the material assistance they can give," he favored a waiting game. He had tried to trade ASDIC for the Norden bombsight and failed; now he preferred to hold off "until the moment [was] ripe."[16]

Playing at this point for extremely high stakes, Churchill seems to have accepted a policy of heightening anxiety and keeping the pressure on. He was not alone. The American Division of the Foreign Office had quickly noted the value of Lothian's argument that the destination of the British Fleet depended upon the state of American belligerency. The concept, although admittedly "rather like blackmail, and not very good blackmail at that," was developed that Britain should force America's hand by using the fleet as a prize. The line should be that "unless the United States were a belligerent—and that too very soon—we should probably elect to send our fleet to Australia and New Zealand."[17] Churchill was pursuing this line, with his own twist—the appeasers, bargaining amid the ruins, might determine the fate of the fleet.

Unfortunately for the British, the fears that had been raised up to this point had only made the Americans reflect in panic on their own gossamer defenses. Reports began to filter into London that even the U.S. War Department was "giving out some very gloomy stuff," implying that the war was already lost and creating the impression that aid would be wasted, or, worse yet, fall into German hands and "strengthen the future enemy of the United States."[18]

The War Department was not the only center of concern. On 21 May a meeting was held at the State Department to discuss various possibilities, including the possibility of moving the U.S. Fleet back to the Atlantic.[19] The consensus was that the fleet was presently performing its most valuable service by keeping the Japanese checkmated; one participant, however, suggested that U.S. naval dispositions would ultimately depend on whether Britain surrendered its fleet, sank it, or sent it to Canada. At the Navy Department, meanwhile, a detailed memorandum on the consequences of Britain's likely defeat was being circulated.[20]

The military planners were also hastily reviewing their options. Until the start of the new German offensive, RAINBOW 2, which called for American concentration in the Pacific during any war against a coalition, had received priority consideration. With things falling apart in Europe, the United States might soon face an aggressive coalition alone. Moreover, since the British and the French fleets might be in enemy hands there would be an immediate threat to the Western Hemisphere. This situation seemed to call for conservatism, avoiding commitments outside the hemisphere, and preparing to defend South America and the Caribbean. These pessimistic views were presented to the president and Undersecretary Welles by Admiral Stark and General Marshall on 22 May. The president did not disagree with the assessment, so the Joint Planners immediately began preparing RAINBOW 4. To counter the threat to the Caribbean, this plan called for, among other things, seizure of key British, French, Dutch, and Danish possessions in the Western Hemisphere.[21]

Lothian, apparently unaware of the unpleasant forms American anxiety was assuming, kept the pressure on. He sincerely believed that the Americans would do little to aid the British until their own security was threatened, so he lost no opportunity to suggest that that time had arrived.[22] At a dinner party on 21 May he spoke as though England were practically invaded. If the Germans got a "foothold" in the islands, he said, and "demanded the surrender of the British Fleet," instead of seeing the English people suffer "some excruciating punishment," the British government would "surrender the Fleet." After dinner, Lothian talked to Breckinridge Long, an assistant secretary of state, who found him "frankly gloomy about the whole situation and permitted the inference that he expected England to be defeated."[23]

Long suspected that Lothian was being a "good British Ambassador" who was trying to scare the Americans into entering the war. Perhaps he was, but within several days Lothian was willing to leaven fear with other inducements. During the night of 23–24 May, the ambassador made a suggestion to his government that would profoundly affect the course of the negotiations. In essence, his suggestion was a variation of the old generosity theme. Why not, he asked, expand upon the base rights already granted to America in August–September 1939? In his view, America would eventually ask for those bases anyway, so it would be wiser to be generous and offer them spontaneously. The ambassador made no connection between the bases and Britain's material needs, but he doubtless intended the gesture to influence American attitudes as well as involve "active cooperation between the United States and [the] British Commonwealth in naval and air defense."[24]

Lothian's concept was definitely not original. For years various groups in the United States had been casting covetous eyes on European colonial possessions in the Western Hemisphere. Eagerness in this regard was so obvious that in April 1939 Ambassador Lindsay had suggested ceding all or part of the West Indies to the United States in return for cancellation of the war debt. Better give freely now, he reasoned, than be pressured to do it later. The Colonial Office had been appalled, while the Admiralty based its rejection on the argument that "we want to make it difficult, not easy, for the U.S. to remain neutral in a war between Germany and ourselves."[25] Lindsay's idea went no further. In May 1940 the United States was again considering the seizure of the islands, and Lothian was merely seeking to make a virtue of necessity.[26]

It took the British government one week to answer Lothian's suggestion, and when it did so it was with one voice—but that voice concealed a wide divergence of opinion. The Chiefs of Staff, perhaps sharing Lothian's view about the beneficial effects of any cooperative defense measures, favored the proposal. The Colonial Office, not surprisingly, still opposed it. The Foreign Office, in general, supported Lothian. The prime minister held a somewhat different opinion, and he prevailed. At the War Cabinet meeting on 27 May, Churchill said that he opposed offering the facilities "except as part of a deal." In his view the United States had given Britain virtually no assistance, and now that they perceived the imminence of disaster "their attitude was that they wanted to keep everything which would help us for their own defense."[27] Churchill's hard line, or quid pro quo approach, was to be one of the major stumbling blocks in the course of the early negotiations over the bases. The War Cabinet met again on 29 May and agreed to advise Lothian to go no further with the offer of bases.[28]

A telegram, drafted at Cabinet direction, was sent to Lothian on 2 June. It followed the general line of Churchill's argument, pointing out that Britain wished to consider no arrangement unless there was "definite assurance of concrete results sufficiently advantageous to us." In that regard, the Cabinet wished to know what "really substantial advantages would accrue" to Britain in return for their generosity. But no matter what advantages there were, Britain would act with caution since the offer might imply panic and thus encourage the Americans to concentrate on their own defense rather than help England.[29] The Cabinet surely did not want that.

With that message, the West Indian bases issue moved into the background until later in June. This did not mean it had been forgotten by the Foreign Office, where Lothian had friends and relations who agreed that America could be more influenced by open-handed generosity than by hard bargaining.

Events were exerting a pressure all their own. On 27 May, Ambassador Kennedy indicated that collapse of Churchill's government was a distinct possibility. The Western Front was falling apart; it now looked as though the French might sue for peace. If they did, Kennedy believed Churchill and some others would opt to fight on till the death, but, Kennedy added, "there will be other numbers [members?] who realize that physical destruction of men and property in England will not be a proper offset to a loss of pride." The public did not realize how bad the situation was, and he concluded: "When they do, I don't know which group they will follow—the do or die [group], or the group that will want a settlement."[30]

On 4 June the prime minister rose in the House of Commons to give one of his most stirring speeches, intended to induce the public to follow him. The prime minister informed the members of the House and the world that the British Expeditionary Force and remnants of the French army had been withdrawn from the beaches at Dunkirk. After describing the heroic character of the retreat he dramatically called to mind the valiant defense that might be fought in the towns, beaches, and hills of Britain. He chose not to conclude with that, leaving this vision of home defense as the only possibility. His last lines were: "If, which I do not for a moment believe, this Island or a large part of it were subjugated and starving, then our Empire beyond the seas, *armed and guarded by the British Fleet*, would carry on the struggle, until, in God's good time, the New World, with all its power and might, steps forth to the rescue and liberation of the Old."[31] Aside from its historical significance and dramatic punch, this statement kept open a possibility Britain's potential allies were extremely interested in—the movement of the British Fleet. In the long negotiations to come, Churchill would have reason to reflect at length on these words.

We now know that Churchill was trying to make the best of a

bad situation. As he had told the Cabinet several days before, it might be easier to defend the home islands once England was freed of Continental responsibilities. Moreover, a valiant defense might evoke "an immense wave of feeling, at least in the U.S.A., which, having done nothing much to help . . . so far, might even enter the war."[32] At the same time he realized the delicacy of the balance to be struck. For, as he wrote Canadian Prime Minister Mackenzie King the next day: "We must be careful not to let Americans view too complacently [the] prospect of a British collapse, out of which they would get the British Fleet and the guardianship of the British Empire, minus Great Britain." If the United States were a belligerent they would automatically get the fleet, but, as Churchill had earlier warned Roosevelt, if they remained neutral and the British Isles were overrun, he could not tell "what policy might be adopted by a pro-German administration such as would undoubtedly be set up."[33]

Roosevelt was also using the Canadians as a conduit for ideas. In his communications with them he made it clear that he was not complacent nor had he given up on getting the fleet, or at least having it serve American interests. As he told Pierrepont Moffat, the newly appointed American minister to Canada, the Canadians should urge the British never to surrender, for the Empire could go on fighting if the British Fleet were dispersed. He suggested, for example, that "twenty percent only would be needed in Canada, ten percent would do for South Africa, twenty percent for Bombay, and fifty percent for Singapore." This large force in the Far East would "checkmate" Japan and insure a force to supplement American units. There had long been concern about British naval assistance in the Far East; maybe adversity could succeed where persuasion had failed.[34]

Although Roosevelt appeared narrowly opportunistic at this crucial moment, he had to be deeply concerned about the fate of the French and British fleets. Moreover, he was leading a deeply divided country and, although he was unwilling to propose that America enter the war or freely provide the destroyers, he was willing to take very generous action. On 4 June he had ordered the service chiefs to "scrape the bottom of the barrel" and provide private firms with all available surplus guns and ammunition for resale to England. The reaction to this order illustrates Roosevelt's dilemma. His directions were followed, but they were not welcomed by all of America's military elite. To many in the War Department it seemed almost treasonous to be giving away any war matériel when America's own needs were so great. As Major Walter Bedell Smith, assistant secretary of the general staff, put it in a memorandum left at the White House, if, after giving equipment away, the United States had to mobilize and was found short, "everyone who was a party to the deal might hope to be found hanging from a lamppost."[35]

Despite this kind of reaction, and the military was probably less inclined to balk than was the mass of citizens, the president was also willing to provide public indications of his support. On 10 June he delivered the commencement address at the University of Virginia. In one of his most stirring speeches, he condemned Italy's declaration of war against the rapidly collapsing French and pledged to "extend to the opponents of force the material resources of this nation."[36]

Next day, in a very private conversation, he took an even more momentous step. He agreed to Lord Lothian's suggestion that Britain and the United States hold staff conversations.[37] This was something influential parties on both sides of the Atlantic had long seen as a minimal prelude to collaboration; yet even on this move there was no unanimity. Secretary Hull, for one, was not enthusiastic about staff conferences, even though Lothian suggested that they would cover that issue which so intrigued the Americans —the movement of the British Fleet.[38] Neither opponents nor proponents should have worried; Roosevelt took no immediate action, and only later would staff conferences become entangled in the bargaining over the destroyers, the bases, and the fleet.

Meanwhile the president provided one more form of indirect support. The U.S. Fleet had completed its annual spring exercises in Hawaiian waters in early May. The expectation was that the fleet would return to its West Coast bases, but the president decided to keep the ships in the mid-Pacific. It was not a neat, firm decision that was arrived at on any certain day, it was rather a process of not deciding when to bring them back to the United States. The fleet commander, Admiral J. O. Richardson, was advised in early May that his fleet might delay its departure "for a short time." Then he was told the delay might be two weeks, and by June the fleet's stay in Hawaiian waters appeared indefinite. The policy was improvisational, but the intent obvious. The United

States was using its navy as a warning to the Japanese not to take advantage of the European chaos and advance its interests in Southeast Asia. This warning, if the desired effect was achieved, was to benefit the United States and other countries, including Britain, that had possessions in the Asian area.[39]

The British were pleased with the president's positive actions, even though he had not yet gone as far as Churchill had hoped. There were many Americans who would not have been as generous as Roosevelt, especially in light of pessimistic reports on British defenses. On 12 June Ambassador Kennedy reported that England's only remaining defense was "courage, and not . . . arms." If America entered the war, and Churchill said he expected the United States to enter immediately after the November elections, Kennedy thought there would be little for U.S. forces to work with.[40]

The strength or weakness of the British military posture was pivotal in determining American actions; thus the professional views of Captain Alan Kirk assumed new importance. On 11 June he wrote Admiral Anderson:

Invasion of Great Britain seems fantastic to people who were brought up on "1066" and all that, but I can assure you from where I sit here in London that the Germans will be all around and all over these Islands before the first of August. The people here say that the Navy will stop invasion, but the Navy won't be able to do that. They will be mined in, torpedoed by submarines, harassed by the air and hamstrung by political considerations. This Island is no more fortified or prepared to withstand invasion in force than Long Island, New York. There will be plenty of grief, and a great deal of destruction of historical monuments but I just don't see what is going to stop this German machine.[41]

Kirk correctly estimated that the Allies were short of planes, tanks, antiaircraft weapons, motorized transport, and all the other supplies needed to conduct modern war. Before rushing to aid the beleaguered democracies, however, Kirk thought the United States should attend to its own strategic interest. Kirk suggested that a reorientation in strategic thinking might be required, for he was especially fearful lest the country make the "very serious mistake" of becoming involved in a Far Eastern war. Instead of reinforcing the Pacific fleet, units should be sent immediately from the Pacific to the Caribbean. "Our vital interests are far more concerned," he wrote, "with the preservation of the Panama Canal and the Caribbean than with the Philippines or the Dutch East Indies." He anticipated that the Germans would beat the French, take their fleet, and then do the same to the British. "All these remnants, added to the German nucleus and the Italian ships, will create a Naval Force in hostile hands which we cannot afford to ignore." He was convinced that "these fellows over here are out to conquer the World. After they have finished over there [on the Continent] this summer, they will be prepared to take time by the forelock and move in on South America and the Caribbean, or perhaps even Canada so rapidly that we won't realize what is happening."

Despite this estimate, the naval attaché favored providing all possible aid to the British. Although he continually told the British that providing destroyers was a "political" matter and thus out of his province, when he wired a list of British ship losses to Washington, he urged that the destroyers be sent immediately. His plea was so convincing that it was shown to the president.[42]

The president did not immediately heed this advice, for he was of two minds about the situation. He did not take as pessimistic a view of Britain's chances as did the military experts, but on the other hand he was not inclined to be profligate. His attitude can be inferred from an outline he provided the senior army and navy intelligence chiefs on 13 June 1940. Among other things, he hypothesized that within six months (1) the British would still be holding; (2) the U.S. Navy, with surviving remnants of the British and French navies, would control the Atlantic, the Persian Gulf, the Red Sea, and the Western Mediterranean; (3) Russia and Japan would not be in the war, but the United States would be, with air and naval forces only; (4) American shipping would be supplying the Allies, while the U.S. Navy maintained the Atlantic blockade. If these hypotheses were correct, Roosevelt wanted to know what effects—economic, political, psychological, and military—could be anticipated.[43]

While the president awaited a response, dark reports continued to come in from American officials in London. On 14 June Ambassador Kennedy observed that "very calm rational people in England believed that Hitler might occupy and hold Canada as a hostage until Britain had paid a huge indemnity. At the same time, he added his interpretation of the talk about the British government moving to the North American continent. Even if they did leave England, Kennedy wrote, the problem was not solved, for "another government will be set up to represent the 45,000,000 people [left behind]." For the first time, he thought the realization was sinking in that the British were in for a "terrible time with little hope for eventual victory." These conditions, the ambassador continued, could lead to an "upheaval . . . against the Government" if the people got the idea that there "was a chance of peace on any decent terms."[44]

On the same day, Captain Kirk cabled Washington suggesting that the rapid collapse of the French forces and the likely surrender of the French fleet might be a preview of coming events in England. Therefore, he suggested that the United States look to her own "vital interests" with "special reference to strategic dispositions [of] our naval forces," so that it would be possible "to assume immediate control over all British, French and Dutch possessions in [the Caribbean area]."[45]

With the worsening situation Churchill picked up the tempo of his requests. On 15 June he sent the president his longest message to date; it contained the most detailed request for the destroyers.[46] Churchill began his message by noting the precarious position of the French. Then he turned to a related problem:

Although the present Government and I personally would never fail to send the fleet across the Atlantic if resistance was beaten down here, a point may be reached in the struggle where the present Ministers no longer have control of affairs and when very easy terms could be obtained for the British islands by their becoming a vassal state of the Hitler empire. A pro-German government would certainly be called into being to make peace and might present to a shattered or a starving nation an almost irresistible case for entire submission to the Nazi will.

Churchill went on to suggest that if the British Fleet was ever joined to the fleets of Japan, France, and Italy, and the "resource of German industry," Hitler would have overwhelming sea power in his hands. Thus America would face a "United States of Europe under the Nazi command far more numerous, far better armed than the New [World]."

Without waiting for a reply, Churchill dispatched another message that evening. He was still hoping, he said, for a declaration of war by the United States. Lest this seem too precipitous, he explained that when he spoke of America's "entering the war" he was not thinking in terms of an "expeditionary force." He knew that that was "out of the question." What he had in mind was the "tremendous moral effect" that America's declaration would have.[47]

These messages arrived in the wake of news that the plucky Pierre Reynaud had been replaced by the doughty Marshal Henri Pétain. The specter of an appeasing government had materialized in the Republic of France. This provided Roosevelt with a point of departure when he discussed Churchill's message with Lothian on 16 June. The president used his now-familiar argument for dispersing the British Fleet; Lothian used his familiar response about war fleets not fighting for neutrals; and no one even mentioned the destroyers or the proposed declaration of war.[48]

In London, Ambassador Kennedy met with the prime minister. Churchill said that he would like to know "one way or other" about the destroyers. The ambassador did not give a definitive reply, but it was his distinct impression that British planning (and resistance) might depend upon "whether they do or do not get the destroyers." Churchill stated that even if the destroyers did not come the British would fight on, but Kennedy saw behind this latest request "a great desire to know what cards they can count on."[49] Churchill was scheduled to make a speech on 17 June, and Kennedy knew the prime minister was being urged to aim the speech directly at the American press, stating clearly that England would fight on to eventual victory. Churchill said to Kennedy, "Why, if I don't say that the people of England would tear me to pieces." Kennedy was not sure how accurate that statement was, but he conveyed Churchill's requests.[50] For some reason, the president apparently never replied to this request for the destroyers.

One reason may have been the depressing reports the president was getting from his military advisers. At this point American military officials seem to have been concentrating almost as much on what to do after Britain fell as on how to keep it from falling. Thus, when General George Marshall, the chief of staff, met with his officers on 17 June, the primary topic seems to have been timing. Major General George Strong, chief of army war plans, stated that Germany might be able to launch an attack on South America within sixty days. Therefore, it was decided that there were two critical dates for planning by the United States. The first was the date the British and French fleets would cease to function;

the second was six months later. For planning purposes they concluded that "the date of the loss of the British or French fleets automatically sets the date for our mobilization."[51]

General Marshall perceived the situation as dictating a total reorientation of American military planning. The army had never had much enthusiasm for the ORANGE plan and the time now seemed right for reframing naval policy by assuming that action should be defensive in the Pacific, thus allowing for concentration on the Atlantic.[52] The navy, although very disturbed about European developments, was not yet ready to make such a fundamental shift.

The prime minister of Canada, uniquely positioned to sense reactions on both sides, was becoming increasingly disturbed by British scare tactics. On 17 June he wired his observations to Churchill. During the past several weeks, King wrote, he had found a growing American tendency to interpret British statements to mean that the fleet would not be sent to Canada *unless* the United States entered the war. King knew the president and the American people, and if the suspicion took root that the British government was trying to use the fleet as a bargaining "lever" for American entry into the war, it would become "harder for the President to give aid to Britain in this hour of need." Blackmail, he was saying, could backfire. Apparently he was not totally optimistic himself, for he suggested that "as we must always envisage what would happen if anything went wrong," the time had come for specific planning regarding the "practical questions that would arise if a large number of the surviving units of the British fleet should suddenly arrive in Canada."[53]

Churchill did not mind talking grimly about disasters, but he seemed at times almost incapable of making specific plans for future unpleasantness.[54] Thus he bristled at Mackenzie King's suggestions for planning. In his reply to Ottawa he noted that a careful reading of his telegram would reveal that there was "no question of trying to make a bargain" with the United States over the ultimate disposition of the fleet.[55] In fact, he said he "doubted the wisdom" of dwelling on the possibility of defeat. He was confident and saw "no reason to make preparations for or give countenance to" a fleet transfer. At the same time, although he would never negotiate for a peace with Hitler, he naturally could not bind a "future Government which, if we are deserted by the

United States and beaten down here, might very easily be a kind of Quisling affair" ready to follow German direction. Instead of minimizing the negative aspects of this development, Churchill thought Mackenzie King should "impress this danger upon the President." This final comment follows somewhat illogically upon Churchill's statement about doubting the wisdom of dwelling on the possibility of defeat. The apparent contradiction well illustrates the duality of Churchill's thinking at this critical juncture.

King was not satisfied. He knew Roosevelt was already concerned about Churchill's 5 June telegram, in which the British prime minister had discussed the possibility of a pro-German government parleying amidst the ruins. Moreover, he felt frustrated in his efforts to avoid a "psychological" misunderstanding, disturbed by Churchill's unwillingness to plan for disaster and depressed by the atmosphere of trading that could so easily become infused with bitterness.[56]

Had he known how right he was about trading, Mackenzie King might have been even more upset. Churchill was searching for a way to strike a multifaceted bargain with the Americans. He hoped to settle these matters simultaneously: the British need for the destroyers and the American reluctance to lend them; the American desire for information and the reluctance of some British officials to give it; and the status of the invitation that Lothian had issued for more joint staff talks. Churchill made the connection between the various issues quite precise when, in discussing technological exchanges on 19 June, he proposed making exchanges "part of a general deal."[57]

In the United States Lothian kept pounding away on a now-familiar theme. On 19 June the ambassador delivered the commencement address at Yale University. His primary topic was the naval situation and he warned that America would be in great danger if Hitler secured the British Fleet. He went on to suggest that there was no assurance that the vital ships would cross the Atlantic if Great Britain were defeated; moreover, if the fleet were sent to North America it would only be after it had sustained heavy losses in defense of the home islands. The ambassador said, in essence, that the only way to insure the transfer of the fleet to American waters was for the United States to enter the war as a belligerent.[58]

Even as Lothian alluded to American belligerence, France was making plans to end theirs. At 3:00 P.M. on 21 June 1940, French officials signed the armistice in Foch's *wagon-lit* at Compiègne. The terms were not made public, but it soon became apparent that the fleet would not be immediately, or totally, surrendered. Some units were seized by the British, others made for colonial ports like Oran, Mers el Kèbir, and Martinique, while those in French mainland ports were kept under naval control. Only time would tell whether the Germans would try to gain through force what they had eschewed diplomatically. No matter—the shudder of France's collapse sent seismic waves through the governments of Great Britain and America. In Washington, military pessimism deepened, while in London there was brave talk about how much easier it would be to defend an England now relieved of Continental responsibilities.

* * *

The collapse of France ended the first phase of British-American negotiations over the destroyers, the bases, and the British Fleet. The analogy was clear to all, yet all did not derive the same lessons. And here it would perhaps be wise to say something about the perceptions and attitudes of the main actors in the drama.

Roosevelt was obviously a man in a most awkward position. He had decided by 21 June 1940 to seek an unprecedented third term in the White House; this decision added an immediate political dimension to his dilemma. How best were American interests to be served? By providing all-out aid to England or by conserving everything of value, as some members of Congress urged? Surely Roosevelt was emotionally involved, but not so involved that he took his eye off the main chance, which in this instance was American national self-interest.

Joseph Kennedy's position is more complicated to analyze. Deeply pessimistic about British chances, he has been roundly condemned as a defeatist, or worse. The truth is, however, that Kennedy had not one view but several. His basic position was that Britain was defeated *unless* the United States gave immediate and massive aid. Being well aware of public attitudes, and it should be noted that Kennedy was an above-average political analyst who had once entertained presidential aspirations, he doubted that a massive aid policy was likely to get public support. Given that presumption, and since he apparently could not envisage a policy by which aid could be secretly provided, his conclusion that Britain was lost until American opinion had changed seems quite logical. Viewing the scene from England, moreover, where to the ranks of the Civil Defense Force the bedraggled and unarmed British Expeditionary Force was being added, it was also logical to assume that almost any aid would arrive too late. Hence, Kennedy's conclusion that it was wiser to concentrate on the defense of positions closer to home.

At the same time it is reasonable to conclude that Kennedy's perceptions of disaster were heightened by his contacts within the international business community. The view from the City must have been darker even than the view from Whitehall. The financial community's world was being torn apart and stood on end for the second time in ten years—only a fool could view it complacently. Kennedy was no fool, and in retrospect it seems that he was not even first among the alarmists. Many thoughtful people in America shared his view. The professional military, for instance, was taking an extremely conservative course, and even some close friends of Great Britain like Adolf Berle and Harold Ickes, the secretary of the interior, seemed convinced that Britain was lost.

Finally, Kennedy accurately sensed a subtle development regarding attitudes toward aid in Britain. Precision was essential, he thought, in conveying our intentions, "particularly if at some later date we might want the British to take action regarding the Navy that might be of service to us."[59] Some animosity toward the United States was already apparent in Britain, since the feeling was growing that all Britain got from the United States was "conversation," which was hardly sufficient when Britain was fighting for America as well as for herself.[60]

All of the preceding are attitudes consistent with American national self-interest. Kennedy was, after all, American ambassador to the Court of St. James, not a spokesman or an apologist for the British government. A good deal of the criticism he later received was based primarily on the fact that he proved to be wrong in his judgment of the future. But asking him to anticipate Roosevelt's skillful handling of the aid question, Churchill's ability to rally public opinion, the failure of the Luftwaffe to defeat the Royal Air Force, and Hitler's decision to turn on Russia, seems more than a little unfair, so unfair indeed that one wonders whether there was not some concerted effort to discredit him by some group or groups that wanted him silenced. At the very least it can be said that he was not helping the British cause, and it would have been in the interests of the British government and of those in America who strongly favored aid to Britain to undermine his credibility.

Where was Kennedy getting his military advice? Primarily from Alan Kirk, who had his office in the Embassy and who worked directly for the ambassador. Kirk and Kennedy got along well personally as well as professionally; indeed, so close were the opinions of these two men that it is hard to tell who was influencing whom. Kirk said, and apparently meant, that he did not like to be pessimistic, but from a military point of view things looked extremely bad. However, he did urge that aid be provided and specifically he encouraged the transfer of the destroyers. The British —especially Admiral Godfrey—made it their business constantly to encourage Kirk; and although they were not entirely satisfied, they could hardly call him a defeatist. He, too, was trying hard to take an objective view of the situation and trying to do what was best for his country. In this regard, he was definitely not averse to getting something from the British in return for American help.

For those who were not downhearted, the nexus of the case was the potential for bargaining. Or, to be more precise, what to bargain. In the weeks since his ascension to office, Churchill had been pursuing a course vis-à-vis the United States on this subject that in retrospect appears maladroit. First, there had been references to carrying the war on from Canada, then requests for declarations of nonbelligerency, then specters of appeasement, and, finally, more suggestions for continuing the war from the New World. He was not being consistent, and possibly he was not being realistic, but it was an unprecedented situation and he was searching for a net to ensnare his prey. Surprisingly, Churchill may not have been as qualified for the task as is commonly thought. A man of tremendous talents, he was oddly unaware of other people's emotions or reactions. As those who knew him quickly realized, Churchill was not much interested in others. He was much more interested in talking than listening, and so preoccupied with his own world that he had failed to develop sensitivity or curiosity about the hearts and minds of others.[61] The prime minister seemingly lacked those antennae so essential to students of human nature.[62] He was not insensitive, but rather asensitive. Obviously that lack would make personal diplomacy extremely difficult—especially when negotiating with someone like Franklin Roosevelt.

Moreover, although he was steady in his determination to tough it out, there were fluctuations in Churchill's own reactions toward the situation he faced. He was not consistently optimistic; in fact, his most eloquent statements were about what to do when things got worse. Whether these statements reflected, as some have suggested, a strain of melancholia, or whether they were simply dramatic expressions of a reasonable man's doubts, it must be admitted that if one took Churchill's assessment of the future seriously, it would be hard to be sanguine about what lay ahead. Actually, many of Churchill's comments could only serve to support the conclusions of Kennedy and Kirk. And whereas talk of fighting in the streets might inspire Londoners, it was hardly the scene to comfort potential allies.

Lothian, whose duties included interpreting Churchill for the Americans and expressing British purpose through his own actions, did not want the Americans to become complacent, and although he was willing to pay more in terms of scientific assistance and bases than was Churchill, he was by no means unduly generous. At the same time, he favored putting the worst possible face on the British predicament. And it is here that we come upon another personal enigma. How much of Lothian's gloom and doom was real and how much pose? As an individual he was not timid, but he was not courageous, either. Although not a pacifist, Lothian on several occasions had shown himself more willing to talk than to fight. He had strongly supported appeasement and he had long championed an international body to control man's more violent impulses. A deeply religious Christian Scientist, Lothian impressed many people with his spiritual qualities and strength of personal conviction.[63] With his round, clear-rimmed glasses and rather tubby frame, the British ambassador presented a mild-mannered appearance, but conveyed the impression that he would stand up for his beliefs. In the summer of 1940 Lothian also conveyed the impression that he might soon be standing up for them in some colonial capital where his government had sought refuge. Even if it is assumed that his attitude partially reflected policy, one comes away with the impression that his convictions about Britain's chances occasionally wavered. Lothian's problem, no matter what his own mental state, was to find a way to wrench loose from

America the aid Britain so badly needed. To do that, it was becoming increasingly clear, the British would have to answer the query: Why should America give Britain fifty destroyers, thus jeopardizing its neutral status and its own defense without receiving something substantial in return? Now a lien on the entire British Fleet might be a bit much to ask, and insuring that 50 percent of it would go to Singapore was perhaps too clever a move to pull off, but Roosevelt was trying. After all, he had his problems too. He could not afford to have his opponents accusing him of playing fast and loose with national defense. If Roosevelt was going to be moved beyond fear and sympathy by Lothian or by Churchill, it would be by deals that could be represented as, or best of all actually be, to America's net advantage.

7.

From "As Black As Possible" to "As Good As Possible"

22 June 1940–8 August 1940

With the fall of France, moves toward Anglo-American co-operation assumed new urgency. The issue was no longer one of alerting the president to the dangers; he was already alive to them. But judgment of British chances had to go beyond professional assessments of how British forces would fare against the Germans. Now Roosevelt had to be convinced not only that Britain could repel invasion but also that Churchill was more than a fighting facade.[1]

Events in France had shown how easily political changes could be made; and there was Norway's Quisling, to whom Churchill had several times referred. The analogy continued to be driven home by despairing telegrams from Kennedy in Grosvenor Square and disturbing ones from Churchill in Downing Street. Britain's own appeasement policy was not mentioned, but it had left a shadow in American minds. If Britain could renounce honor and Czechoslovakia to avoid war in 1938, what might she renounce to avoid destruction in 1940? To find the answer Roosevelt settled upon one of his favorite devices, a private fact-finding mission.

Within the British government there was no sign of flagging

determination. There were still, however, considerable differences of opinion over how best to woo and win the United States. The dilemma was exquisite. The precise balance between dependence on American aid and self-sufficiency had yet to be struck. Some argued for open-handed generosity, others for hard bargaining, while still others thought holding out for a grand arrangement whereby destroyers, scientific exchanges, and staff conferences could be handled jointly was more prudent. Even in their hour of need the British were acting with calculation and circumspection; they would meet an equal amount of both on the other side.

* * *

Although there was talk of how the loss of their ally across the channel had simplified their problems, within twenty-four hours after the French surrender the British again were seeking closer relations with a potential ally across the Atlantic. Lord Lothian's immediate reaction to the French collapse was to reopen the issue of offering America base facilities in the West Indies. On the night of 22–23 June he wired London his reasons. Arrangements for America to operate out of British bases would not only stimulate "defensive collaboration" between the two countries, but also it would "cut away part of the ground from under [the] growing demand in [the] popular press that the United States should take over all islands off [its] coasts."[2] Had the ambassador known that the service chiefs had just approved a memorandum calling for preparation to seize the principal British and French possessions in the Western Hemisphere, it might have made his argument even more persuasive.[3]

Lothian's message arrived in London as pressures mounted for action on various cooperative moves. The Foreign Office thought it would be the "height of folly" to ignore Lothian's suggestion. The king wrote to Roosevelt about the destroyers, while the air minister, Sir Archibald Sinclair, urged Churchill to reconsider the first lord of the Admiralty's month-old memorandum recommending technical cooperation.[4] Several days thereafter, the ultimate in pressure was applied when Lothian telegraphed that President Roosevelt himself favored some form of agreement on technical and scientific matters. The ambassador urged that although America might well get the "better bargain," the British government should immediately make a "generous offer."[5]

Such an offer was becoming increasingly essential from some Americans' perspective. To pragmatic military officers the fall of France made Britain's position more precarious and America's course should, therefore, be more cautious. On 22 June Admiral Stark and General Marshall recommended conserving military equipment in anticipation of British collapse, concentrating on hemispheric defense, and maintaining a purely defensive posture in the Pacific.[6] Several days later the Joint Planners supported these views with their pessimistic response to the hypotheses Roosevelt had proposed at the first of the month. For one thing, they did not think that Britain, which seemed open for invasion, would be an active combatant six months hence. But their primary argument was directed against the proposition that the United States would be participating in the war. They were particularly concerned that America was totally unprepared and that involvement in a European war might prompt Japanese aggression in the Pacific.[7] Conservatism and priority for America's own defense was the military's message.

Since these attitudes were current in Washington, although not fully accepted by the president or precisely conveyed to Lothian, it is little wonder that the ambassador and the Foreign Office came to favor the "generous offer" approach. The Royal Navy did not. This became clear at an interdepartmental meeting called on 1 July to discuss Lothian's suggestion that additional bases be granted the Americans. John Balfour, the Foreign Office representative, strongly supported Lothian. The Air Ministry and the War Office could see no objection, and even the Colonial Office took a "wait and see" approach. The Admiralty representative, however, took a hard line. It was the Admiralty's position that no offer should be made to the United States except as part of a more balanced arrangement in which the United States would offer something in return. The destroyers, he suggested, might be suitable. In the wider context, he maintained that "it would be a mistake to make it easier for the USA to provide for her own hemisphere defense, thereby lessening her incentive to interest herself in our own fate." Balfour opposed this view, but he could not budge the navy.[8] Therefore, when the draft paper was drawn up for Cabinet consideration, it noted that although it would be best to avoid the impression of "haggling," a quid pro quo— possibly "a less intransigent attitude" toward making the destroyers available—might be suggested to the Americans, in return for which they would get the bases.[9]

The Admiralty was hoping in the crisis atmosphere to clear the deck simultaneously on several issues and that the staff conferences which the Americans had agreed to might provide "the ideal forum." At such a general bargaining session, Britain's experience in international diplomacy and superior organization should put them at a real advantage. In the interim reply sent to Lothian, therefore, the Foreign Office suggested that the providing of the bases might best be considered at the staff conferences, where the whole range of issues confronting the Anglo-Americans could be settled at one time.[10]

* * *

The most significant British bargaining point was their continued stand against the Nazis. The question was, How long could they hold out?[11] There was doubt on that very subject not only in Washington but also in Canada. The Canadians were even proposing talks with the United States, "hypothetically, of course," about the possible "grave changes" that might soon take place.[12] In Ottawa, Pierrepont Moffat learned that the head of the Canadian navy was not waiting for talks, but was going ahead "making advance preparations in case the British Fleet in whole or in part should fall back on Canada." The Canadian told the American that he was preparing "anchorages, with the nets, buoys, and other protections against submarines, and air attack." He also was urging the British government to send him specifications on various kinds of equipment needed for ship servicing and repair.[13] This positive action, and the eventualities that it suggested, was at once welcome and ominous.

It was in this atmosphere that President Roosevelt decided to dispatch Colonel William J. Donovan to survey the situation in England and bring back a firsthand, confidential, unbiased report. Actually, Sir William Stephenson, chief of British intelligence in America, initiated Donovan's trip and found ways to make it suit England's needs as well as Roosevelt's. Stephenson had decided that the "bleakly defeatist" attitude in Washington, where he had multiple contacts, could best be countered by concentrating on a single individual. The man he chose was Colonel Donovan.[14]

Donovan's early fame came from conspicuous valor under

fire during World War I. For this service, he acquired the sobriquet "Wild Bill" and the Congressional Medal of Honor. During the years after the war he became a successful lawyer and a prominent Republican. For a time he served as acting attorney general under President Calvin Coolidge and some expected that Herbert Hoover would appoint him attorney general, but that was not to be. He also ran (unsuccessfully) for governor of New York in 1932. As a millionaire Wall Street lawyer he had wide economic and social contacts, including one with Franklin Roosevelt, whom he had known since law school. Thus Donovan had prominence, place, and entrée to the White House—all qualifications Stephenson sought.

Donovan's demeanor was somewhat unorthodox, but that too might work to British advantage. As would become clearer, Donovan observed diplomatic and bureaucratic formalities mainly in the breach. He railed at constraints on his freedom of action and hungered for the excitement of secret meetings, plots, and intrigue. Something of a human dynamo, he combined resourcefulness with "indefatigable energy and wide-ranging enthusiasm" according to his wartime colleague Allen Dulles.[15] Moreover, Donovan had supreme confidence in his selection of proper ends and did not mind pursuing unconventional routes to them. All of this enthusiastic dynamism was confined in a stocky frame topped by an open Irish face that looked out at the world with twinkling eyes. The British were only the first to see the use that might be made of Donovan in clandestine operations.[16]

Stephenson properly judged Americans to be debating two courses in the summer of 1940—either to provide Britain material assistance or to give her up for lost and concentrate upon their own rearmament. "That the former course was eventually pursued," Stephenson recalled years later, "was due in large measure to Donovan's tireless advocacy of it."[17] According to Stephenson, Donovan instinctively believed that Britain could survive if granted enough aid. It seemed to the British agent that the most useful service he could perform was to make British requirements known in appropriate quarters, and that this could be done most effectively by furnishing Donovan with "concrete evidence in support of his [Donovan's] contention that American material assistance would not be improvident charity but a sound investment."[18] If Donovan could be armed in this way, it seemed to Stephenson that the president and other prominent Americans could be suitably influenced. In June 1940 the president appointed Henry Stimson secretary of war and Frank Knox secretary of the navy. Since Stimson was a lifelong Republican and Knox had run as that party's nominee for vice-president in 1936, these appointments helped build a bipartisan political base for the impending crisis. The president selected Stimson after considering Donovan for the position, but it was through the appointment of Knox that Donovan became involved in national policymaking.[19] The new secretary of the navy was an old friend of Donovan's. He also was an ardent "war hawk." By June 1940 Knox was convinced that America would be actively involved in the war within a year and felt that "the sooner we declare war the sooner we will get ready."[20]

When Stephenson asked his assistance, Donovan, who was staying at Knox's house, readily agreed to arrange a meeting between Stephenson, Knox, and Stimson. At that meeting Stephenson candidly discussed the critical shortage of destroyers and other war supplies. The secretaries pointed out the legal barriers to a transaction involving the destroyers and the necessity for a bargain if Congress were to accept the deal. However, they had an ingenious solution for this problem. Since Congress was being balky, why not bypass it by convincing the president that action could be taken by executive order? Stimson and Knox thought that Roosevelt would not sign such an order unless he was convinced that chances were very good indeed that Britain would stand resolute under Nazi attack. Therefore, Stephenson suggested sending Donovan to London so that he could give the president a "firsthand report on conditions." Knox was enthusiastic about the idea and referred it to the president, who "immediately agreed" that Donovan should make the trip and that he should travel as the president's "'unofficial representative.'"[21] Thus Donovan was sent off to gather information that would help decide the American course and specifically to determine whether it would be safe to act by executive order. The president was seeking an objective estimate and to get it he was sending a congenital optimist, handpicked by the British Secret Service.[22]

Although he was in fact a personal representative of the president, Donovan traveled to England officially as a special envoy for Secretary Knox. That arrangement gave him special status with the Admiralty, with whom the matter of the destroyers would be discussed. But Donovan would investigate more than military matters. Ambassador Kennedy's reports and Churchill's messages had fed fears that Britain might collapse internally, and Donovan was instructed to form a judgment not only on whether the British *could* withstand the German onslaught, but also on whether they *would*.[23]

Despite Donovan's many qualifications, he did not feel well enough acquainted with the British "establishment" to conduct his important mission alone. Secretary Knox was able to assist him in this matter as well. For many years one of the most reliable and astute reporters on international affairs had been Edgar Ansel Mowrer, of the *Chicago Daily News*. Mowrer was well informed on European personalities and politics, and his published attitudes on the Nazis had made him hated by the Germans but popular in Britain. Since the Germans had put a price on Mowrer's head when they invaded France, he had fled to Portugal. It was there that a telegram from Knox, the former owner of the *Daily News*, found him. Knox wanted Mowrer to go to London and put himself at Colonel Donovan's disposal. He was given no details on the mission, but was told that the job was vitally important, and he was requested to help Donovan in every possible way. Obviously, having a journalist along on the trip would not hurt any publicity given the mission upon Donovan's return to the States. At the same time Mowrer, like Colonel Donovan, was hardly an unbiased investigator.

Donovan arrived in London on 19 July 1940 and quickly looked up Mowrer. The colonel got right to the point, explaining the mission and his lack of familiarity with British politics and personalities. Donovan thought that Mowrer could go places where he could not go and ask questions he could not ask. Since a large part of the job was to evaluate morale and the desire to fight, Mowrer's trained sensitivities should prove invaluable. Indeed, it was Mowrer's impression that the most important aspect of the investigation was to determine not Britain's ability to resist but rather its will to do so.[24] Mowrer naturally agreed to help all he could, and the two men began their two-week series of appointments and inspections.

The official arrangements for Donovan's tour were made by the naval attaché's office.[25] Donovan checked in with Captain Kirk the day after he arrived in London and outlined the president's instructions. Kirk knew Donovan and was eager to help. He began by giving him a full briefing on the situation from the attaché's perspective. Kirk then explained the arrangements he had made, but warned Donovan that the British were prepared for his visit and would show him the "best side of the picture." Kirk did not want the president's envoy taken in by window dressing, but he assumed that "Wild Bill" was "sufficiently keen to realize the magnitude of the problem faced by the British Empire."[26]

Kirk's anticipation about the British preparations was undoubtedly correct. And it is now known that added to the natural tendency to show one's best side to a visitor, Stephenson had added another stimulus. "I arranged," wrote the intelligence agent, "that he [Donovan] should be afforded every opportunity to conduct his inquiries." Stephenson also endeavored to marshal his friends in high places to "bare their breasts" to the American. "Donovan learned," wrote Stephenson, "that Churchill, defying the Nazis, was no mere bold façade but the very heart of Britain which was still beating strongly."[27] It was important to the British that Donovan reach this conclusion; in fact, one source suggests that the need was "desperate" to convince the president that Britain was "determined to fight on and to win . . . ," for without American aid "victory would be impossible."[28] With this urgency added to official and unofficial assistance, Donovan had an opportunity to see all he wanted and all the British wanted him to see.[29]

One of the first people Donovan saw was Kirk's valued contact at the Admiralty, Rear Admiral John Godfrey. Godfrey found that Donovan was interested in several issues and favored collaboration more or less across the board. The primary object of Donovan's mission, as Godfrey understood it, was "to discover if we were in earnest about the war, and if we were worth supporting." At the same time he had a "particular request" from Secretary Knox to "establish intimate collaboration with the British Navy, both in the spheres of technical development and intelligence."[30] Godfrey was pleased by Donovan's mission and by Donovan's attitude, which he sensed to be optimistic, positive, and pro-British.[31]

The mission naturally caused repercussions at the American Embassy, where cooperation and coordination were already poor. For one thing, Captain Kirk and Colonel Raymond E. Lee, the newly arrived army attaché, did not work as a team. Interservice rivalry, plus other differences of opinion, seems to have retarded their cooperation. Lee maintained a consistent, but guarded, optimism about British chances, and Kirk had his ups and downs. Since Anglo-American cooperation was primarily naval during this period, Kirk did not feel it was necessary to keep Lee informed on things like the Destroyer-Bases-Fleet transfer. Furthermore, Lee was not as close to Ambassador Kennedy as Kirk was. Lee found Kennedy depressingly defeatist and had at least one open and very unpleasant discussion with "His Excellency" on the subject.[32]

Ambassador Kennedy had not been consulted about the Donovan mission. Instead, he had been informed on 11 July that Secretary Knox, with presidential approval, had decided to send Donovan over for a "brief survey and report on certain aspects of the British defense situation."[33] Kennedy immediately contacted Sumner Welles in Washington and told him that he could not understand how Donovan could gain any valuable information "except through our existing military and naval attachés." Therefore, Kennedy believed that the mission would simply "result in creating confusion and misunderstanding on the part of the British." There is no way that Kennedy could have guessed how Donovan's trip was arranged, but it must have been obvious to the ambassador that the British would not expose Donovan to negative attitudes or experiences. They would try to counteract the pessimism they knew was coming from the Embassy; little wonder Kennedy bridled. Welles advised the president of Kennedy's reaction. Roosevelt, who seemed to enjoy the discomfort his Byzantine tactics sometimes caused, turned the problem over to, of all people, Secretary Knox, observing "somebody's nose seems to be out of joint."[34]

Naturally not sharing Kennedy's concern about confusion, the British toured Donovan and Mowrer widely, and the two Americans learned a great deal. Mowrer knew many of the important ministers personally and went to see everyone whom he thought could assist him in making a judgment. "I wanted to do a thorough reporting job," he later recalled, "so I asked about everything under the sun that would help me determine the British will to resist."[35] He had visited with Churchill at Chartwell before the war and now they lunched together at No. 10. The prime minister told Mowrer that "if worst came to worst, he, after defending Britain to the last, would send the Fleet and the Air

Force to Canada and fight from there."[36] That was what the emissaries wanted to hear.

However, it was nothing specific that anyone said that made Mowrer's mind up for him. He was a professional observer and realized that intangible, unspoken factors often determined events. The military situation in England seemed to him "abominable." The defenses were weak; the equipment, what little there was, was old; the Royal Air Force was untested in big battles; the fleet was the only certain shield. Despite all these negative factors, Mowrer became convinced, and so reported to Donovan, that the British, if supplied, could and would hold. "You might call it intuition," he recalled.

On the evening of 2 August Godfrey and Donovan dined together, afterward talking far into the night. Donovan said that he had a special charge to establish close liaison in the areas of naval intelligence and technical development. While discussing these issues Godfrey learned that Donovan sensed the "spiritual qualities of the British Race—those imponderables that make for victory which have evaded Joe Kennedy." Donovan admitted that Kennedy was preaching to Washington that "all is lost." Quite to the contrary, he himself believed that there was still time for American matériel and economic aid to have a "decisive effect" on the war. That was the first message that he would carry to the White House.

Next, Donovan would urge the appointment of a new ambassador to replace Kennedy. There were indications, he said, that Kennedy would be leaving of his own volition, since he figured the big attack was coming and he wanted to clear out before it materialized. "A sensible Colonel House" was needed to search for ways by which cooperation and liaison could be established. At the same time the ambassador would have to find methods to work around the "prickly matters" that involved national sovereignty and prestige and to avoid the "ignorant and too insistent demand for concession." While that man was being sought, Donovan was prepared to impress Roosevelt with the British need for bombsights, flying boats, destroyers, motor torpedo boats, guns, and other war matériel.[37] Thus Donovan and Mowrer were leaving London in an optimistic frame of mind, which was the same frame of mind that Donovan, at least, arrived with.

* * *

Discussion of the Destroyer-Bases-Fleet transfer had been going forward during the time Donovan was in England investigating whether it was safe to make any deals with the British. Within the British government there was still serious disagreement over the form any deal should take. On 8 July 1940 Lothian had advised London that Secretary of the Navy Knox had suggested canceling Britain's war debt—in return for Britain's Caribbean possessions. Knox's suggestion provided the ideal springboard for Lothian to prod London again about offering base facilities to the United States. Aiding this argument was the upcoming Havana Conference, at which he anticipated that European possessions in the Western Hemisphere would be discussed. Lothian calculated that demands for rights in British possessions could be effectively countered if a generous offer had been made spontaneously.[38] In forwarding this suggestion to the Chiefs of Staff, the Foreign Office summarized its argument by stating that, in their view, Britain's main objective should be to take action promptly, action that would "minimize the possibility of our being confronted with demands of a more extensive character and [would] show a forthcoming attitude towards America's defense requirements."[39]

Not everyone at the Foreign Office agreed with this tactic of controlling the nature of the bargain by acting with apparent generosity. When on 12 July Lothian repeated his estimate that unless Britain offered bases to the United States "we shall be confronted with a far more formidable demand if the situation in Europe deteriorates," he drew the fire of Sir Robert Vansittart, chief diplomatic adviser to Lord Halifax, the secretary of state for foreign affairs.[40] Vansittart was a senior, but very controversial, official. He had been kicked upstairs to make room for Sir Alexander Cadogan who, among others, entertained a low opinion of him. However, Vansittart could not be ignored because of his personal access to many influential people, including the foreign secretary. Sir Robert bridled at the idea that the United States might be preparing to make "imperious demands" on Britain and felt that Lothian had "lost his balance" and was viewing things in far too "panicky" a light. He assumed, furthermore, that the British would not be "such fools as to make any concession to the United States in this matter except by way of hard bargaining," which should net some very ample material support. Indeed, he wrote that "for once . . . we are *vis-à-vis* of the USA in the position of bargainers and not supplicants. Lord Lothian apparently doesn't like that position. I do."[41]

In fairness to the acerbic Sir Robert, we know that Lothian did sometimes take too pessimistic a view of the situation. In this case, however, he was quite right in guessing that the Americans were prepared, if necessary, to demand the bases. What that demand would have netted is another matter, since there was formidable opposition to any deal concerning the bases. The Colonial Office, more specifically Lord Lloyd, the colonial secretary, saw any grant of rights as the first step toward the assumption of sovereignty, and opposed it. Lord Lloyd's view, furthermore, as expressed by Mr. Poynton, of the Colonial Office staff, was that if Britain wanted to bring America into the war "we must not relieve them of their anxieties as to their own defenses."[42]

In countering this argument Lord Halifax, who favored a positive response to Lothian, wrote to Lloyd, denying that the grant of rights would be so extensive as to allow the United States to lose interest in Britain's fate. Instead, the effect would be "to bond the Americans closer to us by giving practical evidence of our unity of interests." However, Halifax preferred to rest the issue on the wider base of goodwill and mutual cooperation. The Americans must be convinced not only that England was going to stand and was thus worth supporting, but also that England had "every intention to collaborate with them to their own advantage as well as ours."[43]

The same points had been made in a memorandum drawn up at Halifax's request for presentation to the War Cabinet. In addition, that memorandum argued against asking for any quid pro quo since the good feeling and defense cooperation resulting from the base agreement would provide more in terms of immediate advantage and eventual collaboration than any material that might be gained.[44]

Meanwhile, favorable replies had been received from all the colonies involved and the Foreign Office was ready to push for War Cabinet approval.[45] Unfortunately, Prime Minister Churchill and the first lord of the Admiralty, A. V. Alexander, were absent from the next War Cabinet meeting and consideration was delayed until the meeting on 29 July. At that meeting it was decided to offer to lease to the United States the facilities that Lothian had suggested without requiring any quid pro quo.[46] It would be several days before Lothian would convey this offer to Roosevelt, and when he did he would misstate his government's intentions. Meanwhile other steps toward cooperation were being taken.

On 8 July Lothian had presented the United States with a memoir on scientific cooperation. Churchill had finally been won over by those who saw cooperation in this field as another method for winning American goodwill. With indications that the United States welcomed Lothian's move, the prime minister called a meeting at No. 10 Downing Street on 25 July to discuss procedures for the exchange. It was quickly decided that a scientific mission headed by Professor Tizard would be the ideal vehicle. There was much discussion, however, over the rationale behind exchanges. It was restated, apparently persuasively, that such cooperation would bring the United States "even closer to us materially and morally." Bargaining was roundly decried, but it was decided that two lists should be prepared, one showing *"in precise* detail" what the mission could give and the other listing "what we should like to get."[47] On 29 July the United States responded favorably to Lothian's memoir so all seemed ready. But Churchill said no. He sensed, he said, some "holding back" by the Americans (apparently on the destroyers) and he saw no reason to do more for them until they were in a more generous mood.[48]

The prime minister's reluctance held up the departure of the Tizard mission and although the War Cabinet had agreed to offer the base rights without reference to the destroyers, Churchill apparently was unwilling to await meekly American generosity on that subject either. Churchill perceived the moment to be right to "press the President," so he drafted a telegram intended for that purpose.[49]

Those who had advised couching requests in terms not quite so dramatic may have had an effect, for in this 31 July telegram Churchill gave a brief, but specific, list of recent losses, referred to this as a "frank account of our present situation," and asked for fifty or sixty of "your oldest destroyers." Furthermore, although he described conditions as grim, he made no reference to moving fleets or falling governments.[50] Churchill included a note saying he was sending this message via Ambassador Kennedy, whom he described as "a grand help to us and the common cause."[51]

Churchill's more positive approach was part of a new official line. Lord Beaverbrook told Kennedy on this same day, 31 July 1940, that until recently the British government policy when seeking American aid had been to make things look "as black as possible." Beaverbrook said he had opposed this approach and he was happy that now they were trying to make things look "as good as possible." The government, Kennedy thought, had become somewhat disturbed to find that "America might not be interested if they were doing badly." "Don't let anybody make any mistakes," he wired. "This war, from Great Britain's point of view, is being conducted from now on with their eyes only on one place and that is the United States."[52]

This shift in British tactics was to be met by an equally significant one on the American side. Theoretically, at least, an official decision had been made in London to provide base rights freely and to consider the destroyers and bases as separate entities. By the time Churchill's message arrived, however, the Americans were considering offering the British destroyers in return for the bases. How did this coincidence, which should have been especially gratifying to the British, occur? The record is not clear, but it would appear that personal contact between Lord Lothian and pro-British elements inside and close to the Roosevelt administration facilitated this development.

The idea may have been hatched by some of the more ardent Washington Anglophiles, but it was suggested to Lothian by Secretary of the Navy Frank Knox.[53] Knox had already accepted the concept that the United States should enter the war at the earliest possible date and in his anxiety to help England he may have offered more for the bases than was necessary.[54] In any case, during the course of a 31 July discussion on British needs with an "almost tearful" Lothian, Knox suggested, as he had done before, that England should transfer her Western Hemisphere bases to the United States. This time, however, his argument was different. If Britain transferred those bases it would make it easier to get a bill through Congress concerning the destroyers. The administration could argue, Knox said, that the bases were of greater value than the ships and hence that an advantageous bargain had been struck.[55]

Lothian, not revealing that his government had already agreed to provide the desired bases, said he would query London about such a trade.[56] When Lothian reported this conversation to London he added his personal support for the concept of selling to the United States sea and air bases in Newfoundland, Bermuda, and Trinidad.[57] The new American approach would be welcome. The major controversy surrounding the agreement to provide America with base facilities—admittedly more limited facilities than the Americans now had in mind, but bases nevertheless—had been whether to ask for something in return. Now some Americans were asking for bases and offering destroyers in return.

The British ambassador was promptly advised of his government's favorable reaction, but the terms should be indefinite leases, not sale. It also was noted that the Dominions would have to be consulted again before this widened agreement could be finalized.[58] In his draft of this message Churchill could not restrain himself from reminding Lothian that England had already freely offered the base rights.[59]

Roosevelt had been cautious up to this point. However, when the Cabinet met on the afternoon of 2 August, he must have known that the forces for action were gaining strength. Ickes, Knox, and Stimson had agreed to support an exchange plan, and Morgenthau would probably back them.[60] Thus when Knox suggested that the destroyers be traded for the British island bases, he knew he had a majority. Roosevelt, perhaps sensing that fact, offered minor objections, but ultimately agreed, on condition that the sites be leased.[61]

Then the question of the British Fleet was introduced, and the importance of that consideration is indicated by the fact that Roosevelt, uncharacteristically, drew up a detailed memorandum on the subject after the meeting. The president emphasized that before any agreement could be finalized a public commitment had to be made guaranteeing that the fleet would come to Empire ports.[62] Ickes agreed, suggesting that to accomplish that end it might be wise to increase the offers of asylum for British children. The more English children in America, he reasoned, the more "hostages to fortune we would have and the greater the disposition on the part of the English to send their Fleet." The president agreed.[63]

Knox and Stimson, who previously had discussed with Stephenson and Donovan the possibility of an executive order as a manner of circumventing Congress, apparently did not raise the point at that meeting.[64] The president, therefore, assuming some form of congressional action, was concerned about the political ramifications of the exchange and said it was essential that Republican support be assured.[65] A plan was immediately formulated by which William Allen White, an influential Republican, would secure the support of Wendell Willkie, the Republican presidential nominee, and would use that support as an argument on Capitol Hill for Republican approval.[66] The president called White and received his agreement.

The next day the president proposed the deal to Lothian. Referring to British concessions as "molasses" that would be useful in sweetening up Congress, Roosevelt made two stipulations. The first dose of molasses was a "public assurance by the present British Government that if things went badly, in no circumstances would the British Fleet, or such of it as remained intact at the end of the battle for Britain, be handed over to Germany but would, if necessary, leave British waters and continue the fight for the British Empire overseas." The president admitted that everyone would realize that such a declaration would not bind any government that might succeed the present one, but he wanted the declaration anyhow.

The other dose of molasses was that the British government "give air and naval facilities to the United States for hemispheric defense." At this point Lothian apparently made a mistake. According to his report of the conversation he said that he had been authorized to say that "naval and air facilities in question would be made available to the United States *as soon as we obtained destroyers.*" In fact, he had been expressly authorized to offer the bases without linking them to the destroyers. On the subject of a fleet guarantee he was more circumspect, saying that he would have to query London before making any comment.[67]

Before the British government could react to the president's wishes, Lothian received a shock. On the morning of 4 August he went to the State Department to talk with Secretary of State Hull about the possible transfer arrangement. The old Tennessee judge was in one of his more prickly moods, suggesting that the whole arrangement sounded illegal.[68] But whether legal or not, Hull thought the chances of congressional approval were nil. Moreover, the secretary proposed doing nothing until after the November elections. Sumner Welles, who was also present, was somewhat more helpful. He supported the president's plan and suggested a simple, straightforward guarantee that the fleet would come to North America if necessary.[69] Lothian was not encouraged, and when he met a member of the Century Group (an organization of ardent interventionists) for lunch, he appeared "haggard and worn."[70]

At this point no one seemed to know whether the deal was on or off. Lothian's emotional state probably contributed to the confusion, and when he advised London of Welles's statement, he helped not a bit by getting his syntax garbled. All that was needed, the ambassador wired, was a simple declaration that the fleet would go on fighting for the Empire "even if it is compelled to evacuate Great Britain if and when the President asks for it."[71] Churchill hit the ceiling. He interpreted Lothian to mean that England might have to turn the fleet over whenever the president asked for it.

A public guarantee regarding the future of the fleet was a very delicate matter that the prime minister wanted to approach cautiously. Thus he objected to the Foreign Office draft telegram, drawn up in reply to Lothian, which seemed to imply acceptance of the American proposition. He wanted it made clear, he said, that "only a war alliance" could justify "any stipulations about the disposition of the Fleet." And, under any circumstance, England must be the sole judge of when the fleet should cross the Atlantic. Any other course he thought would be "disastrous on British morale," and, furthermore, the colonial leases seemed to him more than enough to give for fifty or sixty "old destroyers." The Foreign Office had made the point, and the prime minister undoubtedly agreed, that nothing should be done through the administration of molasses that would allow Congress and public opinion to become complacent and allow the United States to "relax in its efforts to assist us."[72] With this point and the prime minister's comments in mind, a new telegram was drafted during the afternoon of 6 August, incorporating what were thought to be Churchill's opinions.

Later that evening, John Balfour, who had helped compose the new message, was summoned to No. 10 Downing Street. When he arrived he found the prime minister, the first lord of the Admiralty, and the first sea lord. They had been talking, he soon learned, about the fleet, and the prime minister's nautical friends had driven him to a new peak of indignation concerning the required guarantee. After chiding Balfour about the lack of "feeling" in the Foreign Office telegram, Churchill proceeded to dictate his own version. He was in fine form, striding up and down, jabbing at the air with his cigar, and punctuating his dictation with dramatic flourishes that brought approval from the Admiralty officials. "It doesn't do to give way like this to the Americans," he informed Balfour. "One must strike a balance with them." At this point the prime minister, looking resplendent in his evening clothes, suited his actions to his words by spreading his arms and rocking them up and down. "Show them that you are ready to meet reasonable requests from them," he said with a benign smile, but "also alive and in fighting form" said he, jutting out his chin. A startled Balfour took the prime minister's message and retreated. [73]

However, the next morning, before Churchill's message could be dispatched, another request for the fleet guarantee came in from Lothian. "It is evident," he reported, "that this argument is the one which has the most effect on Congress in the matter of destroyers."[74] He was sent an interim reply and Lord Halifax set to work trying to mollify the prime minister. Halifax advised Churchill that a "sharp" reply to Lothian would serve no useful purpose and proposed instead a more diplomatic approach. The passage of time and perhaps the absence of his naval friends moved Churchill to be somewhat more agreeable. But he advised Halifax that he still opposed any discussion of the fleet that might give the Americans a blank check that they could present for collection, saying "we think the time has come for you to send your Fleet across the Atlantic." He thus insisted that the American request for a public statement had to be refused and the deal confined to the colonial bases.[75] The prime minister also preferred that Halifax, rather than he himself, reply to Lothian.

Halifax's reply was less stirring than Churchill's, but it pointed out that there was great difficulty in making any statement more specific than the one the prime minister had made on 4 June about the New World "armed and guarded by the British Fleet" fighting on if Britain collapsed. Any declaration on the matter would provoke unfortunate rumors of irresolution in England. Could Lothian, he asked, see any way to reconcile British difficulties and American desires? As a guidepost in his search he was advised to make as few concessions as possible.[76] Halifax made no attempt to deny the connection between the destroyers, the fleet, and the bases, realizing perhaps that it was Lothian who had linked them by saying that the United States could have the bases "as soon as" Britain got the destroyers.

Lothian was even a little more conciliatory than Halifax when he addressed a letter to Sumner Welles, acting secretary of state during Hull's vacation. The letter presented what were purported to be Churchill's views and quoted him as saying that "if Great Britain were overrun, the present Government would certainly send the Fleet . . . to defend the Empire overseas and would neither sink nor surrender it."[77] Lothian then reiterated the contention that any public statement in England or America regarding the fleet would stimulate unhealthy fears. The ambassador may have realized that if a guarantee, which seemed to mean so much to the Americans, was again referred to as mutable and nonbinding, the whole deal might collapse. He did, however, reemphasize the quotation from Churchill's 4 June speech.

Welles, always cool in a crisis, did not take the ambassador's suggestions well. The acting secretary of state realized that the statement on 4 June was limited in scope, and he advised the president that it was "no commitment whatever" and bound no government other than the one presently in office.[78] Furthermore, Welles thought that the base rights that were offered were "restricted and entirely unsatisfactory suggestions" for granting "limited facilities."[79]

Welles might have been more generous had Britain's military prospects looked more promising. By early August there were ominous signs that the Luftwaffe was preparing to turn its might against England. Some bombs had been dropped already; more were sure to come. At this critical juncture Donovan and Mowrer returned to Washington with their firsthand report. They talked initially to Secretary Knox, who in turn briefed them on developments in the United States. What Roosevelt wanted to know, the secretary said, was, Were the British prepared to fight on and, if defeat came, would the fleet cross the seas to North America? The two envoys repeated their optimistic appraisal. The "extreme depression" they sensed in Washington was not justified. The British would "stick it," and, Donovan stated positively, they would win. In his view, British appeasement should not be a major concern.[80]

Donovan and Secretary Knox then went to call on the president. According to Donovan, Roosevelt started off with one of his traditional monologues. Kennedy's reports had left their mark and the president was obviously not as convinced as Donovan of British chances. Intent upon presenting his case, Donovan interrupted the president several times to "dwell upon [Britain's] excellent prospects of pulling through." Since he felt this was the case, he judged there was no danger in providing the destroyers and other military equipment that would make the British task easier. It was difficult to gauge the immediate impact of his statements, but he had surely provided the president with a different point of view that brimmed with immediacy and abounded with factual information.[81]

Stephenson reported to London on 8 August that Donovan was saying "positively and convincingly that we shall win" and it was Donovan's impression that the deal was moving toward a satisfactory conclusion.[82] That news was welcome in London, which had been encouraged several days before with the announcement that an American delegation was preparing to come to London for staff talks.[83] In this improved, but not yet ideal, atmosphere, Churchill withdrew his objections to the dispatch of a scientific mission. Professor Tizard, consequently, hastily packed his instruments, plans, and models, including a mysterious "black box," and on 14 August departed on his scientific *qua* diplomatic mission.[84] The bargaining deadlock had yet to be broken, but progress was apparent on several fronts.

8.

Learning to Play Zero-Sum Games

14 August 1940–25 September 1940

While Donovan was doing his best in Washington to convince Roosevelt of British stamina under attack, the air battle over England moved into a new phase. August 9 to 23 marked Phase II in the Battle of Britain. The first few days of this period were spent in preparation and then, even though 13 August dawned with some cloud and drizzle over the Channel, "Adlertag" opened on schedule. The target was the Royal Air Force Fighter Command itself and for two weeks waves of ME 109s, ME 110s, Junkers, and Heinkels attacked air bases and communications facilities. Spitfires and Hurricanes were destroyed on the ground and heavily engaged in the air; it was an all-out effort that almost succeeded. During much of August the outcome was in doubt and although the task had not been completed in the four days originally projected, Air Reichsmarshal Hermann Goering and his Luftwaffe intelligence staff believed that they were well on their way toward attaining air superiority over England. Churchill thought differently, but could the Americans be convinced?

The Americans were already badly frightened by developments in Europe. Churchill's initial policy of attempting to hasten aid by hinting at collapse had done little but make them more cautious.

Now, with Britain under direct attack, they had to be reassured. Missions like Donovan's helped, and some suggested overwhelming the Americans with "data," for which they seemingly had a passion.[1] The destroyer deal, however, was going to be the measure of things, and it was becoming increasingly confused. The British government had agreed to offer bases without asking for destroyers. Before learning of this initiative the United States government, at the instigation of Knox, had offered destroyers *in return for* bases *and* a fleet guarantee. The question was, Could Britain reject those conditions without bringing down the whole elaborately developed cooperative structure, which now included technical exchanges and possibly staff conversations?

It would appear that in August 1940 political considerations were outweighing, or at least balancing, military considerations on both sides of the Atlantic. Churchill could not give assurances about the fleet that might seem defeatist and thus undermine morale and his own position of leadership. However, he could use the destroyers not only for their strategic value but also as an indication of American commitment. Roosevelt, on the other hand, was in an election campaign and could not appear too eager to aid Britain. A public guarantee concerning the fleet would disarm Roosevelt's critics, and until he got that guarantee the president stalled.

* * *

Roosevelt's political problem was centered in Congress, where there seemed real possibility of obstruction. Therefore, attention in Washington now focused on an executive order to accomplish what Congress might prevent or delay doing. Legal arguments and behind-the-scenes maneuvering culminated in a letter to the *New York Times* signed by Dean Acheson, a member of the militant Century Group, and three other prominent attorneys. The letter, printed on 11 August 1940, argued persuasively that the president had the legal authority to transfer the destroyers. Since the Century Group had been advised as early as 24 July that some legal "flimflam" might be necessary to gain support, the objectivity of this opinion is questionable. Nonetheless, formidable legal support had been mustered and the president was said to be "very, very much encouraged" by the news.[2] Furthermore, William Allen White reported that Willkie would not only not say anything against the transaction but might even say something favorable, which would defuse adverse reaction by Republicans in Congress.[3]

Waiting for word that congressional opposition could be circumvented was not the only thing delaying action. Sumner Welles had not been too pleased with the leases the British were offering for the destroyers, and, to make matters worse, Lothian presented a list of additional items the British wanted, including motor torpedo boats (MTBs), 50 flying boats, and 250,000 rifles.[4] On 13 August Roosevelt held a long meeting with Welles, Stimson, Knox, and Morgenthau, who all agreed that Britain's chances were growing slimmer and that the destroyer exchange, "while a very serious step," would have to be undertaken. But anxiety did not make a bad deal any more desirable. Therefore, the president and his advisers collaborated on a message to Churchill that suggested a reduced list of items the United States might offer and noted that this equipment could be furnished only "if the American people and the Congress frankly recognized that in return therefor the national defense and security of the United States would be enhanced."[5]

To convince the American public that the deal would enhance their security, the president still wanted, first, an unequivocal guarantee that in the event of defeat the fleet would make for Empire ports. And, second, he wanted more bases than the British had offered, as well as clearer, more encompassing rights to their use. To make things easier, the president had changed his mind about the type of fleet declaration that was required. Now he thought a public statement unnecessary. A "reiteration to me of your statement to Parliament on June 4" would be sufficient.[6] Either the suggestion Lothian had made about the parliamentary speech had been picked up, or the president had decided to handle the publicity from his end.[7]

The War Cabinet met on 14 August to discuss Roosevelt's message and Churchill's reply. The prime minister began by saying that since the sale of the destroyers was an unneutral act, it would go a long way toward bringing the United States into the war. Thus the effect on Germany would be "immense." In other words, as he was to say later, the real reason for favoring the exchange was that as an unneutral act it would, "according to all the standards of history, have justified the German Government in declaring war."[8]

The unspoken commitment by the United States would actually enhance British security while allowing the Americans to think it was enhancing theirs. The War Cabinet was generally of the view that the United States was making a "hard bargain." However, it was pointed out that the deal might be the first step toward constituting an "Anglo-Saxon *bloc*" and thus be a "decisive point in history." After considering all these factors it was agreed that a favorable response should be made. But the "crucial point" was what President Roosevelt might say publicly about the fleet.[9] Therefore, in his message to the president, Churchill suggested that it was not in America's interest to emphasize the possibility of British defeat.[10] On the matter of the fleet he said: "I am of course ready to reiterate to you what I told Parliament on June 4th. We intend to fight this out here to the end and none of us would ever buy peace by surrendering or scuttling the Fleet." No mention of quislings here. Concerning the bases, he agreed in principle with the American proposal.[11]

The president considered Churchill's message "entirely satisfactory" and discussed the matter at his press conference on 16 August. He told reporters that there was no connection between the bases for which the United States was negotiating and the destroyers—an unfortunate and unnecessary misstatement of fact[12] since public opinion had come to favor the deal and with Willkie's agreement it certainly appeared politically safe.[13] Lord Lothian was pleased in any case and wired London: "I think the trick has been done. At least the President told me on the telephone this morning that he thought it was. Donovan has helped a lot, and Knox."[14]

Secretary of the Navy Knox had been in the forefront of the advocates, but up to this point the professional navy had been playing a small role in the negotiations. With the time drawing near for signing the papers and declaring the destroyers surplus to American needs, Admiral Stark had to be approached. Secretary Knox met with Stark on the afternoon of the president's press conference and asked him to prepare to transfer fifty "old destroyers to the British in return for certain 99-year leases." Stark, in looking over the paper outlining the procedure, noted that the transfer was to be justified under a law (Section 491 of Title 34 of the U.S. Code) that required a statement declaring the destroyers "obsolete and useless." Stark, who was somewhat more objective than Knox, said that he could make no such statement.

Stark was in an awkward position. Although he never said so

directly, he was personally unenthusiastic about the deal. He may or may not have shared the view of his chief intelligence officer, Admiral Anderson, who was reported to believe that Britain was finished and who wanted to keep the ships to defend America rather than risk them in a "lost cause." At any rate, Stark did not want to lose the vessels.[15] One reason was that as the Navy Department's primary professional spokesman before Congress, he had just asked for appropriations that would increase naval expenditures by 92 percent. Stark had posited his case on two major premises: first, world tensions made increased U.S. naval forces absolutely necessary if the American interests were to be protected;[16] second, the United States should have a navy second to none. In that regard, he had pointedly referred to the need for staying abreast or ahead of Great Britain. When asked, for instance, whether the principal purpose of a certain increase was to keep up with Great Britain, Stark replied: "We are going along in that direction as far as we can." He enthusiastically endorsed the concept, he said, of keeping up with all the world's naval powers.[17] There had been no implication that America might have to fight England, but that made it only slightly less incongruous to provide them now with 75,000 tons of combat shipping. Moreover, if the U.S. Navy needed ships as badly as Stark had said they did, how could he afford to give anything away? Against this background Stark's reluctance becomes more understandable.

Stark later said that he doubted any board of officers would declare the destroyers useless, and even if they did, he, as chief of naval operations, would disallow their finding. In strictly military terms, Stark pointed out, "such an opinion would be false else the British would not be so anxious to get the same destroyers." Stark had apparently contacted the president and told him the same thing and, according to Stark, Roosevelt had agreed that Stark should not make such a certification "independent of other considerations." However, Stark did see a way of changing the proposed arrangement so that the trade would be legal.

The admiral, who had little interest in Churchill's political rhetoric, believed that a "clear-cut trade" of fifty destroyers for the bases would be to American advantage. However, by a "clear-cut trade" he did not mean the 99-year leases the Secretary had mentioned. Stark wanted a complete "transfer of sovereignty." Furthermore, Attorney General Robert Jackson had told Stark that the question of disposition of fifty overage destroyers was more "political than legal." Since that was the case, the admiral thought the terms should leave "no doubt whatever in the lay mind that what we have is bona fide beyond all conjecture and doubt, and a good horse trade." Therefore, instead of separating the two exchanges in any way, he recommended that the arrangements for the destroyers and the bases be tied together in the same document. He had discussed this arrangement with the attorney general, and the single-document formula they worked out seemed practical as well as legal. Even so, Stark's preference was to obtain congressional approval; but he was a naval officer and the president was commander-in-chief, and if the president were to decide to bypass Congress and order him to sign the necessary papers, the chief of naval operations would naturally obey.[18]

Since General Marshall might have to sign a similar statement if any army matériel were included in the exchange, Stark had discussed the situation with him. Marshall agreed completely with Stark's position, stressing that if the admiral did anything that jeopardized his reputation for "honest, frank, open dealing" with Congress, he might just as well resign as chief of naval operations.[19]

The president had gone to Ogdensburg, New York, after his 16 August press conference. When he returned to Washington, Sumner Welles gave him a draft of the letters to be exchanged between the British and the American governments. These letters provided for a fleet guarantee, stipulated the nature of the leases, and made the connection between the bases and the destroyers quite clear.[20] The president raised no objections.

The American military chiefs had yet to be convinced, but otherwise things seemed settled and the United States was preparing to make the arrangement final when the prime minister stepped into the limelight again. In a speech delivered to Parliament on 20 August he offered the bases to the United States as a gift separate from the destroyers and with no strings attached. This statement was not welcome in Washington.[21]

Part of Churchill's difficulty was obvious. The American request for compensation was heavily weighted in its favor to assure congressional and military agreement; however, it was hardly an agreement that the prime minister could term a fair trade; in fact, if it had been, the Americans would not have been interested. Therefore, Churchill acted to inform the English people of the arrangement in a politically defensible manner—which was, as a gift graciously given. Unfortunately, the United States could not accept the bases on those terms. But in the eyes of the British government, and specifically of the prime minister, unless it were done that way it would appear to be, and would be, an indefensibly hard bargain.

In the Cabinet discussions about the matter the point was also made that Britain had originally freely offered the United States limited base facilities and it seemed unreasonable not to connect the two deals when the benefit to the grantor was not equal to that of the grantee.[22] But beyond those practical realities there was a more subtle point. If Britain were to give bases to the United States, then they, as donor, could determine the extent and nature of the gift; if, on the other hand, the bases were part of a deal, the United States might assume some prerogative over what they received in return for their destroyers.[23]

In his speech Churchill had attempted to overcome these problems with rhetoric, but his solution served only to sharpen Admiral Stark's dilemma. The next day, 21 August, Stark and Marshall met with Attorney General Jackson. He assured them that they could legally sign the papers certifying the equipment as not essential for the national security, since American security would be enhanced by the receipt of the bases *in return for* the military equipment.[24] Unfortunately, this approach was useless if Churchill's contention that the bases were gifts unconnected with the destroyers were allowed to stand. At the same time, it was extremely important that the service chiefs sign the releases, for if they did, Congress could safely be bypassed by way of an executive order. If they did not, an opportunity for awkward questioning might arise. Someone might ask, for example, whether it was necessary for the United States to provide destroyers since the British seemed willing to provide the bases without them. A good question.

Even before the ramifications of Churchill's speech were evident, Sir William Stephenson described an atmosphere of delay in Washington that he attributed to "strong opposition from below and procrastination from above." Presumably, he referred to Stark's negative attitude and the lack of initiative shown by Roosevelt. The British agent cabled London on 21 August that Donovan had urged the president to take personal charge of the negotiations.[25]

The president did not take personal charge of the negotiations, but he did write to Senator David I. Walsh (Democrat, Massachusetts), chairman of the Naval Affairs Committee and author of the legislation proscribing the transfer of usable war materials. In a "Dear Dave" letter, Roosevelt made his case for the exchange in terms of national interest. He also drew an analogy between the proposed transfer and the Louisiana Purchase, which he noted had been consummated by Thomas Jefferson, "the founder of the Democratic Party." After explaining what a great handicap America's lack of off-shore bases was, he suggested that the deficiency could be "largely cured" by trading fifty destroyers, "which are on their last legs," for base rights in Newfoundland, Bermuda, the Bahamas, St. Lucia, Trinidad, and British Guiana. In case Walsh did not know how decrepit the destroyers were, the president drove the point home. "The fifty destroyers," he wrote, "are the same type of ship which we have been from time to time striking from the naval list and selling for scrap for, I think, $4,000 or $5,000 per destroyer." Thus, the president computed, the United States was getting seven bases for the "extremely low" price of $250,000. He concluded by saying he hoped Walsh would not oppose the deal, which "from the point of view of the United States" Roosevelt considered "the finest thing for the nation that has been done in your lifetime and mine."[26]

On the day Roosevelt wrote Walsh, a telegram arrived from Churchill. In it the prime minister made his point equally explicit. The British government, he wrote, would like to "give you the facilities mentioned without stipulating for any return." He even opposed the exchange of letters that Lothian and Welles had talked about "or in admitting in any way that the munitions which you send us are a payment for the facilities." He went on to say that he trusted the Americans to be generous in their provision of war matériel and saw no need to bargain.[27]

When this message arrived Lothian went to see Sumner Welles to determine whether the American position had changed. It had not. The president had said that an exchange of letters was the only course, implied that he had done all he could, and suggested that further delay might doom the whole project. Lothian supported this argument in his report to London and said he fervently hoped the prime minister could meet the president's requirements.[28]

The prime minister could not see his way clear to meet the

president's desires. In fact he got quite excited when on the afternoon of 23 August Sir Alexander Cadogan approached him with Lothian's appeal. Churchill feared that if England agreed to provide America with imprecise rights to British bases, the Americans might expect more than Britain was prepared to give and things might degenerate into an "unseemly wrangle." This might do great harm to the spirit of Anglo-American harmony. Then, completely spontaneously, the prime minister said that "if necessary he could do without the American destroyers." He had been painting the picture in "rather vivid colours in order to persuade the Americans," he said. In fact, England, with her new construction, would be in a perfectly safe position by the end of the year. Therefore, he did not need to offer anything he did not want to. But what he did offer should be couched in the most generous terms and in fullest possible detail. Thus the Roosevelt administration, the prime minister believed, would be "shamed" into giving England the destroyers.[29]

In Washington things were going almost as badly, with Roosevelt evincing no shame about not meeting Britain's needs. When Secretary Hull, fresh from his vacation, called at the White House he was advised that the negotiations had "bogged down." Furthermore, instead of taking charge himself, the president wanted Hull to assume responsibility for the negotiations.[30] Hull had not been particularly sympathetic toward the deal; he realized, however, that if things dragged on much longer any psychological benefit derived from the cooperative effort would be lost; he probably also realized that any political or military benefit would be hazarded as well. Therefore, he determined to push the negotiations to completion as quickly as possible. The old Tennessee judge, however, thought the British were "crawfishing."[31]

Churchill did not see it that way.[32] On 25 August he sent a message to the president, again making clear his generous intent; at the same time he wished to define the "gift" very carefully lest he provide the United States with what he referred to as a "blank cheque on the whole of our transatlantic possessions."[33] To avoid this unfortunate development, he proposed offering at once "certain fairly well-defined facilities," and then "your experts could ... discuss these or any other variants of them with ours—we remaining the final judge of what we can give."[34]

Lothian met with Hull and Roosevelt on the same day Churchill sent his wire, and reflecting the spirit of that message, suggested that the matter be treated as a mutual gesture of friendship with gifts exchanged all around. Hull explained that the president could not make gifts, and Roosevelt "at once agreed" with the secretary, stating flatly that "another and different arrangement would be necessary."[35] Moreover, something more precise than a "bare declaration" that Britain intended to provide some bases to the United States would be necessary to appease Congress and Admiral Stark. For his part the president indelicately pointed out that there might be a "change of Government in Britain"[36] and then presumably the base declaration would mean nothing. After reiterating that there would have to be some connection made between the destroyers and the bases, the president turned the matter over to Hull, leaving the solution to him and Lothian.

The next day, 26 August, Hull conferred with his advisers in the State Department. The solution was proposed by Green H. Hackworth, the department's legal adviser. Once posed, it seemed simple. Why not, said Hackworth, split the deal and make some bases a gift and trade the rest for the destroyers? This would give Stark the bargain he wanted while allowing the British to be generous. Hull promptly accepted this idea and a new draft letter was prepared incorporating Hackworth's suggestion. One aspect of the arrangement was thus changed, but the matter of primary importance to the United States—the fleet guarantee—remained the same. The American draft began with the statement: "If the waters surrounding the British Isles became untenable for British warships, the British Fleet would in no event be surrendered or sunk, but would be sent to other ports of the Empire." Hull said he knew Churchill had made a similar statement on 4 June, but he wanted a "formal repetition."[37]

After the Cabinet meeting of 27 August the president, Hull, and Stimson discussed the State Department draft and Churchill's most recent message, in which he continued to refer to the bases as gifts. Then the president left for a brief vacation. On the same day Attorney General Jackson officially ruled that the president had the legal right to act by executive order on this matter, thus removing the last potential congressional roadblock.[38] That evening, however, Lothian went to Hull's apartment and tried to change the draft agreement. It took more than an hour of argument to convince the ambassador that the United States government could not accept gifts.[39] Hull wanted to consummate the deal with the least possible delay, suggesting that a storm of protest was brewing over its dubious legality. Best to get it over with quickly, he counseled, before congressional critics realized that Churchill was saying that the bases could have been obtained without the destroyers—which, of course, was the fact. Lothian finally agreed to urge his government to accept the American version.[40]

The British Cabinet discussed the new drafts at their meeting on 29 August, where Churchill continued to argue for providing all the bases "in friendship and good will."[41] However, finally someone had a "touch of statesmanship" and declared that the real benefits from the arrangement were intangible and lay in the demonstration of solidarity between the two countries.[42] It was not Churchill but Lord Halifax who demonstrated this ability to see matters in their broadest terms. Churchill, as Ambassador Kennedy reported, had been convinced by Lord Beaverbrook to take the view that "if we are going to make a gift, well and good; if we are going to make a bargain, I don't want to make a bad one and this definitely is a bad one."[43]

Lord Halifax convinced Churchill to see things his way, and Kennedy reported that the British were "inordinately happy" about the deal. He was still somewhat worried, though, and suggested that the president make his statement and sign first so that the "direction of Churchill's remarks will be more or less channeled." As for himself, Kennedy viewed the matter from a national security angle and felt it was a good deal.[44]

The Americans did not want the exchange delayed further, and with the receipt of the British Cabinet's view, Lothian, Hull, and Knox quickly reached final agreement. On 2 September 1940, the American secretary of state and the British ambassador signed the papers regarding the bases and on the next day Admiral Stark signed the release for the destroyers. The important fleet guarantee was formalized by an exchange of aide-mémoire between 29 August and 2 September. The language of the original American note was used and the British government replied in prearranged fashion.[45]

Since the issue of a public guarantee had been so important, the handling of that issue is instructive. There had been some last-minute discussion between Hull and Lothian about how the announcement would be handled and apparently it was agreed that the fleet guarantee would not be announced until after the destroyer transfer was made public.[46] However, as the documents were being signed in Washington, the president was holding a press conference at which he made the connection explicit.[47] Since the British had considered fleet guarantee publicity as "crucial," London hoped that the president would not emphasize that aspect of the exchange.[48] Roosevelt, however, had pointedly called the guarantee to reporters' attention, and any idea that it would be soft-pedaled was dispelled by the *New York Times*, which proclaimed in bold headlines: "ROOSEVELT TRADES DESTROYERS FOR SEA BASES / TELLS CONGRESS HE ACTED ON OWN AUTHORITY / BRITAIN PLEDGES NEVER TO YIELD OR SINK FLEET." The article went on to note that the United States had received a "solemn pledge" from the British government "not to scuttle or surrender the British Fleet under any conditions."[49] The report stated that unnamed but "informed" individuals in "official circles" contended that the arrangement "assured the British Fleet as an Atlantic sea-screen for the United States."[50]

But no matter how it was handled in the press, the fleet guarantee was exceedingly important to the Americans. Their desire for assurance on the fleet's ultimate destination had appeared in the earliest messages concerning Britain's fate, and it obviously would have been foolish to add the destroyers to the equipment that might be handed over to the Nazis if England toppled or folded. As we know, the ultimate destination of the British fleet never had to be decided. Churchill denied that there were ever any plans for its movement, and technically he may have been correct; however, the head of the Admiralty Plans Division later pointed out that no "plans" were actually needed. Oil in the bunkers and a single order could have sent the remnants of the fleet steaming to other ports.[51]

The culmination of the negotiations brought relief and satisfaction to most American officials. Hull told Berle that the real advantages for the United States were the "less tangible considerations arising out of the national defense and closer cooperation in the hemisphere."[52] Berle thought that the American public should be very pleased, for "in a single gulp we have acquired the raw material for the first true continental defense we have had since sailing ship days."[53] There would be little public reaction against the exchange, and the storm that had been feared in Congress never materialized.

Thus the administration was satisfied. Undeniably valuable base sites had been acquired at an incredibly low monetary outlay. But what of the intangible price, the moral commitment to aid the British further? There is no evidence that the president or any high administration official considered the United States to be so committed. There is little doubt, furthermore, that the president honestly saw the exchange in terms of national interest. For several years he had been considering ways to insure the United States against transfer of any European possessions in the Western Hemisphere; by September 1940 he had obtained a declaration proscribing such transfers, plus bases for hemisphere defense. In this sense, the agreement could be considered as insurance against Britain's possible demise. Furthermore, as Roosevelt had suggested in his letter to Senator Walsh, a flattering analogy could be drawn between the Destroyer-Bases-Fleet exchange and the Louisiana Purchase, where Jefferson had taken advantage of Napoleon's European preoccupations to strike a favorable deal.

On the British side, Churchill thought the deal could be presented as a British victory worth far more than its face value. As he told his colleagues, they had exchanged "a bunch of flowers for a sugar cake."[54] Churchill obviously was thinking in political terms, terms that allowed him to consider the exchange as a down payment on further aid, and he clearly was not referring to the fifty decrepit destroyers, some of which barely made it across the Atlantic, when he spoke of a "sugar cake."

Certainly the consummation of the exchange tied Britain and America more closely together. But despite the atmosphere of cooperation that was fostered, perhaps the most important aspect of the transaction was the bargaining involved. After the four months of negotiations, marked on both sides by considerable maneuvering to gain advantage, what they eventually realized was that they were not involved in a zero-sum game. Something gained by one was not automatically subtracted from the other's security. Both sides did of course continue to strive for advantage, but the first step away from an adversary relationship had been taken.

At the same time it should be noted that the Americans had consummated their first major negotiation of World War II in very creditable fashion. At a minimum, they had not been taken advantage of and it might even be suggested that Uncle Shylock had shown that he was not averse to advancing his cause at Britannia's expense. From Britannia's perspective, solace could be taken from the "intangible factors" argument and from the fact that the bases had almost been given away without getting the destroyers. Furthermore, doubts about Britain's internal stability and military defenses had been aired, investigated, and, though not entirely dispelled, at least mitigated. The fleet guarantee, which was the most tangible evidence of these doubts, remained in effect.

British policy about how to use those doubts oscillated. Despite the decision in August to make things look "as good as possible," the black side of things was always available for use when necessary. Doom and gloom would still be part of Britain's repertoire, to be trotted out whenever it was judged that American fears needed stimulating. Not much stimulating would be necessary, however, since many Americans were convinced that collapse was still imminent, and American military planners began to consider contingencies accordingly.

9.

Early Moves toward Staff Talks: "A Curiously Muddled Business"

16 April 1940–10 August 1940

With the Destroyer-Bases-Fleet negotiations completed it is necessary to go back and pick up the thread of the staff talks story. American plans during the late 1930s and early part of 1940 had been based upon the supposition that the United States would have allies to rely upon for assistance. The Ingersoll conversations had given substance to that supposition and some planning was done for coalition war. The plan that seemed most applicable in the spring of 1940 was RAINBOW 2, which called for the United States, if attacked, to fight an ORANGE war against the Japanese in the Central Pacific while relying on the British and the French navies to secure the Atlantic frontier. Since this plan would require close coordination with the Allied forces, the planners concluded in April 1940 that staff conversations should be held with the British, the French, and the Dutch as soon as possible.[1] Among other things, American strategists needed to know precisely what the European "colonial powers" intended to contribute toward the defense of their possessions in the Far East.[2] Whereas this question was academic to the navy, it was vital to the army, since coalition war in the Far East would raise the "politically explosive question of sending U.S. Army forces to defend European colonial possessions."

Finding out what contributions potential allies would make was not easy. Misinterpretations, ambiguity, caution, and differing priorities all made progress halting and uncertain. A variety of considerations needed weighing and no doubt the initial British desire to use staff conversations as a medium for settling all outstanding issues contributed to the delay. But when Holland was overrun and France left the war, both England and America began to think less about what held them apart and more about what drove them together. In such an atmosphere coordination became more likely, if not more easily achieved.

* * *

The planning conversations held during Commander Hampton's visit to Washington in June 1939 had been the last formal staff contact. At that time it had been tentatively suggested that the United States might send a fleet to Singapore if the British sent an "adequate token force" as well. The next step toward cooperation in the Far East was taken by Captain Alan Kirk in April 1940. Presumably acting on his own initiative, Kirk went to see Admiral "Tom" Phillips, now deputy chief of the naval staff. Kirk was concerned about repercussions in the Pacific if the Germans overran Holland. People at home were worrying about Holland's Western Hemisphere possessions, but Kirk was more worried about a dangerous escalation of tensions in the Pacific if the Japanese tried to seize the Netherlands East Indies. Since in his view it was vital that the United States forestall any such escalation, he proposed moving the U.S. Fleet from Hawaii to the Philippines, thus threatening Japanese communications should they move on the Dutch possessions. He was disturbed, however, about the lack of docking and repair facilities at Manila.

Phillips guessed that Kirk was asking indirectly whether the British facilities at Singapore would be available for servicing U.S. ships. The British admiral assured Kirk that America could count on the Royal Navy's "fullest assistance." This offer was so significant that Kirk thought he should advise President Roosevelt directly. He had a private line of communication to the White House, he said, which he sometimes used without consulting Ambassador Kennedy. In this instance, he would not ask Kennedy's views, assuming that the ambassador was "too neutral." Kirk knew that Churchill (at this point still first lord of the Admiralty) had been corresponding with Roosevelt, and he wondered whether the first lord wanted to put the Singapore suggestion forward or whether he should use his special line. Phillips promised to find out.[3] The first lord replied: "We should of course offer them every facility; and I see no reason why N.A. [naval attaché] should not say so on his own."[4] Presumably Kirk did.

There was no immediate response, but the Naval Plans Division in Washington was already concerned enough about the deteriorating situation to suggest exploring the "possibilities of effective intervention by the United States." Specifically, the suggestion was that army and navy missions be sent to Britain and France without delay. These missions should consider "concessions" to be received in exchange for U.S. assistance. It was in American interest, but "it is to the interest of England and France as well that the United States be paid, at least in part," for its help. The missions also "must go into the question of military commitments during war as well as in the event of peace—with special reference to the British Fleet."[5]

The British were thinking in much more limited terms. Attention, in the Foreign Office view, should be directed primarily toward the Far East.[6] Holland had fallen on 14 May, and on 25 May Lord Lothian was instructed to ask the president whether he would approve discussions "between our respective naval authorities" about joint action should the Japanese occupy the Netherlands East Indies.[7] Anticipating the request for concessions, the ambassador was instructed to reiterate that the facilities at Singapore would be at the disposal of the United States Navy.

Lothian promptly did as directed, but Roosevelt was not enthusiastic. He doubted the United States would go to war with Japan over an attack on the Dutch possessions, but he had been thinking of resurrecting his blockade-embargo scheme, last discussed in January 1939, to try bringing Japan to its senses through economic coercion. He ducked the question of staff conversations, however, suggesting that the issue was "too full of political dynamite."[8]

Neither his hesitation nor his embargo was welcome in London. The British fully recognized what the president meant by "political dynamite," but they could not understand why he did not see the explosive potential of his economic embargo plan. Surely Roosevelt had not thought this plan through, minuted the Far Eastern Division. Could there by any doubt that Japan would fight if forced to the wall economically? The president's impulsive scheme, if ever acted upon, instead of making staff talks less necessary, made them essential.[9] At the same time there was fear of pressing the Americans too hard. Leaving further moves to Lothian's discretion seemed the only practical option.

The ambassador's discretion led him next to approach Secretary of State Cordell Hull. Lothian raised the issue of staff talks with Hull on 11 June and received a discouraging response. The secretary of state said that he "doubted whether there would be any occasion for staff conferences."[10] Lothian could not have disagreed more. With French armies collapsing en masse and Panzer divisions racing for the Channel coast, it definitely seemed the occasion for consultation, so, despite Hull's rebuff, Lothian went to Roosevelt again. The ambassador proposed secret staff discussions "as to how the British and American navies, and if necessary, air forces, should deal with the various situations which might arise in the near future." This time the president's response was prompt and positive. Obviously more impressed by the deteriorating situation in Europe than he had been three weeks earlier, Roosevelt said conversations would be a "good thing" and could be held immediately.[11] There was no mention of embargoes, political dynamite, or Hull's objections.

The suggestion was quickly taken up by the British military in London and on 20 June Captain Kirk reported that a very high-ranking naval officer had said to him that "the time had come perhaps to hold staff conversations." Kirk had not been informed of Lothian's conversations with Roosevelt and was surprised at the mention of staff talks. His surprise must have been evident because the British officer hastily assured him that conversations would be "in no sense binding." With that caveat accepted, they proceeded to discuss the best location for talks, if they were held. The British officer suggested Washington, "because of President Roosevelt's enthusiasm." Captain Kirk countered by proposing London, and recommended it to his superiors, reasoning that talks be held "where we can see exactly what the position is and what responsibilities we would be assuming."[12]

Secretary Hull apparently had not been advised of the president's enthusiasm for staff conversations either, and several days later he discussed them with Lothian in a distinctly conditional fashion. Hull noted that Lothian had mentioned staff conferences to him previously, but the secretary's interpretation had been that there "might well be" staff conferences "between appropriate military and naval persons in our two governments with a view to discussing the question of policies that might or might not be pursued in the light of various possible developments that might arise at a latter stage of the war." It is hard to imagine a more conditional phrasing of the possibilities. However, Lothian had an appealing bait—the fleet. As Hull put it, the ambassador referred to the "possible disposition of the British Fleet in the event— which neither he [Lothian] nor I [Hull] contemplated at all—of British defeat." Lothian proceeded to discuss the hypothetical case in which the British government "accompanied by more or less of the British Fleet" might come to Canada. Then he added, *"It might be very important to have conversations with respect to these possible future movements so that each Government would know what was in the mind of the other."*[13] Since the fleet was a principal pawn in Anglo-American discussions over the destroyers during June-July 1940, this suggestion would do nothing to make staff conversation less appealing to the Americans. Hull could hardly have missed the reference, but caution was still paramount for he proposed using diplomatic rather than military channels for any exchanges. Diplomatic talks would appear less provocative if there were any leaks although secrecy was essential in any case "even though nothing would be said in such conferences that would need to be concealed from the public if correctly interpreted and understood."[14] Lothian reported this conversation to London, failing to mention that he had baited Hull with the fleet.[15]

Churchill, the man expected to be most receptive to overtures from the United States, said no. As he wrote in a note to Lord Halifax: "I am doubtful about opening staff talks at the present time. I think they would turn almost entirely on the American side upon the transfer of the British Fleet to transatlantic bases." In Churchill's view, such defeatist talk should be avoided lest public confidence in Britain be undermined.[16]

Lord Halifax, the foreign secretary, disagreed; he felt that it would be foolish not to take up promptly what the British now referred to as the president's suggestion. Halifax's opinion was that "sound policy" dictated going as far as possible to meet any of Roosevelt's proposals. Furthermore, he believed that the menacing situation in the Far East called for immediate Anglo-American collaboration. For several reasons, therefore, he hoped that the prime minister would reconsider and allow the talks to proceed.[17] That sentiment was shared by the Chiefs of Staff, who enthusiastically endorsed the staff conference proposal. The Joint Planning staff had already drawn up a draft aide-mémoire that the chiefs had accepted with only minor amendments. The general principle enunciated was that the United States should "reinforce or even replace British forces in those areas where America's own interests lie and in areas where they have bases from which they could secure British interests within their orbit." More specifically, it was proposed that the United States should assume responsibility for the whole Pacific, including the British China station, while the British would cover the Atlantic. Under this arrangement Singapore would become part of the American command area.[18] They also placed on record the "great importance" they attached to holding conversations at the "earliest possible moment."[19]

At this point one of those peculiar delays occurred that led a participant in the Anglo-American liaison to describe the staff conference negotiations as a "curiously muddled business."[20] Both sides were being cautious, but the initiative at this point lay with Britain. Churchill feared for the fleet. He may also have been holding out for a grand conference at which outstanding issues such as technological exchanges and destroyers could be discussed as well. In such a conference Britain could hope for major concessions instead of dribbling out her advantages piecemeal. For whatever reasons, it was almost two weeks before Lothian was instructed to reinforce Roosevelt's enthusiasm by welcoming military staff talks (not diplomatic ones as in Hull's proposal) and suggesting that they be held in London, where secrecy (which Hull had stressed) could more easily be maintained.[21] Roosevelt again responded positively and accepted London as the location.[22]

* * *

With this acceptance the wheels began to turn on both sides of the Atlantic, but they turned faster in London. In fact, the Admiralty had been making preparations for staff talks since Lothian's 17 June message. Those preparations were tailored precisely to the task of working persuasively with the United States. The first move was to recall Admiral Sir Sidney Bailey to active duty to head an Admiralty Planning Committee. Admiral Bailey, who had been director of the Admiralty Plans Division, was married to an American, which was thought to give him some negotiating experience, and was noted for his tact and diplomatic talent. Assisting him, among others, was Captain Curzon-Howe, a former naval attaché in the United States and a party to the Leahy-Ghormley-Phillips discussions of May 1939.[23]

The Bailey Committee's assignment was simple: Examine the naval situation as it stood in June 1940 and determine what assistance was going to be needed from the United States. France was practically gone and Britain would soon be fighting alone. Full American participation seemed at least doubtful in view of statements by prominent Americans, but there was always the hope that when things got bad enough the "Yanks" would come in again. Until that time, there was valuable aid needed short of America's entering the war. In any case, plans for all contingencies could, and should, be made.

On 20 June, ten days before Churchill formally agreed to hold talks, the Bailey Committee held its first meeting.[24] The members discussed the areas of operations most desirable for the British and American forces, the definition of responsibilities in the areas assigned, and the various forms that the desired U.S. matériel and logistic assistance should take. For the time being it was to the advantage of both for the United States to keep a strong fleet in the Pacific. If the United States entered the war in the European theater it might make the Japanese less aggressive, thus freeing more U.S. Navy units for the Atlantic. However, if the Japanese remained threatening, the United States could send more capital ships to be based on Singapore, thus assuming responsibility for Pacific and Australian waters. In that way the American presence would fulfill the British commitment to protect the Dominions in the Far East.

The British planners also had optimistic assumptions concerning the Atlantic, but these were to prove more astute. They thought the United States should take responsibility for their Atlantic seaboard and at least that part of the South Atlantic west of the Azores. If the United States could not take on these Atlantic responsibilities because of the Pacific commitments, the Royal

Navy could and would accept them. However, Bailey and his associates recognized that the Americans might not welcome British assumption of sweeping responsibilities in the Atlantic; it might be that they would insist on protecting the convoy routes and the North Atlantic coast of North America themselves by occupying Greenland and Iceland.[25] The British planners also anticipated that the U.S. Marines might occupy the various Atlantic islands, including the Canaries, the Cape Verdes, and the Azores. These moves would be highly desirable, as the United States could then assume operational control over all the Allied forces in these areas as they came under American strategic control, thus freeing the Royal Navy for duty elsewhere.[26]

Convoying, submarine operations, and troop commitments were other matters the Bailey Committee considered. Since U.S. vessels would be expected to augment the Royal Navy and the Canadian escorts in the Atlantic, combined command arrangements would be necessary. But the American submarines, needed for duty in the Bay of Biscay and in the western Mediterranean, would be under British command. Initially the American ground forces would pose no jurisdictional problems since they would be used for seizing and holding bases only within the vicinity of the continental United States and thus would naturally come under American commanders.[27]

When the Bailey Committee met on 21 June to discuss liaison and other cooperative moves they had before them a précis of World War I experience.[28] Since it would be necessary to discuss questions of high command and grand strategy with the Americans, naval missions should be exchanged; but it would be best, the Bailey Committee concluded, to hold major strategy discussions exclusively in London. The English wartime controls over the press would assure secrecy while the negotiators could draw on British experience. To British planners it seemed logical and likely that British experience, strategy, and operations would strongly influence American officials. Assuming that President Roosevelt would take a lively interest in naval developments, it was decided that a naval officer should be dispatched to Washington to do some personal influencing. The officer selected would serve as Roosevelt's own liaison with the Royal Navy.[29]

If, despite British preference, the American capital were selected as the scene for the talks, the planners suggested that the

British naval officer sent as Roosevelt's liaison man should take a skeleton staff, to establish several liaison groups. Since assistance would initially be naval, the naval officer in Washington was to be designated "Chief of Mission and Liaison Director." In London, following the precedent set during World War I, the head of the U.S. mission would be designated "Commander of the U.S. Naval Forces in British Home Waters." His control would be exclusively administrative, because all the forces in British home waters would be under British operational command.

Whatever his duties, it was essential that Britain's man in Washington be carefully chosen. The care the British expended in this regard illustrates the thoroughness of their preparations. The Washington press corps's inability to keep secrets was given prime consideration during the selection process. America was not only at peace but also preparing for the periodic madness of a political campaign—a campaign in which British-American relations would be a pivotal issue. It would not do to have a prominent, high-ranking officer identified at the next Foggy Bottom cocktail party or, even worse, to be seen entering the Navy Department. Therefore, what was needed was an officer with enough knowledge and experience to speak with authority, but one not yet prominent enough to stir the Washington columnists to action.

The officer selected fitted the requirements perfectly. Captain Arthur Wellesley Clarke had enjoyed a brilliant and active career. The son of a distinguished family (his father was Captain Sir Arthur Wellesley Clarke, K.C.V.P., K.B.E., and an Elder Brother of Trinity House), he was a graduate of the Royal Naval Colleges at Osborne and Dartmouth. During World War I he had served with conspicuous bravery, taking part in the Gallipoli invasion and the Battle of Jutland. In the years between the wars he had done sea duty on a number of Britain's most famous ships, serving on the staffs of Admiral Sir Roger Keyes and Admiral Sir Frederick Field. On shore he had moved along the route marked out for young officers of unusual capability, passing in succession the Staff Officer course at Greenwich and, six years later, the Senior Officer Training course. In 1933 he was appointed assistant naval secretary to the Committee of Imperial Defense (CID). His interview for the job was conducted by the intense little man who was the mainspring of the British defense machine.[30] Sir Maurice Hankey sat almost hidden behind his desk. "Do you take shorthand, Clarke?"

he asked the nervous young commander. The answer, which Clarke expected would send the assignment out the window, was a simple "No, sir." "Good," said Hankey, "we don't want stenographers here."[31]

Thus began four years of experience at the highest levels of British military planning and organization. Clarke was, of course, an "onlooker," a recorder of events, not a mover of them; the experience, however, acquainted him with the procedure and detail of the work done by the CID and by the War Cabinet Office. During duty with the Cabinet Office he dealt with varied matters, including planning for home defense and attending the negotiations that culminated in the Anglo-German Naval Treaty of 1935. Then, after a two-year tour of sea duty he returned to work in 1939–40 with the Anglo-French Military Liaison Committee.[32] For several months he shuttled back and forth between London and Paris, performing the duties of assistant secretary to the Supreme War Council. He knew what was going on and he knew those responsible for the conduct of the war.[33]

All this made Clarke a natural choice for the job in Washington. He had been made a captain in June 1939 and therefore had the rank to associate as an equal with the senior American naval officers. In fact, because of differences in promotion procedure, Captain Clarke, a young-looking forty-two, may have been considered to be quite an unusual officer, since at his age brilliant young officers in the U.S. Navy were still lieutenant commanders. Furthermore, there were row upon row of combat ribbons adorning the uniform of the articulate, affable Britisher. Thus professionally and personally he was all that could be asked for in a confidential contact.

. In preparation for the mission he met with the Bailey Committee and was thoroughly briefed on Britain's plans and hopes. Among his instructions was an explicit admonition that might rank as a classic bit of British understatement. Clarke was to do "nothing which will make it harder for the Americans to enter the war." That should be easy enough and Clarke, who had no doubt that England would eventually defeat the Germans, would also have no trouble appearing optimistic and certainly his manner would do nothing to put the Americans off. He was very much aware, moreover, of the need for tact and secrecy.[34]

Meanwhile discussions on the nature of the talks had been

proceeding in other quarters. The Joint Planning Committee of the Chiefs of Staff welcomed the opportunity for frank conversations. For their part, they were willing to run the strategic gamut, but they were aware of American sensitivities about questions that implied the use of land armies. In fact, the planners thought that all discussions of land forces should be avoided in view of American reluctance even to consider sending troops to Europe.[35] The British Chiefs of Staff accepted the planning group's warning, perhaps because the Foreign Office had added further words of caution. The diplomats thought it would be best to limit the talks to naval matters and then let them "develop" to include other service areas. The Americans were jumpy, and it would be imprudent to begin by pressing them to "widen the scope of talks."[36] Pressure could be applied later.

The Bailey Committee Report, which was completed on 15 July, reflected that sensitivity. The 115-page document incorporated many of the points mentioned in the preliminary discussions, and much more—in many ways it was a remarkable piece of work. Its primary purpose was to outline the situation that would arise "if naval cooperation with the United States eventually came about."[37] Drawn up during some of Britain's grimmest days and eventually discussed during the height of the Battle of Britain, it was a masterpiece of conception. Not surprisingly, the report was not correct on every point, but it was accurate enough to foreshadow clearly many important events. Furthermore, it provided a basis for the strategy talks that would go on between September 1940 and March 1941 and it furnished Captain Clarke, who on 20 July boarded the liner *Britannic* bound for America, with a valuable review of British priorities and plans.[38] But great care had to be taken in wording a strategic overview of this nature. It was the old problem of striking the proper balance between telling the Americans enough to make them take an interest in England's problems but not enough to scare them off.[39]

* * *

In Washington, Lothian was doing everything possible to keep Roosevelt in a positive mood by mixing practicality with the naval allusions for which the president was known to be keen. Thus, in discussing the matter of representation at the conversations, Lothian reminded Roosevelt of Rear Admiral William Sims's valuable efforts in the cause of Anglo-American cooperation during World War I. The ambassador noted that it might be helpful if another American admiral could be sent to London.[40] Intrigued by the suggestion, Roosevelt proposed to Admiral Stark on 12 July 1940 that Rear Admiral Robert L. Ghormley, assistant chief of naval operations, be dispatched to England.[41] By going in mid-summer of 1940 Ghormley could first handle the staff conversations, at which there would be both army and navy representatives, and then remain to conduct the purely naval liaison operations.[42]

These operations would be delicate. When Lothian had alluded to the Sims mission in a positive way, he may not have been aware that Admiral Sims, a renowned Anglophile, had gotten himself into serious difficulty during his tour in London. To some it seemed that he was more British than the British, and since some U.S. Navy officers would just as soon have fought the British as the Germans in 1917, Anglophilia could be an unpopular malady. There had been a dramatic investigation of Sims after the war, and although some young officers like Lieutenant Harold Stark, who served on his staff in London, admired the stern, opinionated Sims, there were plenty of others who would have gladly hung him by his beard. Thus Sims served as both a model and a warning that would significantly influence the Ghormley mission.[43]

When the matter of sending a mission to London was first discussed in the summer of 1940, it was assumed that the officer chosen would be titled "Naval Attaché," but when the subject was mentioned to Admiral Ghormley, he understood that he would probably end up doing Sims's job.[44] There were obvious complications in any arrangement, since Alan Kirk was already serving very effectively in London. Unless care were taken, the liaison he had established might be jeopardized with overlapping responsibilities and confusion could result. If no one else worried about the situation, Kirk did, and he expressed his misgivings when Colonel Donovan visited London in July 1940. Kirk, who had first learned of the mission through cocktail party gossip, thought things "awkward" and "embarrassing," especially since Ghormley, an Annapolis classmate and good friend, outranked him.[45]

For his part, Ghormley wanted to go to sea and was not anxious for the London assignment under any title, but, as he said, "I have been raised to say 'aye, aye,' so there is no other answer."[46] Therefore, he accepted his nomination philosophically and was briefed on his duties by Stark, Rear Admiral Chester Nimitz, and, on 14 July, by Secretary Knox. The secretary talked in very general terms about the mission, intimating that Ghormley could expect to leave in less than a month.[47] He would spend the intervening weeks reviewing plans, talking with senior officers, and making other preparations, but no comprehensive strategy review, such as the Bailey Committee had accomplished, would be undertaken.

Conversely, a great deal of thought was devoted to the important, but essentially minor, detail of Ghormley's title. Kirk had appealed to Donovan, and Donovan had advised Stark, and Stark wrote to the president, suggesting that Ghormley be called "Special Naval Observer" rather than "Attaché." Stark had written: "I know the high opinion that you have for the performance of duty as Naval Attaché in London being rendered by Captain Alan Kirk. . . . While it was not intended to detach Kirk, or change his designation, nevertheless Admiral Ghormley reporting with orders as Naval Attaché does supercede Kirk."[48] The change in designation was finally accepted. Since Ghormley and Kirk would work closely together for several critical months, confusion was worth avoiding, but energy expended on this issue might have been better used in briefing Ghormley more thoroughly.[49]

Since by nature a conciliatory sort and an eminently practical man, Rear Admiral Robert Lee Ghormley would doubtless have wished to spare Kirk's feelings. Indeed it was his amiable practicality that made Ghormley a natural selection for the post, whatever it was to be called. At fifty-six, tall, spare, graying with heavily lidded blue eyes, Ghormley was a diplomatic negotiator who, it has been said, "would not reveal his plans but still convince you of his good will." His empathy and his facility for compromise made him a good committee man. He seldom sought the limelight or took unpopular stands, but Ghormley was not weak-willed— he just instinctively sought the middle ground. Unlike Donovan, Secretary Knox's representative who was still in London when Ghormley was selected, the admiral was unlikely to espouse causes or enthusiasms passionately, but he would be equally thorough and eminently more cautious.

Not surprisingly, Ghormley had spent much of his professional career in staff positions. He had seen combat, both in the Nicaraguan Campaign of 1912 and during World War I. But of the fifteen years between 1920 and 1935 he had spent almost ten in administrative posts. After completing the Senior Officer Training course at Newport, Rhode Island, in 1939, he reported back to Washington to serve jointly as director of the War Plans Division and assistant chief of naval operations. In that capacity, he had attended the exploratory staff conversations held with the British in 1939.[50] His experience, therefore, fitted him well for the mission to England. His work with the General Board and the Plans Office gave him insight into U.S. plans and capabilities; he was close enough to the top to know the attitudes of Admiral Stark as well as those of the fleet commanders; and his manner, with its combination of candor and caution, made him a good bargainer and reporter. He was not, on the other hand, particularly decisive. The relative lack of command experience in his career and that same caution that made him a good bargainer would not incline him to exercise much independence. The failure to prepare him better for his new duties would only reinforce his natural proclivities.[51]

On 25 July he and Admiral Stark went to the White House for a briefing intended to prepare Ghormley for his mission.[52] The discussion ranged widely as Roosevelt reviewed the world situation. American plans should be based on one of three alternatives: (1) that Britain would be defeated by air attack, ask for peace terms, and allow her forces and the control of Europe and of the Atlantic to pass to Germany (Roosevelt thought that if these things happened Germany might move on Latin America within six months); (2) that Britain would be weakened by air attacks and an invasion might partially succeed, but that the British would be able to fight on defensively, probably from Canada, but perhaps from the other Dominions as well; (3) that Britain would successfully defend the home islands, thus providing a base for training and air attacks from which they could maintain control of the Atlantic and European waters. With such a base, preparation could also be made for the "ultimate return to the continent."

The president realized that if either (2) or (3) were to come about "Britain would require greatly increased aid from the United States." Roosevelt was ready to provide material assistance, for he discussed supplying Britain with equipment, food, and raw materials. The president also told Ghormley that he wanted some estimate of Britain's chances of survival, which Roosevelt rated at about fifty-fifty.[53] Despite these doubts he was "not convinced that the United States would be forced to intervene as a belligerent in the war against the European Axis, or would be forced to fight Japan in the Pacific to prevent continued Japanese expansion." Precisely what else he said in the two-hour-and-thirty-five minute conference is not recorded, but future references make it quite clear that Ghormley was specifically cautioned against making any commitments. Furthermore, as was becoming increasingly obvious, an unstated but understood quid pro quo in all the British-American discussions was that in case of British collapse surviving units of the British Fleet would make for ports out of German reach.[54] After the presidential audience, only a few delays remained before Ghormley's departure. The prospect must have elicited mixed emotions. His orders were general, even vague, and he would be asking the British to share their most vital secrets with someone whose primary instructions were not to become too committed to his hosts.

Whatever his misgivings, Ghormley began assembling a small personal staff to assist with his delicate task. He had been slated to command a cruiser division in the Pacific and had chosen Lieutenant Commander Bernard L. Austin as his flag lieutenant. In the summer of 1940 Austin was finishing an assignment as Navy Department press relations officer and was eager for sea duty. Plans had been made, orders cut, and things were proceeding smoothly—until Ghormley received his orders to London. After the meeting at the White House, he summoned Austin, told him the change in plans, and asked him to serve as his personal aide.

Austin was not immediately enthusiastic, but after Admiral Stark assured him that his mission would not hurt his chances of sea duty later and suggested that the assignment would be of short duration, Austin gladly agreed to go. He did, however, request permission to tell his wife, in secrecy, of the mission. The admiral agreed and Austin was able to break the news, thus preparing his wife for what in fact proved to be a very long separation.

The selection of the poised and brilliant Austin was providential. Ghormley came to rely on him heavily, taking him to all meetings and conferences, and often detailing him to handle delicate matters with which the admiral could not become associated. Austin's quick, retentive mind was especially useful since Ghormley had decided not to take a secretary. He knew the British would keep minutes of all proceedings and assumed they would consider it "bad form" or a mark of suspicion if the Americans kept their own records. Therefore, part of Austin's job was to keep cursory notes during meetings and write out any salient details after returning to the office. Austin also considered it his duty to help his commanding officer avoid the difficulties that Admiral Sims had fallen into, which meant not appearing too pro-British, while he worked to establish the same good relations the old admiral had enjoyed in England. By all accounts Austin was good at his job. The British liked his style (which earned him the nickname "Count") and learned to respect his competence and to trust his instincts. For his part, Austin, who found high-level negotiations and trading secrets much to his liking, came to realize that Stark had done him a favor by convincing him to go with Ghormley.[55]

On 7 August 1940, almost two weeks after the conversation with the president and almost three months after the navy memorandum of 22 May that recommended talks, the American Naval Mission, composed of Admiral Ghormley, Lieutenant Commander Austin, Lieutenant Donald J. MacDonald, a communications expert, and a chief yeoman, sailed for England aboard the *Britannic*.[56] Also aboard was Major General Delos Emmons. General Emmons, a U.S. Army Air Corps officer, and Brigadier General George V. Strong, chief of the U.S. Army War Plans Division, had been designated to represent the army in these staff discussions.[57] The purpose of these meetings, they were advised, would be to form an "objective estimate of Great Britain's ability to resist invasion" and to gather information for future planning.[58]

From the composition of the group and the manner in which the preparations were coordinated it is obvious that the Americans did not consider this a staff conference delegation. In addition to Ghormley's extremely vague instructions, the various service representatives had no consultation prior to departure; they did not even travel together, for Strong flew to England. Ghormley's primary assignment was to promote long-range naval liaison, while Strong at least seemed intent on discussing supply problems. Some of the confusion can be attributed to inexperience in military diplomacy, but if nothing else, this lack of a unified objective indicates that the group was not expected to enter into strategic planning negotiations. A fact-finding mission, maybe; a sop to the British in their hour of need, perhaps; but not a group designed to deal with America's most delicate military, diplomatic, political problems.

* * *

It soon became obvious that the British were anticipating just such high-level negotiations and the imminent arrival of the Americans caused a flurry of excitement in England. Even before the *Britannic* sailed, Colonel Raymond Lee, U.S. military attaché, found that the chief of British military intelligence, Major General Frederic "Paddy" Beaumont-Nesbitt, was in a flap. "Paddy" assumed that, at a minimum, the generals were coming for staff talks and thought it would be convenient to move them right into the War Cabinet Office.[59] He realized, however, how sensitive the Americans were about secrecy and there was real concern among the British about concealing the presence of Ghormley and his group. In fact an interdepartmental committee had been established to set procedures for keeping the talks secret. Four pages of elaborate instructions had been drawn up, all intended to keep the mission "hush-hush" until after the elections in America. Lee told his friends in military intelligence that he thought it unlikely that they could get away with the ruse. His advice was that they allow the newspapers to print what they wished, take the new arrivals on a series of tours, and when the initial excitement waned, all necessary conversations could be held without arousing curiosity.[60] He was concerned, though, about the significance attributed to the mission and feared that the British were going to be greatly disappointed.

Lee was right. The British had assigned a "cover" title, the "Anglo-American Standardization of Arms Committee," as well as a very high priority to the mission. On 4 August, Lothian called attention to the "very strong team" that the Americans were sending and requested "all possible information" be provided. At the same time he noted that the Americans had been instructed to be "perfectly frank" and to "withhold nothing" from their British counterparts.[61] The Joint Planning Subcommittee intended to be equally frank with the Americans, preparing material for the discussions on the assumption that the Americans would confer on staff problems "as active allies," although reassuring them by saying that the "political situation did not in fact warrant any such assumption."[62] The Americans would be told enough to make them take an interest in England's problems, but not enough to make them "unduly pessimistic" about England's chances.[63]

J. V. Perowne, of the Foreign Office, had a shrewder estimate of the situation. In his view, and in the view of the Foreign Office, the Americans were coming "first and foremost to see how we were getting on here and to gauge our chances of military survival." Furthermore, "on the impressions made on the Officers by what they saw and heard would in large measure depend not only the answer to the question whether there would be any staff conversations as we meant them at all but also the measure of assistance that we would get from the U.S. It was therefore most important that the correct impression should be created. (It is possibly unfortunate in this connection that the Officers are to begin with three or four days of undiluted Mr. Kennedy.)" Thus it was critical that the Americans should be "shown the right things in the right way" and that the arrangements for their tours should be scrutinized with infinite care.[64]

Getting the talks started had been too difficult to hazard a wrong move. Now that an admiral and two generals were on their way, it must have seemed in London that things were moving toward a favorable conclusion. However, either because of individual propensity, presidential instruction, or historical precedent, Admiral Ghormley, the most important of the visitors, was going to be coy. He was no war hawk, but his caution also bore the stamp of official White House approval. The president had heartily endorsed the staff conversations and had waited patiently while the British muddled through their misgivings; but now he was sending representatives proscribed from making anything but the most tentative cooperative suggestions. It was all very puzzling. Were there going to be staff talks or not? Confusion was apparent and disappointment seemed the inevitable result.

10.

"Acting on My Own":
Initial Meetings in London

15 August 1940–28 September 1940

When the *Britannic* entered Liverpool harbor on 15 August it was met by Embassy personnel, who rushed the military party through customs and onto a train for London. Along the route Ghormley saw all the trappings of war—invasion defenses, antiaircraft guns, and barrage balloons. In London the train was met by Ambassador Kennedy, Captain Kirk, and Colonel Lee. Kirk took the new arrivals out to his comfortable quarters for the weekend, and on the way Ghormley experienced his first air raid. The evening was passed in a long and serious conversation that continued the next day after lunch at the Kennedy estate. Ghormley noted that "they all think England is licked."[1] Kirk confirmed the problem with the mission's title, and both Kennedy and Kirk made it clear that the unorthodox manner in which the Donovan and Ghormley visits had been handled prejudiced existing liaison.[2]

Ghormley was probably prepared to hear that, but he probably was not prepared to be told by Kennedy that Winston Churchill was the cause of many of Britain's current problems. It was Churchill, Kennedy said, who had directed the British move into Norway in April 1940; it was Churchill who had ordered the Allied forces to abandon the water-line defenses in northern France and attack into Belgium; and it was Churchill who thought the French army to be the finest mobile fighting force in the world. In Kennedy's opinion, these errors had brought Britain to the brink of military defeat and now the only chance was a salvage operation by the United States. Kennedy implied that the current attempts to draw America into staff talks was part of this operation.[3]

The British had already significantly inflated the importance of Ghormley's duties, for Kennedy said that the Admiralty expected the American officers to "begin staff talks immediately leading to our entry into the war" or at the very least to discuss "detailed plans for naval help." Kennedy viewed these prospects with scant enthusiasm; indeed, he may have allowed his personal sentiments to color his reporting. Moreover, he was trying to put Ghormley on guard against British, and especially Churchillian, blandishments. But Ghormley was already more than prepared to be cautious, having decided, he said, to tell the British that he was in England only to "obtain such information as they were willing to impart on subjects such as their future plans and Fleet disposition . . . and such information [as] they would not usually give an attaché." In order to avoid misunderstandings, among other reasons, he had decided to delay any staff talks until he received indications from Washington that "Congress is more inclined to take part than is now the case."[4]

While awaiting that day, there were immediate benefits America might reap from closer association with the British. "I am impressed," Ghormley cabled the Navy Department, "that under the present conditions we are getting advantage of priceless information from [an] actual war laboratory which will not be available to us in case of German victory." Although much information was being gained, still more was available, "some on an exchange basis, some available without exchange." He suggested that the technical bureaus of the Navy Department make specific requests for data that then could be used as "entering wedges" for obtaining more.[5]

Ghormley could not estimate the precise dividends of such technical exchanges, but it obviously was fertile ground where the United States could reap substantial benefits from a country sometimes thought to be only a recipient of American largess. The Tizard mission, soon to arrive in Washington, would reinforce this image of Britain as a repository of technical expertise.

When Ghormley's party left Kirk's on Monday, 19 August, and moved into London, they found that part of their English experience would be pleasant. An office had been prepared for them in the Embassy, and after making some of the required formal calls and finding Mr. A. V. Alexander, the first lord of the Admiralty, "delightful," they went to Claridge's for dinner. Later, Ghormley saw the apartment that had been selected for them. "It must be the King's," he noted. "It is a wonder." There was plenty of room for all three officers. It was on the top floor, though, and the air raids made this seem rather exposed, but Ghormley characteristically had checked and found a way down.[6]

The next day was devoted to formalities. Admiral Ghormley, General Emmons, and General Strong met in conference with the three British Vice-Chiefs of Staff. Ghormley, the ranking American, opened by stating that he and his colleagues were not a unified mission and that they were not empowered to make any commitments. General Strong then went into a long discussion of the need for coordinating production schedules. While not referring to it specifically, he implied that American entry might mean less in the way of supplies for Britain. The United States, he pointed out, wished to help the British, but production for them would have to be coordinated with American rearmament. He knew the enormity of the problem faced when outfitting modern armies; and he warned that when Britain moved to the offensive difficulties would increase. After some general discussion, Ghormley raised the question of the Pacific, a strategic area on which he said U.S. planners were concentrating. This issue and many others were too involved for discussion in one meeting, so further talks would have to be held. In the meantime, as Lee had suggested, a tour had been arranged to distract the reporters.[7]

After three days of touring Ghormley felt prepared to report more of his impressions to Washington. He was convinced the British were determined to fight on. Resolution was not everything, however, and after "talking to our own representatives here, and through them getting the reactions from those higher up in the British Government, it is not so reassuring." Ghormley considered it too early to make a valid estimate of their chances but he did offer a typically cautious assessment. "If determination will win," he wrote, "the British should win; however, I presume the powers that be in Germany have a similar determination."

He had been equally careful, he reported, in his personal relations with British officials, making his status and responsibility clear from the beginning. Although they had made "no suggestions as to the participation of the United States in the war as yet," he had been receiving some very special treatment. For instance, the first lord of the Admiralty had taken him through the War Room, commenting that "no other foreign officer" had ever been there. Ghormley thought that a "bit overstated." Then the prime minister had invited Ghormley, Strong, and Emmons, the attachés, and the ambassador to dinner at No. 10. Ghormley had sat on the prime minister's left and found Winston Churchill a "wonderful man." Churchill talked about "the war situation and . . . British strategical possibilities," a topic on which he was at his most wonderful. The admiral, though stimulated, remembered his duty. Stark, as well as Kennedy, had warned him that the British would "put the heat on" and Ghormley referred to this dinner as their first effort in that direction; however, he felt that he was and could remain "fireproof."[8]

By this time Ghormley was even more convinced of the value of British technical information. "This laboratory," he reported to Stark, "is invaluable to us, if we can use it." He remarked on how efficient, quick, and well coordinated the British Fighter Command was; in fact, he concluded that the British were way ahead of the United States in the whole area of air operations. He described a new type of cruiser, the armoring of carrier flight decks, delayed-action fuses, and air-dropped depth charges. He was so impressed with this latter device that he suggested allowing the British to test the new American depth charge for effectiveness under combat conditions. Such generosity might have the added advantage of inducing his hosts to be more magnanimous.[9]

The British might have been more helpful generally if they had been able to determine what Ghormley and company were up to. Colonel Lee had advised the Chiefs of Staff that the visitors wished to learn about: (1) the British "strategic concept" of the war; (2) their "tactical concept" of the present and subsequent phases; (3) steps they anticipated taking with regard to the Western Hemisphere; and (4) the "material requirements beyond the production capacity of Great Britain."[10] But despite this request for a lengthy and detailed briefing, the British could still get no clear indication regarding the Americans' specific assignment or the degree of commitment they were prepared to make. Ghormley's comments at the preliminary meeting implied that they were not even a team but rather individual observers and their differing interests seemed to bear this out. It was all very puzzling. However, the Joint Planning Subcommittee thought it still possible "to lead them [the Americans] into the staff conversations proper, which the President appeared to have had in mind in the first place, and which we expected that the American Delegation would be empowered to undertake."[11]

The British got their only opportunity to "lead" the Americans into "staff conversations proper" when Admiral Ghormley and the American generals met with the Chiefs of Staff on 29 August 1940. The purpose of this conference was to allow the Americans to raise questions concerning Anglo-American strategic cooperation. The issues touched upon ranged from the Atlantic to the Pacific and included political, military, and economic factors. Matters discussed included: How strong was Hong Kong? Did the British want the United States Fleet to stay in the Pacific? What ship-repair facilities were available in Egypt and what was the possibility of the Italians blocking the Suez Canal? To what extent were British plans based on the supply of industrial and economic commodities from the United States? Did they plan for the eventual entry of the United States? Did the British think the final issue of the war would be decided on land? If the British could not withstand enemy attack, had they made alternative plans? What was the relative importance of Singapore? For instance, would the British send units of their fleet to reinforce Singapore if some U.S. Pacific Fleet units were moved to the Atlantic?[12] Ghormley and his associates, by raising these points that hinted at American anxieties, clearly forecast the future, for these same issues would arise again and again in Anglo-American strategy discussions.

During the next two meetings the British attempted to answer these questions by presenting a comprehensive paper on the strategic situation, the economic outlook, the European political picture, anticipated enemy action, and British production requirements.[13] Although this review did not cover all of Admiral Ghormley's questions, it dealt with most of them, and it is obvious that the Bailey Committee report had provided the British chiefs with a comprehensive and useful overview of England's military posture.

The American questions and hints about offensive action also provoked a lively discussion in which the British took the classic position that even though Hitler controlled the Continent, the Royal Navy ruled the seas. The British anticipated that by early 1942 Germany might be so weakened by sea blockade and air bombardment that British forces could move to the offensive. They emphasized, however, that it was essential, both during the present defensive stage and in the later offensive one, that Britain should be provided with American supplies, which meant that supplies would have to be coordinated, much as General Strong had suggested. Despite their immediate problems, British planners saw time as their ally and were generally optimistic about holding the home islands and Egypt, from which they could control the Mediterranean.[14]

The British emphasized that Germany was the center of their difficulties. They hoped the Italians could be knocked out of the war soon, but even if not, the Royal Navy would continue to operate in the Mediterranean. In the current stage of the war that area was of great importance because it was the key to the Middle East and ranked just behind the home islands in strategic importance. Other aspects of their European strategy included: stepping up economic pressure, increasing air attacks, and making plans to take the offensive. In addition, some amphibious thrusts would be made from time to time to keep the Germans guessing and to encourage the captured nations. They did not hedge on the question of invading the Continent—eventually land forces would have to decide the issue—but it was hoped that a combination of bombing and economic warfare would wear the Axis down considerably before that was attempted. The latter was a touchy point. Obviously, an invasion would eventually have to be made, but the chiefs had been specifically cautioned not to scare the Americans off by talking of land armies.[15] It was a dilemma— either they scared the Americans by talking of land armies, or they risked seeming unrealistic by discussing victory without invasion. They solved the problem by emphasizing how bombing and economic warfare would weaken the German ability to resist.

Finally, the two biggest questions were raised. Ghormley wanted to know whether the British, in making their future plans, were relying only on the continued "economic and industrial support" of the United States or whether they counted upon the "eventual active cooperation" of U.S. armed forces. Air Chief

Marshal Sir Cyril Newall, chairman of the Chiefs of Staff, responded that American economic and industrial cooperation was "fundamental" to all British strategy. But he reassured Ghormley that no account had been taken of the "possibility of active cooperation by the United States."[16]

Ghormley then raised the most sensitive issue. All future plans the chiefs had outlined were based on the assumption that the British could withstand attack on the home islands. Had any plans, he wondered, been prepared for "failure to withstand such attacks"? Sir Cyril Newall said that "no alternative plans had been prepared." All British strategy was formulated on the assumption that such attacks, if they came, would be repelled, and "it was the fixed determination of the whole Nation to do so."[17]

They next discussed the vital and vexing Far East. Britain was determined to hold Singapore, but things had changed so dramatically in Europe that the naval forces originally planned for Far Eastern defense could not now be sent. Admiral Pound preferred basing capital ships in the Indian Ocean unless a force could be sent to Singapore that would be equivalent to the Japanese force, less one battleship. Any British ship sent to Singapore would have to be withdrawn from the defense of Gibraltar, and that was unthinkable at present. Clearly, Singapore was vulnerable, but the first sea lord revealed that, for the time being, reliance was being placed on air power. There were, however, several possibilities for the future. Presently it was in British interest to have the U.S. fleet in the Pacific, but in certain contingencies it might be moved, to Britain's further advantage. For instance, if Japan entered the war against Britain, and if the United States would shift a portion of its fleet to the Atlantic, that would free British battleships to reinforce Singapore.[18] On the other hand, it would be less disruptive if the Americans would simply agree to shift their fleet so that Singapore could be included within the American defense perimeter.

Although not stated explicitly at this meeting, protecting Singapore was another British dilemma. Comprehensive staff studies in June and July had revealed that little other than air power could be spared for the Far East. Pound had implied that, but he had not implied the degree of commitment the British government had to that area. Less than a month before, Prime Minister Churchill had sent a guarded but reassuring report to the prime ministers of Australia and New Zealand. In it he stated:

"If . . . contrary to prudence and self-interest, Japan set about invading Australia or New Zealand on a large scale, I have the explicit authority of the Cabinet to assure you that we should then cut our losses in the Mediterranean and proceed to your aid, sacrificing every interest except only the defense and feeding of this Island."[19] Thus Churchill was saying that if the security of the Commonwealth were threatened, the order of priorities remained home islands, Far East, Middle East. But how was the Far East to be defended? Even with the discouraging staff studies in front of him, Churchill continued to insist, to the distress of the chiefs, on ultimately building that defense around a fleet.[20] Where was the fleet to come from? Indirectly and very delicately Ghormley, Strong, and Emmons were being told.

If contingencies became realities and if the Americans would not take Singapore under their wing it could lead to a redirection of American effort from the Pacific to the Atlantic. As far as Ghormley knew, American planners were not preparing for an Atlantic war. No detailed American response to the British plans was made, but General Strong observed that the exchange of information between Britain and America should now take place on a "regular basis."[21] This meeting, however, was the last formal Ghormley-Strong-Emmons session with the Chiefs of Staff.

The much-heralded conferences had turned out to be rather anticlimactic. A great deal of planning and effort, particularly on the British side, had gone into arranging and conducting these meetings with the Americans. Many had anticipated that Ghormley and his group would engage in formal staff conversations, but, although helpful in a general way, these tentative and vague talks did not constitute such conversations. Still, if the British were discouraged, they did not show it; instead they waited for Ghormley to conclude for himself that more formal contacts were necessary.

* * *

They did not have long to wait. On 2 September Ghormley, recalling the president's verbal instructions, decided that the time was right to raise some hypothetical questions. Therefore, on that day he asked Admiral Pound how cooperation could best be accomplished between the two navies if the United States were "forced into active participation in the war." Pound told Ghormley that, interestingly enough, the Bailey Committee "had already submitted proposals and recommendations based on the experience of the First World War."[22] How convenient.

Ghormley, who had done no such preparation, was naturally interested in the British conclusions, but he was initially told that they had been prepared for British eyes only. However, there were some hasty revisions and within the week the report was delivered to Lieutenant Commander Austin, who, at Ghormley's request, began cabling portions of its 115 pages to Washington.[23] The report, which had provided the chiefs with part of their strategic overview, would now form the basis for a series of meetings at the Admiralty between Ghormley and Bailey. The unstated purpose of these meetings was to modify the report in light of American reactions and to allow Ghormley and Bailey to locate potential problem areas.

While Ghormley was awaiting his copy of the report, the concentrated bombing of London began. Goering's promise to destroy the Royal Air Force and thus gain the air superiority necessary before invasion had not been fulfilled. Though sorely wounded, the air fighters rose to counter each attack by the Luftwaffe. The only recourse seemed to be luring the British into showdown battles by forcing them to defend their most vulnerable asset—London, the center of commerce and the seat of government. At the same time bombing raids against London would give the Germans a shot at British morale. If morale should crack, "Sea Lion" might yet prove unnecessary. If it were necessary Ghormley was not certain what the result would be. He had visited Dover with the prime minister, whom he found "a delightful host and a brilliant man," to tour the coastal defenses. These he found to be "ingenious, but not particularly strong."[24]

But the Wehrmacht, hoping for an easier way, was not ready to test those defenses yet. On 7 September Austin noted in his diary: "The air blitzkrieg has begun." And begun it had. Colonel Carl Spaatz, who had come to England in July to gather information on bombing techniques, observed the raid from a rooftop, and Hermann Goering obliged him with quite a show. The raid began as a formation of bombers swept by at dusk. The Luftwaffe had penetrated the defenses for the first time and kept up the attack continuously until 5:00 A.M. Although there were probably five hundred bombers in the area of London, it seemed to Spaatz that they kept only five or six of them over the city at a time. There were broken clouds at eight to ten thousand feet, which made the searchlights and antiaircraft guns completely ineffective, as the German planes dived in and out of the clouds. The procedure that the Luftwaffe followed was to start fires in a number of places and then use those as coordinates for further bombing, which caused more fires. At times the light was so bright that Spaatz could easily have read a newspaper on his roof. Eighty-six of the raiders were eventually brought down, but fires had been numerous and damage had been done to the West Indian docks, the Battersea power plant, Woolwich arsenal, and oil storage tanks. Spaatz guessed that there were numerous casualties in the tenement districts, where many of the fires still raged at dawn. He laconically added that during his observation "some bombs seemed quite close."[25]

Ghormley was impressed by the bombing, but it made him more certain that the United States should use its period of peace to prepare for war. Germany posed a serious menace that "if it must be met, must be met with determination and skill promptly." He wrote Admiral Stark that the "transition from peace to war for us must be instantaneous. Our preparatory period is now." This preparation should not be devoted solely to activity in the military sector, for, he said, "the pent-up energy of the civilian population" could perhaps be harnessed to an Air Raid Precaution System, which Hanson Baldwin might be "stimulated" to suggest.[26]

As to his own activity, Ghormley did not believe that his talks with Pound could be labeled staff talks. He had tried to make it clear that he was "acting on [his] own" (a claim that his hosts must have found hard to believe). However, in Ghormley's view, any talks were a valuable service that helped prepare the ground for further exchanges by "giving the British the benefit of my own viewpoints and observations." He clearly felt uneasy about the responsibility of his position and he saw the dangers inherent in acting without specific directions. He said, "Staff talks should not be conducted without definite approved policies being established by the Navy Department in regard to such staff talks, and it should not fall entirely upon the shoulders of one man to carry out this responsible duty in case definite commitments are to be made."[27]

The "no commitment" principle was difficult to handle tactfully because Ghormley did not want to appear suspicious of

British attempts at entrapment, even though he was. The British were so hard pressed that they would probably stop at nothing, and they were becoming increasingly open in their pleas. Churchill, for instance, had given Ghormley the distinct impression that all hopes now rested on the American entry into the war. In the face of this campaign, Ghormley was painfully cautious about appearing too agreeable. The Anglo-French staff conversations of 1906–14 and the commitment of honor to which they led before World War I were a constant reminder of the snares awaiting the acquiescent parties, so even though he was sympathetic, Ghormley was determined to take no such fateful step without full, specific authorization.[28]

It was in this atmosphere of caution and hope that Ghormley and Austin met with the Bailey Committee on 17 September for the first formal discussion of the report, which became in effect a review of strategy and planning. The meetings were held at the Admiralty in what Austin describes as a "typical British conference room," that is, a cold, damp conference room. There was a heating grate at one end, but its pitiful output was not sufficient for keeping all of the participants comfortable, at least not the American participants. The British committee seemed capable and well organized, with a large support staff as well as a full range of available experts. For minute-keeping they had a military secretary, trained in the same way Captain Clarke had been. He gave copies of the notes to Admiral Ghormley, who, it will be recalled, had not brought a secretary with him so as not to impugn British reliability.

Ghormley opened by restating his official (and unofficial) position, and then he turned to Pacific operations. He tried to show how difficult communication would be if the U.S. fleet moved toward Singapore. American action was not out of the question, though, and Ghormley asked for specific information on Singapore's defenses, fueling, and repair facilities.

Next, Ghormley discussed the Atlantic. Although he could fully understand why the British wanted more American ships there, he doubted whether many units would be transferred from the Pacific soon. All that the United States had available in the Atlantic were three old battleships, two carriers, two light cruisers, four eight-inch cruisers, three six-inch cruisers, and various supporting units.[29] Since the possibility of occupying Portugal's Atlantic island possessions was raised in the report, he wanted to know what forces the British thought were required to take and hold the Azores, Cape Verdes, and the Canaries. In this connection, he mentioned American reluctance to send U.S. ground troops outside the Western Hemisphere, yet implied that America might eventually occupy Greenland.[30]

The discussion of the report continued on 18 September. Ghormley reviewed the problems of using the old battleships in the Atlantic for patrol, fortifying Guam for use as a base for flying boats, training crews for reconditioned submarines, and providing cruiser protection for the carriers *Ranger* and *Wasp* so that they could be used effectively in the Atlantic.[31] In regard to the Far East, he suggested that the committee report be modified to specifically indicate that the "attitude of Japan would be a governing factor to the availability of U.S. Forces outside the Pacific."[32]

The problems of staff talks, liaison, and command were brought up at the 19 September meeting. Ghormley agreed with the British choice of London as the site for staff talks—if it were agreed to hold them. If held, the talks should be primarily naval, since the British did not envisage using large land armies and since there would be no American commitment to fight on the Continent. Therefore, he questioned the necessity of even having U.S. Army representatives present. It was finally agreed, however, that for planning purposes it would be desirable to have all services represented.

Command functions should not be difficult, for the precedent established during World War I would set the pattern. Close liaison would be maintained with the Admiralty; American units in British waters would be under Royal Navy command, with administrative control being exercised by the senior U.S. naval officer. When the organization was fully operative that officer would have separate offices, retaining only liaison officers in the Admiralty. In the interim, however, the British suggested that it would be best for safety, ease of communication, and camaraderie for the Americans to share accommodations in Whitehall with the Royal Navy. In the Pacific area, if the United States became involved in war with Japan and if that were an American area of responsibility, U.S. naval officers would be in operational control. This should also be the case in operations and in escorting convoys around the coasts of the American continents.[33]

Although the British were always careful to put things in conditional terms, suggestions about American involvement were becoming harder and harder to dodge. Ghormley's personal reactions can be gleaned from his letters to Stark. He found the committee to be "keen and bright" and not inclined to "miss any tricks."[34] The report they had drawn up reflected that talent; it was "full of sound lessons," as Stark would gather when he reviewed Austin's cables and the notes that Ghormley would forward. There were many areas on which agreement seemed easy, including command, liaison, and technical exchanges, but there were the problems of commitments and priorities.

The Pacific was the geographical area where dispute seemed most likely to erupt. Ghormley had not expressly stated American distaste for assuming responsibility over "colonial" regions, but the British may well have sensed it from his tentativeness. He knew that his attitude on such issues was disappointing to the committee; they obviously had hoped that he would be more forthcoming. Since they expected, he wrote, that the United States would be in the war "as soon as Roosevelt is elected," they could not understand his noncommittal stance.[35] They wanted formal staff talks, but Ghormley repeatedly told them that such conversations "should be based on policies and commitments approved by the Navy Department."[36] Obviously such policies and commitments had yet to be approved, so he had to be tentative. As he wrote Stark, he had gone about as far as he could go, and the United States would soon have to decide whether to "hold things as they are, making studies of the suggestions contained in this paper or go ahead with formal staff talks." Ghormley was not recommending staff talks, nor was he necessarily pro-British, but he was "sitting here in the midst of a real war" and that bred a certain degree of affinity. Affinity aside, Ghormley was not going to do much more about staff talks without information, direction, and decision.[37]

* * *

General Strong and General Emmons were not participating in the discussions of the Bailey Committee report, so they left for home on 19 September. When they arrived in New York, General Strong told waiting reporters, with British understatement, that the bombings had been "rather severe" since September 7 but that they had not "affected the morale of the British people." "When we left London two days ago," he went on, "the British apparently were quite prepared to stick it out."[38] The next day Strong granted another interview, which was given prominent coverage in the British papers. The London *Times* headlined the story "Britain Will Win—U.S. Observer's Verdict," and quoted Strong as saying: "Britain is determined to win if it is humanly possible. If she cannot win, she is going down with every man fighting and the flag flying." In his considered judgment, victory could be achieved "without military intervention on the part of the United States" although access to American industrial production would "undoubtedly be necessary for sure accomplishment of the British effort." He also predicted that if the Germans attempted invasion they would get the "surprise of their lives," for the time had passed when invasion could be launched without "appalling loss."[39]

These same attitudes were reflected in the initial report that Strong and Emmons made to General Marshall. They emphasized the calm, unhurried manner that characterized the British when under attack and commented on the effectiveness and efficiency of British defense procedures. General Marshall, however, reminded them that they should not "jump to conclusions" based on the "specialized situation" existing in England at the moment. The chief of staff noted that the English stand on the defensive was all well and good, but offensives won wars. On the subject of dealing with the British, General Marshall was equally restrained, mentioning the trouble General "Black Jack" Pershing had had during World War I with their "confirmed beliefs"; and he reminded them that the Germans had stayed ahead of the Allies constantly. The official army history of the period suggests that "perhaps as a result" of Marshall's admonishment, Strong and Emmons were "at pains to be cautious" in their final report.[40]

In that report, which was forwarded to the president, they noted that they had found British public morale to be quite high; the British government was confident, "perhaps overconfident," that it could decisively defeat any invasion attempt. Industrially, conditions were "not bad at present," although the British seemed uncertain of their needs. The financial outlook was "dubious if not distinctly bad," and the shipping situation was "serious." Militarily, things looked "fair" as far as the home islands were concerned, but if the invasion were delayed beyond 15 October, conditions would improve significantly. In the air the situation was "not too bad" but on the seas the naval position was "unfavorable" because of a lack of destroyers and the "relative weakness of the Naval air arm." How Britain would protect its vital sea lanes had "*not* been solved in spite of the fact that the Royal Navy has supreme confidence in its ability to maintain control of the seas."

The British made no secret of their dependence on American manufactured goods; Churchill had personally asked Strong and Emmons to convey the need for more machine tools, 50 more PBYs, 20 MTBs, more rifles, more airplanes, and some sixteen-inch coast defense artillery. The prime minister also offered to provide any U.S. Army or Navy pilot on a leave of absence for a few months with "actual combat experience." All in all, the final report ran to twenty-two pages and included the observation that both Strong and Emmons had the "very definite feeling that sooner or later the United States will be drawn into this war." They made no final evaluation of Britain's chances nor did they make any recommendation concerning staff talks, which they obviously did not think had been conducted.[41]

* * *

The man who was under the most pressure to conduct such talks was Ghormley. He had received neither the pessimistic rebuff that had awaited Strong and Emmons nor any other direction from Washington. He had written Stark on 20 September summarizing his activities and suggesting the need for further instructions. His next letter from the chief of naval operations was not much help. Stark professed to have little more information than was available in London: "The Plot seems to thicken a little all the time," Stark wrote, "and goodness knows what will happen. We do, however, feel a little encouraged over the situation in England and hope it is not unwarranted."[42] But there were innumerable questions to be answered and Stark urged Ghormley to discuss strategy for the Mediterranean, supposing, for the sake of discussion, that the United States was in the war.[43] Ghormley continued his almost daily trips to the Admiralty where he reviewed various aspects of the report, including communications, minesweeping, convoy protection, ship-to-ship and ship-to-air communications, harbor defense, intelligence, and liaison. Everyone was cordial and helpful but Ghormley continued to be vague and noncommittal.

On 28 September 1940 he had an opportunity to put Anglo-American naval cooperation in historical perspective. It was the centenary of the birth of that pragmatic Anglophile, Rear Admiral Alfred T. Mahan, and Ghormley was the featured speaker at a commemorative luncheon. He first noted that Mahan had appreciated the "common bond" that sea power provided between the United States and Great Britain. Mahan had seen, Ghormley said, that Anglo-American supremacy in sea power was the "greatest hope" for lasting peace. He had perceived as well the overriding importance of good relations between England and America, and Ghormley accepted and applauded that view.

While praising this friendship, he also pointed out the great advance that the United States was going to make in the coming years, as it incorporated into its ships and planes the technological advances developed in the "laboratory of the present war." These advances, he recognized, were due in part to the sacrifices and assistance rendered to the United States by Great Britain. Ghormley concluded by saying how unfortunate it was that many of the improvements had to be learned in the schoolhouse of war, but until a "better and a brighter day dawned those people who had precious heritages to preserve would do well to remember and heed the teachings of Admiral Mahan."[44]

Ghormley did not mention it, but Mahan had also offered some guidance regarding the Far East. Writing in 1897, Mahan the academic sailor had foreseen the need for using sea power to control the ambitions of awakening powers in Asia. In his view no country was "charged with weightier responsibilities than the United States" when it came to policing the Pacific.[45] In the fall of 1940 the British would have heartily agreed, particularly since they were eager to have the United States do their policing as well. The day before Ghormley spoke, events had occurred that would increase the urgency of controlling the aggressive impulses of one awakening power in the Far East.

11.

Reactions to the Tripartite Pact; Or, Staff Conversations Anyone?

27 September 1940–16 November 1940

During late September 1940, progress on Anglo-American naval collaboration was negligible. There had been no formal staff conversations, and Ghormley, who had been in England for more than a month, continued to represent himself as a quasi-official fact-finder. Then, as had happened so often, the Axis powers took the initiative, which, if it did not stimulate immediate action, did at least serve to focus the Free World's attention.

* * *

On 27 September 1940 Germany, Japan, and Italy united in the Tripartite Pact. Under the terms of that agreement Japan's sphere of influence in Asia was recognized in return for Japanese recognition of German and Italian interests in Europe. Furthermore, each pledged to assist the other if any one were attacked by a "power at present not involved in the European War or in the Chinese-Japanese conflict."[1] The Japanese had been inspired to conclude the agreement partially through fear that the Americans would follow the Destroyer-Bases-Fleet deal with a similar arrangement in the Pacific.[2] Some Americans, like Secretary of State

Hull, read the signs right and realized that the Tripartite Pact was intended to intimidate, or at least constrain, the United States.[3] It confirmed the latent suspicion, moreover, that the aggressor nations were working in collusion, thus making the danger of a two-ocean war frighteningly real.

The threat of potential Japanese aggression drew Anglo-American attention to the Far East, and the Pacific defenses were a cause of great anxiety. The military strategies of both Britain and America were in a state of flux, each waiting for the other's commitment. The British chiefs had assigned priority to the Atlantic, but this luxury of concentration could be enjoyed only if America would accept Pacific responsibility. Since no previous agreements were binding, the British still sought some form of bilateral staff conferences in the course of which they could pin the Americans down. The Americans, in turn, still sought to elude commitment, partially out of a legalistic sensitivity to anything labeled "staff talks" and partially because they had no strategy.

An additional problem for the Americans was their lack of a procedure for coordinating national defense policy. Each of the services had its planning staff and the Joint Board was supposed to coordinate those plans; however, if serious differences arose, there was no formalized method for reaching decisions. To help compensate for this deficiency, a Standing Liaison Committee, made up of the undersecretary of state and the service chiefs, had been established in 1938. But the committee had no executive authority and it met irregularly; during 1940, for instance, it met only nine times. The president could have exercised authority in this situation, but he was apparently not concerned by the drift, preoccupied as he was with his reelection campaign. The result was a hasty redrafting of the war plans in the wake of each crisis but little that could be dignified with the name of national defense policy.

* * *

In the wake of the Tripartite Pact announcement, Lord Lothian called on Cordell Hull to discuss British policy regarding the Burma Road. The British had agreed to close this vital route to China in July 1940 to avoid provoking Japan. The agreement would expire on 18 October and the ambassador wished to know American views on this matter. Hull emphasized that the United States wanted the Burma Road opened and, if that were to be arranged, he doubted that the Japanese would use the opening as a pretext for war. Lothian, obviously wishing to involve the United States as deeply as possible, asked what help the United States would provide if the Japanese did react aggressively. Hull hedged. He was concerned, however, and he suggested that it might be wise for the United States, Australia, Great Britain, and the Dutch to hold "private staff conversations on technical problems" of common defense. He emphasized that these talks were to be "technical" and would not be concerned with "political policy."[4] In his report to London, Lothian strongly endorsed the suggestion for "non-political" talks.[5]

Hull was always cautious, but now on the eve of the November election, he was especially careful. Roosevelt's Republican opponent, Wendell Willkie, had agreed not to use the Destroyer-Bases-Fleet deal as a campaign issue. He also was in general agreement with the president's policy of aiding Great Britain. The only foreign policy issues in dispute were the manner of providing assistance and Roosevelt's motives. Was Roosevelt trying to maneuver the United States into war, as his enemies contended, or was he honestly attempting to use aid to Britain to keep America out of war? Roosevelt would seek to clarify his position regarding the war in a speech delivered just two weeks before the election. "I hate war," he said. "I have one supreme determination—to do all that I can to keep war away from these shores for all time." Roosevelt also strongly endorsed and often quoted the Democratic party's foreign policy plank: "We will not participate in foreign wars, and we will not send our army, naval, or air forces to fight in foreign lands outside of the Americas, except in case of attack."[6]

These ringing phrases made Hull's caution understandable although the distinction between "technical" and "political" talks seemed niggling. But the British were not going to argue over semantics when it seemed that Hull's suggestion offered an opportunity to draw America closer to war. Britain's Chiefs of Staff recommended that the proposal be quickly accepted, since, "once conversations had been held, the chances of the United States giving us total military support in the event of Japanese aggression would be increased."[7]

It had not always been official British policy to involve the United States in a war in the Pacific. In fact, there had been some difference of opinion concerning the merits of such involvement as late as September 1940 when some, like Sir Robert Vansittart and Sir Alexander Cadogan, reasoned that America's active participation in a Pacific war should be discouraged since it might limit the amount of material aid available to Great Britain.[8] The issue was decided, however, on the same day that the Chiefs of Staff recommended accepting Hull's initiative.

A telegram from Sir Robert Craigie, the British ambassador in Japan, in early October 1940 elicited the new policy declaration. Craigie had been advised by an unnamed American source that war with Japan might so increase American military requirements that aid to Britain would be curtailed.[9] In the light of conflicting opinion on the effect of American entry, Craigie asked for some official reaction. Reaction he got. On 4 October 1940, Winston Churchill directed the foreign secretary to inform all ambassadors that American entry into the war with either Germany, Italy, or Japan was "fully conformable with British interests." Churchill viewed any reasoning to the contrary as a "very serious misconception" since "nothing in the munitions sphere can compare with the importance of the British Empire and the United States being co-belligerents."[10]

With all the principal parties in Britain agreed on talks and policy it appeared that the conversations would begin speedily. The Americans certainly appeared ready. On the same day that Churchill wrote his policy-setting minute, Lord Lothian was called to a meeting with Undersecretary of State Sumner Welles. Welles referred to the staff conference suggestion as the "President's" and expressed the hope that this "very important and far-reaching proposal" would meet with no delays. Lothian needed no prompting and they quickly agreed that Washington would be the ideal spot. Welles presumably wanted an American venue for negotiating prestige, but Lothian later revealed that he wanted talks in Washington because the inefficient American security system would prove unable to contain the secret. A leak revealing Anglo-American collaboration could only be beneficial. The British ambassador did suggest that preliminary talks be held in London between Ghormley, the British, and the Dutch.[11]

In the first week in October activity was apparent at all levels. At the top, Winston Churchill contacted the president. The prime minister wanted to know if the United States could send an American naval squadron, "the bigger the better," to visit Singapore. "If desired," he wrote, "occasion might be taken of such a visit for technical discussion of naval and military problems in those and Philippine waters, and the Dutch might be invited to join."[12]

Mr. Churchill had not informed the Americans of his reasoning on the relative merits of their involvement in a Pacific war, but the subject was clearly on the minds of Admiral Stark and General Marshall when the American Liaison Committee met on 5 October to discuss Churchill's message. In Stark's view, the prime minister's request should not be granted unless the United States were prepared to risk war. "Every month, every week and every day that we are able to maintain peace and still support Britain," he said, "is valuable time gained." Marshall agreed, suggesting that it was a most inopportune time for provocation. Stark then enunciated a principle that would become increasingly apparent in American planning. In the final analysis, he said, "we may have to fight in the Atlantic and treat Japan as a side show." England's survival was "vital," and being drawn into the Pacific might "shut off the flow of munitions to Great Britain." Marshall agreed, capsulating this idea in the phrase, "if we lose in the Atlantic we lose everywhere." For these reasons the group agreed that no squadron should be sent to Singapore.[13] There does not appear to have been any discussion of staff conferences concerning common defense in the Pacific but, in light of the committee's discussion, opposition can be assumed.

Presumably unaware of the service chiefs' reactions, Ambassador Lothian was anxious that the iron not cool on the subject of staff talks, Singapore visit or no. Therefore he telephoned the Foreign Office for instructions. No formal Cabinet decision had been made, but he was advised that the Chiefs of Staff had reacted favorably, and he knew that that was tantamount to approval. He, therefore, could tell Secretary Hull that the British government welcomed the talks and that a formal reply would be forthcoming.[14]

With the decision made, the British characteristically moved quickly to make preparations. Not only were the preparations extensive but they once again anticipated more commitment than the Americans had intended. The Joint Planning Staff drew up a draft outline for the talks. The planners recommended that the discussion proceed on two levels: (1) talks in the Far East between the British, Dutch, and Americans (the British had already been planning a conference at Singapore with the Dutch), the primary purpose of these talks being a commitment from the Dutch and a determination on what naval forces the United States would bring into a Pacific war; (2) talks first in London and then in Washington between the Americans and the British, the purpose of which was to be a discussion of the broader strategic implications of American involvement in the war. The planners had six pages of ideas that the conversations might cover, but they had already decided that the Americans should be pressed to "concentrate a powerful battle-fleet in the Far East." The British planners anticipated a public clamor in the United States to concentrate on the Atlantic frontier, but they felt that the "requirements of the Far East should come first."[15]

In Washington, Lothian was ecstatic. He saw the proposal for staff talks as the "most important and far-reaching which had ever come from the United States about the Pacific." To him it appeared that America was prepared to "put its whole weight behind our security in the Pacific." The ambassador's enthusiasm was not dampened by Hull's increasing eagerness to press forward. On 6 October and again the next day, Hull expressed in strong terms the urgency of the situation. On 7 October he was particularly emphatic and urged starting immediately. Lothian was so encouraged that he went into great detail sketching the strategic connection between the Pacific threat and the dangers in the Atlantic. He used these observations as a springboard for suggesting wide-ranging conversations covering world strategy. Hull seemed to agree.[16] Two days later the bottom dropped out of the staff conference proposal.

When Lothian met with Hull on 9 October he found that "extreme caution" had replaced the secretary's previous enthusiasm. Hull explained that a recent flurry of statements expressing American determination to stand firm in the Far East had produced congressional and public anxiety. Even those who ardently supported the British cause were worried lest a war in the Pacific deny Britain essential materials. (If they had known of Churchill's enthusiasm for American participation, perhaps they would have felt differently.) In any case, the secretary now opposed any formal conference in Washington, London, or Singapore. He apparently had read Lothian's mind, for he suggested the possibility of press leaks "inflating [the] significance" of such talks. He did, however, want Pacific problems examined and information exchanged. Lothian inferred that Hull wanted Admiral Ghormley to determine what resources and dispositions Britain, Australia, New Zealand, and Holland had in the Far East and to discuss "naval problems as to possible common defense."[17] Hull did not say how he distinguished these discussions from preliminary staff talks.

The election was on Hull's mind, and he now felt that no formal talks could be held until after election day on 5 November. The explanation that he offered—adverse public reaction—was surely part of the reason for his change of heart. It is possible, however, that the proposed broadening of the talks to embrace world strategy put him on guard while the very warmth of British enthusiasm might have cooled his ardor.[18]

As has been suggested, however, the "full development of the projected staff conferences is not clear" from American records. Part of the explanation for the mystery is that Hull made a conscious effort to cover his tracks. There is no hint in his account of the period 30 September through 9 October that he initiated the staff conference proposal (at the president's suggestion) or that he repeatedly urged Lothian to press forward. For example, in his record Hull states that on 7 October he made it clear, when pressed by Lothian, that a formal staff conference could not take place until after the election and that he was thinking only of "technical" discussions.[19] To be sure, Hull often used the ambiguous term "technical," but Lothian's report of the 7 October conversation does not record the important caveat about the election; instead, it twice quotes Hull as saying "how important it was that the staff talks he had already suggested should begin as soon as possible."[20]

Lothian may have misinterpreted Hull, but that seems doubtful. Hull was willing at this time to mislead people, even some within the hierarchy of the American government, concerning his actions. For instance, he told Adolf Berle, who thought that conversations about basing at Singapore would lead to a "unilateral obligation to defend the British Empire," that Lothian had pressed him hard on talks but that he had always staunchly resisted his advances.[21]

On the same day that he talked with Berle, Hull again met with Lothian. From his review of Admiral Ghormley's reports it appeared that there had already been "a good many conversations with the Admiralty about common Pacific problems," the secretary said. Since this was the case, neither he nor Admiral Stark believed that it was necessary to send any further instructions to Ghormley. Hull did suggest that the Dutch be advised that "joint defense" against Japanese aggression was being discussed—of course, "without any political commitment." The Dutch might be asked to contribute privately to these talks. Although Lothian was undoubtedly discouraged, he concluded that even though Hull was now opposed to a formal conference, he wanted the problems explored in "technical circles" in Washington and in London.[22]

* * *

In London, meanwhile, the blitz was continuing with unrelenting fury. Bomb craters blocked roads, and empty, gutted buildings were becoming commonplace sights for weary Londoners and for the ancient city's visitors. Ghormley had continued to rent rooms at Claridge's throughout the opening weeks of the campaign because the hotel, though exposed, provided easy access to the Admiralty. Despite the bombing, there also was considerable socializing, and Ghormley frequently dined with Ambassador Kennedy or other members of the American community. Lunch was often at the United Services Club in Pall Mall where, even after a bomb came through the roof into the entry hall, business could be conducted in dignity as generations of British officers stared down from their frames on the paneled walls.

The strain of the continued bombardment soon began to take its toll and it became increasingly difficult to get a good night's rest. Captain Kirk and Commander Hitchcock had already moved out of town and Ghormley decided to seek similar lodgings. The home of the dowager Lady Smiley, located in Wentworth, a few miles from London, was ideal. The house was not large, but it was sufficient to accommodate Ghormley, Austin, and MacDonald. It was far enough out to be safe, yet close enough to allow him to be at his Embassy office daily. But even in the country there were cocktail parties, dinners, and movies at the Kennedys' place, for as Ghormley had noted in a letter to Stark, "the British do put a great deal of emphasis on the social side."[23]

These lighter activities made the task more bearable, but Ghormley was also becoming a serious student of bombing and its effects. Although his own experience had surely been disquieting, he was coming to the conclusion that it would take more than air attacks to beat the British. "The Germans will never win the war by bombing London," he wrote Stark, "unless the morale of all the people is undermined to a marked degree which I do not believe is possible."[24] In a similar letter to Secretary Knox he noted: "There has been considerable damage, some to military objectives, but the damage is so scattered that one must look for it. Even along the Thames . . . the total destroyed in comparison with the total possible objectives is small."[25] Still, Ghormley was not one to be overly optimistic. Invasion, he told Stark, was unlikely unless Hitler could gain air superiority, which he did not presently have, "but by a series of bad breaks for England he might obtain it . . . very unexpectedly."[26]

At the moment Hitler was seeking those breaks through night bombing, but during the day activities in London proceeded at an uninterrupted pace. For Ghormley that meant continuing his meetings with Admiral Bailey to review various aspects of the committee report. For Bailey and the British it meant pushing forward with staff-conversation preparations almost as though Hull had not backed away from his original initiative. Since Ghormley had not been advised yet of any of the Hull-Lothian discussions, the British were able to prepare at their own pace, only informing Ghormley of the role he was to play when they were ready.

After Hull's change of attitude the War Cabinet officially agreed to honor American wishes.[27] As nearly as they could understand, those wishes were for bringing the Dutch up to date and for exchanging information on a purely "technical level." The Joint Planners, however, could see little reason why "technical" could not be interpreted liberally, so they drew up detailed papers for the British conferees. Thus the practical result of Hull's vacillation was forestalling American preparation while the British went forward with unabated enthusiasm.

The papers turned out by the Joint Planners give a clear indication of their intentions. The Roosevelt administration's preference for subterfuge would delay a single, formal, all-inclusive conference, but preliminary conferences could proceed as were originally proposed. The basic assumption—for planning purposes only, of course—was that the British, the Americans, and the Dutch would be allied in fighting the Germans, the Japanese, and the Italians. This meant that any conversations would have to be broad in scope, for although the primary function would be to coordinate plans for a Pacific war, the conference representatives would have to cast that war in its global, two-ocean context.

The principal Far Eastern question to be explored with the Americans was how much they would be able to compensate for British naval deficiencies and whether they would operate from Singapore, Hong Kong, Manila, Guam, or Pearl Harbor. Anticipating a large American contribution, Britain recommended that all naval forces in the Far East be placed under American strategic command. The place to discuss such command arrangements was at the Singapore Conference between the British and the Dutch, which, conveniently, had already been scheduled. If this were agreeable to the Americans, the Joint Planners thought there should be two conferences: one in Singapore to deal solely with the Far East and one in Washington to consider the "wider implications" of American involvement. While preparations were being made for this big conference, which presumably would take place after the elections, Ghormley could be conducting preliminary talks in London.[28]

At the working level the Admiralty had not even waited for the planning papers but had moved on with unrestrained alacrity. Basing his actions on Ambassador Lothian's reported conversations with Hull, the first sea lord told Rear Admiral R. M. Bellairs on 9 October to prepare to "go to America to conduct staff conversations on her coming in."[29] Bellairs had one of the best minds in the Royal Navy and it was now to be put to work on one of Britain's most delicate problems.

In many ways it was an opportunity for Bellairs to redeem himself. Marked by his brilliance for high command, his career had received a staggering setback in 1931. Having just arrived at Invergordon to serve as commander of the H.M.S. *Rodney*, Bellairs was in command on 15 September 1931. Unfortunately for the young captain and for the reputation of the Royal Navy, rebellious seamen, unhappy over a reduction in pay, chose that moment to stage the notorious Invergordon Mutiny. Although he was in no way responsible, and despite his skillful handling of the explosive situation, Bellairs shared the blame heaped upon the navy by the public. In 1932, when he was just thirty-two years old, he was promoted to rear admiral and placed on the retired list. He served as an adviser on naval arms limitations during the 1930s and when war broke out was brought back to active duty.[30] Various planning operations had occupied him at the Admiralty, but this was a dramatic break in his fortunes, which naturally surprised and pleased him. He realized that much work lay ahead and he immediately busied himself reviewing position papers and plans. He was, as he wrote in his diary, "in a flat spin."

On 10 October, the day after Hull had supposedly changed his mind, a committee was formally constituted and designated the ADA (Anglo-Dutch-American) Committee. The membership consisted of Bellairs, Lord Moyne from the Colonial Office, Air Commodore John Slessor from the Air Ministry, Major General John Dewing from the War Office, and Commander J. C. Norfolk, who acted as secretary. This group was supposed to prepare plans and set priorities for what the British were calling the "U.S.-U.K.-Dutch Technical Conversations."[31]

The plan that emerged from these sessions was for Bellairs to conduct preliminary conversations with Ghormley in London, then proceed to Washington for more formal talks. In Washington he would join Captain A. W. Clarke and Air Commodore Slessor, who by that time would have conducted preliminary talks there. The Singapore talks initially presented a greater problem as the Americans were still reluctant to send a representative. Precisely how the decision was made cannot be ascertained at this date, but the result was that after repeated requests from Ghormley, among others, Captain W. R. Purnell, chief of staff to the commander of the Asiatic Fleet, did attend the conference at the British base.[32] By 16 October the ADA Committee had held several sessions and all concerned had their roles well rehearsed.[33]

It was at this point that the British advised Ghormley of the role they had in mind for him. At lunch on 16 October Admiral Bailey introduced Ghormley to Bellairs and informed him of Lothian's conversations with Hull, apparently omitting the part about Hull's recent rush of caution. Instead the British admiral said that the agreed-upon procedure was for Ghormley to meet with British experts to work out a formula for cooperation in the Far East. Bailey envisaged the talks as "more or less a continuation of the Ingersoll conferences" of 1938, but with the added advantage of having the Dutch views. Ghormley said he had received "no definite instructions" concerning "secret and informal conversations." However, he realized how important talks on common Far Eastern problems could be and he did have a "fairly free hand." He said that he would help all he could—with the familiar reservation about "no commitments."[34]

He then asked what the British wished to discuss. Their questions were specific: What units would the United States send to Singapore? After "zero day" how many days would it take that force to get there and how would the units proceed? These questions implied that a fleet would be sent to Singapore, but Ghormley was not at all certain that that had ever been agreed to. He thought talks were necessary, but he did not feel he had the authority to initiate them, so he cabled Washington requesting further instructions.[35]

Since ambiguity was the order of the day for the Roosevelt administration during the preelection weeks, it is not surprising that Ghormley was confused about what to do. Hull had said that he did not want staff talks, but his reference to "technical" conversations in London and Washington was sufficiently vague to allow several interpretations. The president was not being much more precise. On 17 October he talked at length with Richard Casey, the Australian minister in Washington. In reference to staff conversations, Roosevelt emphasized the "undesirability of anything interpretable as commitments or indeed any publicity regarding collaboration on defense questions." At the same time he agreed that Australia could send a naval officer to Washington for secret talks. Publicity and public interpretation of commitment obviously bothered Roosevelt, but was he willing to make a commitment in fact?

The president had made no specific comment to Casey regarding the possible talks in Singapore, but he definitely wanted the base reinforced. In his view, however, the ideal relief would come from the British Mediterranean fleet. Roosevelt said that he "hoped and prayed" that the British would not allow any ships to be trapped in the Mediterranean. For this reason he had requested Lothian to ask Churchill whether "eight capital ships with some cruisers and a few destroyers" should not be transferred to Singapore. Although he did not mention it, units at Singapore would have the added advantage of being well out of German reach if anything happened to British resolve.

But what was America willing to do to back up British resolve? Roosevelt was not saying, but Secretary of the Navy Knox, whom Casey visited after leaving the White House, said that once the election was over (and he was confident of Roosevelt's victory), "many things could and would be done that could not be done now." The impression was that the "no commitment" stance was purely for public consumption. Casey passed Roosevelt's and Knox's comments on to London without interpretation.[36]

In London, Ghormley's first meeting with Bellairs apparently went well, although the British admiral was not satisfied that the reticent Ghormley was telling all he knew.[37] The problem was that Ghormley still had no further word from Washington regarding talks, but on 25 October he presented Bellairs with a paper designed to reach the heart of British plans for the Far East. Although Ghormley expressed his belief in this paper that the American people would oppose the extension of Japanese control over all of Malaysia, he raised some related points that would bedevil British-American naval relations for months. He suggested, for example, that "relative interests in the Far East are now such that any armed assistance from the U.S. should be predicated on a firm determination on the part of the British and the Dutch to provide vigorous and effective means for defensive action by strong and well-coordinated British and Dutch military, naval, and air forces operating under conditions which preclude success of native rebellions, natural or inspired." In other words, he wished to be assured before committing the United States to anything that the British were prepared to help themselves and would receive Dutch assistance. Furthermore, his reference to native rebellions, "natural or inspired," was an oblique allusion to American sensitivity on colonial issues. His other points were less subtle; he wanted to know, for instance, whether the British would actually be able to supply and service ships sent to the Far East.[38]

Now it was the British turn to be cautious. Bellairs met with Ghormley on 29 October to discuss the questions further, and it was not until four days later that the first draft of his answer was finished.[39] Prior to handing the paper to Ghormley, Bellairs discussed it with the Chiefs of Staff, to whom he pointed out the insecurity of the Singapore area. As a result the chiefs instructed Admiral Bellairs to modify his paper to emphasize not the insecurity of the base but rather the difficulties the Japanese would have in attacking it.[40] This change would make the paper more realistic, they felt, yet it would not weaken their case for American support.

* *

Despite the increasingly critical situation in the Atlantic, the Far East was fast emerging as the immediate problem for discussion at any staff conference. Ghormley was the obvious liaison for making preparations for these conferences, yet he was left isolated, often out of date, and generally without a clue concerning the sentiments of the Department of State, the U.S. Army, and sometimes even the U.S. Navy. Moreover, there was no clear course, for, as he wrote Stark, he knew that the popular cry in America would be that the United States was "pulling British chestnuts out of the fire again," while the British view was apocalyptic.[41] Much of the Empire was washed by the Pacific and indications of insecurity in that area could result in Australia's and New Zealand's withdrawing their vital support from the common cause and concentrating on home defense. Therefore, British strategy called for Singapore being held at all costs. Unless the Americans took a firm stand, a "worst possible case" scenario would show the Japanese sweeping up the Dutch East Indies and Singapore, spilling into and across the Indian Ocean, probably overrunning India and possibly Aden in the process, and linking up with the Germans. The Empire would be halved like an orange, the sections gobbled up at leisure. Already overcommitted in the Mediterranean and at home, the British had to rely upon America. Aversion to colonialism aside, Ghormley recognized Britain's plight and saw some validity in British strategy and views. As he suggested to the chief of naval operations, Singapore was the only base in the Orient "ready and available to us to protect our own interests there." So protecting Singapore might be seen as a matter of enlightened self-interest.[42]

Other American officials had other views on American self-interest. The army planners during the fall of 1940 thought, as the official history puts it, that supporting Britain "might well amount to supporting, at first indirectly and then directly, British positions throughout the world," in other words, acquiescing "in British grand strategy." Not surprisingly, army planners were "very uneasy over the prospect."[43] And Adolf Berle, one of the president's closest advisers, voiced another suspicion of British motives: "I have a distinct feeling," he noted, "that while we want to give every help to the British we must not make the mistake we made in 1917 and become virtually their adjuncts."[44]

Roosevelt himself was hardly devoid of suspicion regarding the British, but what were his real desires regarding joint planning with them? If one reads between the lines it is difficult to avoid the impression that the president wanted Ghormley to interpret his instructions very liberally and do everything short of committing the country to an alliance. But either because the president was being too obtuse or because Ghormley was too cautious there were few specific results to be seen. The admiral, despite his anxiety and his feelings that staff talks were essential, was a poor choice if initiative and independence were the requirements for the job.

And as if dealing with the British was not enough, Ghormley was fast learning that the Dutch as well had to be considered. He had asked Bailey about British-Dutch commitments in the Far East, for those commitments or lack of them could be a major stumbling block. The issue is complex and it is difficult to put all the loose ends together, but from a series of comments an accurate picture can be reconstructed. The British were willing to agree to fight with the Dutch, but only if the Americans would agree— preferably publicly—to come to the aid of the British *or* the Dutch if they were attacked by the Japanese. The Americans were, and continued to be, very hesitant about making any such declaration, ostensibly because it might provoke the Japanese. Moreover, they contended that no American commitment to fight in the Far East could be made without a *prior* pledge of Anglo-Dutch cooperation, which the Americans wanted as an indication of earnest intent, and maybe not even then.[45] The situation was vintage Alphonse-Gaston and it made reaching any decision about the Far East more difficult and Ghormley's job more delicate.

But something was going to have to be done and very soon. The Battle of Britain was obviously only the beginning of a long Anglo-German war. British success in such a war, especially when her exposed communications lines in the Atlantic were considered, was at least problematic. It was already apparent that help would be necessary, and was expected, in that ocean. At the same time the Tripartite Pact made Japan seem so menacing that the British were pushing the Americans toward staff talks on the Pacific. Any move might be provocative, yet failure to move might be disastrous. As Ghormley was finding, unless alternatives to British grand strategy could be determined, only two courses seemed to remain—acquiescing to their views or standing back and watching them fall to a coalition of aggressors. The British were careful to do nothing to help solve the riddle; indeed, they were so careful that one might suspect them of deception.

12.

Developments in Washington: Putting National Priorities in Perspective

September 1940–16 November 1940

Ghormley might have felt less isolated had he realized how poorly defined American policy was in Washington. No Anglo-American strategy could be settled upon until internal controversy over Pacific operations was resolved. To appreciate the situation, it is necessary to go back and pick up the thread of this story from the Washington end.

As of fall 1940, new RAINBOW plans were being drawn up, but any Pacific war would still be fought basically on the ORANGE plan model. Admiral J. O. Richardson, commander of the fleet that would fight the war against Japan, was extremely skeptical about that plan. In Richardson's view ORANGE had only been an expedient to justify appropriations and was, in the fall of 1940, almost criminally illusionary. For its part, the U.S. Army had never been enthusiastic about the ORANGE plan and the changes in the world power balance that occurred during the summer of 1940 reinforced its pessimism.[1] Slowly, as we have seen, the conviction was taking hold in both services that the United States should concentrate its efforts in the Atlantic rather than in the Pacific, particularly if Britain were as weak as her spokesmen continued to insist. Complicating matters was the suspicion that the wily British would involve the United States in their troubles, first in the Pacific, then in Europe. Still more disturbing to the military was the fact that such developments were laden with political considerations on which they could get little guidance. Traditional American doctrine held that the military should leave politics to the civilians. However, any Anglo-American planning for a two-ocean strategy, no matter how disingenuously labeled "technical," would have wartime and postwar political implications. So how could the American military planners chart their course without correcting for political tides? One answer was to forgo considering how to advance America's political interest and think instead about how to avoid advancing Britain's.

Suspicion of British machinations was a sentiment that the American services shared. They also could agree that America had not yet made the root-and-branch changes necessitated by the altered world situation and they realized that procrastination beyond a certain point would turn out to be acceptance of British initiatives. If the national leadership could settle on an Atlantic rather than a Pacific orientation, it would have the added advantage of laying to rest the interservice disputes over the ORANGE plan. Surely sufficient justification for both services' programs could be found in the vital Atlantic theater.

The president, unfortunately, found it difficult to be decisive or helpful during this critical period. Never one for tiresome detail, Roosevelt was particularly inattentive during the fall of 1940. If he were not going to offer leadership on national security preparations, who was? The U.S. Navy accepted the task.

* * *

The officer most immediately affected by plans for any Pacific war was the commander in chief of the U.S. Fleet based at Pearl Harbor, Admiral J. O. Richardson, of the U.S. Naval Academy class of 1902, a senior and experienced officer. Immediately prior to accepting command of the navy's primary force afloat, he had served as chief of the influential Bureau of Navigation. In this bureau, later more accurately titled the Bureau of Naval Personnel, he had become intimately acquainted with the politics of the Navy Department as well as of Washington. A direct, even blunt, officer of keen mind and strong convictions, Richardson became accustomed to pursuing what he understood to be the navy's interests with more vigor than tact. With his assignment to the U.S. Fleet, Richardson received four stars and what he considered to be the most prestigious post in the navy. With broad experience and no office to aspire to, Richardson could speak his mind as candidly as he felt necessary. Never one to suffer fools or incompetents silently, he felt that the situation in the Pacific required candor. Furthermore, he was familiar with the corridors of power and was not averse to venturing into them.

Richardson's concern over planning for an ORANGE war had preceded his assignment as commander in chief of the U.S. Fleet. As early as 1938, when serving as assistant chief of naval operations, he had assisted in drafting a modified ORANGE plan that the navy had used to justify a 20 percent increase in naval strength.[2] Richardson had also repeatedly emphasized that no war in the Pacific should be undertaken unless the British were so committed to a coalition effort that they could not leave America "in the lurch."[3] Immediately after taking command of the fleet, Richardson wrote to Admiral Stark, outlining the practical difficulties of carrying out the ORANGE plan.[4] Several moves were made to meet his objections, but basing the fleet at Pearl Harbor in May 1940 was not among them. In Richardson's view, that decision only increased the chances of a war for which the navy was not prepared. By fall 1940, he was convinced that planning was still unrealistic and that deficiencies in ships and personnel "vitiated completely the prospects of a successful campaign."[5]

One problem was that in case of war with Japan the ORANGE plan was practically all he had. RAINBOW 1, which had contemplated concentrating on hemispheric defense, had been promulgated in June 1940. RAINBOW 2, which contemplated fulfilling the responsibilities of RAINBOW 1 and projecting U.S. naval forces into the Western Pacific in company with the British and the Dutch, was never received by the commander of the U.S. Fleet in anything other than tentative form. Preparations had begun on RAINBOW 3, but that would not even be approved by the chief of naval operations until 7 January 1941. Thus, in the closing months of 1940, Richardson was left in case of a Japanese attack to operate with a war plan in which he had no confidence.

The admiral did not suffer that unsatisfactory situation passively. During a visit to Washington in July 1940 he had told

Secretary Hull and Undersecretary Welles that in his view the ORANGE plan was "useless," and he implied that it was dangerous to try to intimidate Japan with an inadequately supplied fleet based at Pearl Harbor.[6] The president had assured Richardson that he had no intention of sending strong naval forces into the Western Pacific, but the admiral left the capital unconvinced of Roosevelt's candor. Indeed, it was Richardson's view that the president was determined to "put the United States into the war, if Great Britain could hold out until he was reelected."[7]

In September 1940 Secretary Knox made a visit to Pearl Harbor that heightened Richardson's anxieties. Knox expressed privately his conviction that the country would be in the war by spring 1941. In view of his feelings concerning the state of naval preparedness, this was not welcome news to Admiral Richardson. Consequently, he presented the secretary with a lengthy memorandum that outlined his views on America's vague, impractical approach to operational planning. He charged that ORANGE had been drawn up originally in order to have some basis upon which to justify increasing the size of the navy.[8] He did not object to this approach, but he clearly believed that facing, or possibly even courting, war when this was the only available plan was extremely unwise. He did not place blame; he merely observed that the lack of coordination between departments meant that there was no clear picture of "national policy, national commitments, and national objectives."[9] He also expressed the hope that this lamentable situation would soon be rectified.

Knox did not respond to Richardson's memorandum, but he did suggest that the admiral come to Washington in October. By the time Richardson arrived on 7 October, the Tripartite Pact had been signed and there was much discussion concerning possible Japanese action when the British would reopen the Burma Road on 17 October. Richardson had three primary concerns: first, the impracticality of basing the fleet at Pearl Harbor; second, the need to build up the fleet, particularly in regard to personnel; and third, the conviction that Roosevelt was playing fast and loose with U.S. security.

After a series of meetings with Navy Department personnel, Richardson and Admiral Leahy lunched with the president. Conversation soon turned to the matter of returning the fleet to the West Coast. Richardson argued for it; the president disagreed;

presumably that settled the issue. Roosevelt then mentioned his recent talks with Lord Lothian. The British ambassador had told him, Roosevelt said, that "Ghormley was busy transmitting information regarding technical materials, and the British Admiralty felt that they [we?] should have officers prepared for staff conferences."[10]

That was significant news, but Richardson had other things on his mind. It had long been his conviction that Admiral Stark was not adequately representing the views of the professional navy to the president. It also was his impression that the president, through goodwill and ignorance, was capable of blithely and irresponsibly committing the navy to tasks to which it was not equal. Finally, he believed that the president was misleading the American public for political purposes. Richardson therefore had decided to shock the president out of his irresponsible course. It was with this object in mind that Richardson said: "I feel that I must tell you that the senior officers of the Navy do not have the trust and confidence in the civilian leadership of this country that is essential for the successful prosecution of a war in the Pacific."[11] The president was shocked indeed. But he did not alter his course; instead he apparently made a mental note to get rid of Richardson at the earliest possible opportunity.

Richardson's unpleasant confrontations were not over, and here it should be noted that the admiral had undertaken his actions only after long and careful thought. He had such strong feelings on the subject, and he had made so many less direct attempts to remedy the situation, that he had now decided to allow his emotions full rein. On 10 October he and several other officers met in Secretary Knox's office. Knox informed the group that if the Japanese took drastic action when the British reopened the Burma Road, the president was considering establishing a naval blockade to sever Japanese trade lines. Richardson asked if the president was also considering a declaration of war. Knox said he did not know. Richardson registered amazement, suggesting that the U.S. Fleet was not ready either to impose a blockade or to fight the war that would certainly result. Knox was displeased. "I am not a strategist," he said. "If you don't like the President's plan, draw one of your own to accomplish the purpose."[12]

Stark and Richardson set the Plans officers (Commander V. R. Murphy and Captains C. M. Cooke, C. J. Moore, and Harry W.

Hill) to work on this request. Since none of the officers were enthusiastic about the prospect of a trans-Pacific blockade, they probably did not welcome the task. Within twenty-four hours, however, they had developed what they considered a reasonable variation on the president's scheme and a list of assumptions that the country should be willing to accept if any blockade were put into effect. Stripped to its fundamentals, the proposal included blockading ports in South America and Southeast Asia where shipments for Japan originated, sweeping the Northern Pacific trade routes, reinforcing the Asiatic Fleet with up to four aircraft carriers, and preparing to defend American Pacific bases against almost certain retaliation.[13]

The ten assumptions that they proposed were what they conceived to be the realities American officials would have to accept in imposing any blockade. There is a tongue-in-cheek quality to these assumptions, as though Richardson and company did not believe the president had considered all ramifications of his proposed action. In summary, the assumptions were that Japan would react aggressively to the reopening of the Burma Road, the United States would institute a blockade, the U.S. Navy would cooperate with Britain and Holland in interdicting Japanese trade in the Western Pacific, and Japan would declare war in retaliation.

The ninth assumption was the most controversial. If war erupted in the Pacific it would require a major American effort, including reinforcement of the Asiatic Fleet, which could be justified only if it were assumed that "Great Britain will prevent any naval aggression in the Western Atlantic against the Western Hemisphere by the Axis powers." That was the heart of the problem; Atlantic responsibilities would have to be wholly entrusted to the British if war in the Pacific were invited.[14] There was no immediate reaction to either the proposal or the assumptions and Richardson left Washington for Pearl Harbor on 11 October.

* * *

Part of the reaction to Richardson's visit took the form of a forward-looking and portentous paper known to history as "Plan D" or "Plan Dog." Although he had not said so explicitly, it was not difficult to infer criticism of the chief of naval operations from Richardson's actions and comments. The War Plans Division operated directly under the chief of naval operations so inadequacies in planning could be attributed to him. The president's provocative blockading scheme was only a symptom of a serious absence of priorities and direction. In any case, shortly after Richardson's visit, Admiral Stark undertook a sweeping reevaluation of American naval policy that was to have a significant effect on American planning preparatory to and even during the war.

There is no denying that an ordering of national security policy was long overdue. At the same time Stark's difficulties should not be minimized. In 1940 the navy was still a decentralized organization in which the various bureau chiefs held the balance of power.[15] The chief of naval operations was a relatively new and not totally accepted administrative position ("imposition," to some), and the holder of that office was not able to dictate policy. He needed to work with and through the secretary of the navy and the assistant secretary, and he depended upon persuasion and logic to sway the relatively autonomous bureaus. To a large extent his authority was determined by his personality and his ability to win influential officers to his side.

By nature Stark was amiable, well-intentioned, and hardworking. He was also junior to several of his commanders at sea and his bureau chiefs and hence in a somewhat disadvantageous position.[16] That he recognized this is clear from the length and frequency of his letters to Ghormley and other officers in the field. He wanted those who would have to fight and die to know that he was aware of the deficiencies, that he was trying, and that he needed their support. Stark's problems were far from simple. He had become chief of naval operations in January 1940, had shepherded through Congress two significant appropriations bills, had dispatched the assistant chief of naval operations (Admiral Ghormley) for talks with the British, had signed away, against his better judgment, fifty overage destroyers, and was trying, with some success, to increase the numbers of naval personnel.

Furthermore, Stark was caught in a dilemma. He was obsessed with the desire that the navy not be caught as ill prepared as it had been in 1917.[17] At the same time he knew that obeisance had to be paid to political realities—one of which was the country's lack of willingness to enter another foreign war. Another was Roosevelt's hesitance to counter that attitude frontally. Stark was well aware that Roosevelt was not being as neutral as he proclaimed, but Stark also knew the frustration of trying to find ways to meet emergencies without arousing public suspicion.

Richardson may have been right about Stark's inadequacy in representing the views of the professional navy to the president, but Stark did try. He and Roosevelt got along superficially well and Stark had plenty of chummy, "Dear Betty" (his Academy nickname) notes from the president in his files. Roosevelt could be both friendly and elusive when he did not wish to be pinned down, so those notes contained more jokes and anecdotes than sound advice or decisions; indeed, it would seem that the president used his personal relationship with the white-haired, bespectacled Stark to fob off responsibility. In this case the responsibility for answering Richardson's criticism and ordering national priorities devolved upon the chief of naval operations.

As rudimentary as it may seem in these days of cost analysis, war gaming, and computer programming, the head of the navy sat down by himself and, in one day working from early in the morning until 2:00 A.M., drew up a rough outline for a national policy review. Then he called in his top aides and proceeded to rewrite and polish his paper. This work took approximately ten days and was accomplished, in part, on the dining-room table in Stark's home in the Washington suburbs. The group was not entirely satisfied with what they had when they finished, but they had accomplished a much-needed exercise in orientation. The paper they had produced could at least be the basis for further planning and was an exceedingly significant step in the evolution of American military policy.[18]

Stark took time out from working on this paper to write to Ghormley on October 16. The issue was British plans and how much reliance could be put on the Royal Navy's assistance. If Japan entered the war on the side of the Axis and the United States undertook a Pacific offensive, could the Royal Navy be counted on to carry out all mutual responsibilities in the Atlantic? Stark clearly had in mind the contingency plan worked out during Richardson's visit and he enclosed the list of ten assumptions with his letter. Beside assumption number nine, the suggestion that Britain could prevent any naval aggression in the Western Atlantic, someone had written: "Is such an assumption warranted? I doubt the wisdom of this setup—Doubt if we can afford (no matter what the British promise) to reduce our forces in the Atlantic to so great an extent."[19] To determine Britain's position fully, Ghormley would have to enter more deeply into strategy talks, and Stark added: "I am assuming that you are continuing your staff talks with the British, keeping up for the moment, at least, the fact that you are doing so entirely on your own responsibility and not committing us in any way."[20]

Perhaps realizing that the body of his letter contained no clear instructions, Stark added a postscript: "Get in on any and all staff conversations you can—go as far as you like in discussions—with the full understanding you are expressing only your own views as what best to do—"if and when"—but such must not be understood to commit your government in any manner or to any degree whatsoever."[21] To stimulate some form of discussion at the Washington end, Stark decided to embark simultaneously on a somewhat audacious course. Although Captain A. W. Clarke (RN) had been sent to Washington in August 1940 to act as a personal liaison officer for President Roosevelt, he had not yet been involved in any high-level negotiations. Now Stark decided to use him as a sounding board for his ideas. The procedure used was to have Captain Richmond "Kelly" Turner, one of the officers working with Stark on Plan D and soon to become chief of the War Plans Division, keep Clarke personally briefed on developing naval strategy. Turner was ideal in this role, for he was brilliant, blunt, somewhat irascible, and could never be considered pro-British; thus he could be counted on to discourage unduly optimistic assumptions the British might have.[22]

Turner started the series of meetings, Clarke recalls, with a long exposition on world politics that, though not entirely pleasant, "bore the stamp of a professionally objective approach without fear or favor." Clarke and Turner met several times during mid-October. On 25 October the British officer was called to Admiral Stark's office preparatory to being shown a copy of the U.S. Navy's current war plan, RAINBOW 3. In Clarke's words:

The Chief of Naval Operations opened the conversation by almost casually saying that they proposed to show me the American Navy's plan for war against Japan, something which he added no outsider had so far ever read. I stammered my thanks and just retained sufficient composure to ask whether I was allowed to tell the Admiralty of what I might hoist in. The reply was a simple one. "You wouldn't be much use if you couldn't," adding with a twinkle, "I hope your cyphers are secure." With that I was sternly led away; not sure from Captain Turner's attitude whether I was a criminal going to the last drop, or a pet who should be humored!

In the Director of Plans' room a safe was opened and I was handed a huge tome and invited to sit down and digest its contents at my leisure. Captain Turner, in passing over the volume, observed with a kind of wry smile: "We've other plans in this safe—war with Great Britain is one of them." And of course very sensible too, but in the circumstances I didn't ask whether I could have a glance at that also, just as a matter of personal interest!

The Director then excused himself, said he had other work to do and the room was mine, and vanished. To this day I have wondered whether this was a tactical hint that if he wasn't there I would feel free to take surreptitious notes. Certainly I did not. After all, I felt that would be going too far, apart from the security angle. But what faced me was stupendous. The "Plan" was comprehensive to the last degree. Chapter after chapter; ranging from principles through strategic intentions to allocation of forces, command structures, responsibilities, communications, logistic support and so on. I could necessarily do little more than skim the outlines and try and get some overall picture in my mind, and twenty years after I remember very little of what I read. It was, however, enough to impress me with certain salient points amongst which, again if I'm not confusing that occasion with later events, was the intention to keep the main U.S. naval strength concentrated in the central Pacific—to wit, Pearl Harbour—and carry forward from there a step-by-step offensive advance westward to Japan. Just as in reality the American Pacific strategy ultimately took form. What the Plan did not cater for, nor at the time did I, for one, even think of such a thing, was the treacherous initial blow which at once severely circumscribed the opening phases.

After about two hours my reading came to an end, and late into the night I shut myself up in the Chancery and composed the telegraphed and follow-up written reports. I recollect that Admiral Stark was that evening giving an At Home at which I and my wife were to be amongst the guests. I think he will have realised why I excused myself at the last moment.[23]

Clarke was invited to the Navy Department four days later to complete his unique orientation. This time he was shown a preliminary draft of Plan D. He immediately reported his observations to London.[24] His report should have been no surprise to Washington, for, as Stark had told him, to fulfill his mission he would have to report his findings to the Admiralty. But why would the chief of naval operations want the British kept current on the most secret of all American contingency plans?

The answer to that question must remain speculative; what we do know is what Clarke reported. The American view he characterized as "gloomy." The reason was the perception that Britain's position was precarious. Ultimate collapse would be preceded by Axis domination of the Mediterranean, which would nullify British blockading efforts, bringing economic and then military disaster. The only way to avoid these developments was by "very considerable direct Naval, Military and Air assistance" from the United States in the Atlantic area. At the same time Britain would continue to need American material assistance. The demands of these combined efforts would be so taxing that an offensive war against Japan was out of the question. The concluding recommendation was that "every political expediency" should be expended to avoid war with Japan.[25]

* * *

Before this report could be fully digested London was cheered by the news of Roosevelt's reelection. As Ghormley wrote Stark, the election results were "very pleasing to the British." He continued:

What they really expect I do not know unless it is that we will come into the war, which, of course, the President has said we will not. This all leads up to the question [to] which I have been giving a great deal of thought. First, will Japan come in, and second—how much naval assistance we can give the British. From the enclosure to my serial 15 [the Bailey Committee report] you have seen what the British would like, but, of course, that paper was drawn up before Japan joined the Axis Powers. I have reiterated to the officials of the Admiralty that our disposition depends upon Japanese action. I am firmly convinced that real staff talks should be held to decide the questions which will come up, and most important of all is that the staff talks should be predicated upon instructions from Washington. We are too far away and our information is too one-sided and incomplete for me to make even sound tentative commitments. Your 221830 [this message cannot be located] gave me some policy in regard to our part of the world, namely—the American people do not want to pull certain "chesnuts [sic] out of the fire." I realize it is difficult in these changing days to define policy—but whenever you can give me some, be it regarding the Atlantic or the Pacific, it is a great help.

I hope that War Plans is now working on these possible staff talks not only as concerns the Atlantic, but also the Pacific and the Dutch East Indies.[26]

With the elections over, the British proceeded with renewed vigor to plan for staff conversations with the Americans. To coordinate preparations, Lord Lothian, who had tactfully returned to England during the final weeks of the campaign, held several meetings at the Admiralty where he provided insight and guidance on American attitudes. Rear Admiral Bellairs attended these sessions as well and his planning papers formed the basis for part of the discussion. Admiral Pound opened the meeting on 8 November by outlining the progress with Admiral Ghormley who, Pound made it clear, had been something of a disappointment. According to the first sea lord, Ghormley seemed to have "no specific instructions" concerning staff talks on the vital matter of "strategical and tactical employment of the combined Fleets."[27] Lothian found this hard to believe. Roosevelt, Lothian said, had been extremely cautious about publicity before the election, but "very keen" for everything short of a formal conference. Therefore, upon his return he would impress the president with the desirability of "strengthening Admiral Ghormley's hand" and, if necessary, reinforcing the delegation.

Lothian also said he would advise the Americans that they were already "fundamentally" allied with Great Britain and that the time had come to get the economic and military priorities in order. He would therefore advocate collecting all British requirements and presenting them, even though they might not be met immediately or *in toto*. Since the Americans, in his opinion, had accepted the view of saving America by helping Britain, he thought that his country should "strike while the iron is hot."

Since the time was right, Admiral Pound wanted Lothian to impress upon the Americans some of the Admiralty's strong opinions concerning the Far East. The Royal Navy's planners had already decided that the Atlantic was the primary theater and there they proposed expending their foremost effort; however, the Far East had to be protected lest hostilities ensue there and divert attention from the main theater. The first sea lord felt the best way to retard Japanese aggression was for the Americans to base a fleet at Singapore. A fleet there would protect the Netherlands East Indies, the Philippines, and Hawaii, which the Japanese would not dare attack with a menacing force on their flank. Pound's impression from Ghormley was that one of the U.S. Navy's primary arguments against using Singapore as a base was the preposterous suggestion that the Japanese might then attack the West Coast of America. All present agreed that assaulting America from six thousand miles away was beyond Japanese capabilities. Lothian, however, suggested that a naval appreciation pointing up the improbability of such an attack be prepared immediately. This appreciation could then be used to "educate" Admiral Ghormley, the U.S. Navy Department, and the American public. Lothian would start the process by educating the president.[28]

The next day, on 9 November, a further session was called to discuss Bellairs's estimate of the naval assistance that Britain needed from America if the United States entered the war. This time consideration centered on requirements in the Atlantic. Convoy protection and augmentation of British patrols with submarines and destroyers topped the list. There was some discussion about whether America could help protect convoys without entering the war. On this point Lothian emphasized American constitutional difficulties. Congress would balk at declaring war, he thought, but "short of that . . . the U.S. would help [us] to the fullest extent possible." Merchant shipbuilding was another way in which America might help, and Lothian was advised to stress the growing danger to Britain's lifeline in the North Atlantic.

The ambassador warmed to the point and expanded on the proper way to influence American opinion. The thing to do, he said, was to convince the Americans that "without [help] we might lose the war and their last remaining advance line of defense would thereby be overrun." This same approach could be used in requesting construction of an American flying-boat base in Ireland and naval protection for vital supplies for the Middle East. It was a variation on the theme used during the initial stages of the Destroyers-Bases-Fleet negotiations; refusal to grant aid should be presented in terms of insuring British defeat.[29] With that policy settled, Lothian was prepared to return to the United States. Hopes were high that Roosevelt's election and England's extreme need would insure more material aid and greater cooperation. With such aid, there was confidence that the Atlantic frontier could be held.

* * *

On 11 November Admiral Stark submitted the final version of Plan D to the secretary of the navy for transmission to the president. Stark hoped that the president would "give some definite pronouncement on it" so that he could give his commanders in the field "something more authoritative."[30] Stark then wrote those commanders about his actions and his hopes. He referred to the plan as a "general estimate" and told Ghormley that he hoped it would elicit some "basic decisions." He was painfully anxious lest the navy be "caught napping." It was to be hoped, he said, that the president, who had revealed nothing further to date, would give the navy "some direction" after he had studied the plan. Stark also said that for the time being everything Ghormley did must be "without definite commitment" and that if he (Stark) could send Ghormley a copy of Plan D, he would, but it "should not appear that the President has seen it—call it my personal study." With that study for reference, Stark believed that a "theoretical plan, which can be a practical plan," could and should be drawn up immediately.[31]

The plan that Stark had developed was a significant document; it not only outlined the alternatives America faced in the fall of 1940, but it also presaged the strategy the country was to follow for the next five years.[32] Its tacit premise was that insufficient attention had been paid to American priorities in the months since the German offensive began in Western Europe. Its plea was for direction before time ran out.

Stark opened by stating that America's future was tied to Britain's defense. If Britain lost the war America might not "lose everywhere," but it stood in danger of not "winning anywhere." He did not believe that Britain's situation was "encouraging" and it was "easily possible" that without American assistance the British would be defeated. To make matters worse, the British were "over-optimistic" about their chances, for even if the home islands could be held, and that was not at all certain, they did not seem to realize the danger of losing elsewhere. Miscalculation by the British was serious for the United States, the naval chief thought, since the "prevention of the disruption of the British Empire" came second only to Western Hemisphere defense in his list of American national objectives. If Britain lost, the "military consequences" as well as the economic repercussions would be serious; therefore, America had to support the "vital needs" of the British Empire.

As a realist, Stark saw that to support those vital needs meant to help the British defeat the German Reich. He realized that this objective could not be accomplished merely by bombing and blockading, the only offensive actions the British had been willing to propose when pressed about their plans. The only way to assure military success was to undertake a "land offensive." However, since the British lacked the "manpower and material means" to defeat the Germans in that kind of struggle, she must be assisted with men, munitions, and supplies. In preparation for the ultimate offensive Britain needed to maintain the blockade and continue to provide the geographic base from which a land offensive could be launched.

He next turned to Far Eastern strategy. It was Stark's judgment that Japan would prefer not to engage in war with the British or the Dutch. But if war came, he was not certain that the British and the Dutch would support each other. Without assistance from the Dutch, the "external effectiveness" of the British bases at Hong Kong and Singapore would quickly evaporate. Moreover, if the United States sought to assist her potential allies by applying RAINBOW 3 (or presumably any other variation of ORANGE) serious problems would arise. The RAINBOW 3 offensive would be expensive and difficult; for instance, the essential first step, taking the Marshalls and the Carolines, might require 75,000 men. Was it realistic to plan for actions of this magnitude when a crisis in the Atlantic was impending? If Britain appeared likely to collapse, the United States would have to cancel or curtail operations in the Pacific and incur a "great loss of prestige." Furthermore, Stark considered the difficulties of fighting in the Pacific so serious that careful consideration should be given to the chance of failure. But the most portentous consideration was that any plan that involved moving strong army and navy forces into the Far East meant accepting "considerable danger" in the Atlantic and probably curtailing assistance to Great Britain.

Since the support given Great Britain in the Atlantic might determine the outcome of the present war, Stark suggested a compromise. Why not plan for a war in the Pacific with a "more limited objective than complete Japanese defeat?" This would be a war undertaken "only in cooperation with the British and the Dutch, and in which they undertake to provide an effective and continued resistance in Malaysia." This "limited war" would require absolute assurance that the British and Dutch would cooperate in resisting Japanese aggression. Even if assurance were gained, Stark did not believe that they could defend the Malay Barrier for long without help from the American Asiatic Fleet, reinforced by ships and planes from Hawaii, and "possibly even by troops." However, he thought it was out of the question to send the entire fleet to Singapore. The facilities were too limited, supply too difficult, and Hawaii, Alaska, and the United States mainland too open to Japanese raids.

Admiral Stark realized, though, that no plan for Pacific war would be entirely satisfactory. For example, there was always the bothersome issue of public opinion. If Stark's "limited war" were being fought in the Pacific and there were serious reverses, the American public might bring "great pressure to bear" to turn full attention to that region. By insisting that an all-out effort be made in what had been planned as a limited war, the public might force a fight to the finish against Japan. In that case, all American strength might be vitiated in the Far East with little remaining for "eventualities" in the Atlantic.

Even if the United States entered the war as an ally of Great Britain and it were possible to keep Japan out, the task of winning the war in Europe would be formidable. The British, Stark knew, were expecting extensive naval assistance, but naval assistance would not *assure* victory. He believed that the United States would need to assist at sea *and* to send "large air and land forces to Europe or Africa, or both, and to participate strongly in this land offensive."

With this detailed statement as prologue, Stark moved to his conclusions. He realized that the United States wanted peace; however, since there was a strong likelihood of war, he recommended determining expeditiously a "national policy with mutually supporting diplomatic and military aspects" to assure that any involvement would "ultimately best promote our own national interests." Until such a policy was developed and "authoritatively" approved, he could not determine "the scale and the nature of the effort" required by the U.S. Navy. He then proceeded to pose four alternative plans for American action: Plan A: hemispheric defense and security in both oceans; Plan B: offensive action in the Pacific with assurance of British and Dutch assistance, while remaining on the defensive in the Atlantic; Plan C: assistance to allies in the Atlantic and Pacific and preparing to fight on two fronts; or Plan

D: an eventual strong offensive in the Atlantic in alliance with the British and a defensive posture in the Pacific. For the moment the United States should concentrate on hemispheric defense (Plan A), but efforts and plans should be directed toward Plan D (or Plan Dog). He made this recommendation in full recognition that an Atlantic First policy might require a "full-scale land offensive" made especially costly "should Great Britain collapse." He also realized that adoption of Plan D would limit American influence in the Pacific, but since neither Plan A, Plan B, nor Plan C offered enough assistance to assure British survival, there was no other reasonable alternative. Even full assistance in the Atlantic would not assure Allied victory, he wrote; chances, however, were in America's favor, "particularly if we insist upon full equality in the political and military direction of the war."

Whatever decision the president made, the chief of naval operations believed that a "complete Joint Plan for guiding Army and Navy activities" should be drawn up immediately. Basic to this plan should be the concept that no operations should be undertaken in the Far East or mid-Pacific that would "prevent the Navy from promptly moving to the Atlantic forces fully adequate to safeguard our interests and policies in the event of a British collapse." Furthermore, and most important for judging his attitude toward British intentions, he did not believe that the United States should "willingly engage in any war against Japan unless we are certain of aid from Great Britain and the Netherlands East Indies."

To be certain that the United States received aid, he recommended a "clear understanding between the nations involved as to the strength and extent of the participation which may be expected in any particular theatre, and as to a proposed skeleton plan of operations." Therefore, he concluded that "secret staff talks on technical matters with British military and naval authorities in London, with Canadian military authorities in Washington, and with British and Dutch authorities in Singapore and Batavia" should begin at once. As well as being prudent, these staff talks were vital to the realization of "full equality in the political and military direction of the war." Without staff talks the United States would be caught between its own lack of preparation and British miscalculation. Richardson's hand was evident in much of Stark's paper, but the credit for development rests with the anxious, insecure Stark. Despite the frustrations of his position, he had been able to cut through the years of misgivings about the ORANGE plan and point the way to a new course.

Even while applauding his accomplishment, one does wonder what really prompted Stark to settle the dispute by not only accepting, but proposing, an Atlantic orientation for the U.S. Navy. The primary factor undoubtedly was that he believed that policy to be best for the country no matter what the narrower interests of his service dictated. At the same time he may have had some ulterior motives. One important factor that he could hardly have ignored was that while offering a route around dissension among his senior commanders and with the army, Plan Dog also made it more likely that the president could be spurred into action. Positive moves were especially desirable for Stark who was probably as anxious about America's defense posture as anyone in Washington. If the admiral had serious difficulty selling the navy on his strategy, he could have pointed out that any agreement was changeable. If events dictated, or if the British became too difficult, it was always possible for the United States to return to its time-honored posture of Pacific First. But for the moment there was only one strategy upon which agreement was possible with the army and possible with the British and Stark was courageous enough to push it.

One of Stark's most practical reasons for seeking some form of agreement was British vulnerability. In light of British inability to assure security on the Atlantic frontier, all other objections to a Pacific offensive shrank to insignificance. British weakness was the best argument for the assertion of American strength in the Atlantic.

Plan Dog was not the place to mention it, but it could hardly have escaped Stark's notice that this assertion, coupled with the 92 percent increase in naval strength approved by Congress, would eventuate in America's becoming the world's primary naval power. The ships that naval enthusiasts had been seeking for fifty years were now authorized, and when that additional 1.3 million tons came through, America would rule the waves. Plan Dog outlined a mission second to none for a navy second to none. No more searching for a role in the liquid wastes of the Western Pacific. No more bickering with the army over how long before the Philippines could be relieved.

But before those happy days would dawn, America must keep Britain from faltering through weakness or miscalculation. From letters he wrote on 12 and 16 November it is obvious that Stark was less than impressed by British intuition and reliability. Upon learning that the British expected the United States to enter the war soon after the presidential election, Stark suggested that this assumption was

merely another evidence of their slack ways of thought, and of their non-realistic views of international political conditions, and of our own political system. They have been talking in a large way about the defense of the Malay Barrier, with an alliance between themselves, us, and the Dutch, without much thought as to what the effect would be in Europe. But we have no idea as to whether they would at once begin to fight were the Dutch alone, or were we alone, to be attacked by the Japanese.[33]

But, as he noted in another letter, "[W]hen I think over their diplomacy for the past several years I am not surprised at their present guess-work."[34] With Britain faltering so badly it was high time for the United States to play a more prominent role; indeed, America's positive course was based largely on negative views about Britain's ability and future. Now if they wanted staff talks the U.S. Navy at least was ready.

13.

Agreement at Last

With Admiral Stark settled on a policy for advancing America's interests while safeguarding Britain's, all appeared ready for Anglo-American strategic cooperation. Even so, some complex problems remained unresolved, and as Stark's paper was circulating between the departments of State, War, and Navy, new interdepartmental bickering surfaced. Considering the enormity of the decisions, some debate and consequently some delay was to be expected, particularly in a country just recovering from elections.

Lack of leadership and a requirement for subterfuge also inhibited progress, for to an extent the president had become the prisoner of the noninterventionist opinion to which he had catered during the political campaign. Having done little to educate the public either about his covert policies or about America's legitimate interests in the conflict, Roosevelt now faced an electorate that expected fulfillment of his promises. The only solution seemed to be continued deception and increased caution. So cautious was he that for years it was difficult to determine what actions he took or what actions he allowed to be taken in his name.

The record is far easier to trace in London where there was little effort to conceal the enthusiasm for staff talks. But even in London there were unresolved interdepartmental differences about priorities and methods. In the face of these differences, Winston Churchill offered bold leadership. Forget the subtleties, he advised, get the Americans involved—first in talks, then in war. If accomplishing that goal necessitated reinforcing American fears of British collapse, so be it. If British strategic concepts had to be subordinated, so be that also; any nuances or misconceptions could be dealt with after America was involved in hostilities. The Far East was the obvious point of contention, but as Churchill was to recall, that area basked in a "sinister twilight" anyhow. Once the Americans were fighting beside Britain the illumination would improve.

* * *

While Stark and others had been hard at work attempting to give direction to American security policy, Ghormley had dangled at the end of his tenuous communications line. He still awaited detailed instructions concerning staff conversations, although he had finally received on 11 November a copy of the ten assumptions drawn up during Admiral Richardson's visit to Washington. These assumptions provided the basis for a meeting at the Admiralty on 19 November between Captain Kirk, Lieutenant Commander Austin, and admirals Ghormley, Pound, and Bailey. As may be recalled, one important assumption was that the British could hold the Atlantic frontier unassisted while the U.S. Navy engaged in a blockade and possibly a war with Japan. Captain Kirk considered that assumption "dangerous" and Admiral Bailey was asked to comment.[1]

Bailey, who had been informed by Captain Clarke almost three weeks before that the Americans were considering shifting their focus from the Pacific to the Atlantic, found the assumption that America was going to put her major effort in the Pacific confusing, but he replied with a strategic overview. Policy in the Far East should be directed toward containing Japan, if possible, north of the Netherlands East Indies and Singapore, while pinching it economically so it could not assist the Axis. If the situation were handled without provoking war, Japan could be dealt with after Italy and Germany had been defeated. Singapore was the key; the United States should base her Pacific Fleet, or a substantial part of it, at Singapore and thus deter Japan from moving south. This disposition would free any remaining American forces to assist the Royal Navy in the Atlantic. With this reference to assisting the Royal Navy, Bailey sidestepped the question of whether the British could hold the Atlantic frontier unassisted.[2] Ghormley immediately observed that putting most of America's capital ships at Singapore would raise questions in the United States about the security of the West Coast. Lord Lothian had anticipated this problem and Admiral Bellairs answered that studies had shown how difficult it would be for the Imperial Navy to carry out anything other than "tip and run" raids.

But even if the West Coast did not face imminent invasion, where were the ships to be found to perform all the tasks the British wanted the U.S. Navy to undertake? In the British plan, the United States would contain the Japanese in the Pacific and would help in the Atlantic with submarine patrols, escort convoys, and antiraider activities. In other words, full American effort was desired in both oceans. Kirk's concern was well founded.

On 19 November, the day that Ghormley attended this meeting, Admiral Stark wrote him that Plan Dog had not elicited the hoped-for presidential direction. In fact, the chief of naval operations had "no further word of any kind from higher up." Despite this silence, Stark was going to show a final copy of Plan Dog to Captain Clarke, but the British officer would neither be allowed outside the Navy Department while reading it nor permitted to take notes. Ghormley would receive a copy, but Stark wanted the British told that the plan was "strictly unofficial," that it was unsponsored and unauthorized "by either [the] State Department or [the] President."[3]

Stark was as good as his word. On 20 November Clarke was shown what he called the "final version of the naval staff's appreciation." The chief of naval operations expected Clarke to report home what he learned, and he mentioned that it would be "useful if the Prime Minister endorsed the basic suggestions contained in Plan Dog."[4] That Clarke was not allowed to take notes was no obstacle. Sir Maurice Hankey's prejudice against stenographers required an unusual ability to recall and record accurately; that was the job Clarke had trained for, and in which he had operated with distinction for four years. So he sent a lengthy and accurate résumé to London.[5]

In London, Clarke's report quickly made its way to the prime minister, who had studied it and pronounced it "most highly adapted" to British interests. Whereas the president had "shied away" from endorsing the document, the prime minister enthusiastically accepted it almost without reservation. On 22 November he wrote the first sea lord:

1. In my view Admiral Stark is right, and Plan D is strategically sound and also most highly adapted to our interests. We should therefore, so far as opportunity serves, in every way contribute to strengthen the policy of Admiral Stark, and should not use arguments inconsistent with it.

2. Should Japan enter the war on one side and the United States on ours, ample naval forces will be available to contain Japan by long-range controls in the Pacific. The Japanese Navy is not likely to venture far from its home bases so long as the superior battle-fleet is maintained at Singapore or at Honolulu. The Japanese would never attempt a siege of Singapore with a hostile, superior American Fleet in the Pacific. The balance of the American Fleet, after providing the necessary force for the Pacific, would be sufficient, with our Navy, to exercise in a very high degree the command of all the seas and oceans except those within the immediate Japanese regions. A strict defensive in the Far East and the acceptance of its consequences is also our policy. Once the Germans are beaten the Japanese would be at the mercy of the combined fleets.

3. I am much encouraged by the American naval view. *The paragraphs about our being incapable of winning alone are particularly helpful.*[6]

In short, Churchill was very willing to exploit American doubts about British inability to win unassisted. But had his eagerness for immediate aid caused him to overlook the long-range implications of the American naval chief's initiatives and grim forecasts? Had Churchill grasped all the implications of the American presence in the Atlantic or of the eventual land offensive Stark had recommended? Did the prime minister see that if the U.S. Navy shifted major units to the Atlantic the United States would no longer have a "superior" fleet on Japan's flank protecting Singapore? And did he realize that Far Eastern requirements would have to assume a higher priority for the British if they were to assume a lower one for the Americans? These details Churchill was willing to skim over; everything paled next to getting the United States committed to some forward policy.

Neither the Royal Navy nor the Foreign Office saw the issue in such simple terms. The Admiralty in particular was horrified to find that the U.S. Navy was not only willing to give up virtually all Allied positions in the Pacific west of Hawaii, but it was also opposed to basing on Singapore, the best place, in the Royal Navy's view, for checkmating Japan. The Admiralty's point was that logical force dispersal made it unnecessary for either country to give up valuable positions in the Far East. America was not likely to take this more balanced view, however, if British spokesmen continued to emphasize Britain's precarious position. The Admiralty, and some elements at the Foreign Office one assumes, hoped that Churchill could be persuaded to be more reasonable and less pessimistic in his comments.[7]

But the most immediate task was to influence American strategic thinking before it became set. From what Clarke wrote, it appeared that Stark was awaiting a presidential decision before proceeding with staff conversations, thus insuring a coordinated U.S. position. That was logical, but it also would exclude the British from having a say in U.S. policy during its formative stages and the Admiralty objected to that exclusion. The Foreign Office agreed that it would help to be "in on the ground floor" but doubted that Britain could hope to exercise much influence before the talks began. The best procedure was to get the delegates to America before U.S. planners adopted any rigid policy. Thus, despite the Royal Navy's disagreement with Churchill's expediency-is-all approach, speed seemed the only answer.[8] There was one other way in which the Admiralty might advance their case and that was through Ghormley; if the special naval observer could be convinced of Singapore's value, perhaps the U.S. Navy could be influenced. The task of selling Ghormley was renewed on 22 November, when he met again with Admiral Bailey's group. In the discussion that ensued Ghormley said that he was not fully aware of Washington's current planning,[9] but he did know that the Navy Department was reconciled to "temporarily" abandoning Singapore, the Netherlands East Indies, and the Philippines.[10] Then he proceeded to outline the old ORANGE plan under the terms of which the U.S. Fleet based on Pearl Harbor would slowly fight westward.

Admiral Bailey countered by presenting arguments against abandoning Singapore, even temporarily, before starting an offensive. The way to deter the Japanese, he said, was through a demonstration of resolve. Unfortunately, the British had no capital ships available to demonstrate resolve, but American ships would do nicely. Indeed, they had worked out a table calling for ten battleships at Singapore, five in the Atlantic, and none at Hawaii. The British then ran through the familiar arguments for favoring

Singapore over Pearl Harbor as a base. Ghormley countered by warning that the Navy Department would oppose sending that many battleships to Singapore, and, even if they did not, the American public would never stand for it. The British, however, held out for a study of Singapore's facilities and for some staff work on a possible U.S. Fleet movement to that port.[11]

* * *

Meanwhile President Roosevelt was still not giving Stark the direction he requested. Apparently the president was seeking to avoid accountability, public or private, for reorienting American strategy. This avoidance of responsibility could only work if someone else were willing to carry the burden. Stark seemed the likely candidate. Roosevelt did venture his opinion on Plan D to the chief of naval operations but swore him to secrecy on the details; however, we do know that the president asked Stark to coordinate the plan with the army and the Department of State.[12] At the very least, therefore, it can be assumed that Roosevelt did not reject Plan Dog.

Coordination was not easy. In the first place there was the army to deal with. If the ORANGE plan, to which they had long objected, was now on its way out, the army planners wanted to eliminate it completely. Therefore, they reviewed Stark's paper very carefully, lest by oversight they give endorsement to *any* offensive action in the Pacific. This caution was apparent in the preliminary report on Plan D sent by the acting chief of the War Plans Division, Colonel J. W. Anderson, to General Marshall. Colonel Anderson observed that although his office was in "general agreement" with the recommendations, he wanted to be sure of two things: first, in any staff talks it should be clearly understood that "the United States shall retain complete control of its own forces"; second, any American intervention in the war must be "in accordance with alternative 'D,'" which in the Army's view meant "no material commitment in the Pacific."[13] Anderson did agree with Stark that Britain's position was precarious, that she needed military support from the United States in order to win, and that even with that aid, victory would come only after a long war.[14]

Marshall apparently agreed with these objections, for while the Plans Division was working on Stark's paper, he wrote Stark warning that Germany would be pleased to see the United States make a serious commitment in the Pacific. Therefore he fully accepted the concept of relieving the British of obligations in the Atlantic and letting them use the ships thus freed to support their own forces in the Far East.[15]

The other problem came from the Department of State. Roosevelt had asked Stark to get the department's reaction and Stark had tried. However, Secretary Hull was being tendentious again, observing that, although in "general agreement," he doubted the "propriety of joining in the submission to the President of a technical military statement."[16] The department was not averse at times to encouraging the use of the fleet to intimidate the Japanese, but the secretary was very cautious about committing himself on "technical" military actions.

Stark could wait while the plan was reviewed by the army and he accepted the Department of State's recalcitrance, but immediate action was called for on staff conferences. In his view, the British were so dangerously unrealistic that it was essential to learn more about their planning before becoming any more closely committed to them. As he wrote to General Marshall: "I do not know . . . whether or not they have any long-range plan for themselves, or whether they have realistic ideas as to what help they think they need from us to defeat Germany and Italy."[17] Therefore, with a cautious chief executive and a hesitant secretary of state, Stark decided to take, or at least to accept responsibility for taking, the initiative in bringing about the staff talks.

Stark later testified before a congressional committee that "when I asked them to come over initially I did not ask the President's permission nor that of the Secretary of the Navy." He added that the invitation to the British was made on his "own initiative" and that he had not informed the president until January, after the British representatives had arrived, that he was "going ahead."[18] General Marshall later stated that "Admiral Stark brought up the proposition and I acquiesced. He arranged the meeting."[19]

Indeed, Stark displayed so much initiative and so openly discussed the role he played in setting up the conferences that for a long time historians could not tell exactly who had conceived and pushed the talks.[20] It was not until British records were opened in 1972 that the real initiator could be identified. The president's penchant for secrecy has been amply documented in the preceding pages; the fact that his role in this particular development is not so amply documented would seem the result of a calculated oversight. Thus Stark's assertions now appear as attempts to protect his commander in chief.

With the aid of the new records, developments can be accurately summarized and Stark's contentions contradicted. On 25 November Ambassador Lothian, just back from London, called at the Department of State. The ambassador, in conformity with the strategy of gloom that he had urged on the Chiefs of Staff, told Hull that an attack was expected on Singapore. From this and other comments, Hull deduced that Lothian was suggesting "conferences between the naval experts" of Britain and America to make contingency plans in case of war with Japan. Moreover, Lothian said that the present arrangement was not sufficient, for although the Admiralty considered Ghormley a "good man," he consistently declined to discuss possible future plans on grounds that he had no "authority."

Hull replied, with what is described as his "usual circumspection," that "of course, there could be no agreement entered into in this respect, but that there should undoubtedly be collaboration with the view of making known to each other any and all information practicable in regard to what both might have in mind to do, and when and where, in case of a military movement by Japan."

Lothian, possibly lost amidst this rhetoric, said again that "military consultations among appropriate officials" were needed. Singapore, specifically, should be discussed because some British experts believed that the U.S. Navy should base its fleet there. Hull wrote, "I merely remarked that that was a matter for experts to pass on, and he said he hoped that there would be discussion between his and our high naval officials with respect to all phases of the Pacific situation."[21]

Precisely what Hull said will, of course, never be determined, but questions are raised about his or Lothian's veracity by the British ambassador's report of this conversation. According to Lothian, Hull said that "he would immediately take the matter [of staff conversations] up with the President and the Navy Department."[22] No record has yet been found of when and how, or whether, Hull took this matter up with the president. In view of his campaign promises, however, Roosevelt would probably not have wanted records kept that would have implicated him in Anglo-American planning.

The British had no such reservations and their records now reveal that the president himself did authorize the formal staff conversations. On 29 November electrifying news arrived in London that set every wheel in the British conference machinery spinning. Lothian's report read: "The President has now agreed to staff talks taking place in Washington. . . . It is of the utmost importance however that no knowledge of this should be allowed to obtain any kind of publicity. The officers should come over here attached in some way to British Purchasing Commission as if they were here for the purpose of export advice or inspection. Admiral Ghormley is being instructed to accompany them over."[23]

There is no more specific reference to how Lothian learned of this agreement. However, no one would have spoken in such definitive terms without express presidential approval, nor would an experienced diplomat have acted on such a momentous issue without being sure that his source was reliable. Thus we can be sure that, even though he may have hidden behind someone (previously Welles had sometimes been used), the president had spoken.

* * *

Ghormley was not officially advised of the president's agreement to talks until 2 December, when he and Brigadier General Raymond E. Lee (Lee had been promoted in November) were ordered to return to Washington for staff conversations.[24] Prior to coming they were instructed to enter into discussions with the British on some hypothetical situations. The situations proposed clearly mirrored the American shift in emphasis to the Atlantic. For instance, it was suggested that the United States would restrict its offensive action in the Pacific to those areas east of 160° east longitude. This line passes between Australia and New Zealand and would thus exclude Singapore and the Philippine Islands. At the same time it was suggested that the United States, in cooperation with the British possessions and Dominions in the Western Hemisphere, would "discharge allied responsibilities" between 30° and 180° west longitude. That would be from the international date line in the Pacific to the vicinity of the Azores in the Eastern Atlantic. Furthermore, the British chiefs were asked for information on the American forces required in the Atlantic area, specifically in Iceland, and the British Isles. And finally, the Americans wanted to know the general outlines of the British war plans for the next two years.[25]

Although these questions and assumptions presaged more cooperation and aid in the Atlantic sphere and would consume the greater part of the conversations, the Far East would also have to be discussed. If there was any doubt that the Admiralty and the Navy Department had differing priorities regarding that area, it was swept away when Ghormley relayed to Washington a review of Admiralty strategy provided by the first sea lord.[26] The paper began by suggesting that Germany and Italy were the primary objectives and that the goal in the Pacific was to contain the Japanese. However, the British staff believed that Singapore must be held "at all costs." Thus the United States should send at least nine capital ships, with carriers, cruisers, and auxiliaries to be "based at Singapore." Admiral Pound said that the British capabilities were stretched to the limit in the Atlantic. They would continue to do their best, but five United States capital ships would be a big help.

This message was not welcome in Washington. The British paper, Stark wired, "does not provide sufficient support for United States interests and therefore is unacceptable." Ghormley was directed to advise the British that their representatives must come to Washington with instructions to "discuss concepts based on equality of consideration for both [the] British Commonwealth and [the] United States and realistically explore the various fields of war cooperation." This was essential, for Admiral Stark and General Marshall were agreed that if the British representatives were going to be "restricted to the concept stated . . . as the only basis of discussion . . . there will be no purpose in talks."[27]

The Admiralty's ploy of convincing the U.S. Navy via Admiral Ghormley of Singapore's importance had clearly failed and the prime minister acted promptly to head off further debate. After noting how strongly Stark had reacted, Churchill observed: "There is no use in putting before them a naval policy which they will not accept, and which will only offend them and make it more difficult to bring them into the war. If they prefer Hawaii to Singapore there is no more to be said. Pray bring this minute to the notice of the Admiralty."[28]

While Churchill was counseling discretion, Ghormley was suggesting that the Admiralty not take Stark's reaction too much to heart. The day after he sent the Navy Department's comments to Admiral Bailey, Ghormley stopped by to explain. He regretted Stark's implication that the British representatives would take a "cast-iron" position from which they would not budge. He understood the British view, but the Navy Department, he explained, was buffeted from a number of directions. First, there was the press, which would leap on any suggestion that the U.S. Navy was neglecting the West Coast or the Atlantic seaboard. Then, Stark knew that some people were unconvinced that Great Britain could win "even with full United States assistance," so why, they would ask, should the navy defend Singapore while it denuded American positions? It was just the kind of move that critics would brand "pulling British chestnuts out of the fire." Obviously, Ghormley said, these reactions reflected a lack of appreciation for the "vital importance of Singapore to the British Empire, and therefore indirectly to the United States," but the public did not grasp that concept and it possibly was not fully accepted even at the Navy Department.[29]

Reacting both to Churchill's minute and Ghormley's conciliatory visit, Bailey hastened to advise Ghormley that the views to which Stark objected were neither official nor immutable. Perhaps American sensitivities had not been taken sufficiently into consideration, Bailey said, and it was unfortunate that Stark had misunderstood the British position. Ghormley reported these reassuring comments to Washington, adding his conviction that the British delegates would approach the staff talks with a "spirit of full cooperation and willingness to recognize [the] special interests of the United States."[30]

As a further demonstration of cooperative resolve, the director of British naval intelligence told Captain Kirk that the time was "ripe for some general understanding" regarding postwar ship construction, since the two navies "by private prearrangement could create a mutually advantageous situation prior to any peace conference giving us [the United States and Great Britain] together pretty general control of the world's trade routes." Captain Kirk advised Washington of this statement, observing that it was a striking example of British prescience. At the same time it was vaguely disquieting to see that the role of British sea power in the postwar world was never far from their minds.[31]

That postwar world would have to be prepared for without the services of one of England's most faithful servants. Lord Lothian, who had done so much to advance the cause of Anglo-American cooperation, died on 11 December 1940 just as the final adjustments for the staff conversations were being made. As a practicing Christian Scientist, Lothian had not called a doctor when he became ill on 8 December and his death came quickly. It was greeted with shock and remorse on both sides of the Atlantic. The agreement on staff talks that he had signaled just two weeks before was not his last act of service to his country, but it capped a long career of trying to bring the two countries closer together. Untangling the complications between the two nations may have been his important contribution to Anglo-American affairs.

For this very reason it was important, in the view of some Americans, that his death should not be used as an occasion for delaying those talks. General Lee knew the British very well and although he was pleased that the talks were to take place, he was displeased by British plan-changing and backpedaling about the date for the delegation's departure. Presumably the delays resulted from the need to select and brief an ambassador to replace Lothian, but Lee began to suspect an ulterior motive. The British first suggested 19 December, but that was finally pushed back to 15 January, when the British and American officers would sail for America aboard the battleship *King George V*. Lee's basic supposition was that the British would not want the United States to play any larger role in the war than necessary. In the last few weeks the war had begun to go better in Africa where the Eighth Army was driving the Italians back, in Greece where that tiny nation's forces were putting up bitter resistance, and even in England where the air raids had generally tapered off. He sensed that all this contributed to a euphoria in the ranks of the British high command. If they thought that victory might come soon, they would not want any closer alliance with America because, as Lee put it, they would not want the United States at the peace table "for fear some of our soft idealism" would infect the terms. The best way to keep America away from the peace table was to keep America away from the war. Thus the British might be stalling on staff talks, awaiting developments on the battlefield. He relayed his suspicions to Herschel Johnson, chargé of the Embassy, to Admiral Ghormley, and, indirectly, to his superiors in Washington.[32]

* * *

There actually was no need to reinforce suspicions of British motives in Washington where American planners were attempting to put affairs in order for the conference. By 12 December the U.S. Army War Plans Division had finished reviewing Plan D and had forwarded it to the chief of staff. Their objections had not been major; they did believe that there should have been some discussion of alternatives to RAINBOW 3 and they objected to the statement that the United States should not "willingly engage in any war against Japan unless we are certain of aid from Great Britain and the Netherlands East Indies." That was changed to read "the United States ought not willingly engage in any war against Japan." Moreover they thought that counting on Britain still to be available as a staging area for an attack on Germany was overly optimistic.[33]

Stark probably accepted, reluctantly, the army's pessimism about the British Isles. Churchill and Lothian had by now succeeded in convincing some Americans that Britain was on the brink of disaster. Stark, for one, believed that with the current rate of losses in the Atlantic, England could not hold out six months.[34] Under those conditions haste seemed in order and the revisions to Plan D were quickly accomplished. The plan thus became the new basis for American war planning and it was used in preparing the agenda for the forthcoming talks and as the basis for instructions to the American delegations.

Running through these instructions and other relevant papers there is a persistent note of suspicion which makes it clear that caution and cooperation were to be intermingled in the American approach.[35] In this regard the memorandum drawn up by the Joint Planning Committee for use by the Joint Board in formulating the instructions to the American delegates is especially noteworthy. The paper opened by observing that British political leadership, with Churchill among a small group of exceptions, had been none too good. Therefore, the United States could not afford and did not need to "entrust our national future to British direction, because the United States can safeguard the North American continent and probably the Western Hemisphere, whether allied with

Britain or not." The Planning Committee did not think that Britain could defeat Germany without "direct military assistance" and increased material aid, and even with these advantages the results were not certain. The admonition for caution and skepticism was summed up this way: "It is to be expected that the proposals of the British representatives will have been drawn up with chief regard for the support of the British Commonwealth. Never absent from British minds are their postwar interests, commercial and military. We should likewise safeguard our own interests."[36]

Considering the prejudices of Captain Turner, the navy's chief planner who had briefed Captain Clarke, the statement about British interest in protecting the "Commonwealth" could be read specifically to mean British interest in protecting Singapore and generally to mean British interest in protecting the Empire. Inherent, but unstated, was the concept that those interests were not the ones America should be safeguarding. Making this concept especially relevant was the suggestion that Britain could not win without direct American military help and perhaps not even then. Wisdom dictated not being drawn into any commitments in peripheral theaters of war, particularly when the major theater was in such jeopardy. Stated another way: beware perfidious Albion, especially a decrepit, perfidious Albion.[37]

Even Ghormley, who was at least predisposed to be sympathetic toward the British, advised Washington to premise its preparations for the talks on the "sound assumption that the United States and the Western Hemisphere must be protected even though Great Britain may collapse."[38] Presumably Churchill, who had welcomed Stark's doubts about Britain's weakness, would have welcomed this premise as well.

Undoubtedly aware of possible American suspicions, the British were carefully assessing the proper way to present their case. There seems to be no indication that Lee's suspicions about British stalling were accurate, but at the same time, they were expending every effort to make their case persuasively. Lengthy papers were drawn up and care was exercised to see that the method and attitude of the United Kingdom delegation should in no way offend the Americans. One problem was the old dilemma: what to tell the Americans and what not to tell them. The Chiefs of Staff felt that it would be poor policy to allow the Americans to think that information was being withheld. The prime minister agreed that it would be "unwise to withhold pertinent information," but at the same time the delegation should not provide "details of impending operations," confining themselves instead to "general explanations" that were to be shared with the smallest possible circle of Americans.

As far as the attitude was concerned, Churchill felt that the delegation should be deferential to the views of the United States "in all matters concerning the Pacific theatre." "It would be most unwise," he went on, "to try to force our views on naval strategy in that theatre upon the U.S. Naval authorities." In fact, the delegation should openly state that American views on Pacific strategy would prevail. On Singapore they should say that they were not asking the Americans to protect British possessions, but rather that Singapore was there for the Americans to use if they wished. This deferential approach could hardly irritate the Americans, and maybe after they were in the war they would decide on their own that they wished to do more.[39]

Despite their sensitivities to U.S. reactions, the British did manage to antagonize the Americans. As already noted, General Lee was not satisfied that preparations were proceeding with sufficient alacrity. By 2 January 1941 his anxiety had increased. The Chiefs of Staff had scheduled a meeting with Lee, Ghormley, and Austin for that date and the military attaché thought he knew why. The British had been busy since early December drafting instructions, position papers, and answers to questions, but no American had yet seen any of these. As Lee hypothesized to Ghormley on the way to the meeting, the British were going to say that the papers were too secret to be revealed while there was any chance of breaches in security; therefore, they would propose making them available only after the delegates were safely aboard ship. While there was some logic in this approach, it meant that Washington would not be able to prepare counterproposals until after the delegation arrived, since neither Ghormley nor Lee would be able to communicate with their superiors once at sea.

Admiral Pound opened the meeting with an outline of the elaborate arrangements that were being made to transport the delegates to America. (Lee regarded this as "British window dressing," with which he was unpleasantly familiar.) Pound then outlined the plan for providing the documents to the American team. It was exactly as Lee suspected; they would not be given access to the papers until they were at sea. Then, to Lee's amazement, Ghormley not only told Pound that Lee had anticipated this proposal but also told the old admiral why it was unsatisfactory. As Lee said, this "rather queered the point," for Pound naturally replied that there was no need to advise Washington in advance since "it should not take long to agree on principles and the details then could be dealt with later." Lee approached the matter differently. He asked how urgent the British felt the issue of agreement was. Pound hemmed and hawed. General Sir John Dill chimed in, *sotto voce*, that unless they hurried spring would be upon them, but the point was lost and Lee gave up. The British procedure would be followed.

General Lee later recorded his reaction:

What I fear is: (a) our people, with their usual passion for haste, which will be increased in the present keyed-up mental attitude of the United States, will be inclined to accept proposals which the British had been cooking up for six weeks without examination; or (b) if the necessary time is taken to study them, history will catch up and pass us and there will again be reason for the cry "too late" which has dogged the democracies from the start. It is true that Pound made it plain that the British proposals were intended only as the basis for discussion. However, their delegates will hang on to them like leeches if I know the British character at all.[40]

He also reported his views to Washington, where they increased American suspicion of the British and their devious ways.

Although the British do not appear to have been suspicious of American motives, influential forces in the Admiralty clearly disagreed with American logic concerning Singapore and with the soft sell that Churchill was proposing. Despite the flexibility they had indicated to Ghormley and Stark, and despite Churchill's admonitions, Admiralty studies regarding the East Asian bases reflected a certain rigidity. On 7 January 1941 Ghormley informed Washington that Admiral Pound had just advised him that (1) "Singapore is the only naval base in the Far East available to American, British, and other Allied Forces"; (2) the Singapore base is "most important" because of British interests in India, Malaysia, Australia, New Zealand, and Persia; (3) if Singapore were held it would probably prevent the Philippines from being overrun by the Japanese; (4) nine United States battleships, plus support craft, would hold Singapore "until such time as Germany and Italy are disposed of. At that time, if Japan had not already folded up, a United States effort could be made against them"; (5) "Three U.S. battleships, supported by a cruiser, destroyers, and light cruisers, would prevent any raids against the American West Coast or North Pacific holdings"; and (6) the present force patrolling the Atlantic would be enough to assist convoy work, oppose German raiders, and "prevent aggressions against the Western Hemisphere by the Axis powers." Ghormley made no comment to Pound, but he confided to Stark his view that it would be "dangerous" to count on Britain holding the Atlantic without considerable assistance from the United States.[41]

This was another of those admonitions that Washington really did not need. But less than a week remained before the delegates departed and soon U.S. Navy Department officials could themselves comment on the proper Anglo-American naval strategy.

* * *

The preparatory period that was now drawing to a close had been, depending on one's perspective, either agonizingly long or amazingly brief. Mutual suspicions obviously played a role in retarding progress, but there also was undoubtedly a connection between the staff talks and a number of other issues. For instance, the destroyers had been delivered, but they had not been as combat-ready as hoped or as advertised. In part that explained British reluctance to meet American demands as far as the bases were concerned. To untangle the snarl a Base-Lease Commission had been appointed and was to begin meeting in London in January. Scientific and technological exchanges were also stalled. On 25 October 1940 a detailed agreement calling for extensive exchanges had been approved. Included in that agreement were plans for establishing permanent research and development missions in London and Washington.[42] Despite that apparent move toward full cooperation there were still delays in London. The British had a temporary mission in the United States, but no formal invitation for establishing a U.S. mission in London was dispatched until 20 January 1941.

That some aid program for England was urgently needed was also becoming increasingly obvious. On 23 November Lothian, who had advised his superiors in London to "strike while the iron is hot," had followed his own advice. To a startled group of American reporters he bluntly announced "Britain's broke; it's your money we want."[43] The British government followed this general statement on 8 December with Churchill's detailed and eloquent plea to President Roosevelt for aid.[44] No immediate reply was forthcoming. Lothian's unexpected death on 11 December no doubt contributed to the delays and backlog of unfinished business, but it is not difficult to see (with a perspective of thirty-five years after the fact) that the various items on the agenda were connected. When progress was made on one issue, progress was made on all. It was a bargaining relationship that was simply becoming more complex.

Ghormley was hardly the man to coordinate complex agreements. Not only was he out of date and often out of touch with his superiors, but also, as we have seen, he was not inclined, by nature or by training, to make independent decisions. His work in London had, however, provided a good review of the possibilities for strategic cooperation. The review made the situation quite clear: it would be easy to work together in the Atlantic, difficult in the Pacific.

Roosevelt and Churchill might have resolved the Pacific conundrum or at least narrowed the differences. When alliance finally came they often mediated between their staffs; however, the relationship between the two men had not developed to that point yet, so mediation, such as it was, fell to others. Admiral Stark's views about shifting the focus from the Pacific to the Atlantic obviously reflected the president's own strategic thinking although Roosevelt did not care to associate himself formally with Plan Dog. More or less the same can be said for staff talks; Roosevelt was perfectly willing for them to go forward so long as the White House was in no way implicated.

For his part Churchill was not going to get involved in sorting out Pacific differences; he was willing to act as though there were no differences. As far as staff talks were concerned, the prime minister was a later convert to the ranks of the enthusiasts, having originally opposed them on the grounds that they would pivot on the fate of the British Fleet. As he became more eager to ensnare the Americans, however, his reservations faded and he became eager to hold talks, viewing them as a long step down the road to commitment.

Curiously, the secret-correspondence link between the two leaders revealed nothing of these shifting motives and world views; in fact, the subject of coordinated strategy was not even mentioned in their correspondence during this period. Roosevelt did send Harry Hopkins to London as a special emissary in late December 1940, but Hopkins's mission was more personal than professional and by the time he arrived it was too late to influence agendas or procedures.

Indeed by January 1941 America had already made strategic determinations that would have lasting historical significance. The agreement to hold staff talks was, as Churchill hoped, a definite move toward commitment, but it also was a sign that America intended to play an important role in the formulation of Anglo-American strategy. Obviously influencing the talks was the fear that Britain would fall without, and possibly even with, massive doses of American aid. This anticipation had certainly been heightened by Churchill and Lothian, perhaps without full realization of the implications of America's resultant shift of emphasis from the Pacific to the Atlantic. One of those implications was that if a vacuum in world leadership was near or even possible, the United States wanted to be in a position to fill the void; once filled it would be difficult for Britain to reassume her former leadership.

Viewed in this light, the determination of American strategy in 1940 had a significant and lasting effect on the nation's destiny. As long as America had been willing to assume a primary role in a secondary theater, her power position had been compromised. Now the torch of leadership was practically being tossed into her lap; it was an opportunity not to be missed. Thus America's decision to act as the world's primary naval power can be dated from the time when Plan Dog and the Atlantic First concept were tacitly accepted as national policy. The naval construction authorizations of 1940 had guaranteed the largest navy in the world—now there was a plan to use it. The coming staff talks would be either America's last act as a secondary power or its first act as the major power in the Western world, but one thing was very obvious: America was going to plan for and fight the war on her own terms.

14.

"Heavy Weather" at ABC

14 January 1941–12 February 1941

Finally all seemed in readiness for what would be known as the ABC (American-British-Canadian) Conference.[1] These meetings, which would set the strategy for World War II, raised numerous issues and took two months to conclude. Security during the sessions, which ran from 29 January through 29 March, was above average for the Americans and few knew of ABC until the war was over. Then there was a storm of controversy, with some charging that the talks committed the United States to war and others contending that they involved only noncommitting, prudent contingency planning.[2]

In many ways the ABC Conference epitomized Anglo-American naval collaboration in the 1938–41 period because the same charges could have been made about earlier contacts. Most of the issues and problems raised during previous discussions were raised and either resolved or accepted as irreconcilable. All of the old prejudices and suspicions were in evidence as well, and competitiveness and bargaining were always just beneath the surface. Most representative of the competitive spirit was Rear Admiral (recently Captain) Richmond K. Turner. As director of plans, and a well-regarded member of Admiral Stark's official family, he had played a large role in formulating Plan Dog and in the preparations for the conference. Turner had little respect for British planning or performance and he longed for the day when the United States would supplant Britannia as ruler of the waves. On this subject and others Turner's attitude and performance provided a contrast to the cooperative aspects of the meetings.

At the same time, Turner and the other American delegates were determined that the conference should accomplish at least two things: (1) British endorsement for the new concept of a major role for the United States in the Atlantic with the concomitant release from obligations in the Far East; and (2) British recognition that Germany must be fought first and costly diversions in secondary theaters avoided. The British intent was simpler than the American. They wanted to get the United States into the war as quickly as possible. Naturally they had to be tactful about their desires and sometimes attempts at disingenuousness led the British to waver between indirectness, which added to the American suspicions, and heavy-handedness, which led to resentment.

The irony of the conference is that the single-minded British, usually so well organized, in this instance alienated the Americans most by their muddling. The problem was the unresolved difference between the Chiefs of Staff and the prime minister about strategy for the Far East, a debate that centered, it will be remembered, around Pound's determination to reinforce Singapore and Churchill's determination to leave it in limbo if agreement on the issue proved an obstacle to American entry into the war. For a time the British delegation at the conference seemed more intent on forwarding the strategy of the Chiefs of Staff and in the process almost broke up the Washington meetings.

The debate over the Lend-Lease Bill provided a counterpoint for the ABC Conference. On the same day that the delegates left London bound for the United States, hearings in Washington began on H.R. 1776, as the Lend-Lease Bill was symbolically numbered. Defended as the minimum action necessary to keep America out of war and attacked as a deeply laid plot to drag her in, the bill would take two months aborning.

While the debate over the bill proceeded in Congress and in the press, the ABC Conference was being conducted in camera at the Navy Department. Time after time the administration contended that Lend-Lease was essential to keep England fighting and America out of the war. On the floor of the Congress and in press conferences, commitments and plans to convoy or send American troops out of the hemisphere were denied repeatedly by administration spokesmen. But at the other end of Pennsylvania Avenue the military representatives of that same administration were conducting the first prewar staff conferences in American history and laying plans for convoying, building bases in the British Isles, and replacing British Tommys in Iceland with American GIs.

When H.R. 1776 finally passed the Senate on 11 March 1941, by a vote of 60–31, it was seen by friend and foe alike as congressional approval of administration sympathies. This $7-billion investment in British security, and the redevelopment of the American arms industry, may not have been the "new Magna Carta" described by Winston Churchill, but it was an open declaration of America's intent to stand behind Britain—at least with supplies. There would be no news conferences at the beginning or at the conclusion of the ABC talks, nor would there be any congressional debate or vote. This omission was unfortunate, for ABC was a telling indication of the administration's intent to stand behind Britain with ships and men. Although technically noncommitting, there is no doubt that ABC was as significant militarily as Lend-Lease was economically.

* * *

When General Lee and Admiral Ghormley arrived at King's Cross Station on the morning of 14 January 1941, they found a distinguished company assembled, presumably to bid farewell to Lord Halifax, who had resigned as foreign secretary to become Lord Lothian's successor in Washington. Among the dignitaries were Lord Beaverbrook, Anthony Eden (the new foreign secretary), Ernest Bevin, General Ismay, Prime Minister and Mrs. Churchill, and Harry Hopkins, President Roosevelt's special emissary to the prime minister.[3] The British delegation to the staff talks was also there, and included, along with Rear Admiral Bellairs, Rear Admiral V. H. Danckwerts, immediate past director of plans at the Admiralty; Major General Edwin Morris, previously director of plans at the War Office; and Lieutenant Colonel A. T. Cornwall-Jones, secretary from the War Cabinet Office. When they arrived, they would join Captain A. W. Clarke and Air Commodore John Slessor, who would provide background on American planning and attitudes. It was a strong team. With the exception of Clarke, everyone had had experience as war planners and they were assisted by the elaborate studies for an Anglo-American conference that the British had been planning for since July 1940.

The train headed north for Scapa Flow, the main base of the British home fleet. There the conference delegates and Lord and Lady Halifax boarded the new British battleship, *King George V* (*KG-V*, in navy parlance), for a wintry and potentially dangerous trip to America.

On 16 January, the day after the *KG-V* steamed out of Scapa Flow, Roosevelt convened a new U.S. coordinating body. In the wake of Plan Dog's circulation, and possibly to counterbalance British coordination, the old liaison committee had been superseded by an ad hoc national defense group consisting of the service secretaries and Secretary of State Hull.[4] It was this group, plus General Marshall and Admiral Stark, that met in the Oval Office to hear Roosevelt's views on U.S. strategic policy. Roosevelt's discussion was long and somewhat discursive, but he seemed to subscribe to the basic Plan Dog concept. He did not mention Stark's plan, but he did say that he wanted the U.S. Fleet to base on Pearl Harbor and be prepared to fight an essentially defensive war in the Pacific. Admiral Thomas Hart would have discretionary authority about how long to stay in the Philippines, which would not be reinforced, and where to go—Singapore or east—when he withdrew. In the Atlantic, the navy should be ready to convoy supplies to England and tighten the patrol along the North Atlantic coast. The army, according to the president, should pursue a "very conservative" course until its strength was more developed, its first foreign responsibility being protection of Latin America. One of Roosevelt's basic concerns was material aid to England, about whose fate he was pessimistic.[5] If Hitler attacked the United States any time soon, his principal objective would be to limit U.S. aid to England, so the president wanted to do everything possible to frustrate that aim by insuring a continued flow of goods. Although he did not say so, this would mean some form of naval aid to keep the sea-lanes open.

Roosevelt's performance was typical—forceful, but somewhat vague, and implying more (or was it less?) than he said. It was most noteworthy for being one of the very few comprehensive discussions on strategy that the president held with his military chiefs during the fall of 1940 and early spring of 1941. Stark and

Marshall were doubtless relieved to have insight into the president's views, especially since he seemed to be moving toward the Atlantic First concept. General Marshall was also in full sympathy with the conservatism approach, since he was neither eager to see his untrained troops deployed before they were ready nor willing to have equipment drained from his nascent divisions.[6] For his part, Admiral Stark had already accepted the necessity for all steps that the president had suggested, including escorting convoys.

At sea aboard the *KG-V*, which creaked and leaked, as new ships often do, Ghormley and Lee set to work with the British delegation on the planning papers the British had kept so secret. These documents covered the spectrum, but one paper that was to prove especially important asked for an overview of American plans for the Pacific area. That paper and the others proved to be "quite complete," and the two Americans spent considerable time reviewing them with their British counterparts.[7]

The atmosphere on board ship was not always conducive to contemplation, for it was a harrowing journey. For one thing, the weather was not particularly good: "Cold, passing blizzards, ice freezing on deck," wrote Ghormley one day, adding the next, "Ladies not out today and some of the Army not so good." For another, there were marauding submarines about (the warning chart showed seventeen in the North Atlantic on one day).[8] But everyone took the submarines blithely, and there was a stir of excitement when it was learned that President Roosevelt was to meet the *KG-V* as she entered Chesapeake Bay. Ghormley found the entire ship's company preparing for the possible arrival of the president on board.[9]

Charles Peake, Lord Halifax's private secretary, was determined not to leave this to chance. "We were all agreed," Peake noted, "that by hook or by crook the President should be brought aboard the *King George V.*" Peake even had a hoist devised so that the president and his wheelchair could be picked off the deck of his yacht and winched aboard.[10] Right on schedule, at 3:00 P.M. on 23 January 1941, the British battleship anchored off Annapolis, where it was met by the presidential yacht. Unfortunately for Charles Peake, but perhaps happily for the president, Lord and Lady Halifax were invited for high tea on the presidential yacht *Potomac*.[11] The weather was miserable, but Roosevelt's warmth made up for the intemperance of the elements. Halifax found the president to be so friendly and informal that within a moment the visitors were completely at ease and chatting in an intimate manner.[12]

There was not much time for relaxing and storytelling for Admiral Ghormley. On the day after the *KG-V* anchored he had meetings with Admiral Stark, Secretary Knox, and Admiral Turner.[13] It was then that Ghormley received his formal orders for the staff talks. As senior member of the naval committee, which was to act in cooperation with a similar army committee, he was to meet with the representatives of His Majesty's Government for the purpose of "reaching tentative agreement, and recommending engagements, concerning the methods and nature of military collabo-ration between the two nations should the United States decide to engage in war against the Axis Powers in common with the British Commonwealth of Nations."[14]

On the same day, the British received a briefing from Clarke, who spoke of the "stiff attitude of [the] Navy Department and rather intellectual outlook of Turner, Director of Plans."[15] Both sides held preliminary meetings among themselves and on Wednesday, 29 January, the first plenary session convened.

The Americans, perhaps recalling the advice about British guile, had uncharacteristically prepared an agenda for the discussions that provided the framework for the meetings.[16] The agenda called for the first session to be held in the office of the chief of naval operations. Originally, the opening remarks at the conference were to have been made by Undersecretary of State Sumner Welles. However, at the last moment it was decided that he should not appear nor would any representative from the Department of State. That strategy was designed to preserve the traditional American separation between civilian and military authority and at the same time reduce the level of implied commitment.[17] So the U.S. military chiefs, rather than Welles, made the opening statement. It was specifically intended to "discourage the British visitors at the outset from enterprises unacceptable to the United States," while channeling talks into areas of mutual interest.[18]

As written, the opening statement was lengthy and all the details need not be covered here; however, several points do give a clear indication of American attitudes. Priorities, for instance, as described by the chiefs, were to (1) exclude non-American influence from the Western Hemisphere; (2) give diplomatic and material assistance to the British Commonwealth; and (3) contain Japan. The American people, however, wished to stay out of war. Therefore, no "specific commitments" could be made and any plans would be "contingent upon the future political action of both nations." If the United States did decide to make war "in common with the British," the primary objective would be to defeat Germany and her allies. But this aim must be carried out so that the United States could "maintain dispositions which, under all eventualities, [would] prevent the extension in the Western Hemisphere of European or Asiatic political and military power." American power, in short, would not be dispersed in either ocean; it would instead remain ready for either Japanese attack or British collapse. This objective could best be fulfilled and victory most assured by using American strength in the Atlantic and concentrating on Germany first.

These views were obviously predicated on the hope that Japan could be kept out of the conflict. If the Japanese did enter the war in the Pacific, forces should be defensively deployed so that the United States could put primary emphasis on the Atlantic or "navally in the Mediterranean." It was not specifically stated, but the United States clearly had no intention of getting drawn into an offensive or defensive war because of Singapore.

The president had stressed the importance of supplying Britain in case of war in the Far East, and the chiefs' statement noted that the United States would "continue to furnish material aid to Great Britain." Some of the positive effect of this assurance was lost by the next clause, which, though realistic, was blunt: "[B]ut [the United States] will retain for building up its own forces material in such proportion as to provide for future security."[19]

Also frank and realistic was the allusion to the strategic position of the British Isles. Churchill had once feared that staff talks might include awkward questions about the fleet and its destination if the home islands were overrun, and for that reason he delayed the talks.[20] Apparently he had not delayed long enough, for the American chiefs wanted the talks to include examination of the "probable situations that might result from the loss of the British Isles." In fact, an estimate of the current strategic position of the British Commonwealth was requested as a preliminary to the meetings.[21]

In conclusion, Admiral Stark emphasized the need for secrecy, saying that stories in the press would cause a "most serious delay" in coordinating plans, would retard the passage of the Lend-Lease Bill, and "might well be disastrous." In this estimate he was no doubt correct. For although it was usually cloaked in congressional ambiguity, much of the case against the Lend-Lease Bill derived from doubt about Roosevelt's sincerity when he argued that it was intended to keep America out of the war. The president's credibility would have been seriously undermined had it been learned that a few blocks from the Capitol British and American officers were making plans for a coalition war. The British delegates did their best to remain inconspicuous, representing themselves as members of the British Purchasing Commission, and dressing in civilian clothes. However, since several of them looked almost Colonel Blimpish, Admiral Stark felt that further caution was necessary.[22]

With the guidelines established, the first meeting adjourned. There was no meeting the next day, but the British delegation gathered in preparation for the second session as they regularly did before and after every joint meeting. The Americans followed somewhat the same procedure but with less regularity. The preparatory meetings that the Americans did hold often hindered coordination because the two teams usually met separately and were thus prepared during plenary sessions to disagree on their conclusions. In contrast, the British worked as a unit. In fact, they only appointed a chairman, Danckwerts, in "deference to American ideas."[23] As usual, all members worked as equals with everyone's opinion being solicited without regard to rank or service so that, when they entered the conference room, it was an agreed-upon position they presented.[24]

This ability to work as a unit was obviously to the British advantage, but it was not the only factor in their favor. Professional experience, the size of their group, and their personal associations also helped. Furthermore, all were acquainted with the operations of the War Cabinet, where interservice and interdepartmental cooperation was a cardinal rule. They also were familiar with the formal process of minute taking and circulation; in fact, the minutes of this conference were drawn up on the British model and were primarily the product of Cornwall-Jones.

The Americans, on the other hand, had no equivalent to the Committee on Imperial Defense, and although they accepted British help on minute taking, they were neither accustomed to nor sympathetic toward interservice cooperation. All of these factors contributed to the displays of disagreement to which the Americans occasionally treated their guests. The British quickly noted this lack of harmony and tried to take advantage of it.[25]

The British did not, however, dominate the conference. For one thing, although their delegation presented a more united front, it was not nearly as single-minded as Churchill wanted it to be. Some Americans, moreover, were very suspicious of British motives (their efficiency would do little to dispel these doubts) and the Planning Committee had acted to put the U.S. delegation on guard.[26] Also, the Americans were in their capital, and whether it allowed for quick decisions or not, that was a tactical victory in the lexicon of conference diplomacy.

As far as personnel was concerned, the American naval contingent was a strong team. Ghormley and Kirk had been working with the British for months and Ghormley would be more assertive now that he had direct access to the Navy Department. But assertiveness was the specialty of Admiral Turner, widely known (and after this conference, internationally known) as "Terrible Turner," who seemed to see himself as the sole guardian of American national interest. Other members of the team were Captain Oscar Smith and Commander L. C. McDowell, who acted as one of the secretaries.

Heading the army team was Lieutenant General Stanley Embick, the chairman of the American delegation. Embick was an experienced planner, having served as director of war plans and deputy chief of staff. Moreover, like Turner, he was not noted for his openness to British suggestions, having been markedly unimpressed by their strategy during World War I when he had served on the Allied War Council.[27] General Embick was assisted by Brigadier General Sherman Miles, chief of army intelligence; Brigadier General Lee S. Gerow, director of the war plans division; Colonel J. T. McNarney; and Lieutenant Colonel W. S. Scobey, who served as the other U.S. secretary. These delegates were assisted by a number of technical experts, and when the entire group first filed in and introduced themselves the British were stunned. Drawn up behind several tables facing the small British group, the Americans presented a formidable array.[28] Had the British been aware of some of the preconceptions within the American delegation they might have been even more aghast.

At the second meeting, on 31 January, the two sides began to maneuver for position.[29] General Embick set the tone by asking about British policy in case the home islands fell. According to the general, the American public, who were being told by administration witnesses arguing for Lend-Lease that without immediate aid England would collapse in sixty to ninety days, were "apprehensive" about that eventuality. The British dodged this question, preferring to suggest that planning against such an event would be quite difficult because their forces theoretically would have been decimated in the titanic struggle that would precede any surrender. This was the same indirect suggestion that had been made in August 1940, and apparently it was still applicable—no new contingency planning was revealed. It was a little awkward. Churchill, Lothian, and others had been arguing for aid by suggesting that without it Britain would soon collapse. But Churchill had also forbidden planning for that contingency, so, when questioned, British military officers had to answer, whether true or not, that they had no plans.[30]

Now it was the British turn to pose an awkward question. Would the United States enter the war prior to Japanese involvement? The American officers answered that there were two contingencies that might cause the United States to enter the hostilities. The first was overt Japanese action, which would mean war with Japan, and in that event the U.S. military chiefs thought that "war should be declared on Germany and Italy." The other possibility was that Germany or Italy might take provocative action in the Atlantic. In fact, it was suggested that "actual provocation might be on United States initiative or Germany's or Italy's"—an extremely provocative suggestion in itself. But, since the basic American policy was to keep the Japanese out of the war, the chiefs preferred the second possibility—war in the Atlantic—for then the Japanese might decide not to become involved.

The British pressed the point. What would the United States do if the Japanese did become involved in some way short of overt action against the United States? That was the rub; and it was hard for the British to make plans for the Far East without knowing American intentions. The American delegates said that their policy was to "oppose any extension of Japanese rule over additional territory." However, there were various ways of extending rule, including, for example, economic coercion—and the delegates took no position on what would be done if the Japanese adopted such a course. There was discussion about supplies as well as other tangential issues, but the meeting adjourned with nothing resolved.

The problem of Pacific contingencies was emerging as the first order of business and would cause considerable trouble, as it had been doing for months. American views, Bellairs wrote, were considerably different from British views; however, "we are clearing the ground."[31] He also reported to London that the "discussions were taking place in an atmosphere of complete cordiality and frankness."[32]

There were no meetings during the weekend, and the British delegation used that time to hold a private discussion on Pacific strategy. That subject was at the head of the agenda for the session that opened on Tuesday, 4 February.[33] The British suggested that it was impossible to estimate what forces would be available in the Atlantic until the United States clarified its intentions in the Pacific. The Americans responded with a historical overview. Since it had been U.S. policy since 1916 to give the Philippines independence, the military position there had been progressively weakened; however, the islands were still U.S. territory and if the Japanese attacked them it was "possible" that the United States would declare war. The decision would be "political," but the military would recommend that an attack on the Philippines be considered a cause for war against Japan, Germany, and Italy. The best estimates available, however, indicated that the Japanese would avoid the Philippines and attack the British and the Dutch.

There was no guess hazarded as to U.S. reaction to such an attack, but basic U.S. war strategy in the Pacific was outlined. In general, the plan was to cooperate with the British and the Dominions. Specifically, the United States would protect American and British interests east of the 180° meridian. That area included the Hawaiian Islands and the west coast of the United States. South of the equator, the United States was prepared to support Dominion naval operations "as far west as 155°," thus including New Zealand, but not Australia. These major American operations would be undertaken by units of the U.S. Fleet. The weaker Asiatic Fleet would defend the Philippines as long as possible and then fall back on another suitable base, "probably Singapore or Surabaya" (in the Dutch East Indies). The general objective of all Allied fleets should be to "neutralize" those Japanese forces that got past the

U.S. Pacific Fleet and hold them "north of the Malay Barrier." Naturally, all this planning was predicated on the concept that the United States would be in the war against Japan, which the U.S. delegation had already said was problematic.

The discussion next turned to the connection between Atlantic and Pacific action. The American military experts realized that their Asiatic Fleet was not strong enough to meet the Japanese on equal terms, and there were no plans for reinforcing it with ships from the Atlantic. Thus, from the American point of view, it seemed wisest for the U.S. forces to relieve the British in the Atlantic and the Mediterranean, thereby allowing the Royal Navy to transfer its own units to the Southwest Pacific if they wished. Such action had the added advantage of allowing the British to protect their own colonial possessions while at the same time putting naval units out of German reach in case of British collapse.

It was just as well that this last point was not mentioned, since the British delegates took exception to the more tactful suggestion. They pointed out that conditions were so critical in the Atlantic that it would take a sizable American force to replace any appreciable number of British ships. Deployment of too many ships to the Atlantic would only jeopardize American ability to restrain the Japanese. Not surprisingly, the British were most concerned about restraining the Japanese in the Southwest Pacific, the area that included the primary Empire possessions and the one that Americans were least interested in protecting. Instead of accepting the U.S. views regarding the Pacific the British delegation would try to change them. The British team was convinced that either the U.S. Fleet should be more active in restraining the Japanese or the U.S. Asiatic Fleet should be reinforced.

To the Americans the situation appeared exactly the opposite. If the U.S. Fleet were more active it might provoke the Japanese into offensive action, and if the Asiatic Fleet were reinforced with ships from Pearl Harbor two understrength fleets would be created. In any case, as things stood, the Americans did not think the Japanese would move while the powerful U.S. Fleet remained on their flank at Pearl Harbor. Therefore, the shift to the Atlantic that they had suggested was the only practical one. Not much progress was being made.

When the teams met next, on 5 February, only a few minutes were spent on the Pacific, but that was long enough for the British to indicate again their doubts about the strength of the Asiatic Fleet.[34] Kelly Turner quickly cut off debate by repeating that whether it was strong enough or not, no reinforcement was planned —and that was that. Turner, who was emerging as the principal naval spokesman at the conference, dominating and overshadowing Ghormley, spoke with the fervor, logic, and confidence that comes from the support of higher authority. Unfortunately, though, he had personal qualities that led an American officer to describe him as "ornery as hell" and caused a British delegate to suggest that Turner was "rather liable to start from the assumption that he was right and everyone else either fools or knaves."[35] These attributes naturally did not smooth anyone's path.

With the American position regarding the Pacific firmly established, the greater part of the session was spent discussing the Atlantic. Here agreement proved easier. The British attitude was simply put: wear down the Germans through economic pressure brought to bear by air and sea. The British insisted that they could protect England and would gradually shift to the offensive. The Americans, who were "all for pressing on," wanted to hear much more about offensives, and Turner immediately jumped on the point, asking for a current and precise report on the division of effort going into offensive and defensive actions.[36] The answer was not particularly precise, but it appeared that efforts would be primarily defensive until 1942, with the single exception of bombing, which would be progressively increased. That was less aggressive than the Americans had hoped for, so they might have been surprised to learn that the cautious British were pleased by their bellicosity. As one British delegate put it, "the main thing . . . was to get the Americans to subscribe firmly to the policy of offensive action against Germany, no matter by what means."[37]

Although the discussion on 5 February was not oriented toward the Pacific, the American reply to the paper Admiral Bellairs had handed Ghormley on board the *KG-V* was presented to the conference and provided an overview of American attitudes.[38] The paper began by noting the "marked divergence" of view between British and American officials about the Philippines. The issue had been thoroughly reviewed during the debate over the ORANGE plan, and it was the American estimate that supplying and defending the islands was virtually impossible. The Philippines had neither material nor trained personnel; only Corregidor could be held more than a few weeks.

American intelligence reports estimated that as of spring 1941 the Japanese had 1,009,935 combat tons of shipping plus 1,500 airplanes available in the Pacific, whereas the United States had only 917,430 combat tons and 716 planes. In the Atlantic the United States had 285,000 more combat tons and another 329 aircraft—but "no units could be drawn from the U.S. Atlantic Fleet" to redress the balance in the Pacific. Even merchant tonnage was in short supply and the British apparently wanted to lease much of what was available. Therefore, the American planners had accepted the unfortunate realities, which included absorbing the Japanese first strike, losing the Philippines, and then advancing slowly westward from Pearl Harbor. The gradual push west would protect communication lines, eventuate in the recapture of the Philippines, and finally bring a superior force to bear against the Japanese.[39] It was a discouraging picture, and the British were not pleased. They believed the strategy to be a serious misreading of the immediate situation, with even more serious consequences for the future.[40] But with no obvious solution in view the meeting adjourned.

The next day, 6 February, was devoted to answering more British questions.[41] Turkey, Russia, the Mediterranean, and the Indian Ocean were all discussed. Then, as Bellairs put it, Turner gave a "dissertation . . . on the dispositions in the Atlantic."[42] The dissertation was based on the encouraging hypothesis that by 1 April 1941 the United States would be in the war. If so, the United States would take responsibility for the area west of 30° west and to the south as far as Rio de Janeiro. Destroyers and flying boats would augment the escort vessels in the Northwest Approaches. The Atlantic Fleet would be buttressed with converted merchant vessels, new construction, and units from the U.S. Fleet. The last assumption was based on the highly optimistic view that, if Japan entered the war at an "early date," the "movement of U.S. forces from the Pacific to the Atlantic" might be facilitated. In other words, U.S. naval planners assumed that quick work could be made of the attacking Japanese and that the "slow advance west from Pearl Harbor" could be carried out without straining American naval resources. If that proved correct, Turner estimated that by 1 July the U.S. Navy would have strong escort and strike forces in the Atlantic, including units based on Iceland, a force of combat ships in the Eastern Atlantic, perhaps based on Gibraltar, as well as destroyers and flying boats based on the British Isles. With this presentation the first full week of conferences ended.

Despite the theoretical nature of Turner's "dissertation" the outlook for cooperation was better in the Atlantic than in the Pacific. The sometimes acerbic American planner contributed further to this intimation by sending a memorandum to Admiral Bellairs the next day concerning the possibility of establishing American bases on Iceland and Scotland to facilitate escorting of convoys and patrolling. Turner had ordered the problem studied because it appeared to him that the lack of "adequate security" for shipping in the North Atlantic might be the "Achilles heel" in the British war effort.[43]

Turner's concern was no doubt welcome, but the British delegates wished the Americans could become more sensitized to the exposed tendons in the Pacific, and after preliminary talks with Ambassador Halifax, Admiral Bellairs broached the subject to Kirk during lunch on Friday.[44] At the very least, Bellairs wanted to have the matter discussed further. Kirk agreed.[45] A new and potentially serious complication arose that same day when Admiral Danckwerts was taken ill, making Admiral Bellairs chief of the British team. In addition to the loss of Danckwerts there were strong and very convenient hints from London that a Japanese offensive was impending.[46]

With all these problems, the meeting on Monday, 10 February, turned into a mixed affair. It started off well with the U.S. Army delegation putting forth its basis for operational planning.[47] Since the chief of staff wanted U.S. Army land and air forces to operate "in the regions bordering the Atlantic," the U.S. Army would assume all British Army commitments in that area "exclusive of the British Isles." It thus was logical to assume that bases in Greenland and Iceland would eventually be staffed by U.S. troops, thereby relieving British forces for service on more active fronts.

Attitudes on the Pacific had not changed much, but Kelly Turner did explain U.S. opposition to economic sanctions against Japan. The best estimate the Americans could make indicated that an embargo of gas and oil for the Japanese home islands would serve only to "precipitate a Japanese move into the Netherlands

East Indies," or, in other words, a war that neither the British, the Dutch, nor the Americans were prepared for. But estimates were all more or less beside the point since any economic decision would be "political, not military," and thus improper for discussion at the ABC meetings.

Talks then turned to reinforcements for the Asiatic Fleet. Turner had already stated that the sacrifice of the Philippines had been accepted, but the British had not been convinced, so he now added two new reasons for not moving more ships farther west. First, with the majority of ships held at Pearl Harbor it would be relatively easy to reinforce the Atlantic if necessary (an oblique reference to British vulnerability). Second, the Asiatic Fleet did not have the servicing capacity to handle the additional heavy ships (an oblique reference to American doubts about the servicing capacity available at Singapore). Thus it seemed best to move ships to the Atlantic rather than to the Far East, and when that was done the British could shore up their own defenses at Singapore. Turner assumed that this settled the matter and called on the British to work up a strategy appreciation incorporating their views and theories. Bellairs accepted the task.[48] Although tempers wore thin, they held, but Bellairs described the meeting as "sticky."[49]

A note of profound concern ran through Bellairs's report to London on the situation. Several things had become obvious: the Americans wanted to make their main contribution in the Atlantic and the Mediterranean; they were dead set against reinforcing their Asiatic Fleet; they did not want to "appease" the Japanese and therefore wanted to threaten them by keeping heavy fleet units at Pearl Harbor on their flank. Bellairs found the Americans "most reluctant" to recognize the importance of the Far East, not only to British imperialists, but to the total war effort. They were willing if necessary to give up the entire Far East in the early stages of the war, confident that it could be retaken. In an effort to convince them of the folly of this course Bellairs advised the Chiefs of Staff that he was, at Turner's request, submitting an appreciation to them that elaborated the view of the British Chiefs of Staff on the strategic importance of the Far East. Although the Americans would not send their forces there, they wanted to know British plans if the U.S. Navy sent six battleships, eight heavy cruisers, eight other cruisers, eighty-two destroyers, and a large number of submarines to the Atlantic and the Mediterranean. He proposed to tell them and in the process convince them that it was a bad idea.[50]

The prime minister was not pleased with Bellairs's report, which the Chiefs of Staff forwarded to him; however, his displeasure was directed not at the recalcitrant Americans but at Admiral Bellairs. "All this," he wrote in reference to Bellairs's telegram, "seems very confused and they seem to be making heavy weather." Churchill did not disagree with the American plan for leaving their forces at Pearl Harbor instead of transferring them to Singapore, for "once war is declared events will draw them naturally into [a] forward policy for which we should *not* now press unduely." He did think that the U.S. Navy was planning on transferring more heavy units to the Atlantic than was necessary. All that was needed were destroyers, cruisers, and several old battleships for escorting convoys.

As for shifting British ships to the Far East, he found that "quite foolish." For him the principle was simple. The United States should take care of the Pacific in any way they wanted and help the British in the Atlantic with destroyers and escorts; but in no case should they be challenged or offended.[51] In pursuing that course he seemed to minimize the danger to the Far East. Bellairs, on the contrary, did not; he reflected the viewpoint of the Admiralty whose planners had been stewing over the problem since first hearing of Plan Dog. It seemed to the Royal Navy that the Americans were too willing to write off islands and bases, apparently assuming that the Japanese would not prove to be a formidable adversary. Moreover, Churchill did not seem to understand that when the Americans shifted their weight to the Atlantic they intended to play a significant role—maybe even the primary role—in that area. They did not intend to be just adjuncts to the Royal Navy.

At the very least, the ABC Conference was illuminating the problem of establishing priorities in a coalition war. It also was following closely the pattern of disagreement and distrust established over the past three years. The British needed American help to guarantee the security of their interests in the Far East, and, for a variety of reasons, the Americans were not going to supply that help. There were evident, though, some significant changes in attitude and approach. Heretofore the U.S. services had differed over the ORANGE plan and the amount and timing of aid for the Far East. ORANGE had now been deemphasized and the services could unite in resisting British attempts to entangle them in distant colonial regions. Previously, British officers and politicians had agreed on the importance of the American role in the Far East; now Churchill was directing that the American view be accepted, even if it was misguided. Upon these new premises perhaps accommodation could be found, but at what price?

15.

"Get the Americans into the War"

13 February 1941–29 March 1941

The prime minister had not been pleased with Bellairs's "heavy weather" concerning the Far East; the Americans were equally distressed, and it is not difficult to understand why as one reads the long, closely reasoned two-part document that Bellairs prepared. In it he analyzed, first, the importance of Singapore and, second, the proper manner of defending it. As Bellairs put it, Singapore was not only important strategically but also for "political, economic, and sentimental" reasons.[1] Furthermore, Great Britain had made "specific undertakings" to support Australia and New Zealand; Singapore was essential to fulfilling those promises. So significant were these guarantees, the paper stated, that if "Singapore were in serious danger of capture . . . we should be prepared to send a fleet to the Far East, even if to do so would compromise or sacrifice our position in the Mediterranean." In short, the loss of Singapore would be a "disaster of the first magnitude second only to the loss of the British Isles."

Defending the fortress was not as easy as setting the priorities. Forces could be drawn from the Royal Navy in the Atlantic or the Mediterranean but that seemed illogical. The most practical solution would be for the U.S. Navy to dispatch at least one carrier and a division of heavy cruisers from the U.S. Fleet at Pearl

Harbor to defend Singapore. That would leave the majority of the U.S. force on the Japanese flank, thus threatening any offensive move south. Even with that assistance Singapore's defense was not safe, but with American and Dutch help there was a reasonable chance of holding on. The paper concluded by urging the American delegates to accept the British view. American agreement was important because the Far East was essential to the war effort and Singapore was the key to defending that area. In short, "its retention must be assured." Though the paper was the handiwork of Bellairs and the British delegation, the conclusion was an accurate reflection of the views of the Chiefs of Staff.

There was a meeting of the combined U.S. delegation on 13 February to consider the paper.[2] As expected, Kelly Turner was the most outspoken in his discontent. He sensed, he said, a note of condescension and heavy-handedness in the British presentation to which he took umbrage. In Turner's opinion, the paper was so important that it deserved a formal, written reply, which in fact he had already prepared and on which he hoped the army and navy delegations could agree.

According to Turner's reply, the genesis of British hopes for American action in the Far East had been the 1938 Ingersoll Conversations after which the president and the secretary of state had "more or less committed" the U.S. Fleet to cooperate with the British forces in the Far East. During the Ingersoll Conversations, the British had suggested the idea, which the U.S. had tacitly accepted, that in case of war with Japan, the U.S. Fleet would base on Singapore. A British Fleet would join the U.S. forces and the two navies could then move north against the Imperial Navy.

Turner did not comment on the wisdom of this original commitment, but he did observe that the British were now unable to keep their side of the bargain. Yet when the British delegation had first arrived in Washington, they still wanted the United States to send the "whole Fleet, together with a large U.S. Army" to the Far East; in other words, the British wanted the United States to live up to the American side of the bargain even if they could not live up to theirs. Turner, as well as others, opposed the move. He said thankfully that some progress had been made, for the British had now trimmed their requests to air support, some submarines, and considerably less than the whole fleet. However, it still appeared that the British were conducting a "concerted drive" to have the

United States accept their view of strategy in the Far East. Although they superficially accepted the United States Staff Committee's opposition, they persisted in trying to get commitments for more U.S. forces.

But, Turner pointed out, the Americans were in a far different position than they had been when the Ingersoll Conversations had been held. The power balance had perceptibly shifted. The United States now had greater responsibilities and potentially greater opportunities. Turner was determined that U.S. forces not become overextended. Any inaccurate impressions that the British had formed would have to give way to new realities. General Embick agreed. The American delegates were charged with advising the president on the soundest military strategy. Currently that strategy called for an Atlantic concentration, with Pacific requirements given second priority. Therefore, it was decided that a paper, Turner's, with recommendations added, would serve as an outline of U.S. policy in the Far East and that the British would have to work with that.

Turner welcomed the American committee's agreement and proceeded to give his views on British strategy. It seemed to him that it had shown "very serious defects," which had resulted in innumerable problems. Yet despite their reverses and current tenuous position, they continued to insist that the Americans accept their ideas for winning the war. Needless to say, Turner did not consider such subservience wise or prudent.

Although everyone did not share Turner's views, there was general agreement that the primary theater was the Atlantic and, after accepting Turner's paper on the Far East, General Sherman Miles proposed moving the conversations in a positive direction by forcing the British to concentrate on the central issue. The primary objective of the staff talks, Miles said, was to devise a strategy for protecting the British home islands. Attention should be shifted to that problem, and, after making sure that the "citadel" was secure, the talks could turn again to the Pacific.[3] This change in the agenda was no doubt sound, but Miles's attitude was probably conditioned by his view that British chances of survival were only slightly better than fifty-fifty.[4]

Miles was no doubt influenced by what has become known as the "Battle of the Atlantic," in which German submarines, land-based aircraft, and surface raiders were becoming frighteningly effective in constricting Britain's lifeline. The battle cruisers *Scharn-horst* and *Gneisanau* alone had destroyed some 115,000 tons of Allied shipping in less than two months, and the growing use of "wolf-pack" tactics increased the effectiveness of the already deadly submarine.[5] Even as the conferees debated, naval planners in London and Washington anxiously studied the rising curve of shipping losses. No matter what else was done, some relief, perhaps escorting or repairing British shipping in American yards, would have to come soon. All of the American team may not have been as pessimistic about British chances as was Miles, but it agreed that Atlantic needs and strategy should top the agenda for the next plenary session. This procedure would offer a convenient course around dissension at the same time that it forced discussion of the issue many Americans believed to be central—the safety of the British Isles.

The British agreed to consider the Atlantic at the next session; therefore, when the delegates convened on 14 February, the topic was keeping British sea-lanes open. American priorities soon became clear: protecting the home islands from invasion and avoiding their economic strangulation. Although the British naturally shared those concerns, they could not be kept on the topic. They reminded the Americans of their other worries, particularly in the Middle East. Since forces were already heavily engaged there, the British felt it had some legitimate call on their resources and attention. To the Americans, any large-scale allocation of forces and supplies to the Mediterranean area would sap strength from protection of the "citadel."[6]

Furthermore, supplying the Middle East risked shipping, and Kelly Turner, among others, saw the loss of merchant shipping as Britain's greatest danger. To Turner, "even the loss of the Mediterranean position would not be as severe as a decided increase in sinkings." Here again, the British and the Americans found themselves disagreeing and the route of disagreement was the same as it had been. The Americans would provide aid in the area they considered vital—the Atlantic—and the British could protect the Mediterranean as they saw fit.[7]

Since the Germans were making an all-out attack on shipping in the Atlantic, the Americans advocated putting emphasis on air and surface escort, inbound and outbound, from the British Isles as far north as three hundred miles below Iceland and as far west as the Azores. Obviously the British did not have the combat vessels to afford that protection, so the U.S. Navy might provide a large and varied force of battleships, carriers, cruisers, destroyers, and flying boats, thus freeing British units for service in the Mediterranean.

Some of the American units would come from the Pacific, but it was impossible to tell exactly when they might arrive, at least until it was determined when and whether the British would send replacement units to the Far East. Furthermore, Turner stated, when they did arrive there was no intention of breaking them into small groups or placing them under British command. As Turner put it, "the U.S. proposes to accept full responsibility for operations in certain definite areas, or for executing specific tasks in areas of British responsibility." The ships would remain under U.S. command, but the United States would accept strategic direction from British naval authorities.[8] That was sound planning and no surprise. Bellairs believed that progress had been made and that agreement had been reached on basic strategy in the Atlantic.[9]

Despite his optimism, Bellairs did sense American displeasure with his paper on the Far East. He had yet to see Turner's response, but he had learned of "considerable discussion" at the Navy Department.[10] Anticipating trouble, he decided to send a detailed description of his paper to London. Although Bellairs could not know it, his strategy appreciation was fast becoming the glass through which many disparate rays would focus. On the day he sent his description to London, 15 February, the new British ambassador, Lord Halifax, and the Australian minister, Richard Casey, called on Secretary Hull to alert him to the impending crisis in the Far East.[11] Tensions had been increasing for almost a month and the British, doing nothing to minimize the dangers, now tried to force the Americans into action or at least commitment. The pretext for the meeting on 15 February was the unreconciled differences on Far Eastern strategy among the ABC conferees.[12] Since Hull was not aware of the strategic deadlock, Halifax showed him Bellairs's paper, and, to give the secretary of state time to absorb the British point of view, left a copy with him.

Actually, on 15 February the discussion at the conference was proceeding smoothly. Atlantic problems were the issue, and all participants agreed that shipping was vital and that the U.S. Navy should help protect the North Atlantic lanes. As Bellairs understood it, planning was already advanced to the point at which the force could be accurately estimated. The northwestern approaches to the British Isles would be the center of gravity for American naval forces, although they would operate in other waters as well. The forces provided would be distributed as follows: 42 destroyers, 7 Coast Guard cutters, and 36 flying boats for the northwestern approaches; 3 battleships, 8 destroyers, 4 destroyer minesweepers, 4 heavy cruisers, and 12 flying boats for general Atlantic escort and trade protection; 2 carriers, 4 six-inch cruisers and 4 destroyers as a hunting force in the North Atlantic; 3 battleships, 1 carrier, 4 heavy cruisers, 18 destroyers, 20 submarines, and 12 flying boats based on Gibraltar; and 4 old cruisers and 10 armed merchant cruisers based in the Caribbean.[13] An immediate step in establishing the nucleus escorting fleet was taken by Admiral Stark who ordered the creation of an Atlantic Support Force as of 15 February 1941.[14]

Although shielded from the realities of the ABC discussions and the orders of the chief of naval operations, opponents of the Lend-Lease Bill were accurately anticipating developments. Those who opposed the bill argued that convoy escorts would be necessary to effectively aid England, that the escorts would lead to incidents, and that incidents would lead to war. The administration responded with what has been charitably described as a "classic case of misdirection." For instance, instead of answering that escorting convoys would be necessary, which he believed, Secretary Stimson suggested that the Lend-Lease Bill in no way increased presidential authority to escort. Secretary Knox did imply that escorting could lead to war, yet managed to convey the impression that there was no intention to escort.[15] The president had stated categorically at his news conference on 21 January that he had no plans to escort supplies to England. Off the record, he agreed with the logical progression that opponents foresaw, but added "You can see that that [incidents and war] is about the last thing we have in our minds."[16] The next day he stated—this time, privately —that escorting was probably necessary; the establishment of the Atlantic Support Force was the logical extension of necessity.[17]

There was no meeting of the ABC Conference on Sunday, so the next plenary session convened on Monday, 17 February. The Atlantic area was again the topic and the U.S. Navy continued to be cooperative. If Gibraltar became untenable they suggested developing Freetown in Sierra Leone as a major base for which the U.S. Navy would accept full responsibility. They also agreed to bring the Fleet Marine Force up to readiness and to keep it available for assisting the British in seizing the Azores and the Canary Islands. The rest of the discussion dealt with the U.S. Army Air Corps, which would cooperate with the British in bombing Germany. For their part, the army agreed to take over for the British troops in Iceland, Aruba, and Curaçao. It also would send a "token force" of one brigade group to the British Isles to protect the American air and naval bases that would be established in England, Northern Ireland, and possibly in the Hebrides to assist in the convoying effort. The Americans made it clear that few of those forces would be available before September 1941.[18]

Meanwhile, the opponents of the Lend-Lease Bill were either the recipients of some privileged information or they were making some insightful guesses. On 18 February, the day after the productive session of the ABC Conference, Senator Allen Ellender (Democrat, Louisiana) offered an amendment to the Lend-Lease Bill that opposed the use of U.S. forces outside the Western Hemisphere. The administration tried to beat down support for the amendment, with the president declaring that he had no intention of using military forces outside the hemisphere. Doubt remained, and the Senate ultimately accepted a modified version of the Ellender Amendment.[19]

With the two teams in agreement on a number of general points, it now seemed advisable for the army to prepare a paper on command and liaison. Because of Ghormley's previous work and Turner's pertinacity, the navy already had its paper completed. So, instead of waiting for the army's paper, Turner suggested establishing a steering committee to work out specific cooperative agreements between the delegations. The proposal was accepted and Bellairs, Ghormley, and General Gerow were appointed to carry out the drafting.[20]

During the day's discussion the British delegates told their American counterparts that Halifax had left a copy of Bellairs's Far East paper with Secretary Hull on 15 February. There was no immediate reaction and Bellairs thought "very considerable progress" was being made. The calm surface was deceptive, though, and later that evening he heard rumblings of "grave consternation" because his paper had been given to Hull.[21]

The rumors were well founded, but the Americans were not the only ones upset about Bellairs's paper; at approximately the same time Churchill received the detailed description of its contents. The prime minister had reacted badly to Bellairs's cursory review of the paper, but he virtually exploded when he learned the details. The prime minister's reaction took the form of a memorandum to the first sea lord:[22]

This appreciation is far too long, and ought never to have been telegraphed in its present form.

I very much deplore Admiral Bellairs spreading himself in this way and using such extreme arguments as those contained in the last sentence of para. 6.[23] I trust the appreciation has not been sent, and that a short and simple expression of our views may take its place without the need to employ all this redundancy of argument and repetition of facts, which *apart from their proportions* are present in the minds of anyone who has thought about the subject.

What has been the use of all this battling? Anyone could have seen that the United States would not base a battle-fleet on Singapore and divide their naval forces, enabling the Japanese to fight an action on even terms with either one of them. They said so weeks ago, and I particularly deprecated the raising of this controversy. Our object is to get the Americans into the war, and the proper strategic dispositions will soon emerge when they are up against reality, and not trying to enter into hypothetical paper accords beforehand.

I think we should say:—

"We loyally accept the United States Navy dispositions for the Pacific. We think it unlikely that Japan will enter the war against Great Britain and the United States. It is still more unlikely that they would attempt any serious land operations in Malaya, entailing movements of a large army and the maintenance of its communications, while a United States Fleet of adequate strength remains at Hawaii. It would however be a wise precaution in our opinion if the American Asiatic Fleet were somewhat reinforced with cruisers. Perhaps as the war develops, some enterprise with aircraft—carriers strongly supported by fast ships against the Japanese homeland towns might be attempted; but this is a matter better settled on actual contact with the event. In the meanwhile, apart from the admirable dispositions proposed by the United States for the Atlantic, we should be glad of assistance in convoys through the Pacific and Indian Oceans against individual Japanese raiding cruisers."

The first thing is to get the United States into the war. We can then settle how to fight it afterwards. Admiral Bellairs is making such heavy weather over all this that he may easily turn the United States Navy Board into a hindrance and not a help to the main object, namely the entry of the United States.

I do not see why, even if Singapore were captured, we could not protect Australia by basing a fleet on Australian ports. This would effectively prevent invasion.

As for India, if the Japanese were to invade it would make the Indians loyal to the King-Emperor for a hundred years. But why would they be such fools as to get tied up there with vastly superior, unbeaten naval forces on the high seas?

Although Churchill's reaction made his intent of embroiling the United States in the war more explicit than ever before, it offered no new route around the strategic stumbling block in the Far East. Thus, even though the Chiefs of Staff shared Bellairs's sentiments, Churchill's view would have to prevail or there would be a major confrontation. The only course seemed to be to act as though there were no strategic stumbling block and move on to other subjects. The Americans were not willing to follow the same course. It had been bad enough when the delegation had suspected Bellairs of direct pressure, but now it appeared that he was trying to pressure them via Secretary of State Hull. Their reaction was swift and angry. First, they sent the British delegation a written statement concerning American action if the Japanese entered the war and captured Singapore. Then they prepared a letter protesting the British method of problem-solving. Taken together, these two documents provide an overview of American attitudes and strategy.

The written statement began positively, noting that if the United States were an ally of the British Commonwealth and entered the war first against Japan, "it will at once also engage in war with Germany and Italy."[24] Furthermore, if the United States first entered the war against Germany and Italy, "it will thereupon make war against Japan, provided Japan is then at war with the British Commonwealth." If, however, Japan simply moved farther south, say into Indo-China, the staff committee did not believe that the United States would regard that as *causus belli*. Also, and this was the most important reservation, there was "serious doubt" that the United States would "immediately declare war against Japan" if Japan moved to occupy Malaya, British Borneo, or the Netherlands East Indies "unless the U.S. were previously also at war with Germany and Italy."

The paper cited congressional attitudes as a restraining influence on American action. If the Japanese attacked Malaysia, it would take the American legislators a "considerable period of debate" before they decided for or against war. For that reason it would be a "serious mistake" for the British to count on immediate support from the United States. Thus the Americans believed that any preparations for the defense of Malaysia should be made *without* dependence on U.S. intervention.

Even with this dash of cold water from the Americans, it was logical to inquire why the United States could not at least put a battle fleet into Singapore to deter Japanese action. This matter, however, had to be approached delicately, and it was, even though it went to the very heart of American defense strategy and involved its oldest and darkest fears about Britain's chances. The way it was put was that since hemispheric defense took priority, American military power must be deployed so that forces from both the Atlantic and the Pacific could be thrown into the defense of the hemisphere if the British were defeated. In other words, Britain's tenuous hold on life, which Churchill himself had spoken of so often and so dramatically, was the best argument against heavy American commitments far from the major theater of war.

That was part of the reason for the divergence of opinion on the Far East; another was that the Americans held a "less pessimistic view" about the consequences of Singapore's fall. However, differences of opinion regarding the consequences were somewhat academic since the Americans estimated that the great base was vulnerable to attack from the land side no matter how many ships were in the harbor. Thus it would be the height of foolishness to send an American fleet to a vulnerable colonial base, thereby running the risk initially of public criticism and ultimately of disaster.[25]

If despite these risks the British decided to try to hold Singapore, the United States might be able to supply some submarines, a carrier, and four heavy cruisers. But the U.S. delegation thought it wiser to concentrate on the defense of the Western Hemisphere and leave responsibility for the Far East with the British and the Dutch. The reasoning was simple and to the point. If that strategy were followed and either associate were forced to "withdraw from the war, the deployment of the other remains sound."

The U.S. staff concluded their review by noting that while

they considered holding Singapore "very desirable," to do so would require a diversion from the primary theater—the Atlantic—and "might jeopardize the success of the main effort." In view of available forces, the dispatch of units to Singapore might mean the employment "of the final reserve of the Associated Powers in a non-decisive theatre." According to a textbook description of sound strategy, an initial U.S. commitment to Singapore carried a further commitment to "employ the forces necessary to accomplish [the] mission." This strategy clearly indicated that the United States would "undertake the early defeat of Japan," but it ran counter to current American planning because it implied acceptance of responsibility by America to protect a "large portion of the British Empire." That responsibility was antipathetic to American intent, interest, and ingrained prejudices. If the British wished the Empire defended, they could do it themselves. Lest the basic points be missed, when the Americans handed that paper to Bellairs, they reiterated their fears about British defeat and the "political" reasons against basing at an Empire fortress.[26]

The American delegation had also prepared a letter that included a review of the present awkward situation. In the letter they noted that the original instructions for the conference delegates strictly prohibited political commitments and specifically prohibited political supervision. Such supervision, the letter went on, could only retard progress and cause embarrassment, especially when exercised by only one of the governments involved. With the letter went a note stating that the meetings were recessed until a satisfactory answer was received.[27] Bellairs must have thought he had run into a buzz saw. On the same day the American letter arrived at the Embassy, he received the official reaction from London. The chiefs to whom Bellairs officially reported were more restrained in their response to his paper than the prime minister had been. As they put it, there was little purpose in continuing the argument over Singapore. They did not disassociate themselves from Bellairs's paper but they did suggest that, since the British position regarding Singapore had been "adequately represented," he not "press our views further."[28] Bellairs did not respond directly to the message. He did answer the "tiresome" letter from the Americans in the suggested tone of cooperation. That meant promising not to provide the diplomats with any further military papers, thus preserving the theoretical divison about which the Americans felt so strongly. Bellairs also said that the British delegation regretted the incident although it had occurred "through no fault of ours." The reply was ready by late afternoon and Bellairs hoped that the matter would quickly blow over.[29]

It would not if Kelly Turner had anything to say about it. That became clear when the Navy Section met on 20 February to consider the British response. Admiral Ghormley said that he found the British reply acceptable because it promised the desired exclusion of the diplomats; Turner, to the contrary, did not believe that that was sufficiently specific. He wanted ironclad assurance that not only no papers, but also no reports of any kind regarding the talks, would go to the State Department. His interpretation was that the staff conversations were on a "purely military plane"; consequently, until final conclusions were reached, any presentation of uncoordinated views could only lead to confusion. He had taken it upon himself to draft an answer to Bellairs's reply, which stated "political measures should not be employed by either the U.S. or the U.K. with a view to influencing decisions on matters which may be pending before the Staff Conference." That attitude reflected sound procedural training, as well as Turner's suspicions of British machinations.[30]

The U.S. Navy group presented Turner's draft to the joint meeting of the army-navy team that convened later the same day. Despite the previous argument, the business was quickly concluded. It was agreed that the British answer was satisfactory, that "no reply was required, and that the matter would be considered as being closed." With that, the meeting adjourned. It is likely that the alacrity and the unanimity of the decision are explained by the secretary's notation at the end of the minutes: "Rear Adm. R. K. Turner was absent by reason of a previous engagement."[31] The most serious crisis of the conference ended on this anticlimactic note and the two delegations got back to work. The format of the final report was discussed on 24 February, when a steering committee was chosen to agree on its general framework. The procedure adopted was that drafts would be prepared by both delegations for use in drawing up the combined paper.[32]

It still remained to be decided, though, how to reconcile the differing opinions on the Far East. When the matter was discussed on 26 February, the British stated that although they agreed with many aspects of the American approach, there were items upon which they could not agree. It was finally decided, therefore, that unreconciled differences over the Far East should be spelled out in the final report.[33]

Even after the adoption of this approach Bellairs and his team tried assiduously to learn what operational plans existed for the Pacific Fleet. There were actions that could be taken in the Pacific short of defending Singapore, but the U.S. Navy was distressingly vague about any moves in the Pacific. Although the British had accepted American dispositions and plans, they had assumed that the fleet at Pearl Harbor would have to be active in some way so as to restrain the Japanese. To their dismay, they were told that planning for such moves was the "business of the Commander in Chief [of the] Pacific Fleet." No one in Washington professed to have "any clear idea" of just what operations were likely to be undertaken by those ships. There seemed no way around it other than to have a British delegation go to Pearl Harbor, meet with Admiral Husband Kimmel (who had replaced Admiral Richardson as Commander of the U.S. Fleet), and learn his plans. Bellairs recommended following that course.[34]

Despite their differences, both sides assumed that agreement on "unified strategic control" in the Far East could be reached. There was an American naval representative in Singapore with what were described as "full powers to arrange mutual cooperation with the British and the Dutch." In staff discussions there, perhaps some of the difficulties could be resolved.[35]

Despite the warnings about the uncertainty of American support in case of war the ABC delegates did work out a preliminary division of responsibility in the Pacific. In accordance with American wishes and terminology, the area was subdivided into the Central Pacific and the Far East, a division that was convenient for the Americans whose attitude toward the two parts was distinctly different. They would accept strategic responsibility for the Central Pacific area, which was defined as territory as far west as Guam north of the equator, but only as far west as the Fiji Islands south of the equator. Everything west and south of the Central Pacific was the Far East and for that, needless to say, the U.S. Navy wanted no responsibility.[36] The British had been willing to allow American officers strategic command over all forces in the Pacific; the Americans were not flattered enough to accept. Moreover, they would not agree to put Admiral Hart's Asiatic Fleet under

British direction, at least not until after the "fate" of the Philippine Islands had been decided.[37] Because Churchill had decided to "loyally accept" American initiatives in the Pacific there was little to do other than agree.

There were other meetings, most notably one between the two navy sections on 6 March to discuss the complex problem of ship distribution in the Atlantic for effective convoy escort. With issues like this before them, it seemed unlikely that the conferees would meet Bellairs's goal of concluding the conference by 25 March.[38] Then Ghormley submitted part of the U.S. draft agreement to Bellairs on 7 March, commenting that the British suggestions had not been considered "wholly satisfactory" and requesting that the American draft now become the "master."[39] When Bellairs received the "master" he found it to be "not at all what we want."[40] Obviously there was work to be done by the Steering Committee if the meetings were to end on schedule.

Meanwhile, on 8 March the U.S. Senate voted on the Lend-Lease Bill. The debate had been long and at times heated. The final result, 60 to 31 in favor, reflected what many had long suspected —the Administration had the horses. The debate had been allowed to continue in order that all objections could be heard and the appearance of power politics could be avoided. On 24 March the Senate accepted the conference committee's version of the legislation and three hours later the president signed the law.[41]

The drafting of the final report had taken longer than Bellairs had estimated, for Turner had proved obdurate on certain points. In fact, wrote Bellairs, "every paragraph had to be fought."[42] However, on 27 March the two delegations assembled for the closing session. Colonel McNarney chose that moment to suggest the adoption of a special U.S. Army Air Corps report on the allocation of air matériel. Kelly Turner, who did not reserve his acerbity for the British, went through the roof. Why, he wanted to know, should the needs of the air forces be given special consideration? He did not accept the answer Slessor and McNarney gave, so he refused to sign anything. In Bellairs's words, a "stand-up fight" ensued. Slessor was fully as obdurate as Turner, and the "closing session" turned out to be the session before the closing.[43]

The next day Slessor and Turner argued out their differences, and a "battle it appears to have been," recorded Bellairs. Turner was behaving in what was described as an "extraordinary manner," but luckily Ghormley got Stark to bring pressure and settle the issue. The air forces apparently were placated with an air force annex to the final report (formally titled "ABC-2"), for that is what they got.[44] Thus, when the final session was held on 29 March, the signing went off smoothly and Bellairs finally got to deliver the short farewell speech he had prepared.[45] Admiral Ghormley and General Embick responded for the Americans, with Embick expressing the hope that "the immense amount of work which had been put into the agreements would one day be productive."[46] The ABC Conference was over, and perhaps more than he could anticipate, events would justify Embick's hopes.

* * *

The ABC Conference was a fitting conclusion for the important formative phase of Anglo-American naval collaboration and a harbinger of things to come. In recent years the British had not been given everything they wanted at the bargaining table—with the Royal Navy having especial grounds for disappointment—but the conference agreements had provided some grounds for hope. Britain had received assurance of help in the Atlantic, a blueprint for a war against Germany, and with a little luck, all might even come out right in the Far East. Churchill had thought that the concessions made to reach this level of agreement were justified because they might hasten American entry into the war. Of course there is no way of knowing what would have happened had the British not accommodated themselves to American wishes, but there is no evidence that the concessions they did make hastened the fruition of the prime minister's wishes. Most influential members of the Roosevelt administration, including Roosevelt himself, had already decided to enter the contest at the appropriate moment, and nothing Churchill granted or withheld was likely to hasten, retard, or materially influence that decision.

The conference also provided an example of American strategic policymaking. Improvisation was the hallmark of the day-to-day operation, but old doubts and prejudices were recurring themes, and the strains of long-range ambition were never absent. As the proceedings pointed up, policy concerning America's future course was made, characteristically, without public knowledge. The president had demonstrated time and again in his relations with Great Britain that he felt it was necessary to be devious in shielding his actions and intentions from public view. Undoubtedly some forms of military planning could not be openly conducted, but the kind of systematic and continuous deception that marked the Roosevelt administration's conduct of strategic relations is quite another matter. One result of this deception was the development of a pervasive conspiracy thesis that held Roosevelt responsible for the attack on Pearl Harbor. No solid evidence has yet been uncovered that can prove that thesis, but as has been shown in the previous pages, there is ample evidence to suggest that the president did engage in an elaborate subterfuge that verged on conspiracy. The conspiracy was to conceal from the Congress and the public the true nature of American strategic policy regarding the war and America's role in that conflict. No one has yet resolved the dilemma of how democracies can best undertake the undemocratic process of strategic planning; what is clear is that an overly deceptive process leads to suspicion and undermines the credibility of government.

In time the decisions made at the ABC Conference became known and there is no doubt that the major strategic agreement had more impact on the history of the war than did the major disagreement, or the deception. At the same time, the reasons behind the extraordinary crisis over Far Eastern strategy that flared so dramatically in late February bears analysis. How, one may ask, had problems of this magnitude, which actually threatened the continuance of the conference and presumably of Anglo-American cooperation, arisen?

The British contribution to the difficulties is easier to explain than the American side although both are complex. The basic problem for the British was their inability to protect an area that many of their strategists considered vital. The obvious way to compensate for that deficiency was to get the Americans to protect it, but how hard could the Americans be pushed without hazarding the larger prize—American involvement in the war? The British found out, and, if nothing else, the outer limits of coercion had been determined.

But in the process of pushing, Bellairs focused American attention on a basic contradiction in the British position. The issue between the prime minister and the Chiefs of Staff concerning Singapore was Empire priorities—a quintessential problem. It was perhaps wise for the chiefs to acquiesce to Churchill's initiative on the issue, for to have continued wrangling would have meant revealing a bad example of British muddling to an already dubious associate. On the other hand, acquiescence by the chiefs meant consigning to the Far East a priority never to be met.

The Americans probably never sensed the depth of the priority dilemma, but wrapped within their reaction to Britain's original Far Eastern gambit was a mélange of precepts, prejudices, suspicions, and doubts. Their long paper on strategy listed or hinted at the nature of most of these—colonialism, British resilience, the absence of logic in British plans—but it did not include a vital, yet subtle, dimension. In all likelihood the smoothly professional British delegation, with its apparently well-coordinated, well-articulated positions elicited a certain degree of envy in American breasts. The British attempt to bring "political" pressure to bear provided the pretext for the American outburst, but that was only a symptom of the deeper problem. Vanity would not allow some of the old-timers like Embick to see themselves once again, as in World War I, becoming the adjuncts to the proper, but slightly disdainful, British. The fact that the American delegation believed their guests to be wrong as well as overbearing made logic the ally of vanity. Furthermore, being adjuncts to the world's foremost naval power, though galling, is bearable, but only for a second-rate power. The new realities of naval strength necessitated at least full partnership and probably American command.

The end of the conference signaled the end of the first stage of Anglo-American naval relations. The long and difficult process had begun with the Ingersoll-Phillips talks, resumed with the Leahy-Hampton conversations, gained momentum during the agonizing summer of 1940, become more specific with Ghormley's meetings in London, and concluded in March 1941, nine months before the American entry into the war. When the bargaining began the British had debated about how badly they wanted the Americans in the war and the Americans had debated about how much they could afford to trust the British. By the summer of 1940, with French forces swept from the field, a war going badly, and an exchequer running dry, there was no longer any doubt that Britain would pay a high price for American entry into the war. Trust was still far from complete on the American side, but there was no reluctance about driving hard bargains. If the United States were to play a major role in the war, she wanted a major role in determining how and where her power would be expended; if disputes arose she could no longer be bullied. By March 1941 only the plans for exerting American power had emerged; the arms and men would take time to gather, but a great change in international politics was portended.

The major tenet of the strategy agreement—that Germany came first—has been called the basic strategic decision of World War II. Germany was to assume top priority among the Axis countries, and the United States was to assume top priority among the Allies. When the United States turned away from concentration on the Pacific and accepted a major role in the Atlantic it meant, because of her manpower and material, senior-partner status in the European theater. Style and experience would still count, but as the American role increased, British influence would consequently decline. Although the adjustments were not completed until 1944, when America's actual power on the battlefield equaled her promise, the shift in influence had already begun in 1941.

Ironically, the American doubts about British reliability, resilience, and wisdom did as much to advance these developments as anything else. Sensing this, Churchill emphasized Britain's extreme need at every possible opportunity. If sympathy was the anticipated reaction, the prime minister must have been disappointed since, as the Destroyer-Bases-Fleet agreement showed, his American cousins saw in Britain's desperate state an opportunity to help but also an opportunity to advance their own interests. The more the British stressed their vulnerability, whether it be at Singapore, in the Mediterranean, or on the sea-lanes of the Atlantic, the more they justified American doubts about their leadership ability and competence. The British, however, should not be viewed as the helpless victims in this story. They tried to advance their case by any means available, and there is no evidence that Churchill intended meekly to defer to American initiatives once they got the United States in the war. On the contrary, as Churchill himself said, he talked one way when "wooing" America and quite another after he got her "in the harem." Unfortunately for him the power shift that the ABC agreements foreshadowed proved far more immutable than he had anticipated.

Thus the ABC talks epitomized the whole range of Anglo-American relations during the 1938–41 period when conflicting anticipations, motives, and emotions were very much in evidence.

Probably no better example than these talks can be found for why the period is so difficult to characterize and especially for why it is unduly simplistic to label it a time of Anglo-American cooperation. Although there was an amazing degree of cooperative spirit evinced at the conference, the same hobgoblins that had retarded previous agreements were still present. Progress was not made because of mutual concessions; it was made because the British finally accepted American inflexibility regarding the Far East and allowed the United States to plan for a naval role second to none. "Antagonism" no longer properly described the Anglo-American relationship, and "cooperation" may be accepted only as long as it does not imply willingness to subordinate self-interest; "collaboration" is perhaps the best word to describe it, though, for that word implies a relationship based on calculation and convenience.

After the war, and partially because of growing East-West conflict, it was fashionable to look back on most of the Anglo-American disputes as minor and on the alliance as an example of national goals sacrificed in the name of union. In the postwar ambience it was logical to emphasize those things that brought us together and minimize those irritations that drove us apart. It was also generally accepted that the origins of Anglo-American cooperation be sought in the years preceding the war. Unfortunately reality is too complex to be contained by such pleasant generalizations. Careful examination of the period suggests that shadows of the future may be found in the prewar years, but those shadows portended cautious accommodation and constant maneuvering for advantage rather than selfless cooperation for lofty goals.

16.

Epilogue

When the ABC agreement was signed, nine months remained before the United States actually entered the war and many details needed attention. With the exception of further staff talks about the Pacific, and the Atlantic Conference that was held in August 1941, those details fall outside the scope of a study of strategy formulation. However, since the establishment of staff missions, the building of bases in England, Iceland, and Newfoundland, escorting convoys, and the extension of patrolling had been provided for in the ABC agreement, it seems worthwhile to review them, especially since the arrangements concerning those items followed the terms of the agreement so closely. Adherence to the agreement did not occur entirely by chance, as some British officers were to find to their surprise. The prime minister, for instance, was advised that the Americans regarded and quoted the ABC agreement "as the Bible of our joint collaboration," and for the U.S. Navy the document represented a "definite commitment" that it was "inclined to regard as more sacrosanct than is justified." Because of his experiences during the first few months of operating under the strictures of the ABC terms, Admiral Danckwerts warned others at the Admiralty to be careful since the Americans "with their usual suspicious outlook" were quick to accuse the British of bad faith if they departed in the slightest degree from the letter of the agreement.[1]

Staff Mission

The importance of direct contacts between British and American personnel had been evident from the time of the Ingersoll Conversations right through the ABC meetings. Therefore it is not surprising that the conferees had agreed that "to ensure the co-ordination of administrative action and command between the United States and British military services, the United States and the United Kingdom will exchange military missions."[2] Admiral Ghormley was the natural choice to head the naval section of the group in London and he returned to that post in April. Lieutenant Commander Austin assumed the duties of chief of staff and within several months the mission had multiplied ten times in size and complexity.

The Royal Navy ordered Admiral Danckwerts to stay in Washington as commander of their nucleus Naval Staff Mission with Captain Clarke as his chief of staff. Clarke was also charged with establishing a War Office secretariat similar to that with which he had served in London. On 1 June some one hundred Royal Navy personnel arrived in Washington to take up their duties, and on 18 May 1941 Vice Admiral Danckwerts was relieved by Vice Admiral Sir Charles Little.[3]

At times there was duplication of effort, confusion, and some acrimony as several hundred naval personnel in London and Washington tried to coordinate planning, supply allocation, and technological exchanges.[4] Giving practical application to the agreements was far from easy, but the two staffs did valuable work in preparing the two navies to fight together.

Bases

As has already been detailed, the Destroyer-Bases-Fleet exchange of September 1940 was one of the most public indications of Anglo-American cooperation. The destroyers had been delivered immediately, but by early spring 1941 there were still troublesome delays obstructing agreement on the bases. Moreover, as indications of continuing and closer cooperation grew, the list of locations grew as well. Only Western Hemisphere bases had been included in the original deal, but by the spring of 1941 American and British naval representatives were discussing sites in the United Kingdom.

Before the ABC meetings ended, a delegation headed by Captain Louis Denfeld was already on its way to England to search for air and surface stations from which American units might operate. Four bases were selected, although only two, at Gare Loch and Londonderry, were actually developed. There were already facilities available at Londonderry, but Gare Loch had to be built from scratch. Captain Denfeld returned to Washington in April and induced the president to provide $50 million out of Lend-Lease funds for base development. An American construction company began sending materials to England in June 1941 and the bases were ready to accept American troops and ships when the United States entered the war in December 1941.[5]

Escort of Convoys

The ABC agreements had treated the escort-of-convoys issue as follows: "Owing to the threat to the sea communications of the United Kingdom, the principal task of the United States naval forces in the Atlantic will be the protection of shipping of the Associated Powers, the center of gravity of the United States' effort being concentrated in the Northwestern Approaches to the United Kingdom."[6]

As we have seen, Admiral Stark had taken preparatory moves for escorting convoys even before the ABC Conference ended and in early March 1941 the Atlantic Support Force was officially constituted with Rear Admiral Arthur LeR. Bristol, Jr., in command.[7] Bristol's force would operate as a unit of the new Atlantic Fleet under the orders of Commander-in-Chief of the Atlantic Fleet, Admiral Ernest J. King. (The Neutrality Patrol Force had been retitled and Rear Admiral King had been promoted and redesignated on 1 February 1941. As of that date the U.S. fleet in the Pacific had also been redesignated, henceforth to be known as the U.S. Pacific Fleet.)

Just over two weeks later, Secretary Knox informed President Roosevelt that the U.S. Navy would shortly be ready to escort convoys from North America to Great Britain.[8] This degree of preparedness was matched by the eagerness of certain members of the administration, most notably Secretary Stimson, to undertake actual convoying. There was widespread concern that the Battle of the Atlantic would accomplish what the Battle of Britain had failed to do—force the United Kingdom out of the war. But President Roosevelt, possibly thinking of his press conference denials during the Lend-Lease debate, was not willing to act precipitously. However, on 10 April he did announce plans to take several significant steps to assist the hard-pressed Royal Navy. For one thing, he had decided to extend the Security Zone to 26° west longitude, thus enlarging the area patrolled by the U.S. Navy. Furthermore, to make the patrol more effective he had ordered Admiral Stark to transfer three battleships, one aircraft carrier, four cruisers, and necessary supporting destroyer squadrons from the Pacific Fleet.[9] In the president's initial plan, once these forces were on station they were to operate under Hemispheric Defense Plan I, by the provisions of which American ships would attack Axis shipping found in the Security Zone.[10] Moreover, the president had decided to place Greenland under American protection and to construct bases there to facilitate the expanded patrol activities.[11] At the same time Roosevelt removed the Red Sea from the list of areas closed to U.S. shipping.[12] All of these measures carried the risk of incidents and confrontations with Hitler's Reichsmarine.

However, for the Roosevelt administration during the spring of 1941, seemingly bold moves toward involvement often proved less bold in execution. The president was still being cautious about public and congressional reaction to openly interventionist policies. Specifically, he was worried about an Anti-Convoy Resolution that had been introduced on 31 March 1941.[13] Perhaps with that resolution in mind the president backed away from the more bellicose Hemispheric Defense Plan I, selecting instead Plan II, by which American ships would not attack but would rather follow and report the positions of Axis shipping, much as they already had covertly been doing. At the same time he decided not to transfer units from the Pacific to the Atlantic. The result of this backing and filling was that on 24 April 1941 Admiral King and Admiral Bristol began their new patrolling duties with forces obviously inadequate to the task.[14] The pendulum of presidential decision making swung back in a few weeks and he reversed his position again, this time allowing a reduced number of ships to join Admiral King's Atlantic Fleet. By the end of May the ships were on station.[15]

The next move toward escort convoying turned upon a decision regarding Iceland. After considerable pressure by the U.S. Department of State, the Icelandic government invited the United States to relieve the British garrison occupying that Atlantic island. The ostensible purpose of the occupation was to deny Iceland to Germany, but in reality the occupation provided a rationale for escort convoying. This indirect approach became somewhat clearer when Admiral King prepared to issue his Operation Plan VI on 19 July 1941. Under these orders ships of the Atlantic Fleet were to support the defense of Iceland and to "escort convoys of the United States and Iceland flag shipping, including shipping of any nationality which may join such United States or Iceland flag convoys, between United States ports and bases, and Iceland." The U.S. Task Force was to "provide protection for convoys in the North Atlantic Ocean as may be required by the strategic situation."[16]

This seemingly decisive move was vitiated by more White House vacillation. Isolationists, like Senator Burton K. Wheeler (Democrat, Montana), had been kicking up so much fuss about convoying that the president did not feel secure enough to face the issue head-on. Furthermore, there was increased Japanese pressure on Indo-China that made him reluctant to remove more ships from the Pacific. For whatever reason or reasons, at the last minute Roosevelt directed that the clause containing the words "ships of any nationality" be struck from the order, thus theoretically restricting the convoys to American and Icelandic shipping.[17] It was not until the Atlantic Conference in mid-August 1941 that the anomalous escort-of-convoy situation was clarified.

Despite the stops and starts, from midsummer on, convoying operations intensified in direct relationship to the U.S. Navy's capacity for execution. A base of operations had been established at Argentia, Newfoundland, as early as February 1941, and on 15 July 1941 a United States Naval Air Station and Naval Operating Base were officially commissioned there. Two months later (19 September), Admiral Bristol transferred the headquarters of the support force to the base on the remote peninsula bordering Placentia Bay. From that base American ships and planes could range out across the North Atlantic, protecting British and American shipping.[18]

In line with agreements reached at the Atlantic Conference, on 1 September orders were issued by Admiral King for the U.S.

Navy to take responsibility for escorting convoys from a point off Newfoundland to the vicinity of Iceland. Eastbound convoys would be handed over to the U.S. Navy by the Canadian Royal Navy off Newfoundland and then passed on to a Royal Navy escort off Iceland. Then the U.S. escort force would pick up a westbound convoy or drop off to shepherd ships into Reykjavik. Thus in September 1941 the United States assumed total responsibility for the mid-Atlantic portion of British-Canadian-U.S. convoys.

The isolationists and the "America Firsters" were convinced that Roosevelt was conspiratorially or stupidly exposing American ships to German torpedoes. Perhaps not surprisingly, some British officers cherished the hope that Senator Wheeler and his ilk were not far off the mark. As Admiral Little, the head of the British Liaison Mission in the United States, wrote to Admiral Pound on 15 July 1941: "I have said before [that] the brightest hope for getting America into the war lies in the escorting arrangements to Iceland, and let us hope that the Germans will not be slow in attacking them." "Otherwise," he continued, "I think it would be best for us to organize an attack by our own submarines and preferably on the escort." World War I and the Spanish-American War were both on Little's mind, for he added that in both those conflicts the "pretext" for American entry had been the loss of American ships or lives at sea. "So," he concluded, "let us hope it will be the same again."[19]

Little had to wait for his wish to come true, but while escorting procedures were being developed, and actually right up until 7 December 1941, the U.S. Navy was engaging in steadily intensifying patrolling activities. Broken into three task forces, U.S. ships patrolled the North Atlantic, Central Atlantic, and South Atlantic. An area of special concern was the Denmark Straits, through which it was anticipated the German commerce raiders might debouch into the North Atlantic shipping lanes. In November 1941, when it was reported that capital ships of the Reichsmarine were about to break out into the Atlantic, an American task force rushed north to confront them. The reports proved to be unfounded, but if the *Prinz Eugen* and the *Tirpitz* had entered the North Atlantic, American ships would have been placed under temporary British command in order to hunt them down.[20]

If American ships under British command hunting down German ships smacks of undeclared naval warfare, it should not be surprising. On 4 September 1941 the U.S.S. *Greer* en route to Iceland had met a German submarine. The *Greer* trailed the submarine and after five hours of cat-and-mouse the German boat turned and fired two torpedoes. The *Greer* dodged these and replied with depth charges. After failing to reestablish sound contact the *Greer* retired to Iceland to report the incident. Filled with indignation, President Roosevelt declared in a nationwide radio address on 11 September that "from now on, if German or Italian vessels of war enter the waters the protection of which is necessary for American defense, they do so at their own risk."[21] The U.S. Navy interpreted this speech to imply "shoot on sight" and issued orders accordingly. As the foremost authority on this phase of U.S. naval history suggests, "From the date of the *Greer* incident, 4 September 1941, the United States was engaged in a *de facto* naval war with Germany on the Atlantic Ocean."[22]

Atlantic Conference

Some of the decisions that led to the extraordinary undeclared war were made between 10 and 15 August 1941 in Placentia Bay off Argentia, Newfoundland, at the meeting known to history as the Atlantic Conference. At that conference, President Roosevelt and a small staff met with Prime Minister Churchill and a large British delegation. That dramatic meeting, which was the first of a series of summit conferences between American and British leadership, had several products. They included the Atlantic Charter, decisions on Russia's share of Lend-Lease supplies, and the less tangible, but extremely important, establishment of personal ties between the leadership of the two countries.[23]

Although there is no denying the importance of its benefits, it would be incorrect to ascribe too great a significance to the results of the conference. In many ways the meeting was inconclusive and public relations considerations seem to have outweighed concrete accomplishments. This characterization is especially appropriate in relation to the military strategy developed at the conference. While a number of important contacts were made and many critical issues were raised, only one specific decision was made. After months of vacillation, the president agreed to allow the U.S. Navy to escort convoys, including British and Canadian merchant shipping, as far east as Iceland. That was definitely an issue that naval authorities in both countries had wanted settled, and settlement they got; however, the other strategy aspects of the conference were noteworthy primarily for their inconclusiveness.[24]

The lack of decisiveness was particularly frustrating to the British participants. The chiefs of staff had come to the meeting, hoping, optimistically, to be sure, for some American commitment to fight somewhere at some specified time. Failing that, they hoped to get American comments and views on some important matters of strategy and divisions of responsibility. Disappointingly, the senior American delegates, Admiral Stark, General Marshall, and Major General H. H. Arnold, were unwilling to discuss these matters at length and, incredibly, seemed at times actually to lack interest in strategic matters, preferring to discuss matériel and supplies. The junior members of the American staff, though pumped assiduously by their British counterparts, appeared more intent on having a drink or two (after days of confinement and teetotalism on the U.S. Navy's ships) and engaging in friendly banter than in discussing military topics. To the disappointment and amazement of some British officers, the Americans seemed simply unconcerned about the war. There were a number of informal meetings and dinners among the officers involved, but there were only two staff conferences as such during the six days the British and American ships were anchored together in Placentia Bay.

Despite British efforts to arrange an earlier session, the first meeting took place on 11 August, when the British chief's memorandum "Review of General Strategy" formed the basis for discussion. This paper stressed the importance of the Atlantic area, the Middle East, and Singapore. At the same time it emphasized the importance of American aid and spoke quite explicitly about the significance of American intervention which would "revolutionize the whole situation." The American officers would doubtless have agreed with that assessment, but Admiral Stark said that "General Marshall and I are of the opinion that this meeting today is one for discussion and not a meeting for reaching new agreements or accepting new commitments."[25]

It soon became apparent that neither Stark nor Marshall was willing to provide assurance of intervention as the British had hoped or to agree to the British plan for offensive action once the defensive phase of the war was concluded. The British chiefs still counted heavily on blockade, subversive activity, and bombing as the tools with which to weaken and ultimately wreck the Third Reich. Especially important in the British view was bombing, and they wanted more American planes to carry out the planned air offensive. With the exception of General Arnold, who not surprisingly was quite enthusiastic about air operations, the American officers were not convinced that the war could be won without landing large armies on the continent of Europe. Furthermore, as Stark had indicated, General Marshall and the majority of the others in the U.S. delegation were loath to get into any wideranging discussion of Grand Strategy. The Americans had come to the meeting without extensive preparation and insofar as they were ready for anything they were ready to discuss production and supply allocation under the Lend-Lease Act. Admiral Stark summed it up when he said that in the American view the ABC agreement should "continue to serve as the basic guide for the military effort of both the United States and the British Commonwealth."[26] He did agree, however, to peruse the "Review of General Strategy" with the British, although no detailed response would be forthcoming until it had been subjected to careful scrutiny.

General Marshall agreed with his navy colleague, but did unburden himself of some fairly explicit, perhaps intemperate, comments. For one thing, it was his view that the British were putting too much emphasis on the Middle East. Priorities would have to be established between the Russian demands for aid, the Middle East, and the Far East. In that regard Marshall said he was preoccupied with the developing situation in the Far East and wanted to insure that the American garrison in the Philippines was not starved because of diversion of material to secondary theaters. As far as shipments of aid were concerned, Russia was primary and the Middle East was far down the list again. In a demonstration of poor coordination between the branches of the American military staff, Admiral Stark's comments revealed that he did not share Marshall's interest in the Far East. It was Stark's view that "we can afford to see it all 'go West' without bothering ourselves unduly."[27]

That remark did not cause the open opposition that such comments had elicited from Admiral Bellairs during the ABC Conference. Perhaps the British were becoming more subtle or perhaps they realized the futility of confronting American prejudices head-on. Their strategy review highlighted the importance of

Singapore and although Churchill had stated emphatically that nothing that could happen in Malaya "could amount to a fifth part of the loss of Egypt, the Suez Canal, and the Middle East,"[28] there is little evidence that naval thinkers like Pound shared his view. Nevertheless, for the moment at least, the British had decided to concentrate on getting the United States into the war in the Atlantic and on gaining "collaboration" in the Mediterranean area.[29] Marshall and Stark might have differed about the Far East, but they could agree on circumventing British desires concerning any commitment and they managed to convince the chiefs that commitments would not be made. Therefore, after some further discussion of priorities and an agreement by Stark to replace British ships at Gibraltar by American ships "in case of war," the meeting adjourned.

There was one other brief conference on Tuesday morning. After a foul-up in communications the staffs got together at 11:30 A.M. on board the *Prince of Wales*. The British tried to gain more specific information about American intentions and there was some brief discussion of the status of the ABC talks. Again the Americans were not very forthcoming, preferring to talk about supply. Accordingly, most of the time was spent going over material assistance and distribution priorities. Time was now growing short before the British departure, and the meeting broke up without any definite agreement.

In terms of strategy development, the Atlantic Conference was insignificant. The British had concluded few agreements with their U.S. counterparts and, with the exception of the convoy issue, few things were decided. The ABC agreement still stood as the basis for Anglo-American cooperation and to many of the Britishers present the Americans seemed little closer to war than they had been five months previously when that agreement had been concluded. The U.S. Navy was becoming progressively more involved in the major theater and that was satisfying, but they were still far from joining in hostilities and thus decisively altering the balance. Furthermore, after Stark and Marshall reviewed the chiefs' strategy review they reported that they found many of its proposals "unacceptable."[30]

Singapore Conferences

The major strategic legacy of the ABC Conference was a series of meetings concerning strategy in the Far East. It had been agreed at Washington that the Pacific, and most explicitly the Far East, was to be a secondary theater; however, agreeing on strategy in that secondary theater had proved far more difficult. In an attempt to work out the differences of opinion two moves were taken. First, Admiral Danckwerts and Captain Clarke went to Pearl Harbor to consult with Admiral Kimmel, the commander in chief of the Pacific Fleet. Second, another conference was convened in Singapore to discuss Far Eastern strategy.

The Danckwerts-Clarke visit to Kimmel was as unproductive as the Atlantic Conference. Admiral Kimmel was unwilling to talk in detail about offensive action and implied that aside from the outdated concept of a step-by-step advance in the Marshall and Caroline islands *after war began*, he planned no action that might be construed as bellicose. To the British it appeared that the attitude common at Pearl Harbor was hope that their "mere existence" would restrain the Imperial Navy. After a series of meetings, it was Danckwerts's conclusion that, unfortunately, the British government could not count on "any active demonstrations in Japanese waters" by the Americans.[31]

Shortly after the ABC Conference ended, Admiral Stark and General Marshall asked the Chiefs of Staff to hold another strategy session in Singapore "as soon as practicable."[32] The meetings were duly held between 21 April and 27 April 1941, with Captain W. R. Purnell, chief of staff to Admiral Thomas Hart, the commander in chief of the Asiatic Fleet, as the U.S. representative.

Purnell had attended two previous sessions in Singapore, one in October 1940 and the other in February 1941. At the first meeting Purnell had merely been an observer, but at the second one he had been empowered to "agree to a joint plan of operations of U.S.-British-Dutch forces, but without making political commitments." He had further been warned to advise the British and the Dutch that plans based upon American entry into a Far Eastern conflict "would not be sound" because there was doubt that Congress would declare war if the Japanese attacked territory not under U.S. control.[33] Perhaps because of the very conditional attitude of the Americans, little had been accomplished. Actually, the Americans thought themselves ready to go further than the other representatives, for they believed that the "conference ended at about the agreements which we expected to begin [with]."[34] The British commander at Singapore, Air Vice Marshal Sir Robert Brooke-Popham, was not impressed by the results of the meeting either, despite the fact that it had been conducted in an atmosphere of "friendliness, full cooperation, and complete frankness."[35]

Thus Purnell could approach the new meetings from a position of good personal relations and very little else. The ABC Conference had stipulated that authorities of the United States, the British Commonwealth, and the Netherlands East Indies should collaborate in the "formation of strategic plans" and that was the charge facing Captain Purnell, Air Vice Marshal Sir Robert Brooke-Popham, Vice Admiral Sir Geoffrey Layton, British naval commander in chief of the China Station, Major General H. ter Poorten, chief of the general staff, Netherlands East Indies, and the delegates from Australia and New Zealand.[36] Purnell had been directed to tell this group that there had been few changes in the basic war plan of the Asiatic Fleet. In case of war with Japan there would be little attempt to hold Luzon or the Philippines. Admiral Hart's ships would leave Manila and retire toward the southwest, where they would combine with the British and Dutch fleets. If this situation evolved and if some general cooperative agreement had been reached, the American ships would be placed under British strategic command. What Purnell wanted to discover was the initial deployment proposed by the British and the Dutch. The basic assumption concerning American action that the British and Dutch could make was that Japan would be America's enemy "just as soon as we enter hostilities against Germany-Italy."[37] What Purnell could not assure his counterparts about was what would happen if the Japanese attacked British or Dutch territory without engaging the United States. In similar fashion, they could not tell him what action their governments would take if the Japanese attacked American territory and avoided British and Dutch possessions.

The conferees did make certain recommendations to their governments on this delicate subject. They recommended that Japan be engaged by all the powers represented in any one of these contingencies: (1) "direct act of war" by Japanese armed forces against American, British, or Dutch territory; (2) movement of

Japanese forces into Thailand west of the meridian of Bangkok or south of the Kra Isthmus; (3) occupation of Portuguese Timor or the Loyalty Islands off New Caledonia.[38]

There was insufficient agreement, however, to make recommendations on deployment of naval units once hostilities began. The British saw everything as pivoting on Singapore and wanted to concentrate on protecting convoys in and out of the Malayan base. The New Zealand and Australian representatives wanted to use their forces to protect the vital sea-lanes around their coasts and the Dutch would only agree to assign a small portion of their forces to a unified command. Fulfilling all these desires would result in an impossibly wide dispersal of forces, and the emphasis on convoy struck the Americans as unduly defensive. Purnell's reactions can only be judged by those of Admiral Hart, who was later to characterize the British obsession with convoy and escort as "a basic disagreement" that resulted in a failure to "make the most of our combat power by the concentration of our ships and maintaining readiness to attack." Admiral Hart also totally disagreed with the idea of allowing Commonwealth forces to retire to their respective coasts once shooting began. It was his opinion that they should "work on the fighting front."[39]

There was also apparent in the proceedings a disturbing degree of "maneuvering by the home-land British, in the direction of gaining control." Naturally, this was resisted by the Dominion representatives but it contributed to an atmosphere in which everyone was "keeping the guard up" and there did not seem to be enough "trustfulness" to insure unity. Even Admiral Layton, whom the Americans liked and respected, held back any information he had on long-range planning.[40] Part of the explanation for this reticence was that long-simmering British debate over a commitment to the Dutch. No decision had yet been made and the British were still hesitant to make any formal commitment until they had a commitment from the Americans.[41]

Brooke-Popham was almost as displeased with the Americans as they were with him. For one thing the British commander found the U.S. representatives to be "remarkably afraid of the Civil authorities in Washington and very shy of expressing any opinions on any subject that touched on the political sphere." Furthermore, he was disappointed that the Americans had not sent more senior officers—he had hoped that Admiral Hart himself would attend rather than delegating a mere captain. Since the topics had been primarily naval, Brooke-Popham had been at pains to impress the Americans with the need for the U.S. Pacific Fleet to take "a more active part" in any Far Eastern war. On the other hand, Brooke-Popham did feel that the Americans were "fully impressed with the importance of Singapore to the whole of the Far East."[42]

With Brooke-Popham trying to impress the apolitical Americans with the importance of Singapore and with the Americans sensing that the British were too defensive and not forthcoming enough, it is surprising that any agreements were reached. However, by the time the conference adjourned on 27 April there was a joint document ready, known as ABD-1 (American-British-Dutch-1).[43] The British may not have been pleased with the American unwillingness to discuss political factors, but to Admiral Stark and General Marshall it appeared that this document incorporated too many political considerations and with that as their stated reason they disapproved it on 3 July 1941.[44]

There were other inconclusive meetings in the Far East during the summer, but on 11 November 1941 Admiral Stark advised the commander of the Asiatic Fleet that "ABD-1 and ABD-2 are dead and a completely new approach will be required."[45] Admiral Hart and Admiral Thomas Phillips were meeting on 6 December 1941, at Manila, to try to work out such an agreement when news of a Japanese force steaming south brought an end to their discussions.

But unfortunately for the Allies, war did not bring an end to the debates about Pacific strategy. The Japanese proved to be an implacable foe, fully prepared to take advantage of American, British, and Dutch confusion. The military forces of the Australian-British-Dutch-American Command (ABDA) proved to be no match for the forces of His Imperial Majesty, the Emperor Hirohito; within four months the product of hundreds of years of European and American colonialism had been swept away. Perhaps nothing could have saved it, but there can be no question that the lack of unified goals, the absence of coordinated plans, and the inability of commanders to subordinate narrow national interests to the common good contributed to the disarray and ultimately to the disaster.

Appendix

So many individuals played a prominent role in this study that it seemed only fair to give the reader some idea of the future careers of the "dramatis personae."

Vice Admiral Bernard L. ("Count") Austin. Austin continued to serve with Admiral Ghormley in London until the spring of 1942. At that time he was reassigned to the Pacific where he first commanded several destroyers and then a Destroyer Division in the Marshall Island campaign. He next served on the staff of the commander for all destroyers in the Pacific. Following that service "Count" was moved up the administrative ladder to the Joint Chiefs of Staff and National Security Council where the lessons in procedure he had learned from the British served him and his country well.

Major General William Joseph ("Wild Bill") Donovan. Donovan performed a number of prewar special missions for President Roosevelt in Europe and in the Middle East. In July 1941 he was appointed coordinator of information, a cover for a secret intelligence unit. A year later the nation was at war and Donovan was made director of Strategic Services, the wartime forerunner of the Central Intelligence Agency.

Vice Admiral Robert L. Ghormley. Ghormley continued on in London until April 1942, when he was assigned as commander of the South Pacific area. In that role it fell to him to direct the attack at Guadalcanal in the fall of 1942. Unfortunately for Ghormley, that operation did not go well and in mid-October he was replaced by the more aggressive Admiral William "Bull" Halsey. Although he served throughout the war, Ghormley's career was finished.

Admiral Royal E. Ingersoll. Ingersoll served as assistant chief of naval operations until January 1942 when he replaced Admiral King as commander in chief of the Atlantic Fleet. He remained in that position throughout the war and thus worked closely with the British in carrying out the Atlantic First strategy.

Vice Admiral Alan Kirk. Kirk returned to Washington in December 1940 and in 1941 was appointed director of naval intelligence. In the fall of 1941 he was detached from that post to participate in the escorting operations going forward in the North Atlantic. When war broke out he was sent back to London, this time as chief of staff for the commander of the U.S. Naval Forces in Europe. In 1943 he was designated commander of the amphibious forces of the U.S. Atlantic Fleet. In that role he commanded the task forces that invaded the European continent, first at Sicily in July 1943 and then at Normandy in June 1944.

Vice Admiral Sir Tom Phillips. Phillips was detached from his position as vice chief of the naval staff in November 1941 and given command of the Far Eastern Fleet. He arrived at Singapore on 2 December 1941 and flew immediately to Manila to attempt a coordination of plans with Admiral Thomas Hart's Asiatic Fleet. Word reached Phillips in the Philippines that a Japanese striking force had been sighted off Malaya. He hastened back to Singapore just in time to put his under-strength command in the path of the Japanese forces. The result was the loss of the *Repulse*, the *Prince of Wales*, Phillips, and thirteen hundred men on 9 December 1941.

Admiral J. O. Richardson. Richardson had done much to redirect American naval policy and call attention to its deficiencies; he was rewarded for his pertinacity and his impertinence by being removed from command of the U.S. Fleet in January 1941. His replacement, Admiral Husband Kimmel, had his career ruined when many of Richardson's fears materialized on 7 December 1941. Richardson served briefly as a member of the General Board and then retired in October 1942.

Admiral Harold Stark. Stark was removed as chief of naval operations in the wake of the Pearl Harbor attack and assigned, fittingly, considering his Plan Dog, as commander of the U.S. Naval Forces in Europe. He served in that post until August 1945 when, by order of the secretary of the navy, he was removed from command because of his role at the time of the initial Japanese attack on the Pacific Fleet. Thus Stark, who had tried so diligently to prepare the U.S. Navy for war, was dishonored for not having done enough.

Admiral Richmond Kelly Turner. Turner left the War Plans Division in the spring of 1942 and went first to the Southwest Pacific, the area he wished the British to defend. From the Southwest he went to the Central Pacific where he commanded the amphibious forces that attacked the Gilbert Islands and Marshall Islands. Then, in February, he directed the amphibious assault on the Japanese forces on Iwo Jima. Captain Turner ended the war as a full admiral.

Abbreviations

ABC	American-British-Canadian Conference
ADM	Admiralty Records
Cab	Cabinet (or War Cabinet) Office Papers
CMD	Classified Microfilm Dispatches, U.S. Navy
CNO	Office of Chief of Naval Operations
ComNavEu	Commander, Naval Forces Europe
C.O.S.	Chiefs of Staff
F.O.	Foreign Office
FR	*Foreign Relations of the United States: Diplomatic Papers*
JP	Joint Planning Committee (Royal Navy and British Army)
JPC	Joint Planning Committee (U.S. Army and U.S. Navy)
Naval Archives	Operational Naval Archives, U.S. Navy
NID	Naval Intelligence Division
OpNav	Operations Division, U.S. Navy
PHA	*Pearl Harbor Attack: Hearings of the Joint Congressional Committee on the Investigation of the Pearl Harbor Attack*
PPF	President's Personal File, Roosevelt Papers
PREM	Premier, Prime Minister's Operational File (PREM 3)
PRO	Public Record Office
PSF	President's Secretary's File, Roosevelt Papers
S.D.	State Department
S.D.F.	State Department Files

WM   War Minutes or Conclusions of the War Cabinet
W.O.   War Office
WP   War Cabinet Memoranda
WPD   War Plans Division (U.S. Army and U.S. Navy)

Notes

1. Stephen Roskill, *Naval Policy between the Wars*. Volume 2, published in 1976, is entitled *The Period of Reluctant Rearmament, 1930–1939*.

2. Harry Hopkins found that many Britons confidently expected American entry into the war in April 1941. See Robert E. Sherwood, *Roosevelt and Hopkins*, p. 263.

3. Roskill, *Naval Policy between the Wars*, 1:314, 330.

4. For a contemporary view see Dudley W. Knox, *The Eclipse of American Seapower*. For a more analytical opinion see Samuel Eliot Morison, *The History of United States Naval Operations in World War II*, 1:xxxii–lxii and 3:19. (The introduction to the first volume is written by Captain Knox.) Japan made more progress at the London Naval Conference when her cruiser ratio was raised from 3 to 3.5. At the same conference, Britain and the United States accepted parity in all categories. See Raymond G. O'Connor, *Perilous Equilibrium*.

5. Henry Morgenthau, Jr., *From the Morgenthau Diaries*, 2:95.

6. For information on the Vinson-Trammel Act see Charles F. Elliot, "The Genesis of the Modern U.S. Navy," pp. 62–69.

7. U.S. Congress, House, Naval Affairs Committee, *Hearings on the Sundry Legislation Affecting the Naval Establishment*, 76th Cong., 3d sess., 1940; of special interest are comments on pp. 3353–54. See also U.S. Congress, Senate, Committee on Naval Affairs, *Hearings on Construction of Certain Naval Vessels*, 76th Cong., 3d sess., 1940.

8. These observations are taken from several sources, but all are included in Donald C. Watt, *Personalities and Politics*, p. 42.

9. See Letter, Admiral J. O. Richardson, commander, U.S. Fleet, to Admiral Harold Stark, chief of naval operations, 26 January 1940, in U.S. Congress, Senate, *Pearl Harbor Attack*, 79th Cong., 1st sess., 1946, 14:924 (hereafter cited as *PHA*).

10. For negative reactions to what was seen as a lack of British resolution in Asia see especially Henry L. Stimson and McGeorge Bundy, *On Active Service in Peace and War*, pp. 233–37, and Henry L. Stimson, *The Far Eastern Crisis*. Stimson was secretary of state when the Japanese attacked Manchuria (September 1931). The United States adopted a hard-line policy against this aggression and Stimson was disappointed that the British did not consider their lack of support as a demonstration of weakness, which was the U.S. interpretation.

11. Samuel Eliot Morison, *Strategy and Compromise*, p. 22.

Chapter 2

1. Robert A. Divine, *The Illusion of Neutrality*, p. 163.
2. Sumner Welles, *Seven Decisions That Shaped History*, pp. 70–71.
3. Bradford A. Lee, *Britain and the Sino-Japanese War, 1937–1939*, pp. 28–29.
4. See Sir J. R. M. Butler, *Grand Strategy, September 1939–June 1941*, 2:323ff.
5. For information on War Plan ORANGE see Louis B. Morton, *The War in the Pacific*, chap. 1. See also Louis B. Morton, "War Plan ORANGE," pp. 221–50.
6. Morton, *War in the Pacific*, pp. 38–39.
7. Morison, *United States Naval Operations*, 3:22.
8. Ibid., p. 24.
9. See Waldo Heinrichs, Jr., "The Role of the United States Navy," pp. 197–223.
10. Divine, *Illusion of Neutrality*, pp. 221–23. For an interpretation that questions the traditional "storm of protest" view, see Dorothy Borg, "Notes on Roosevelt's Quarantine Speech," pp. 405–33.
11. Lee, *Britain and the Sino-Japanese War*, p. 54.
12. Ibid., p. 55.
13. Jay Pierrepont Moffat, *The Moffat Papers, 1919–1943*, p. 163.
14. Ibid., p. 182.
15. Admiral Richardson to Admiral Stark, 26 January 1940, in *PHA*, 14:924.
16. Sir Anthony Eden, *The Memoirs of Anthony Eden, Earl of Avon*, 1:611.
17. U.S. Department of State, *Foreign Relations of the United States: Diplomatic Papers, 1937*, 4:153 (hereafter cited as *FR*). For background on Davis's conversation and the general subject of Roosevelt's blockade scheme, see John McVicker Haight, Jr., "Franklin D. Roosevelt and a Naval Quarantine of Japan," pp. 203–26. Also see Heinrichs, "Role of the United States Navy," pp. 211–13. The individual most often cited as the originator of the blockade concept is Admiral Harry Yarnell who in the summer of 1937 was commander of the Asiatic Fleet. Interestingly, the British Admiralty considered a similar blockade in June 1937 (see Stephen Pelz, *Race to Pearl Harbor*, pp. 183 and 199). For the full British perspective see Lawrence Pratt, "Anglo-American Naval Conversations on the Far East of January 1938," pp. 745–63.
18. *Eden Memoirs*, 2:536–40.
19. *FR: 1937*, 3:724–25.
20. Ibid.
21. Sir Edward Grey had made this interpretation of the talks (see Samuel R. Williamson, Jr., *The Politics of Grand Strategy*, p. 354). For Williamson's interesting discussion of the whole issue of commitment in which he contends that the degree of obligation has been exaggerated, see chap. 15.
22. One day, in the fall of 1915, H. C. Breckenridge, the acting secretary of war, found President Wilson "trembling and white with passion." Wilson had just read an article in the *Baltimore Sun* claiming that the General Staff was preparing war plans in case there was war with Germany. The president ordered the practice stopped immediately (see Frederick Palmer, *Newton D. Baker*, 1:40).
23. Morton, *War in the Pacific*, p. 40.
24. Haight, "Franklin D. Roosevelt," p. 207.
25. *Eden Memoirs*, 1:617.
26. *FR: 1937*, 3:800
27. *Eden Memoirs*, 1:615–16.
28. William D. Leahy Diary, 13 December 1937, Library of Congress, Washington, D.C.
29. The opinion quoted is that of Moffat on 16 December 1937 (see "Diplomatic Journals of Jay Pierrepont Moffat," in Jay Pierrepont Moffat Diary and Papers, Harvard University, Cambridge, Mass.).
30. The conversation is reconstructed from Ambassador Lindsay's report to London, 17 December 1937, Admiralty Records 116/3922 (hereafter cited as ADM), Public Record Office, London (hereafter cited as PRO).
31. In his telegram to Lindsay, Eden had urged Anglo-American collaboration, believ-

ing that "only thus can the peace of the world be assured without a shot being fired" (*Eden Memoirs*, 1:617–18).

32. Admiralty minutes, 17 December 1937, ADM 116/3922, PRO. The British also went back to the record of World War I cooperation and included an outline of events in staff papers drawn up in preparation for staff talks. Items on which Roosevelt had been helpful were marked, but no reference was made to the activities of Commodore Gaunt. An exhaustive search of pertinent records in the United States and the United Kingdom has failed to turn up any evidence to support Roosevelt's intriguing story. At the same time, internal evidence suggests that there was at least some form of intelligence exchange.

33. Much of the information for this section on the Ingersoll Mission is based on an interview with Vice Admiral Royal E. Ingersoll, Washington, D.C., December 1966. Useful information was also found in the Vice Admiral Royal E. Ingersoll File, United States–United Kingdom Staff Conversations Correspondence, War Plans Division: Office of Chief of Naval Operations (CNO), U.S. Operational Naval Archives, Washington, D.C. (hereafter cited as US-UK Staff Conversations Correspondence, WPD:CNO, Naval Archives). Helpful and of general interest is the manuscript by Captain Tracy B. Kittredge entitled "United States-British Naval Cooperation: 1939–1942" (hereafter cited as Kittredge MS), Naval Archives.

34. A few days later Roosevelt wrote his British friend Colonel Arthur Murray: "Things international still drift in the wrong direction in spite of the success we have had in getting a quick and on the whole fairly satisfactory reply from Japan. I am glad to say that your government people seem at last to be ready and willing to converse with me 'off the record and informally' but I still wish we could have more of that sort of thing without its getting into your papers and ours" (Roosevelt to Murray, 31 December 1937, President's Personal File (hereafter cited as PPF), Box 435, Franklin D. Roosevelt Papers, Franklin D. Roosevelt Memorial Library, Hyde Park, N.Y.).

35. *Eden Memoirs*, 1:619–20.

36. Haight, "Franklin D. Roosevelt," p. 216.

37. Alexander Cadogan, *The Diaries of Sir Alexander Cadogan*, p. 31.

38. Foreign Office (hereafter cited as F.O.) to Lindsay, 1 January 1938, ADM 116/3622, PRO.

39. Lindsay to F.O., 3 January 1938, ADM 116/3622, PRO.

40. Captain Russell Willson, "Notes on Conversation with Admiralty, January 3, 1938," WPD:CNO, Naval Archives (hereafter cited as Willson Notes). Captain Willson was U.S. naval attaché in London and attended the sessions with Ingersoll.

41. Willson Notes, 5 January 1938, Naval Archives.

42. *Cadogan Diaries*, pp. 32–33. Cadogan identifies himself as the author of the telegram and makes his intent explicit.

43. *FR: 1938*, 3:7–8.

44. Stimson and Bundy, *Peace and War*, pp. 400–401. Copies of Roosevelt's and Hull's letters were released to the press.

45. Divine, *Illusion of Neutrality*, pp. 219–21.

46. Haight, "Franklin D. Roosevelt," p. 219.

47. *Cadogan Diaries*, p.34. David Dilks's interpretation appears on p. 33.

48. For background and details of the plan see Sumner Welles, *The Time for Decision*, pp. 61–67.

49. *Cadogan Diaries*, p. 37. For Chamberlain's diary account of his reaction see Iain Macleod, *Neville Chamberlain*, p. 212. Here Chamberlain says the scheme appeared to him as "fantastic and likely to excite the derision of Germany and Italy."

50. Welles, *Time for Decision*, p. 66.

51. The British copy of the Record can be found in ADM 116/3922, PRO. Haight suspects that this Record also influenced Chamberlain in turning down the president's proposed conference (see Haight, "Franklin D. Roosevelt," pp. 221–22).

52. Message, CNO to Commanders, U.S. and Asiatic Fleet, 2 February 1938, WPD:CNO, Naval Archives. A brief description of the Ingersoll Mission can be found in *PHA*, 9:4273–76.

53. See "Periscope," *Newsweek*, 31 January 1938.

54. For Roosevelt's further schemes see Haight, "Franklin D. Roosevelt," p. 222.

55. Welles, *Seven Decisions*, p. 30; *Eden Memoirs*, 1:620 and Winston S. Churchill, *The Second World War*, 1:254.

Chapter 3

1. Morton, "War Plan ORANGE," p. 249.

2. Heinrichs, "Role of the United States Navy," p. 215.

3. Message, CNO to Commanders, U.S. and Asiatic Fleet, 2 February 1938, WPD: CNO, Naval Archives.

4. Minute, 9 February 1938; ADM 116/4302, PRO. Roskill, *Naval Policy between the Wars*, 2:365–66.

5. Minute, 8 March 1938, ibid.

6. Minute, 12 March 1938, ibid.

7. Board Decision 3547, 12 May 1938, ibid.

8. Report of Conversation, 20 May 1938, ibid.

9. Minute, 30 May 1938, ibid.

10. Minute, 14 June 1938, ibid.

11. Minute, 17 June 1938, ibid.

12. The sequence of events is traced in a minute written by the Director of Navy Intelligence, 2 December 1938, ibid.

13. Minute, 27 March 1939, ibid.

14. Sir Llewellyn Woodward and Rohan Butler, eds., *Documents on British Foreign Policy, 1919–1939*, 3:627–28.

15. Lord Halifax, *Fullness of Days*, p. 197.

16. Memorandum, 10 January 1939, ADM 116/3922, PRO.

17. Memorandum, 16 January 1939, ibid.

18. "Record of Conversations with British in Regard to Bringing Ingersoll Conversations Up-to-Date," 13 January 1939, Ingersoll File, WPD:CNO, Naval Archives.

19. Letter, Admiralty to F.O., 23 January 1939, ADM 116/3922, PRO.

20. Telegram, F.O. to Lindsay, 19 March 1939, ibid.

21. Telegram, Lindsay to F.O., 21 March 1939, ibid.

22. Telegram, Lindsay to F.O., 22 March 1939, ibid.

23. Minute, 24 March 1939, ibid.

24. Minute, 27 March 1939, ibid.

25. Minute, 26 April 1939, ibid.

26. Ibid.

27. Note on file in F.O. 371/23560, 2 May 1939, in ADM 116/3922, PRO. Cadogan thought that Lord Halifax, the secretary of state, had ordered him to draft the message, but he was not sure. Lord Chatfield, the minister for the coordination of defense (previous first sea lord), remembered something about a conversation with the American ambassador at some social function, but the details escaped him.

28. Telegram, Lindsay to F.O., 2 May 1939, ADM 116/3922, PRO.

29. Louis Morton, *The War in the Pacific*, pp. 31–32.

30. Orders to Hampton, 22 May 1939, in F.O. 371/23561, PRO.

31. This account has been reconstructed from the American record in the Ingersoll File, WPD:CNO, Naval Archives, and the British record in ADM 116/3922, PRO.

32. Morton, *War in the Pacific*, pp. 71–72.

33. Heinrichs, "Role of the United States Navy." p. 217.

Chapter 4

1. Sir John Wheeler-Bennett, *King George VI*, pp. 388 and 391–92.

2. Lindsay to F.O., 1 July 1939, ADM 116/3922, PRO.

3. Memorandum by Director of Plans, 10 July 1939, ibid.

4. Admiralty to Commander in Chief of the American and West Indian squadrons, 17 July 1939. The date of the cable from Lindsay in which he reported the president's reaction is 8 July 1939, ADM 116/3922, PRO.

5. The Director of Plans concluded that the British questions had caused the president

to "think, for the first time, on this project." The result had been that "His Majesty's Government cannot expect that important help at the outset of the war which the plan in its first form seemed to promise" (Memorandum, 10 July 1939, ADM 116/3922, PRO).

6. Divine, *Illusion of Neutrality*, chap. 9.

7. Churchill, *Second World War*, 1:440–41. The best single collection of Churchill-Roosevelt telegrams can be found in the Premier 3 File (hereafter cited as PREM 3), War Cabinet Office Papers, PRO, but this was not maintained with any regularity until after Churchill became prime minister. Also see the somewhat unsatisfactory *Roosevelt and Churchill*, edited by Francis Loewenheim, Harold D. Langley, and Manfred Jonas.

8. John G. Winant, ambassador to England (1941–45), suggests that Prime Minister Chamberlain "delegated the task" of keeping President Roosevelt informed on the war situation to Churchill (*Letter from Grosvenor Square*, p. 37n.). This may be correct; however, no other reference to this "delegation" can be found. In describing the beginning of the correspondence Churchill said that he replied to Roosevelt's opening message only after "having obtained the permission of the Prime Minister" (*New York Times*, 18 April 1945, p. 18).

9. Letter, Halifax to Lothian, 15 November 1939, F.O. A 7530/5992/51, PRO. There has been confusion about the date of Churchill's first message. When the Foreign Office became concerned about the link and began asking for details the Admiralty said they would not date Churchill's first message but thought it was 2 October. Since Roosevelt's letter did not arrive until 3 October that is obviously incorrect.

10. The first of these was not available to scholars until January 1972 when the British opened their World War II Papers at the Public Record Office.

11. Naval Attaché in Berlin to Navy Department, 4 October 1939, President's Secretary's File (hereafter cited as PSF), Navy Department, Box 4, Roosevelt Papers.

12. Message and information pertaining to it and the receipt of the president's letter can be found in ADM 199/1928, which is still held at the Admiralty Historical Branch, PRO.

13. See Henry Morgenthau, Jr., Diary, especially 9 October 1939 entry and message, Navy Department to Roosevelt, 11 October 1939, PSF, Navy Department, Box 4, Roosevelt Papers.

14. For information on the meeting and the Declaration of Panama, which established the Security Zone, see *FR: 1940*, 5:15–41.

15. Copy of message in F.O. A 7530/5992/51, PRO. See also *FR: 1939*, 5:85.

16. A copy of Phillips's memorandum is in *FR: 1939*, 5:86.

17. Letter, Churchill to Halifax, 16 October 1939, ADM 199/1928, PRO.

18. Copy of message in F.O. A 7530/5992/51, PRO; copy also in PSF, Churchill-Roosevelt File, Roosevelt Papers. Churchill implies that there have been no intervening communications by closing: "this and my former cable give all my news."

19. Memorandum, 2 November 1939, in F.O. A 7530/5992/51, PRO.

20. In a letter General Sir Ian Jacob wrote to General Hastings Ismay (Lord Ismay) years later, commenting on doubts about Churchill when he was first made prime minister, Jacob says: "We (Colonel Leslie Hollis) didn't know him so well as you, and had merely seen his effect on everyone when he was First Lord and the friction he created" (Jacob to Ismay, 24 January 1959, I/14/69, Lord Ismay Papers, Kings College, London.

21. Roosevelt wrote: "Under existing legislation . . . the request you make could not be granted unless the sight desired . . . were made available to all other governments at the same time it was made available to Great Britain" (Roosevelt to Chamberlain, 31 August 1939, Official File, Great Britain, 1939–40, Roosevelt Papers).

22. See notes in File MO/15450/39, ADM 199/1928, PRO.

23. H. Duncan Hall, *North American Supply*, pp. 44–46. At the time of Pearl Harbor the Royal Air Force was still without the highly overrated American device.

24. Halifax to Churchill, 8 December 1939, F.O. A 8146/5992/51, PRO.

25. Churchill, *Second World War*, 1:529. The presidential reluctance is implied by the first lord. The *Graf Spee* had just been sunk off the River Plate and a German merchant ship had been scuttled near the U.S. coast when pursued by British cruisers. The *Graf Spee* incident had sparked a formal protest by the American republics.

26. Sir E. L. Woodward, *British Foreign Policy in the Second World War* (1970), 1:335n. The timing was very close on this message, for the Argentine ambassador talked with Lothian on 26 December.

27. The British had been following Kennedy's attitudes closely and every conversation he had was carefully reported. There also is information in his file which would appear to have only been available if one had access to his private correspondence. See F.O. A 1945/605/45; A 7195/1090/45, and A 6016/98/45, all in PRO. Sir John Balfour suggests that the Foreign Office felt that Kennedy was not only pessimistic about British chances but also very indiscreet (personal interview with author, London, July 1971).

28. Note on File, F.O. A 9128/5992/51, PRO. Months later the Foreign Office official, though still not enthusiastic about the practice, suggested that Churchill may have been using the Kennedy link either (1) to keep Kennedy "in play" or (2) to manipulate the situation so that the Germans will "still get to know and understand how close our liaison with the Americans is" (Note on File, F.O. A 3261/1/51 signed Prowne, 14 June 1940, PRO).

29. Note on File, F.O. A 3261/1/51 signed Prowne, 14 June 1940, PRO.

30. Halifax to Churchill, 6 January 1930, ADM 199/1928, PRO.

31. Halifax to Churchill, 19 January 1940, ibid.

32. Ibid. For Foreign Office view see Woodward, *British Foreign Policy* (1970), 1:335n.

33. The full and complicated story is told in W. N. Medlicott, *The Economic Blockade*, 1:350–66. The Ministry of Economic Warfare was not pleased by this surrender of belligerent rights, but was left to accept it in the interest of the higher goal of Anglo-American friendship. There is a brief reference to the episode in Cordell Hull, *The Memoirs of Cordell Hull*, 1:733.

34. *FR: 1940*, 2:10.

35. William L. Langer and S. Everett Gleason, *The World Crisis and American Foreign Policy*, 1:358.

36. Roosevelt to Churchill, 1 February 1940, in Franklin D. Roosevelt, *F. D. R.: His Personal Letters*, 2:995 (hereafter cited as *FDR Letters*). The reference to "our conversation" in all probability means the extended conversations going on between British and American officials at the Department of State.

37. Churchill had sent Roosevelt a report of the naval action off the River Plate after which the *Graf Spee* had been scuttled (PSF, Churchill-Roosevelt File, Roosevelt Papers). Churchill made a regular practice of sending reports on naval actions to the Naval Attaché and the Ambassador (Kittredge MS, p. 78, Naval Archives). It may well be this practice to which Ambassador Winant referred as being delegated by Prime Minister Chamberlain (Winant, *Letter from Grosvenor Square*, p. 37n.).

38. Churchill, *Second World War*, 1:551.

39. For a general description of this period from the American point of view, see Langer and Gleason, *World Crisis*, 1:354–61.

40. Memoranda by Admiral John Godfrey, 26 February 1940, ADM 116/4302, PRO.

41. *FDR Letters*, 2:29–30. The eliding dots are substituted for a paragraph concerning specific problems with the Moore-McCormack Shipping Line.

42. PSF, Churchill-Roosevelt File, Roosevelt Papers.

43. A good account of the trial and the circumstances surrounding it was written by the presiding judge (see Sir William Allen Jowett, *Some Were Spies*).

44. An extensive treatment of the Kent case can be found in Richard J. Whalen, *The Founding Father*, pp. 310–30. A newspaper article that helped spur speculation appeared in the *Washington Times Herald* on 12 November 1941. The article stated that the secret correspondence was related to British and American policy concerning the war. "Among the questions touched upon," the article continued, "are said to have been a more vigorous prosecution of the war than had been achieved by Mr. Chamberlain and the possibilities of the U.S. taking an active part in support of Great Britain."

45. Memorandum, Roosevelt to Hull, 11 November 1941, PSF, Churchill-Roosevelt File, Roosevelt Papers.

46. Arthur M. Schlesinger, Jr., *The Age of Roosevelt*, 1:356. Churchill forgot this occasion—a lapse that Roosevelt did not appreciate.

47. *FR: 1939*, 1:671.

48. Breckinridge Long, *The War Diary of Breckinridge Long*, p. 113. Long believed that Kent had been passing information to the Russians and possibly the Germans via his girl friend. The fact that Kent's information ever went to a foreign government has never been proven.

49. Ibid., p. 114.

Chapter 5

1. Letter, Kirk to Admiral Walter S. Anderson, 20 June 1939, Admiral Alan G. Kirk Papers, Naval Archives. Anderson was chief of naval intelligence and Kirk supplemented his formal reports with frequent letters.

2. Letters, Kirk to Anderson, 14 August and 10 October 1939, Kirk Papers. Within a short time after his arrival in England Kirk had established good personal relations at the Admiralty.

3. Letter, Kirk to Anderson, 10 October 1939, Kirk Papers. Additional information on this venture was gained through an interview with Captain Norman Hitchcock in Washington, D.C., August 1967. Captain Hitchcock was assistant naval attaché for air during this period.

4. Cable, CNO to Kirk, 12 October 1939, Classified Microfilm Dispatches, U.S. Navy (hereafter cited as CMD), National Archives.

5. Letter, Kirk to Anderson, 3 November 1939, Kirk Papers. Kirk also gives some detail on technical exchanges during this period in his Oral History Project, Columbia University, New York, N.Y.

6. There was fear that Churchill had "queered" the prospects for a deal by offering ASDIC freely (see the correspondence in Naval Intelligence Division [hereafter cited as NID] 02204/39, ADM 116/3922, PRO).

7. Godfrey memorandum on Exchange Situation, 11 December 1939, ADM 116/4302, PRO.

8. Donald McLachlan, *Room 39*, pp. 216–17. Considering the sensitive, subtle work required to fulfill this job, it may be relevant to learn that Godfrey was one of Ian Fleming's models for the super spy "M" in the James Bond series. At least the Americans were taken in by no amateur. Godfrey himself has left an informative account of his career in the form of manuscript memoirs deposited at the Admiralty Historical Branch, London. This portrait of Godfrey has been drawn from information obtained from Godfrey's obituary in the London *Times*, 29 August 1971, and from McLachlan, *Room 39*, pp. 11–18. I am also indebted to Vice Admiral B. B. Schofield who furnished personal insights.

9. Letter, Kirk to Anderson, 3 November 1939, Kirk Papers.

10. Letter, Kirk to Anderson, 13 December 1939, ibid. Kirk at this time did not have a very high opinion of Winston Churchill.

11. Letter, Kirk to Anderson, 22 January 1940, ibid. Godfrey was imprecise in his quote.

12. "U.S. Naval Administration in WW II: Office of CNO: ONI," Naval Archives. See especially pp. 293–96.

13. Letter, Kirk to Anderson, 6 February 1940, Kirk Papers.

14. At one time the British had pressed the Americans hard for performance statistics on a certain undersea mine. The Americans kept stalling, but finally had to admit that they only had several of the mines and had never tested them (personal interview with Captain Norman Hitchcock, assistant naval attaché for air in London, 1939–41, Washington, D.C., December 1967).

15. Despite what he told Kirk, Godfrey was still concerned about security leaks, but he thought that much more could be given without seriously increasing the risk factor (Godfrey Memorandum on Exchange Situation, 26 February 1940, ADM 116/4302, PRO).

16. Minute to the File, 28 February 1940, ADM 116/4302, PRO.

17. Ibid., 1 March 1940, ibid.

18. Ibid., 6 March 1940, ibid.

19. Letter, Anderson to Kirk, 29 February 1940, Kirk Papers.

20. Cable, Kirk to Operations Division File (hereafter cited as OpNav), 31 October 1939, and Cable, OpNav to Kirk, 28 November 1939, Alusna Secret Messages, Com-

mander, Naval Forces Europe (hereafter cited as ComNavEu), Naval Archives.

21. In August 1940 the first full text of a Japanese message was deciphered. Colonel William Friedman, and others, had been working on the project for eighteen to twenty months (*PHA*, pt. 36, p. 312).

22. For information on American radar development see "The History of U.S. Naval Research and Development in WW II," Naval Archives. There were also many officers in the U.S. Navy who were very slow to accept the utility of shipboard radar and it was not until the naval disaster off Savo Island in late 1942 that the device gained wide respect (see especially p. 1093). Kirk's attitude is reflected in Cable, Kirk to OpNav, 25 July 1940, Alusna Secret Messages, ComNavEu, Naval Archives.

23. Kirk Oral History Project. The surprising story of Britain's plans and the resulting battle is told in Sir B. H. Liddell Hart, *The History of the Second World War*, pp. 52–63.

24. Letter, Kirk to Anderson, 11 April 1940, Kirk Papers.

25. Letter, Kirk to Anderson, 16 April 1940, ibid.

26. Letter, Kirk to Anderson, 24 April 1940, ibid.

27. All of this report is taken from McLachlan, *Room 39*, pp. 217–18. McLachlan had access to Godfrey and Godfrey's papers and his account is undoubtedly accurate insofar as it reflects the attitude of Admiral Godfrey and NID.

28. Ronald W. Clarke, *Tizard*, p. 250.

29. Margaret Gowing, *Britain and Atomic Energy, 1939–1945*, p. 45.

30. Hill's suggestion was included in a message from Lothian to F.O., 24 April 1940, F.O. A 3600/2961/45, PRO. Other valuable information on the Hill mission was gained through an interview with Hill in Cambridge in 1968.

31. Clarke, *Tizard*, pp. 250–51. One of Watt's scientific contemporaries, upon reading this quotation, noted: "Nobody could teach W. W. anything. He was an able man, but conceited, opinionated, and often a damned nuisance."

32. Ibid., p. 251.

33. Gowing, *Britain and Atomic Energy*, p. 44.

34. As things turned out, the Germans failed to give high priority to attacks on the RDF stations during the Battle of Britain, a mistake with far-reaching implications.

35. Minutes of the meeting and the recommendations can be found in ADM 116/4302, PRO.

36. See 8 May 1940 Memorandum in ibid.

37. Letter, J. H. Peck [for Churchill] to John Balfour in the F.O., 1 May 1940, PRO.

38. For information on data provided the Poles see Memorandum dated 28 November 1939 in NID 02204/39 and ADM 116/3922, PRO.

Chapter 6

1. Churchill, *Second World War*, 2:24–25. Churchill had had his eye on American destroyers almost since the war had begun. At a Cabinet meeting on 18 September 1939 he had urged that as soon as the U.S. Neutrality Act was repealed the British should do everything in their power to purchase destroyers from the United States. Even if they could secure only twenty of "their old vessels" it would be of the "greatest assistance," War Cabinet Minutes, 1939, Meeting no. 19 (hereafter cited as WM [39], 19), PRO. The numbers following WM denote the year and, usually, the meeting number.

2. *FR: 1940*, 3:30. Kennedy realistically saw that even Churchill's determination was not an unmixed blessing. If the prime minister insisted on England's fighting alone if France fell, the ambassador reported that it might provoke another crisis in the British government (ibid., 1:224). German intelligence reports indicate that movement to Canada had been discussed as early as 2 May (see General Franz Halder, *The Private War Journal of General Halder, 1939–1942*, 3:186). Churchill had made a somewhat different comment to Kennedy in October 1939 when he said that if Germany beat England "one of their terms would certainly be to hand over the Fleet. . . . If they got the British Fleet, they would have immediate superiority and then your troubles would begin" (Kittredge MS, sec. 2, pt. A, vol. 2, chap. 5, p. 72).

3. Kennedy to State Department (hereafter cited as S.D.), 15 May 1940, *FR: 1940*, 3:29–30. Kennedy made this comment after a bracing talk with Churchill in which the apocalyptic image of Britain's falling had again been called to mind.

4. *FR: 1940*, 3:49–50.

5. Franklin D. Roosevelt, *The Public Papers and Addresses of Franklin D. Roosevelt*, 9:198–212.

6. Adolf A. Berle Diary, 15 May 1940, in private possession, New York, N.Y. On the very same day the French prime minister, Paul Reynaud, made some brave statements about French resistance and also requested some "old American destroyers." The similarity between the situations facing France and Britain could not have escaped notice. Therefore, when France collapsed on 17 June, despite brave statements, the parallel very probably was drawn between France and Britain (see *FR: 1940*, 1:221, and *Hull Memoirs*, 1:831).

7. Woodward, *British Foreign Policy* (1962), p. 79. For a copy of Churchill's message see *FR: 1940*, 3:50–51.

8. Woodward, *British Foreign Policy* (1962), p. 79.

9. *FR: 1940*, 3:51.

10. Lothian's report is in F.O. A 3261/131/145, PRO. No official reply by Roosevelt to this message can be located. A draft reply, however, is in the Hull Papers. It may never have been sent, but it was quite direct, saying in part: "In moments like these, I believe that complete frankness is required and I am therefore replying to you in terms as blunt as those contained in your message. If worst came to worst, I regard the retention of the British fleet as a force in being as vital to the reconstitution of the British Empire and British Isles themselves." In other words if the British ceded the fleet they would also cede any rights to Empire after the war (Cordell Hull Papers, Box 47, Folder 113, Library of Congress, Washington, D.C.). A message similar to this was sent by the president to the French on 26 May 1940 (see *FR: 1940*, 2:452).

11. Minutes of 18 May 1940 meeting in ADM 116/4320, PRO. Admiral Pound approved a letter to the prime minister on 19 May, saying: "I think that the time has come when we might greatly influence the American attitude in the right direction by making them an unrestricted offer to pool technical information" (ibid.).

12. Letter, Alexander to Churchill, 20 May 1940, F.O. 371/24255, PRO.

13. The technique consisted of passing cables carrying an electric current under the hull of the ship, thus producing a magnetic field that neutralized that of the ship and rendered it immune from the mine (Kirk Oral History Project).

14. Memo, 14 May 1940, ADM 116/4302, PRO. Kirk had requested the information on the same day (see Kirk to OpNav, 14 May 1940, ComNavEu: Message Folders, Naval Archives).

15. Minutes, 16 May 1940, ADM 116/4302, PRO, contains the Admiralty decision. Kirk's report is in Kirk to OpNav, 27 May 1940, ComNavEu: Message Folders, Naval Archives).

16. Letter, Churchill to Alexander, 21 May 1940, F.O. 371/24255, PRO.

17. Memorandum by Charles Scott, chief of American Division, 20 May 1940, F.O. 371/24192, PRO.

18. Memorandum, 22 May 1940 in F.O. A 3427/131/45, PRO.

19. Berle Diary, 21 May 1940. For further insights on Mr. Berle's attitudes during this period I have relied on a number of interviews with him in 1967 and 1968.

20. Memorandum on World Situation, unsigned, A 14–6, 22 May 1940, WPD:CNO, Naval Archives.

21. Stetson Conn and Byron Fairchild, *The Framework of Hemisphere Defense*, pp. 34–35. See also Mark S. Watson, *Chief of Staff*, p. 105.

22. Letter, Lothian to "an American-born friend," 20 May 1940, in J. R. M. Butler, *Lord Lothian*, p. 287.

23. Breckinridge Long Diary, 21 May 1940, Library of Congress, Washington, D.C.

24. Lothian to F.O., 23 May 1940, F.O. A 3297/2961/45, PRO.

25. Memorandum to File, 3 June 1939, ADM 1/9784, PRO.

26. Langer and Gleason, *World Crisis*, 1:625. This time Roosevelt was suggesting that plans be made for a Pan-American trusteeship over any defeated colonial powers' possessions.

27. WM (40), 141, PRO.

28. WM (40), 146, PRO.

29. F.O. to Lothian, 2 June 1940, F.O. A 3297/2961/45, PRO. The latter point was

made in a memo written by Sir Alexander Cadogan on 30 May and incorporated in somewhat different terms in the message to Lothian.

30. *FR: 1940*, 1:233.

31. Winston S. Churchill, *Blood, Sweat and Tears*, p. 297. Italics supplied.

32. Recorded by Hugh Dalton, 28 May 1940, Hugh Dalton Diary, London School of Economics, London.

33. Churchill, *Second World War*, 2:145. Lothian shared Churchill's sensitivities, yet he feared that the speech might have encouraged "those who believed that even though Great Britain went under, the Fleet would somehow cross the Atlantic to them" (see Woodward, *British Foreign Policy* [1970], 1:345).

34. *Moffat Papers*, pp. 310–11.

35. Smith is quoted in Forrest C. Pogue, *George C. Marshall*, 2:53. For an excellent discussion of the general supply problem see especially pp. 46–79.

36. *Roosevelt Public Papers and Addresses*, 9:264.

37. Telegram, Lothian to F.O., 17 June 1940, F.O. 371/24240, PRO.

38. Memorandum of Conversation between Hull and Lothian, 24 June 1940, Great Britain, Box 7, Roosevelt Papers.

39. For a full description of the debate over keeping the fleet at Pearl Harbor see Robert J. Quinlan, "The United States Fleet," pp. 155–62.

40. *FR: 1940*, 3:37.

41. Letter, Kirk to Anderson, 11 June 1940, Kirk Papers.

42. Cable, Kirk to OpNav, 12 June 1940, ComNavEu Files: Message Folders, Naval Archives. A note on the telegram indicates that it was shown to the president by his naval aide. Kirk said the British needed the destroyers "at once."

43. Hypotheses, questions, and answers can be found in Maurice Matloff and Edwin M. Snell, *Strategic Planning for Coalition Warfare*, pp. 13–15. For a more complete record see WPD 4250–3, National Archives.

44. Kennedy to S.D., 14 June 1940, State Department Files (hereafter cited as S.D.F.), 740.0011, EW 39/3786–½, National Archives.

45. Cable, Kirk to OpNav, 14 June 1940, CMD, National Archives. This cable was similar to the letter Kirk had written to Anderson on 11 June.

46. *FR: 1940*, 3:53. This message was sent at least partially in response to an observation Lothian had sent from Washington. He had it from a good source, Lothian said, that Roosevelt was not convinced the British need for destroyers was serious. Therefore, the ambassador suggested that Churchill send the president a detailed list of numbers and types of destroyers that were lost or under repair. (Kirk had sent such a list three days before.)

47. *FR: 1940*, 1:257.

48. Woodward, *British Foreign Policy* (1970), 1:349.

49. Kennedy to S.D., 16 June 1940, S.D.F. 740.0011, EW 39/3882-½, National Archives.

50. Ibid.

51. Conn and Fairchild, *Hemisphere Defense*, pp. 35–37.

52. General George Strong drew up a memorandum based on this meeting's conclusions. The Naval Plans Staff was in general agreement, so Admiral Stark and General Marshall presented a set of joint recommendations to the president (see Kittredge MS, sec. 2, pt. D, vol. 1, chap. 8, pp. 168–73). The situation looked scarcely more bright to some British officials. Sir Stafford Cripps, British ambassador to Russia, urged planning for all possible contingencies. Unless preparations were made, he warned, the "sudden removal of the Government to, say, Canada would provoke widespread opposition and those remaining might well set up an alternative government to conclude a separate peace with Hitler" (quoted in Cecil Edwards *Bruce of Melbourne*, p. 303).

53. *Moffat Papers*, p. 319. King showed a copy of his message to Pierrepont Moffat. To some, requests for equipment were tacit admissions of improper preparations and they added to the "lack of confidence in the way in which the present British Government has conducted the war" and made people "dubious of what lies ahead during the next six months" (Laurence A. Steinhardt, American ambassador to Russia, to Rudolph Schoenfeld, a member of the American Embassy staff in London, 17 June 1940, Box 79, Laurence A.

Steinhardt Papers, Library of Congress, Washington, D.C. Steinhardt was vacationing in Washington at the time this letter was written.

54. Sir Edward Bruce, in London, said that he found an "incurable reluctance to consider hypothetical cases" (Edwards, *Bruce of Melbourne*, pp. 301–2). In the grim days of April 1941 Churchill "exploded" when he learned that General Sir Archibald Wavell, commander of British forces in Africa, had prepared contingency plans for his forces if the Germans should force the British out of the Middle East. To many high-ranking British officers Wavell's action looked like "soldierly precautions" but to Churchill any plan in the event of defeat smacked of cowardice (see General Sir John Kennedy, *The Business of War*, pp. 103–14).

55. Churchill, *Second World War*, 2:227. Actually, Lothian had tried on 15 June to make the bargain Churchill here denies.

56. Memorandum of Conversation with Mackenzie King, 27 June 1940, Moffat Diary.

57. WM (40), 141, PRO.

58. Butler, *Lord Lothian*, pp. 289–90.

59. Kennedy to S.D., 6 June 1940, S.D.F. 740.0011 EW 39/34874/10.

60. Kennedy to S.D., 10 June 1940, S.D.F. 740.0011 EW 39/34874/10.

61. For intuitive insights see Sir Isaiah Berlin, *Mr. Churchill in 1940*, p. 25; Aneurin Bevan, "History's Impresario," p. 56; and Lord Moran, *Churchill*, p. 13.

62. Two close observers make this same observation. See Violet Bonham-Carter, *Winston Churchill*, p. 9, and Lord Moran, *Churchill*, p. 112.

63. One of Lothian's many admirers was Lady Astor. After Lothian's death in December 1940 General Raymond Lee met her and expected to find her deeply grieved. Instead she talked of him with no visible sign of emotion. The explanation provided by one of Lady Astor's nieces was that "one of the great advantages of these noncarnal attachments is that they are just as good after death as before" (Raymond E. Lee, *The London Journal of General Raymond E. Lee*, p. 191).

Chapter 7

1. Kennedy's reports, Churchill's comments about the uncertainty of his position, and possibly some doubts of Roosevelt's own would soon lead the president to dispatch a pulse-taking mission to assess the stability of Churchill's government. As late as July 1941 Harold Ickes still feared that if the Germans offered peace terms Churchill's government might be "overthrown and a Cabinet formed under Lloyd George or someone else who would come to terms with Hitler" (Harold Ickes, *The Secret Diary of Harold L. Ickes*, 3:574).

2. Lothian to F.O., F.O. A 3297/2961/45, PRO. The Foreign Office had been receiving reports of American press comment including one in the *Wilmington* (Del.) *Morning Star* to the effect that it would be "gracious" of France and Britain to cede their colonies "without delay." A foreign official had noted in the margin "Gawd!" (see F.O. A 3373/131/45, PRO).

3. Matloff and Snell, *Strategic Planning*, p. 20.

4. See reference to Lothian's suggestion in F.O. A 3297/2961/45. The king's 26 June message is in the State Department Files, but cannot be declassified because it originated in a foreign government. Sinclair's letter dated 25 June 1940 is in F.O. 371/24255, PRO.

5. Telegram, Lothian to F.O., 27 June 1940, F.O. 371/2455, PRO.

6. Watson, *Chief of Staff*, p. 110.

7. Matloff and Snell, *Strategic Planning*, pp. 14–16.

8. Summary of meeting, 1 July 1940, in F.O. A 3297/2961/45, PRO.

9. Draft, 4 July 1940, ibid.

10. See Woodward, *British Foreign Policy* (1970), 1:360. Also interim reply to Lothian, 6 July 1940 in F.O. A 3297/2961/45, PRO. It was the feeling at the Foreign Office that the bases might be used as bait to lure the United States into a greater commitment during any staff talks. Presumably the idea was to discuss the destroyers at the same time (see notes at bottom of "Minute on Paper L," 2 July 1940, F.O. A 3297/2961/45, PRO).

11. The doubts about British vulnerability were obviously in Churchill's mind when he ordered the Royal Navy to attack the French ships at Mers el Kèbir and Oran. After the 4 July attack he wrote, "there was no more talk about Britain giving in" (Churchill, *Second*

World War, 2:238–39). For an account of the attack see Stephen W. Roskill, *The War at Sea*, 1:242–45. At the Cabinet meeting on 29 June when the action against the French Fleet had been considered, Lord Halifax reported that he had reason to believe that "any action which we might take in respect to the French Fleet would be applauded in the United States" (WM [40] 187, PRO).

12. Memorandum, 12 July 1940, S.D.F. 740.0011, EW 39/4700, National Archives.

13. Moffat Diary, 13 July 1940. There was a fairly reliable report that Sir Campbell Stewart, a close friend of Mackenzie King's, had been sent to Canada "on behalf of His Majesty's Government in order to arrange for evacuation if necessary" (Unsigned Memorandum dated 24 July 1940 in the Dalton Papers).

14. Harford Montgomery Hyde, *Room 3603*, p. 35. For an intriguing, supposedly "inside," account of Stephenson's activities see William Stevenson, *A Man Called Intrepid*, chaps. 17 and 18.

15. Allen Dulles, *The Secret Surrender*, p. 9.

16. Donovan later came to direct the OSS (Office of Strategic Services), the free-wheeling U.S. espionage-sabotage-unconventional warfare organization in World War II. The portrait of Donovan has been put together from Dulles, *Secret Surrender*; R. Harris Smith, *OSS*; and Corey Ford, *Donovan of OSS*.

17. Hyde, *Room 3603*, p. 35.

18. Ibid., pp. 35–36.

19. Roosevelt had written Knox: "I should like to have him (Donovan) in the Cabinet not only for his own ability, but also to repair in a sense the very great injustice done him by President Hoover" (*FDR Letters*, 3:297).

20. Frank Knox to Mrs. Knox, 15 June 1940, Frank Knox Papers, Box 3, Library of Congress, Washington, D.C.

21. Hyde, *Room 3603*, p. 36.

22. General H. H. Arnold said that Donovan was the one man who never told him that something could not be obtained. "He was incapable of [providing] a defeatist intelligence answer" (Henry H. Arnold, *Global Mission*, p. 535).

23. Not surprisingly, Donovan spent much time with Admiral John Godfrey (RN) while in London. Godfrey's impression was that Donovan's mission was to "satisfy himself that Britain would continue to fight on alone as Churchill had promised" (McLachlan, *Room 39*, p. 225).

24. Interview with Edgar Ansel Mowrer, Washington, D.C., January 1967. Credence is lent to this view since after their return they collaborated on a series of articles on subversive activity in England (see William Donovan and Frank Mowrer, *Fifth-Column Lessons for Americans*).

25. Kirk had been advised on 14 July that Donovan was coming to London (Cable, OpNav to Kirk, ComNavEu Files: Message Folders, Naval Archives).

26. Letter, Kirk to Anderson, 27 July 1940, Kirk Papers.

27. Hyde, *Room 3606*, p. 37.

28. McLachlan, *Room 39*, p. 226.

29. On Monday (21 July), for instance, the attaché had a full series of interviews set up for him at the Admiralty. Between 3 and 4 P.M. Colonel Donovan had appointments with six top people there, including the first sea lord, Sir A. Dudley P. R. Pound, and the director of naval intelligence, Rear Admiral J. H. Godfrey. On the next day he met the second sea lord, Admiral Sir Charles Little, and Kirk was busy arranging interviews with officials in the other ministries (Kirk to Donovan, 23 July 1940, Kirk Papers).

30. John Godfrey, Memoirs of Rear Admiral John Godfrey, vol. 5, pt. 2, pp. 129–30, Admiralty Historical Branch, London.

31. See letter, Godfrey to Cavendish-Bentinck, 2 August 1940, in F.O. A 3582/131/45, PRO. See also Godfrey Memoirs, vol. 5, pt. 2, pp. 130–31. Godfrey made a full report of his meetings with Donovan to his superiors and recorded the essence of Donovan's reactions in his memoirs. The Franklin D. Roosevelt Memorial Library is presently unable to locate a copy of Donovan's report. Donovan appreciated Godfrey's assistance and wrote to him, "I shall always remember most gratefully your many courtesies and kindnesses to me. Certainly you aided me in getting a perspective that I could not have had otherwise" (McLachlan, *Room 39*, p. 227).

32. For information on this subject the author has relied on the *Lee Journal*, the General Raymond E. Lee Journal (in private possession, Washington, D.C.), and Kirk Papers.

33. Cable, S.D. to Kennedy, 11 July 1940, S.D.F. 740.0011 EW 39/4570 A, National Archives.

34. Memorandum, Welles to Roosevelt, 12 July 1940, and Memorandum, Roosevelt to Knox, 13 July 1940, PSF, Knox File, Roosevelt Papers.

35. Mowrer Interview, January 1967.

36. Edgar A. Mowrer, *Triumph and Turmoil*, p. 315.

37. Report by Godfrey of his 2 August 1940 conversation with Donovan, NID 0/154, ADM 199/1156, PRO. One gets the impression that Donovan may have thought of himself as the ideal replacement for Kennedy.

38. Lothian to F.O., 8 July 1940, F.O. A 3297/2961/45, PRO. Lothian had made a similar suggestion on 23 May 1940.

39. Letter, Balfour to Colonel Leslie Hollis of the Chiefs of Staff Committee, 10 July 1940, ibid.

40. Lothian to F.O., 12 July 1940, ibid.

41. Notes dated 13 and 14 July 1940, ibid.

42. Letter, Poynton to Balfour, 14 July 1940, ibid.

43. Letter, Halifax to Lloyd, 19 July 1940, F.O. A 3600/2961/45, PRO.

44. F.O. A 3600/2961/45 and War Cabinet Memoranda, 1940, Meeting no. 276 (hereafter cited as WP [40] 276), PRO. The numbers following WP denote the year and, usually, the meeting.

45. See F.O. A 3297/2961/45, PRO.

46. WM (40) 214, PRO.

47. Memorandum by F.O. representative, J. V. Perowne, 25 July 1940, F.O. 371/24241, PRO.

48. Churchill's reaction is reflected in a memorandum on technical exchange circulated on 1 August 1940. Copy in F.O. A 3631/131/45, PRO.

49. Copies of draft and telegram in F.O. A 3582/131/45, PRO.

50. *FR: 1940*, 3:57–58.

51. Copy in F.O. A 35826/131/45, PRO.

52. S.D.F. 740.0011 EW 39/4929-¼, 31 July 1940, National Archives.

53. Lothian to F.O., 3–4 August 1940, F.O. A 3670/131/45, PRO.

54. Knox to Mrs. Knox, 15 June 1940, Knox Papers.

55. *Ickes Diary*, 3:283.

56. Woodward, *British Foreign Policy* (1962), pp. 82–83. In the *Morgenthau Diaries*, 2:177, Morgenthau quotes Lothian as saying that "he had not discussed this with his Government" but would take it up if Knox desired. Technically, Lothian was correct; he had discussed providing the bases several times, but he did not link the bases to the destroyers.

57. Woodward, *British Foreign Policy* (1970), 1:364–65.

58. Ibid., 1:365.

59. Draft in F.O. A 3600/2961/45, PRO. Initially Churchill had written that he had no objection to meeting Knox's suggestion, but Balfour pointed out to him that the Cabinet had agreed to leases not sales (Balfour Interview, July 1971).

60. *Ickes Diary*, 3:283.

61. One problem on Roosevelt's mind was the stipulation agreed to at the Havana Conference that no Western Hemisphere nation could unilaterally acquire territory from a nonhemisphere nation. For details see *FR: 1940*, 5:180–256.

62. *FR: 1940*, 3:58–59.

63. *Ickes Diary*, 3:293.

64. See p. 99.

65. Benjamin Cohen, an administration intimate, had been arguing for some time that the president was safe if he went ahead on the basis of an executive order, but Roosevelt remained unconvinced. Cohen sent his memorandum to the president on 16 July 1940 (interview with Benjamin V. Cohen, Washington, D.C. March 1966). See also Philip Goodhart, *Fifty Ships That Saved the World*, pp. 152–53.

66. For Roosevelt's account see *FR: 1940*, 3:58–59. Also see *Ickes Diary*, 3:293. The

Century Group had been working on Willkie since 25 July (see Mark L. Chadwin, *The War Hawks of World War II*, p. 87).

67. Lothian to F.O., F.O. A 3670/131/45, 3–4 August 1940. Italics supplied in Lothian's comment.

68. Box 58, Folder 213A, Hull Papers.

69. Lothian to F.O., 4 August 1940, F.O. A 3670/131/45, PRO.

70. Goodhart, *Fifty Ships*, p. 157. Lothian went on from lunch to play golf with the American ambassador to Russia, Joseph E. Davies. Davies also found Lothian very "grim" and contemplating the difficulties of starting a new life in Canada (Joseph E. Davies Diary, 5 August 1940, Library of Congress, Washington, D.C.).

71. Lothian to F.O., 4 August 1940, F.O. A 3670/131/45, PRO.

72. WM (40), 220: F.O. A 3670/131/45, especially Balfour's minutes dated 6 August 1940, PRO.

73. Taken from Balfour's unpublished memoirs and Balfour Interview.

74. Lothian to F.O., F.O. A 3670/131/45, PRO.

75. Churchill, *Second World War*, 2:404–5. The copy of this message in the files is marked "not sent." When Balfour found the telegram printed as though it had been sent he queried the Cabinet Office on this unorthodox and rather unhistoric inclusion. "Oh," the clerk replied, "the message was so stirring and patriotic that Mr. Churchill just couldn't bring himself to leave it out" (Balfour Interview).

76. Halifax to Lothian, 8 August 1940, F.O. A 3670/131/45, PRO.

77. If Churchill made this statement at this juncture in the negotiations, it is nowhere to be found and this sentiment does not seem in line with his "anxiety" theme. Most probably, this was an ambassadorial interpretation.

78. Lothian's letter can be found in *FR: 1940*, 3:64–65. Welles's note to the president appears in Langer and Gleason, *World Crisis*, 1:753.

79. *FR: 1940*, 3:66.

80. This report has been reconstructed from several sources including the Mowrer Interview and Hyde, *Room 3603*. See also Knox to Mrs. Knox, 8 August 1940, Box 3, Knox Papers.

81. Donovan gave a brief summary of his meeting with the president to John Balfour and Professor T. North Whitehead on 21 December 1940 (see summary in F.O. A 5194/4925/45).

82. Hyde, *Room 3603*, p. 38.

83. Telegram, Lothian to F.O., 4 August 1940, F.O. 371/24240.

84. Clarke, *Tizard*, p. 259. Also valuable in reconstructing the chain of events is the Sir Henry Tizard Diary, National War Museum, London.

Chapter 8

1. Cavendish-Bentinck to Captain W. D. Stephens, 1 August, F.O. 371/24240, PRO. The Century Group, it will be recalled, had come up with the idea of joining the bases and the destroyers.

2. See also Chadwin, *War Hawks*, p. 85; Langer and Gleason, *World Crisis*, 1:757; and Philip Goodhart, *Fifty Ships*, p. 163.

3. Langer and Gleason, *World Crisis*, 1:758.

4. Ibid., p. 753.

5. *FR: 1940*, 3:65–66.

6. Ibid.

7. This message was bolstered by instructions to Ambassador Kennedy advising him officially to tell the British that their earlier offer was too limited and their requests too broad (Langer and Gleason, *World Crisis*, 1:758). Kennedy had been left out of the earlier arrangement and had had to wire for information on Lothian's 8 August memorandum so that he would know what offer and what requests were referred to (*FR: 1940*, 3:66).

8. Churchill, *Second World War*, 2:404.

9. Woodward, *British Foreign Policy* (1970), 1:369.

10. *FR: 1940*, 3:67.

11. Churchill, *Second World War*, 2:406–7.

12. As has been suggested, "It is hard to believe that it was necessary to purposely mislead the public as the President did on this occasion" (Langer and Gleason, *World Crisis*, 1:761). The next day, at the Ogdensburg Conference, the president told Mackenzie King that Churchill had "at last" given him a "sufficient pledge" on the fleet. He went on to discuss the destroyers, the bases, and the fleet, seemingly seeing some connection (*Moffat Papers*, p. 329).

13. See *Public Opinion Quarterly*, September 1940.

14. Butler, *Lord Lothian*, p. 297.

15. Anderson's reaction and Stark's general hesitancy were reported to the Century Group late in July (see Chadwin, *War Hawks*, p. 84).

16. U.S. Congress, *Hearings Affecting the Naval Establishment*, 1940, see especially pp. 3553–54. These hearings took place in July and provided for increasing the size of the U.S. Navy by 81 percent. Earlier hearings had discussed the U.S. Navy's request for funds to increase the size by 11 percent (see U.S. Congress, *Hearings on Construction of Certain Naval Vessels*, 1940).

17. U.S. Congress, *Hearings on Construction of Certain Naval Vessels*, p. 20. Stark also noted that during World War I "our neutral rights were severely transgressed upon by both sides" (ibid., p. 21).

18. Memorandum, Stark to Knox, 17 August 1940, CNO Files, folder marked "Destroyer Deal," Naval Archives. Stark had very good relations with Congress and feared its reaction if he certified the destroyers as unnecessary to national defense when he had been pleading for funds to build similar craft. The CNO believed that his discussions with the attorney general on this point laid the groundwork for the final arrangement (Interview with Harold R. Stark, Washington, D.C., December 1966).

19. Addenda to Stark to Knox Memorandum, 17 August 1940.

20. Langer and Gleason, *World Crisis*, 1:762–63.

21. Churchill, *Second World War*, 2:408–9. See also the discussion in Langer and Gleason, *World Crisis*, 1:762–63. It may be that the prime minister received permission to use the president's 6 August press conference remarks as the basis for his statement.

22. WM (40) 231, 21 August 1940, PRO.

23. See notes by Balfour, 29 August 1940, F.O. A 3917/3742/45, PRO.

24. Langer and Gleason, *World Crisis*, 1:763–64. Goodhart, *Fifty Ships*, p. 168.

25. Hyde, *Room 3603*, p. 39. It may be that Stephenson put too much faith in the president's personal drive since Langer and Gleason say that during this period the president "was at a complete loss how to proceed" (*World Crisis*, 1:756).

26. Letter, Roosevelt to Walsh, 22 August 1940, in *FDR Letters*, 2:1056–57.

27. Churchill to Lothian, 22 August 1940, F.O. A 3917/3742/45, PRO.

28. Lothian to F.O., 22 August 1940, ibid.

29. Notes of Conversation, 23 August 1940, ibid. There is a possibility that Churchill misread the Admiralty's optimistic forecasts of destroyer construction.

30. *Hull Memoirs*, 1:834.

31. Langer and Gleason, *World Crisis*, 1:765.

32. Churchill explained to the Cabinet that in his view it was best to be very careful in negotiations with the Americans. (see WM A 3917/3742/45, PRO).

33. The message that is not quite so candid can be found in *FR: 1940*, 3:70–71.

34. Behind the scenes there were British officials who also wanted a quid pro quo arrangement. Vansittart, for instance, described the receipt of the destroyers as a case of "jam tomorrow." "I trust," he wrote, "that we won't sign up and part with our end of the goods without actually having theirs" (see note dated 26 August 1940, F.O. 371/24259, PRO).

35. Memorandum, 25 August 1940, Box 58, Folder 213A, Hull Papers. See also *Hull Memoirs*, 1:836–37.

36. See Lothian to F.O., 25–26 August 1940, F.O. A 3980/3742/45, PRO. On 15 August Ambassador Kennedy had asked the president to consider the situation that might develop if the British surrendered and the British deposed. "Is it too much to imagine," Kennedy asked, the "new government might very well not consider itself bound by promises of Churchill and dispose of the fleet to its own advantage?" (*FR: 1940*, 3:68).

37. *Hull Memoirs*, 1:837–38. This American draft is significant because Churchill claims that he suggested an identical text on 27 August. He also contends that the president

adopted his version. However, the facts do not conform to his interpretation (Churchill, *Second World War*, 2:414). The American version was the first one drafted and the opening statements remained unchanged.

38. Goodhart, *Fifty Ships*, p. 174. A copy of the attorney general's opinion was published in the *New York Times* on 2 September 1940 when the "deal" was announced. His opinion, which followed the lines of the Acheson-Cohen argument, apparently did little to satisfy some lawyers, because when Hull and Green Hackworth discussed the matter they agreed that the transfer was a "violation of international law" (Long Diary, 28 August 1940). For a lengthy discussion of the legality of the matter, see Herbert W. Briggs, "Neglected Aspects of the Destroyer Deal," pp. 569–87. Professor Briggs argues that the exchange was illegal.

39. Memorandum, Box 58, Folder 213A, Hull Papers.

40. Lothian to F.O., 27 and 28 August 1940, F.O. A 3980/3742/45, PRO. He noted that the difficulty was partially attributable to a written constitution and a coequal executive and legislative branch.

41. Langer and Gleason, *World Crisis*, 1:768.

42. 31 August 1940, Berle Diary.

43. *FR: 1940*, 3:72. Kennedy advised Washington that he knew nothing about the background of the negotiations, "but I am sure that there is a complete misunderstanding" by the British Cabinet about the American terms. Kennedy's understanding of what went on in the Cabinet session, though, is quite correct and is borne out by the minutes (WM (40) 236, 237, PRO).

44. *FR: 1940*, 3:73. Kennedy's remarks remind one of the president's letter to Senator Walsh.

45. In the final arrangement the bases in Newfoundland and Bermuda were given without payment; only the bases in Jamaica, St. Lucia, and British Guiana were provided in consideration of the military hardware and destroyers (*FR: 1940*, 3:73–74).

46. Langer and Gleason, *World Crisis*, 1:768.

47. Goodhart, *Fifty Ships*, p. 180.

48. See p. 117.

49. See report of press conference in Goodhart, *Fifty Ships*, p. 185. After telling reporters about the destroyers and the bases the president said: "I have not finished the story. There is also to be given out in Washington, simultaneously—you will have to leave this off the record as coming from me; make it just pure information." And then he gave them the details of the fleet guarantee. He did say that the guarantee was not a quid pro quo, but said it "fortuitously" came along at the same time. See also *New York Times*, 4 September 1940, p. 1.

50. The London *Times*, on the other hand, mentioned the pledge concerning the fleet well down in its article and saw no need to elaborate upon it (4 September 1940, p. 4).

51. Letter to the author from Admiral Sir Charles Daniel, 7 October 1967. Admiral Daniel cannot recall having made any plans, but notes that "after all, no *plan* is really necessary. In a real crisis a simple order to the Fleet is all that is required; oil will go wherever ordered. Everything could be arranged when it [the fleet] got to its destination." However, it is reported that the British representatives in the United States had informed Admiral Stark and officers on his staff of "the plans being made in London for the continuance of the war by Britain, even in the event of an invasion of England." Daniel was director of plans at the Admiralty in 1940.

52. 22 September 1940, Berle Diary.

53. 31 August 1940, ibid.

54. Harold Nicolson, *Diaries and Letters, 1930–1939*, 2:153.

Chapter 9

1. See U.S. Army Files, [Army and Navy] Joint Planning Committee (hereafter cited as JPC), Development of RAINBOW 2, Joint Board 325 Ser. 642–2 (hereafter cited as RAINBOW 2), National Archives.

2. Matloff and Snell, *Strategic Planning*, p. 10. For a discussion of American planning during the 1920s and 1930s see ibid., pp. 1–10.

3. Note of Conversation, 16 April 1940, F.O. 371/24716, PRO. Kirk may well have been officially directed to make this request since the navy planners were working on revising RAINBOW 2 at this time (see RAINBOW 2, National Archives).

4. The War Cabinet confirmed the offer on 18 April 1940 and recommended that Kirk so advise the president, WM 96 (40), PRO. Churchill also advised Roosevelt of Singapore's availability a few weeks later.

5. Memorandum on the World Situation, unsigned, 22 May 1940, CNO Files, A1416, Naval Archives.

6. Memorandum by Ashley Clarke, 18 May 1940, F.O. 371/24716, PRO.

7. Telegram, F.O. to Lothian, 25 May 1940, F.O. 371/24716, PRO.

8. Telegram, Lothian to F.O., 26 May 1940.

9. Minutes on file jacket, 27 and 28 May 1940.

10. *FR: 1940*, 3:36.

11. Telegram, Lothian to F.O., 17 June 1940, F.O. 371/24240, PRO.

12. Dispatch, Kirk to OpNav, 20 June 1940, CMD, National Archives. As will be recalled, the problem of location had delayed talks in spring 1939.

13. Memorandum of Conversation between Hull and Lothian, 24 June 1940, Great Britain, Box 7, Roosevelt Papers. Italics supplied.

14. Ibid.

15. Lothian to F.O., 24 June 1940, F.O. 371/24240, PRO.

16. Minute, Churchill to Halifax, 24 June 1940, ibid.

17. Minute, Halifax to Churchill, 28 June 1940, ibid.

18. Joint Planning Committee (hereafter cited as JP), (40) 276; copy dated 27 June 1940; in ADM 199/1159, PRO.

19. Chiefs of Staff (hereafter cited as C.O.S.) meeting on 28 June 1940 (40), 198, copy in ADM 199/1159, PRO.

20. Air Marshal Sir John Slessor, *Central Blue*, p. 314.

21. Telegram, F.O., to Lothian, 30 June 1940, ADM 199/1159, PRO.

22. Telegram, Lothian to F.O., 2 July 1940, F.O. 371/24240, PRO.

23. See p. 37.

24. Brief mention is made of the Bailey Committee in Butler, *Grand Strategy*, 2:243. Mention is also made of the committee in Watson, *Chief of Staff*, p. 107.

25. A complete copy of Bailey Committee's minutes, etc., can be found in ADM 199/1159, PRO. It may be assumed that such insistence would not have displeased the British, although maritime nations have a vested interest in protecting their own trade routes.

26. Mention of various points in the Bailey Committee's deliberations appear in Kittredge MS, especially sec. 3, pt. B, vol. 2.

27. This discussion of command problems clearly reflected the lessons of World War I. Command had then proved a vexing difficulty with General "Black Jack" Pershing insisting that U.S. ground forces be used as a unit and only under American commanders. Admiral Sims also had some trouble in arriving at a satisfactory division of command responsibilities with the Royal Navy.

28. Kittredge MS, sec. 3, pt. B, vol. 2, chap. 11, p. 251.

29. For further information on the Clarke Mission see pp. 136–37.

30. At this time Lord Hankey was serving in three capacities: secretary to the Committee on Imperial Defense (CID), secretary to the Cabinet, and clerk of the Privy Council.

31. The British secretaries were more than the title implies. They took down what they understood the speaker as wanting to say, not what he said. This eliminated verbiage, but made the post an extremely sensitive and responsible one. Interviews with the following men yielded more information about the importance of this practice: Captain Arthur W. Clarke, London, May 1967; Sir Ian Jacob, Ipswich and London, May and June 1967; and Brigadier A. T. Cornwall-Jones, Henley, England, June 1967. All of these gentlemen were at one time secretaries to the CID. A very good study of the CID is Franklyn Johnson's *Defense by Committee*.

32. Captain Arthur W. Clarke, "Historical Sidelight," pp. 2–3, MS in possession of the author.

33. Ibid., pp. 3–4.

34. Clarke Interview, May 1967.

35. See JP Memorandum on Staff Conversations with Americans, ADM 199/1159, PRO.

36. See Extract from Minutes of C.O.S. (40) 216, 10 July 1940, copy in ADM 199/1159, PRO.

37. A complete copy of the Bailey Committee Report can be found in ADM 199/1159, PRO.

38. Arthur W. Clarke Diary, 20 July 1940, Southsea. It should be noted that for all its strengths, the Bailey Committee Report also bore signposts toward trouble. The British, strong in procedures and preparation, were weak in understanding American sensitivities and prejudices. To suppose that America would agree to send its fleet to a colonial outpost or meekly submit to the principle that initiatives for American involvement would emanate from London was to engage in daydreams bordering on the hallucinogenic.

39. For an explanation of British intent see Extract from C.O.S. (40) 236, 27 July 1940, in ADM 199/1159, PRO.

40. Telegram, Lothian to F.O., 2 July 1940, F.O. 371/24240, PRO.

41. Robert L. Ghormley Diary, 13 July 1940, in private possession, Washington, D.C.

42. For a British review of situation see Butler, *Grand Strategy*, 2:243.

43. For information on the Sims Mission see Elting E. Morison, *Admiral Sims and the Modern American Navy*, chaps. 19–21. For the attitude of Stark and other naval officers the author has relied on an interview with Admiral Harold D. Stark, December 1966, Washington, D.C. For repercussions after war and negative reactions see Tracy B. Kittredge, *Naval Lessons of the Great War*. Kittredge was a young officer who served on Sims's staff. For Roosevelt's relations with Sims see Frank Freidel, *Franklin D. Roosevelt*, 2:40–46.

44. Ghormley Diary, 13 July 1940.

45. Kirk Oral History Project. Ghormley was older than Kirk, but they had been at the Academy together in 1905 and 1906.

46. Ghormley Diary, 14 July 1940.

47. Ibid., 15 July 1940, ibid.

48. Memorandum to President from Admiral Stark (n.d.; on or about 8 August 1940), Kirk Papers.

49. Kirk Oral History Project. Kirk contended that they worked without "any friction of any sort."

50. See p. 37.

51. See, especially, p. 214.

52. Kittredge MS, sec. 3, pt. A, vol. 2, chap. 10, pp. 212–13.

53. On 14 October Roosevelt told his old friend Leonard K. Elmhirst that at one point his betting went as low as three-to-one against. But, he said, "after the fall of Paris, my betting went back to 50:50 and at the moment it's moved in the other direction for the first time" (Leonard K. Elmhirst Diary, Totnes, Devon).

54. Interview with Admiral Bernard L. Austin, Washington, D.C., December 1966. Austin went to London with Ghormley as flag secretary.

55. This information has been gained from interviews with Admiral Austin and from discussions with various British officers who knew him. Unfortunately, one of Austin's closest friends and contacts, Admiral Michael Goodenough, died in 1957, but his widow was most helpful in providing information and insights.

56. Shortly after they sailed they heard a radio bulletin announcing the imminent arrival of Ghormley's "secret group" (Ghormley Diary, 11 and 14 August). The London *Times* also carried items about Ghormley's appointment (see *Times*, 10 and 12 August).

57. General Strong flew to England.

58. Louis B. Morton, "Germany First," p. 31.

59. *Lee Journal*, pp. 29–30.

60. Ibid., 8 August entry. The British Committee had been in existence for at least a week at this point, considering such things as "cover," accommodations, and meeting places.

61. Telegram, Lothian to F.O., 4 August 1940, F.O. 371/24240, PRO.

62. Note dated 8 August 1940 by the JP for the Chiefs of Staff, C.O.S. (40) 604, PRO.

63. Extract from Chiefs of Staff minutes, C.O.S. (40) 236, 27 July 1940, in ADM 199/1159, PRO.

64. Minutes dated 9 and 10 August on file jacket in F.O. 371/24247, PRO.

Chapter 10

1. Ghormley Diary, 16 August 1940.

2. Kirk had been worried about being upstaged by a rear admiral carrying a title which implied usurpation of the attaché's duties. As he wrote Donovan on 14 August: "The decision to call Rear Admiral Ghormley 'Special Naval Observer' was a good answer. It leaves me free and also saves face—which is quite important over here" (Kirk to Donovan, Kirk Papers). Kennedy had wired on 31 July 1940 that it had been "a bit embarrassing to have the entire British Cabinet know that an Admiral was coming here for staff talks when nobody in the Embassy knew anything about it" (S.D.F. 740.011, EW 39/4925 2/4, National Archives).

3. Colonel Raymond E. Lee, Pocket Notebook, 16 August 1940, Raymond E. Lee Journal, in private possession, Washington, D.C. (hereafter cited as Lee Notes).

4. Cable, Ghormley to Stark, 17 August 1940, CMD, National Archives. Lloyd George had been advised on 16 August 1940 that Ghormley was in England for staff talks that could lead to coordinated military activities "if and when Washington decided to enter the war which might be very soon" (David Lloyd George Papers, G/28/1/105, Beaverbrook Library, London).

5. Cable, Ghormley to CNO, 18 August 1940, Dispatch File, WPD:CNO, Naval Archives.

6. Ghormley Official Diary, 19 August 1940, ComNavEu, Naval Archives.

7. Ghormley Official Diary and Minutes of Meeting in Ghormley Secret File, ComNavEu, Naval Archives (see also Butler, *Grand Strategy*, 2:341).

8. Colonel Lee was taken aside at this dinner and quizzed about the instructions given to the visitors. The British were frankly puzzled by the unorthodox procedure of sending an uninstructed delegation to discuss war plans (Lee Notes, 22 August 1940).

9. Letter, Ghormley to Stark, 23 August 1940, Robert L. Ghormley Papers, in private possession, Washington, D.C. Ghormley to Knox, 23 August 1940, Ghormley Papers; Ghormley Diary, 21–23 August 1940. Some of the Ghormley Papers are in private hands, and others are in the Naval Archives.

10. Standardization of Arms Committee (hereafter cited as S.A.), (40) 5, 24 August 1940, ADM 199/1159, PRO.

11. JP (40) 401, 26 August 1940, ADM 199/1159, PRO.

12. Minutes of Meeting of 29 August 1940, Ghormley Secret File, ComNavEu, Naval Archives. This was the type of question Churchill had feared would come up. See p. 132.

13. Kittredge MS, sec. 3, Notes and Appendix, vol. 3, pp. 223–24.

14. Ibid.

15. See p. 138.

16. Minutes of Meeting of 31 August 1940, S.A. (J) 3, ADM 119/1159, PRO. The existence of the Bailey Committee shows that Newall was not telling the literal truth.

17. Ibid. See also Butler, *Grand Strategy*, 2:342.

18. Kittredge MS, sec. 3, Notes and Appendix, vol. 3, pp. 223–24. See also Butler, *Grand Strategy*, 2:341–45. A brief review of the meeting is in Mark S. Watson, *Chief of Staff*, pp. 113–15.

19. Churchill, *Second World War*, 2:385–86. Also see Butler, *Grand Strategy*, 2:334.

20. Ibid., pp. 338–39.

21. Watson, *Chief of Staff*, p. 115.

22. Kittredge MS, sec. 3, pt. A, vol. 2, chap. 10, p. 228. The First Sea Lord apparently did not evince it, but he must have heaved a sigh of relief that some American had finally asked the right question, since the Bailey Report had been available for discussion since 15 July.

23. Admiral B. L. Austin Diary, 8 September 1940, in private possession, Washington, D.C.

24. Letter, Ghormley to Stark, 2 September 1940, Ghormley Secret File, ComNavEu, Naval Archives. Ghormley had sent a Marine officer to inspect other coastal implacements

and had received the report that the defenses were practically worthless against determined German attack (Austin Interview, November 1966).

25. Colonel (later General) Carl Spaatz Diary, 8 September 1940, Library of Congress, Washington, D.C.

26. Letter, Ghormley to Stark, 13 September 1940, Ghormley Papers, Naval Archives. Hanson Baldwin was military correspondent for the *New York Times*.

27. Letter, Ghormley to Stark, 13 September 1940, Ghormley Papers, Naval Archives.

28. Admiral Austin recalls that Admiral Ghormley and his staff knew how the French had drawn the British into a quasi-alliance in 1908 and were, therefore, on guard against commitments. They also were sensitive to the charges made about Admiral Sims being excessively pro-British, and they conducted themselves accordingly (Austin Interview, November 1966).

29. Ghormley may have been in error on two of these points. Serious consideration was being given to moving the fleet back to the West Coast from Pearl Harbor. Furthermore, Stark wrote him on 9 September that he was moving four cruisers to the Atlantic and sending the three (not two) carriers to the Pacific (Stark to Ghormley, 9 September, Ghormley Papers, Naval Archives).

30. Minutes of meeting with the British, 17 September 1940, Naval Attaché, London to CNO: 1940–41, WPD:CNO, Naval Archives. British minutes in Bailey Committee (J) (hereafter cited as B.C.; the "J" is used to signify a joint meeting), 1, ADM 199/1159, PRO. Ghormley said that consideration was being given to extending the Monroe Doctrine to cover Greenland, thus bringing it within the traditional U.S. defense perimeter.

31. Minutes of Meeting with the British, 18 September 1940, Naval Attaché, London, to CNO: 1940–41, WPD:CNO, Naval Archives.

32. B.C. (J) 2d Meeting, 18 September 1940, ADM 199/1159, PRO.

33. Minutes of Meeting with the British, 19 September 1940, Naval Attaché, London, to CNO: 1940–41, WPD:CNO, Naval Archives.

34. Letter, Ghormley to Stark, 18 September 1940, ComNavEu, Naval Archives.

35. Churchill at least watched the election campaign with great interest and anxiety (see Churchill, *Second World War*, 2:553).

36. Letter, Ghormley to Stark, 18 September 1940, Naval Attaché, London, to CNO: 1940–41, WPD:CNO, Naval Archives.

37. Letter, Ghormley to Stark, 20 September 1940, ibid.

38. *New York Times*, 21 September 1940, sec. 1, p. 7.

39. *Times* (London), 23 September 1940, p. 4.

40. Matloff and Snell, *Strategic Planning*, p. 24.

41. The preliminary and final reports of Generals Strong and Emmons, dated 23 and 25 September and titled "Observations in England," can be found in WPD Files 4368-1 and 4368, U.S. Army, Office of Chief of Staff Files, National Archives.

42. At this time Stark was extremely pessimistic about the general trend of events and wrote Admiral J. O. Richardson that "he would not be surprised at anything happening any day. . . . I have long felt that it is only a matter of time until we get in" (Stark to Richardson, 1 October 1940, *PHA*, 14:962).

43. Letter, Stark to Ghormley, 24 September 1940, Ghormley Papers, Naval Archives.

44. *Times* (London), 28 September 1940, p. 2.

45. Harold Sprout and Margaret Sprout, *The Rise of American Naval Power*, p. 216.

Chapter 11

1. For a copy of the Pact see U.S. Department of State, *Peace and War*, p. 573.

2. For Matsuoka's fears in this regard see Langer and Gleason, *World Crisis*, 2:29. The official Nazi press also expressed concern about an Anglo-American Pacific base deal (*New York Times*, 28 September 1940). Obviously, the agreement had many roots and implications, but fear of the United States and intimidating the United States were involved.

3. Hull referred to the pact as a "posted" sign for the Pacific (*Hull Memoirs*, 1:908–9).

4. Telegram, Lothian to F.O., 30 September 1940, Cabinet Office Papers (hereafter cited as Cab), 84/19, PRO. Hull failed to note his suggestion in his *Memoirs* (1:911) or in his official version of the conversation (see Stimson and Bundy, *Peace and War*, pp. 574 ff.).

5. Telegram, Lothian to F.O., 1 October 1940, Cab 84/19, PRO.

6. *Roosevelt Papers and Addresses*, 9:407 ff.

7. C.O.S. (40) 802, 4 October 1940, F.O. 371/24709, PRO.

8. See minute by Sir Robert Vansittart to R. A. Butler, 20 September 1940, and Sir Alexander Cadogan's telegram to Lord Lothian, 21 September 1941; both in F.O. 371/24709, PRO.

9. Telegram, Craigie to F.O., 3 October 1940, F.O. 371/24709, PRO.

10. Minute, Churchill to Halifax, 4 October 1940, ibid. For some reason Churchill identified Kennedy as the source of confusion on this issue. In this same note Churchill declared that "if Japan attacked the United States without declaring war on us we should at once range ourselves at the side of the U.S. and declare war upon Japan." The prime minister was as good as his word and Britain actually declared war on Japan shortly before Congress could act on 8 December 1941. But even after taking that formal step the British could not be certain what effect America's going to war with Japan would have. Despite his brave words, Churchill was still worried in December 1941 that the United States might cut aid to Britain as a result of war with Japan and cited fear in this regard as one reason for his first trip to wartime Washington (see Lord Moran, *Churchill*, pp. 11, 39). The War Cabinet confirmed Churchill's change in policy on 7 October 1940, Cab 84/20, PRO.

11. Telegram, Lothian to F.O., 5 October 1940, F.O. 371/24709, PRO.

12. Churchill, *Second World War*, 2:498.

13. Minutes, Standing Liaison Committee, 6 October 1940, War Department Records, National Archives. It is intriguing to wonder whether the British ever toyed with the idea of giving fate a shove in the Far East. Lord Lothian's biographer, Sir J. R. M. Butler (whose official *History of the Second World War* appeared as vol. 2 of *Grand Strategy*) wrote in regard to the Pacific: "America was, however, most reluctant to be plunged into war even with Japan, and the British could not be sure if they provoked Japan to the point of war America would join in" (*Lord Lothian*, p. 271).

14. Memorandum of phone conversation between Lothian and J. Stendale Bennett, 6 October, F.O. 371/24709, PRO.

15. Planning paper, JP (40) 520 (S), 6 October 1940, approved in Cab 84/20, PRO.

16. Telegrams, Lothian to F.O., 7 and 8 October 1940, F.O. 371/24709, PRO. Lothian apparently had guessed the direction of preparations in London for staff conversations on two planes. He was not formally advised of that approach until 8 October, F.O. 371/24709, PRO.

17. Telegram, Lothian to F.O., 9 October, F.O. 371/24709, PRO.

18. For the divided reaction within the Roosevelt administration see Langer and Gleason, *World Crisis*, 1:40–44.

19. Ibid., 1:46–47.

20. Lothian to F.O., 7 October 1940, F.O. 371/24709, PRO.

21. Berle Diary, 11–14 October 1940; see also Long Diary, 9 October 1940, pp. 138–39.

22. Telegram, Lothian to F.O., 10 October, F.O. 371/24710, PRO.

23. Letter, Ghormley to Stark, 13 September 1940, Ghormley Papers, Naval Archives.

24. Letter, Ghormley to Stark, 11 October 1940, ComNavEu, Naval Archives.

25. Letter, Ghormley to Knox, 11 October 1940, Ghormley Papers, Naval Archives.

26. Letter, Ghormley to Stark, 11 October 1940, ComNavEu Files, Naval Archives.

27. See Minutes, 14 October 1940, Cab 84/20, PRO. The Foreign Office advised Lothian that they found the change in the administration's attitude "not unexpected but nonetheless disappointing" (Telegram, F.O. to Lothian, 14 October 1940, F.O. 371/24710, PRO).

28. JP (40) 545 (S), 14 October 1940. The proposal was embodied in C.O.S. (40) 831; Cab 84/20, PRO. Several sets of planning papers can be found in Cab 84/20; for discussion on the desirability of having American delegates at Singapore see especially jacket F 4732/G, F.O. 371/24710, PRO. The overview of the talk emerges most clearly from C.O.S. telegram to Far Eastern commanders, 15 October 1940, Cab 84/20, PRO.

29. Roger M. Bellairs Diary, 9 October 1940, Hascombe, nr. Godalming.

30. Information on Bellairs's career has been reconstructed from files of the London

Times, conversations with his family, and the Austin Interview, December 1966. For information on the Invergordon Mutiny see Roskill, *Naval Policy between the Wars*, 2:89–119.

31. Information on the Australian-Dutch-American (hereafter cited as ADA) Committee can be found in ADM/199/1232, PRO.

32. There are a number of messages relating to the Singapore Conference in F.O. 371/24710, PRO. For Ghormley's specific request see Cable, Ghormley to Stark, 24 October 1940, CMD, National Archives. Captain Purnell was on the staff of Admiral Thomas Hart, commander of the Asiatic Fleet. No record of the Purnell mission can be located in the U.S. Navy files. From the British record it would appear that he sat as a silent observer. For a brief review of the Pacific staff conferences, see Admiral Kelly Turner's testimony, *PHA*, 4:1931 ff.; also Feis, *Road to Pearl Harbor*, p. 128n.

33. Records in ADM 199/1232, PRO.

34. Cable, Ghormley to Stark, 17 October 1940, CMD, National Archives. Bellairs Minute, ADA, 10th Meeting, 17 October 1940, ADM 199/1232, PRO. The conversation is reconstructed from the British record and from Ghormley's report to Stark. In his cable, Ghormley said he had "no definite instructions" concerning the Dutch. A search of the cables from Washington to London indicates that Ghormley's "no instruction" interpretation is correct. Hull said on 11 October that Stark did not feel that Ghormley needed "any further instructions for the time being" (Lothian to F.O., 11 October 1940, F.O. 371/24710, PRO).

35. Cable, Ghormley to Stark, 17 October 1940, CMD, National Archives.

36. Cable, Casey to London, 17 October 1940, F.O. 371/24710, PRO.

37. Bellairs Diary, 21 October 1940.

38. Letter, Ghormley to Bailey, 25 October 1940, Ghormley Secret File, ComNavEu, Naval Archives.

39. Ghormley and Bellairs diaries, 29 October 1940.

40. Bellairs Diary, 5 November 1940.

41. Letter, Ghormley to Stark, 14 November 1940, Naval Attaché, London, to CNO, 1940–41 File: WPD:CNO, Naval Archives.

42. Letter, Ghormley to Stark, 16 November 1940, Ghormley Conference Data, WPD:CNO, Naval Archives.

43. Matloff and Snell, *Strategic Planning*, p. 21.

44. Berle Diary, 15 October 1940. Berle definitely did not think America should aid the British out of sentiment "but because we realize that we ourselves will be in difficulty if they go under—quite a different thing."

45. For lengthy discussion of issue see historical overview of British position in F.O. minutes dated 18 February 1941 and in PREM 3/326, PRO.

Chapter 12
1. Although General Strong had initially given a guardedly optimistic report on Britain's chances, by mid October he urged continued preparations in case the British were defeated; most particularly, he recommended that consideration of Pacific strategy be subordinated to immediate concerns in the Atlantic (see Watson, *Chief of Staff*, pp. 115–17). Strong had proposed a similar reorientation as early as June (see ibid, p. 110).

2. Ibid., p. 92.

3. See p. 7.

4. *PHA*, 14:924–26. For mention of Richardson's fears and a brief review of problems in the Pacific see Morison, *United States Naval Operations*, 3:46 ff.

5. Admiral J. O. Richardson, *On the Treadmill to Pearl Harbor*, p. 277.

6. Ibid., p. 385.

7. Ibid., p. 387.

8. Notes given by Admiral Richardson to Secretary Knox, 12 September 1940, *PHA*, 14:958–68. Concerning the idea that ORANGE was a justification for naval expansion see also Heinrichs, "Role of the United States Navy," pp. 197–224.

9. *PHA*, 14:968. Since September 1939 the Navy Department had been conducting a periodic series of evaluations called "Are We Ready?". These evaluations covered the spectrum from personnel to plans and contained information on ships, bases, supplies et al. Al-

though no specific recommendations were included in the "Are We Ready?" series about redirecting American efforts, the need for some kind of reorientation was implicit since the answer to the question was always "No." For the series see General Board Files, 1939–41, Naval Archives.

10. *PHA*, 14:962.

11. Richardson, *On the Treadmill to Pearl Harbor*, p. 435.

12. Ibid., p. 400.

13. Richardson describes the process in ibid. See also Letter, Richardson to Commander, Asiatic Fleet, 16 October 1940, *PHA*, 14:1006–11.

14. Assumptions as of 11 October included as enclosure in letter to Commander, Asiatic Fleet, 16 October 1940, *PHA*, 14:1012.

15. One source suggests: "The sum of the organizational situation in the Navy Department from the 1890's until World War II was that the centralizing reformers had their heyday between the Spanish-American War and World War I; at all other times the philosophy of decentralization was dominant" (Vincent Davis, *The Admirals Lobby*, p. 38).

16. The front-page story in the *Washington Post* which announced Stark's appointment on 16 March 1939 called him a "junior" and a "dark horse." The paper also noted that Stark had only reached flag rank two years before and that he was promoted "over the heads" of many senior officers.

17. Stark described his attitude and his relationships during the course of two interviews, December 1966 and January 1968.

18. *PHA*, 14:971; also Stark Interviews, January 1968.

19. Richardson's list of assumptions, with comments, 11 October 1940, in Ghormley's Conference Data File, ComNavEu, Naval Archives. On President Roosevelt's copy of these assumptions there is a handwritten note, possibly in Roosevelt's handwriting, beside assumption nine, "a very important assumption" (PSF, Navy Department, Roosevelt Papers).

20. Letter, Stark to Ghormley, 16 October 1940, Ghormley's Conference Data File, ComNavEu, Naval Archives.

21. Ibid.

22. Clarke, "Historical Sidelight," p. 12.

23. Ibid., pp. 13–14. Clarke apparently was shown a copy of RAINBOW 3.

24. Clarke Diary, 29 October 1940. Obviously the "contingency" was American entry into the war.

25. Telegram, Clarke (via Butler) to F.O., 31 October 1940, F.O. 371/24243, PRO.

26. Letter, Ghormley to Stark, 6 November 1940, Naval Attaché file, London, to CNO, 1940–41, WPD:CNO, Naval Archives.

27. Minutes of 8 November 1940 meeting in Cab 79/7, PRO.

28. Ibid. See also Butler, *Grand Strategy*, 2:418. Bellairs Diary, 8 and 11 November, was also helpful in reconstructing the meeting.

29. Minutes of 9 November meeting, Cab 79/7, PRO.

30. Letter, Stark to Richardson, 12 November 1940, *PHA*, 14:971.

31. Letter, Stark to Ghormley, 16 November 1940, Ghormley's Conference Data File, ComNavEu, Naval Archives. For a short summary of Plan Dog, see Morton, "Germany First," pp. 35–38. See also Morison, *United States Naval Operations*, 1:43–44.

32. Information obtained from copy of Plan Dog in the President's Files, PSF, Navy Department, Roosevelt Papers.

33. Letter, Stark to Commander, Asiatic Fleet, 12 November 1940, *PHA*, 14:972.

34. Letter, Stark to Ghormley, 16 November 1940, Ghormley's Conference Data File, ComNavEu, Naval Archives.

Chapter 13

1. Richardson's assumptions with comments can be found in Ghormley's Conference Data File, ComNavEu, Naval Archives. Ghormley had sent Pound a note saying: "I have recently been informed, unofficially, that in some of the N.D.'s [Navy Department's] studies of possible action in the Far East an assumption has been made that Great Britain can, and will, prevent any aggression in the Western Atlantic against the Western Hemisphere by the Axis powers" (Note, Ghormley to Pound, 13 November 1940, ADM 199/1159, PRO).

2. Minutes of 19 November 1940 meeting with British, Ghormley Secret File, Com-NavEu, Naval Archives.

3. Letter, Stark to Ghormley, 19 November 1940, Ghormley's Conference Data File, ComNavEu, Naval Archives.

4. Clarke's report, dated 21 November 1940, can be found in F.O. 371/24243, PRO. The assertion that Stark wanted Churchill's endorsement is made by Herbert Feis in *Road to Pearl Harbor*, p. 141. No reference is made to this desire in Clarke's report, his diary, his essay on his activities ("Historical Sidelight"), nor does Clarke recall Stark having made this suggestion.

5. Clarke Diary, 20 November 1940.

6. Memo, Churchill to First Sea Lord, 22 November 1940, Cab 84/24, PRO. The underlined portion of the message was not included in Churchill's history (*Second World War*, 2:690–91), but it does appear in the original.

7. Admiralty and Foreign Office reaction is reflected in a note by John Balfour, 26 November 1940, on jacket A-4712G, F.O. 371/24243, PRO.

8. Ibid.

9. Stark had mailed him a copy of "Plan D" on this very day; it arrived on 6 December 1940 (Ghormley Diary, 6 December 1940). The entry says that he received his copy of the plan on this date along with a personal note from Stark dated 22 November 1940.

10. Bellairs, for one, was already fully aware of this plan (Bellairs Diary, 21 November 1940).

11. Minutes of 22 November 1940 Meeting, Ghormley Secret File, ComNavEu, Naval Archives.

12. One source suggests that Roosevelt "shied away from immediate and formal approval of Plan Dog and its implications" while another states that FDR "in no way committed himself to the theory of strategy outlined by Stark" (Langer and Gleason, *World Crisis*, 2:222, and Matloff and Snell, *Strategic Planning for Coalition Warfare*, p. 28). Stark did tell General Marshall that he, Stark, was holding the comment "very tight." At the same time he mentioned the president's expressed wish for coordination by State, War and Navy (see Memorandum, Stark to Marshall, 22 November 1940, WPD 4175–15, U.S. Army, National Archives). No record has been found of what the president's comment was.

13. Memorandum, Anderson to Marshall, n.d., WPD 4175–15, U.S. Army, National Archives.

14. Watson, *Chief of Staff*, pp. 119–20. (There is some confusion concerning Marshall's opinion about Plan D. The problem is that RAINBOW 3 was being reviewed at this same time and some of his comments, those cited here for example, were in reaction to that plan's call for a Pacific offensive. The official history mistakenly attributes these comments as being a reaction to Plan D.)

15. Memorandum, Marshall to Stark, n.d., WPD 4175–15, U.S. Army, National Archives.

16. Matloff and Snell, *Strategic Planning*, p. 28.

17. Letter, Stark to Marshall, 29 November 1940; WPD 4175–15, U.S. Army, National Archives.

18. *PHA*, 5:2332–33; Admiral Stark confirmed this assertion in an interview in Washington, D.C., December 1966.

19. *PHA*, 2:1052. See also Pogue, *George C. Marshall*, 2:126. The matter is complex. At a Cabinet meeting on 29 November 1940, the president said that he had "no objection" to a group of British "experts" coming to the United States to discuss future plans (see *Ickes Diary*, 3:389). Roosevelt had in fact raised no objection to staff talks when the question was first broached in June 1940. The issue may in part be semantic; Roosevelt agreed in principle, but Stark did the arranging. On the other hand, if Stark is correct, he never knew that Roosevelt was aware of the impending visit until January 1941.

20. Watson, *Chief of Staff*, p. 118.

21. *PHA*, 20:4072–74. In Hull's *Memoirs* he cites this meeting as taking place on 23 November 1940 (1:914). Since the ambassador arrived in New York on 23 November, it is unlikely that Hull is correct on this detail.

22. Telegram, Lothian to F.O., 25 November 1940, F.O. 371/24243, PRO.

23. Lothian to F.O., 29 November 1940, F.O. 371/24243, PRO.

24. Cable, Stark to Ghormley, 2 December 1940, CMD, National Archives. The British had learned of the agreement to hold staff conferences perhaps as early as 25 November and at least by 30 November (Bellairs Diary, 25 November, 30 November 1940). The British actually advised Ghormley of this before he received his instructions from Stark (Cable, Ghormley to Stark, 3 December 1940, CMD, National Archives).

25. Assumptions included with Stark's 2 December cable.

26. Cable, Ghormley to Stark, 5 December 1940, CMD, National Archives. Part of the confusion at this point arose because of incredibly slow American communications. The Admiralty paper was partially in response to questions Stark had sent to Ghormley on 16 October, but Ghormley had not received them until 16 November.

27. Cable, Stark to Ghormley, 7 December 1940, CMD, National Archives. When Kelly Turner conveyed Admiral Stark's feelings to Captain Clarke he said that the British plan would leave America "naked" and was like America "proposing to despatch British Mediterranean fleet to Singapore to safeguard the Philippines" (Clarke to Pound, 7 December 1940, F.O. 371/24243, PRO).

28. Undated minute written in reaction to Clarke's 7 December report of Stark's unfavorable reaction, Cab 84/24, PRO. The minute must have been written on or about 9 December.

29. Notes on Disposition of U.S. Naval Forces, 9 December 1940, ADM 199/1232, PRO.

30. Cable, Ghormley to Stark, 11 December 1940, CMD, National Archives. See also Letter, Ghormley to Bailey, 9 December 1940, Ghormley's Conference Data, ComNavEu, Naval Archives. For the official British reaction, see telegram for Stark dated 13 December 1940 in F.O. 371/24243, PRO.

31. Kirk to OpNav, 10 December 1940, ComNavEu Files, Message Folders, Naval Archives. Such pertinacity could inspire caution as well as admiration. For reaction in Washington, see p. 221.

32. 29 and 30 December entries, Lee Journal, pp. 192–94. For his message to Washington, see p. 212. He suspected that the British wanted Americans to play no larger role at any peace conference than was required. The best way to keep America away from the peace settlement was to keep it away from the war.

33. Memorandum sent with copy of Stark's paper by War Plans Division to General Marshall, 12 December 1940, WPD 4175–15, U.S. Army, National Archives.

34. Stark made this comment at a meeting on 16 December 1940 (see memorandum of meeting between Secretary of War, Secretary of Navy, CNO, and Chief of Staff, WPD 4175–18, U.S. Army, National Archives).

35. See Watson, Chief of Staff, pp. 120–25. For the president's attitude, see Sherwood, Roosevelt and Hopkins, pp. 271 ff. For general U.S. planning, see Ray S. Cline, Washington Command Post, pp. 55 ff.

36. Watson, Chief of Staff, pp. 370–71.

37. The official historian states that this document "struck an attitude which was known would be acceptable to higher authority" (Watson, Chief of Staff, p. 370).

38. Letter, Ghormley to Stark, 7 January 1941, Naval Attaché, London, to CNO, 1940–41 File, WPD:CNO, Naval Archives. Secretary Stimson had told a group of government officials who had gathered at his home in early December that America's most immediate danger was the possibility that British sea power would be swept from the Atlantic. "The crucial hour for Britain," he thought, "was only ninety days away. After that, it was very doubtful whether she could hold out without firm assurance or great amounts of material aid" from the United States (Edward R. Stettinius, Jr., Lend-Lease Weapon for Victory, p. 65).

39. C.O.S. 1052, 19 December 1940, Cab 80/24, PRO. Based on Defense Committee (Operations) meeting on 17 December 1940, reported in Cab 69/1, PRO.

40. Lee's account of the meeting is taken from Lee Journal, pp. 197–98. Lee was later advised that the British procedure had been insisted upon by Prime Minister Churchill (ibid., p. 200). The British minutes of the meeting, which generally agree with Lee's account, can be found in ADM 199/1232.

41. Letter, Ghormley to Stark, 7 January 1941, Ghormley Papers, Naval Archives.

42. Rear Admiral Julius Furer, *Administration of the Navy Department in World War II*, p. 797.

43. Sir John Wheeler-Bennett, *King George VI*, p. 521.

44. Churchill, *Second World War*, 2:538 ff.

Chapter 14

1. Despite this title, the only delegates at the conference were the British and the Americans. The Canadians and the Australians had representatives on hand at the British Embassy, but they did not attend the sessions. The British were concerned lest they scare the Americans off with too large a group (see Matloff and Snell, *Strategic Planning*, p. 33n.). See also Telegram, Bellairs to C.O.S., 31 January 1941, Cab 105/36, PRO.

2. The most virulent attack on the talks can be found in Charles A. Beard, *President Roosevelt and the Coming of the War*. A well-known defense appears in Sherwood, *Roosevelt and Hopkins*, pp. 272–74, and a short but well-balanced account is in Feis, *Road to Pearl Harbor*, pp. 165–70. The final report of the conference was printed in *PHA*, 15:1485–1549. For other accounts of the meeting see Watson, *Chief of Staff*, pp. 367–82; Slessor, *Central Blue*, pp. 325–70; Matloff and Snell, *Strategic Planning*, pp. 32–42. For this account the author has depended primarily on the records of the conference held by the U.S. Naval Archives, Washington, D.C., the U.S. Army Files, especially WPD 4402–1, U.S. National Archives; private diaries of participants, including those of Admiral Roger M. Bellairs, Captain Arthur W. Clarke, Admiral Robert Ghormley; other diaries, most notably those of Lord Halifax, Charles Peake, Admiral B. L. Austin, and J. Pierrepont Moffat; and interviews, including those with Captain Arthur W. Clarke and Brigadier A. T. Cornwall-Jones; and the official records of the Admiralty, War Office, and War Cabinet Office, PRO, London.

3. See *Lee Journal*, p. 226; Lord Moran, *Churchill*, pp. 5–6; Lord Birkenhead, *Halifax*, pp. 470–73; Austin Diary, 14 January 1941; Lord Halifax Diary, 1940–41, York; Sir Charles Peake Diary, 1941, London.

4. Watson, *Chief of Staff*, pp. 124–25.

5. As early as 16 December 1940, Stimson, Marshall, Knox, and Stark had met and basically agreed that the "emergency could hardly be passed over without this country being drawn into the war eventually" (Stimson and Bundy, *Peace and War*, p. 366). And as Stettinius recalls, they agreed that the crisis would come within ninety days (*Lend-Lease Weapon for Victory*, p. 65). It should be recalled in this regard that it had not been until mid-October 1940 that Roosevelt had begun giving England a better than even chance of survival.

6. For Marshall's concern see Pogue, *George C. Marshall*, vol. 2, especially chap. 3. Air Vice Marshal Slessor says that the British saw the War Department's desire for a large troop build-up this way: "We fully recognize (though it was an odd feeling) that they had to take into account the possibility of a British defeat and hence the requirements of their own un-aided defence. . . . But we felt they were overdoing it a bit and perhaps even making our defeat less improbable by allocating too much effort to long-term measures at the expense of those necessary to defeat Germany soon" (*Central Blue*, p. 348).

7. *Lee Journal*, p. 228. On 16 January Bellairs handed Ghormley the answers to American questions on British war plans requested on 4 December. Bellairs did not consider the questions particularly relevant nor the frame of reference very realistic, but they did allow him to provide an estimate of the British needs in the Pacific. See also Ghormley Diary, and Memorandum, Ghormley to Stark, 16 January 1941, US-UK Staff Conversations Correspondence, Miscellaneous File, WPD:CNO, Naval Archives.

8. Ghormley Diary, 17, 18 January 1941.

9. Ibid., 21 January 1941. Some regarded the president's move as another indication of growing Anglo-American partnership, but some of Roosevelt's intimates thought they recognized his normal curiosity about ships (see Sherwood, *Roosevelt and Hopkins*, p. 246).

10. Peake Diary, 20 January 1940; Birkenhead, *Halifax*, p. 473.

11. Contrary to the report in Feis, *Road to Pearl Harbor*, p. 165, the president did not come on board the *KG-V* nor did the military experts remain hidden in their cabins. In fact,

they were all elbowing for position at the ship's rail (Clarke Interview, April 1967). Feis gives no source for this information.

12. Birkenhead, *Halifax*, p. 474. Halifax later came to feel that Roosevelt's charm was "faintly synthetic" and instead of promoting intimacy actually interposed "a screen" between the president and others. There also was a "faint aroma of hypocrisy, a whiff of the *faux bonhomme*" about Roosevelt that put Halifax off, although he continued to admire his political talents. But he perhaps best summed up his feelings about Roosevelt when, after listening to a speech that epitomized those talents, Halifax suggested that it was an example of "the fatal gift of manipulation bestowed by a bad fairy which disposes him to manoeuvre" (pp. 502–3, 525).

13. Ghormley Diary, 24 January 1941.

14. Memorandum, Stark to Ghormley, 24 January 1941, Ghormley Papers, Naval Archives.

15. Bellairs Diary, 24 January 1941.

16. Agenda for Staff Meetings, 27 January 1941, United States–United Kingdom Staff Conversations, U.S. Serial 011512–2, U.S. Navy, Naval Archives (hereafter cited as US–UK Conversations Minutes). These are the U.S. minutes kept during the Joint Conference sessions. This one-page paper was presented at the first meeting and consisted of eight procedural points: (1) presentation of agenda and agreement on it, (2) presentation of statements, (3) discussion of general situation, (4) discussion of major strategic lines "for cooperative military and naval action between the United States and the British Commonwealth (a) in the Pacific, (b) in the Atlantic, and (c) in the Mediterranean and Middle East" [this last item had been added in pencil], (5) operations to bring that strategy into effect, (6) "agreement upon the principal regions of responsibility, forces to be committed, skeleton plans, and general command arrangements," (7) discussion of details, and (8) adoption of a written report.

17. It was decided that Welles's presence might have implied too formal a commitment (see WPD 4402–89, U.S. Army, National Archives). Herbert Feis contends that Roosevelt himself decided that Welles should not attend (*Road to Pearl Harbor*, p. 165n.).

18. The U.S. Planning Staff had expressly suggested this approach (see Watson, *Chief of Staff*, pp. 372–73).

19. British officials had spent considerable time worrying over the exact proportion the United States would retain. For instance, on 30 November 1940, Anthony Eden had written a memorandum to the prime minister regarding American material aid. He had noted that "the United States Administration is pursuing an almost entirely American policy, rather than one of all possible aid to Britain" (*Eden Memoirs*, 1:176). Ironically, in light of the president's expressed concern, when war did come to the United States in December 1941, Churchill stated that one of his primary concerns was the fact that America had "stopped the stream of supplies" that were so vital to the British survival (Moran, *Churchill*, p. 11).

20. See p. 132.

21. Statement of Chief of Naval Operations and Chief of Staff, drafted 27 January 1941, US–UK Conversations Minutes, U.S. Serial 011512–3, U.S. Navy, Naval Archives. See also Watson, *Chief of Staff*, pp. 372–73.

22. Slessor, *Central Blue*, p. 341. Colonel Blimp was the cartoon creation of David Low. He became a figure who represented the British military at its stagiest and most conservative.

23. Slessor, *Central Blue*, pp. 340–41.

24. Cornwall-Jones Interview, May 1967. Slessor suggests that in some ways the American system was less formal and efficient than the British. However, "in others, they are strangely rigid and inflexible when compared with our often rather casual, informal and empirical way of doing things" (Slessor, *Central Blue*, p. 354).

25. Slessor comments on the "muddled condition" of American policymaking and speaks of how it allowed the British to get away with inaccurate estimates of aircraft needs (Slessor, *Central Blue*, pp. 349 and 321). Even after the war began the British were nonplussed at American procedures, in which there was evident a disorganization and a lack of system that seemed terribly inefficient. As General Sir John Dill observed: "There are no regular meetings of their Chiefs of Staff and if they do meet there is no secretariat to record

their proceedings. They have no joint planners and executive planning staff. . . . At present (January 1942) this country has not—repeat not—the slightest conception of what the war means, and their armed forces are more unready for war than it is possible to imagine" (Sir Arthur Bryant, *The Turn of the Tide*, pp. 292–93).

26. See p. 210.

27. Pogue, *George C. Marshall*, 2:132.

28. Cornwall-Jones Interview, May 1967.

29. US–UK Conversations Minutes, 31 January 1941, U.S. Serial 09212–6, U.S. Navy, Naval Archives.

30. For problems when trying to plan for contingencies see General Sir John Kennedy, *The Business of War*, pp. 91–97.

31. Bellairs Diary, 31 January 1941.

32. Bellairs to Chief of Staff, 1 February 1941, F.O. 371/26147, PRO.

33. US–UK Conversations Minutes, 3 February 1941, U.S. Serial 09212–7, U.S. Navy, Naval Archives.

34. US–UK Conversations Minutes, 5 February 1941, U.S. Serial 09212–8, U.S. Navy, Naval Archives.

35. Slessor, *Central Blue*, p. 356. Later in the negotiations the British team dedicated a series of verses to their American opposites. Kelly Turner's read:

The U.K. delegation have had the luck to learn a
Great deal of naval strategy from Admiral Kelly Turner
No piteous entreaties or objurgations harsh'll
Induce him to put P. B.Y.s under an Air Vice Marshal.
[Slessor, *Central Blue*, p. 342]

36. Cornwall-Jones Interview, May 1967.

37. Slessor, *Central Blue*, p. 345.

38. See p. 220.

39. US–UK Conversations Minutes, 5 February 1941, U.S. Serial 011512–6, U.S. Navy, Naval Archives.

40. Slessor, *Central Blue*, p. 347.

41. US–UK Conversations Minutes, 6 February 1941, U.S. Serial 09212–9, U.S. Navy, Naval Archives.

42. Bellairs Diary, 6 February 1941.

43. Memorandum, Turner to Bellairs, 7 February 1941, Miscellaneous File No. 5; WPD:CNO, Naval Archives.

44. Halifax Diary, 7 February 1941, and Bellairs Diary, 7 February 1941.

45. Clarke Diary, 8 February 1941.

46. Bellairs Diary, 9 February 1941.

47. US–UK Conversations Minutes, 10 February 1941, U.S. Serial 09212–10, U.S. Navy, Naval Archives.

48. Bellairs Diary, 11 February 1941.

49. Ibid. Slessor says that the Americans only accepted this policy because the British made it "quite clear that it was no good their doing anything else" (Slessor, *Central Blue*, p. 425).

50. Bellairs to Chief of Staff, 11 February 1941, ADM 116/4877, PRO.

51. Minute, Churchill to General Ismay for C.O.S. Committee and the First Lord and First Sea Lord, 12 February 1941, ADM 116/4877, PRO. As the head of the Joint Intelligence Committee, Victor Cavendish-Bentinck, put it, "Whilst it seems rather silly that in the event of the U.S. entering the war, the Americans should send naval forces to the Atlantic and the Mediterranean, and that we should be compelled to send forces from those seas to the Far East, on the other hand there may be considerable psychological advantages in the U.S. Navy being strongly engaged in warfare in the Atlantic and the Mediterranean" (Minute on folder containing Bellairs's telegram, F.O. 371/26147, PRO).

Chapter 15

1. A copy of the paper sent by Bellairs to Chiefs of Staff, 15 February 1941, can be found in ADM 116/4877, PRO; copy in U.S. files is dated 11 February 1941 (see file B.U.S. (J) 4113, WPD 4402, U.S. Army, National Archives).

2. Minutes of Joint U.S. Military Delegation, US–UK Staff Conversations Minutes, 13 February 1941, U.S. Serial 09212–11. U.S. Navy, Naval Archives. These are minutes kept during joint meetings of the U.S. team; as noted previously, such meetings were held irregularly.

3. Ibid.

4. Less than two weeks before Miles had commented that by 15 April the United States would face a choice of "saving England by going to war or letting England go in order to concentrate on our own defense" (Moffat Diary, 1 February 1941).

5. Langer and Gleason, *World Crisis*, 2:423.

6. There were also British officers who feared that allocation of material to the Mediterranean Theater was a diversion from the major theater (see Bryant, *Turn of the Tide*, p. 241, and Kennedy, *Business of War*, pp. 100–105). When problems arose over this theater later in the war General Marshall saw victories won in the Middle East as primarily "victories for the British Empire," and hence could not become too enthusiastic about them (Pogue, *George C. Marshall*, 2:349). When Hopkins visited London in July 1941, he explained to Churchill that the American Chiefs of Staff thought the "British Empire [was] making too many sacrifices in trying to maintain an indefensible position in the Middle East" (Sherwood, *Roosevelt and Hopkins*, p. 314).

7. Admiral Stark would soon cite the "very grave threat" to England's sea communications as the first of two "principal dangers" immediately threatening her survival (Letter, Stark to Fleet Commanders, 3 April 1941, *PHA*, 17:2463). The U.S. Navy would soon begin helping to patrol portions of the Atlantic for German submarines.

8. US–UK Conversations Minutes, 14 February 1941, U.S. Serial 09212/12, U.S. Navy, Naval Archives.

9. Bellairs Diary, 14 February 1941.

10. Ibid., 13 February 1941.

11. Halifax Diary, 15 February 1941. Newspaper reporters had been pursuing the ambassador and he noted that meeting Hull in company with Casey would give the "journalists good ground for guessing what we have been talking about." The journalists would not be the only ones guessing, he would find.

12. The Japanese were trying to pressure the French and Dutch for concessions while bargaining for bases in Indo-China. It would seem that London inflated the crisis "beyond all reasonable proportion" (see Langer and Gleason, *World Crisis*, 2:330; for a full discussion of developments during this period, see pp. 319–31).

13. Bellairs to Chiefs of Staff, 17 February 1941, ADM 116/4877, PRO.

14. Turner had recommended the development of a "British Isles Detachment" made up of 27 destroyers plus support craft less than a week before (see Stark to Commander in Chief, Atlantic Neutrality Patrol, 15 February 1941, and Turner memoranda in WPD 4175–18, U.S. Army, National Archives; also see Navy Serial Op–12A–4 (SC) A16CR–5, U.S. Navy, Naval Archives).

15. Warren Kimball, *The Most Unsordid Act*, pp. 180–81.

16. Franklin D. Roosevelt Press Conferences, Microfilm Roll #9, Franklin D. Roosevelt Memorial Library, Hyde Park, N.Y.

17. Kimball, *Most Unsordid Act*, pp. 180–81.

18. Bellairs to Chiefs of Staff, 17 February 1941, ADM 116/4877, PRO.

19. Kimball, *Most Unsordid Act*, pp. 214–16.

20. US–UK Conversations Minutes, 17 February 1941, U.S. Serial 09212–14, U.S. Navy, Naval Archives.

21. Bellairs Diary, 17 February 1941.

22. Minute, Churchill to First Lord and First Sea Lord, 17 February 1941, ADM 116/4877, PRO.

23. This was the paragraph in which Bellairs had said that Singapore had priority in Empire considerations. The issue broke into the open in England a few weeks later. Churchill had written a minute suggestion that the loss of the Middle East would be a disaster of the first magnitude, second only to invasion and conquest of the home islands. General Sir John Dill, the C.I.G.S., formally disagreed, observing that although the loss of Egypt would

be terrible, Egypt was "'not even second in order of priority,' for it had been an accepted principle in our strategy that in the last resort the security of Singapore came before that of Egypt." Churchill was almost as displeased by this observation as by Bellairs's memorandum (*Grand Strategy*, 2:506).

24. Statement of U.S. Staff Committee on Far East, 19 February 1941, US–UK Conversations Minutes; U.S. Serial 011512–8, U.S. Navy, Naval Archives.

25. Paradoxically, American doubts about Singapore were reinforced by the British themselves. In a memorandum for the president's naval aide, Admiral Ingersoll noted that by requesting American help in repairing the British carrier *Illustrious*, the British proved that "Singapore is not considered as a suitable place by the British for the repair and upkeep of aircraft carriers or large cruisers and shows the difficulty that we might have if we sent aircraft carriers or large cruisers to base on Singapore" (Admiral Royal Ingersoll to Captain Daniel J. Callahan, 21 February 1941, Navy File, 1941, Roosevelt Papers).

26. Bellairs included these comments in his message to the Chiefs of Staff several days later (see Bellairs to Chiefs of Staff, 23 February 1941, F.O. 371/26219, PRO).

27. Copy of letter to Bellairs, U.S. Serial 011512–7, WPD 4402, U.S. Army, National Archives.

28. Chiefs of Staff to Bellairs, 19 February 1941, ADM 116/4877, PRO.

29. Bellairs Diary. Herbert Feis contends that Halifax and Hull continued to exchange papers (see *Road to Pearl Harbor*, p. 166n.). Letter, Bellairs to Embick, can be found in Executive 4, Item 11, U.S. Army, National Archives.

30. Minutes of U.S. Navy Delegation to US–UK Staff Conversations Minutes, 20 February 1941, U.S. Serial 09212–16, U.S. Navy, Naval Archives.

31. Minutes of U.S. Navy–U.S. Army Delegation, 20 February 1941, U.S. Serial 09212–17, U.S. Navy, Naval Archives.

32. US–UK Conversations Minutes, 24 February 1941, U.S. Serial 09212–18, U.S. Navy, Naval Archives.

33. Slessor, *Central Blue*, p. 355.

34. Bellairs to Chiefs of Staff, 4 March 1941, F.O. 371/26219, PRO.

35. US–UK Conversations Minutes, 26 February 1941, U.S. Serial 09212–19, U.S. Navy, Naval Archives. As the officers pointed out at this meeting, part of the U.S. Navy's hesitation about basing their ships at Singapore was that the fortress seemed vulnerable to attack from the land side.

36. The lines were: north of the equator to longitude 140° east; south of the equator to longitude 180°, the International Date Line. This delineation would seem to exclude the Philippines. American intransigence on the terminology is pointed out in a special report submitted by the British (see C.O.S. [41] 250, 2 April 1941, Cab 80/27, PRO).

37. Bellairs to C.O.S., 13 March 1941, F.O. 371/26219, PRO.

38. Minutes, U.S. Navy–U.K. Navy Delegations to US–UK Conversations Minutes, 6 March 1941, U.S. Serial 09212–20, U.S. Navy, Naval Archives; see also Bellairs Diary, 3 March 1941.

39. Letter, Ghormley to Bellairs, 7 March 1941, WPD:CNO, U.S. Navy, Naval Archives.

40. Bellairs Diary, 7 March 1941.

41. For summary of developments, see Kimball, *Most Unsordid Act*, pp. 219–20.

42. Bellairs Diary, 15 March 1941.

43. US–UK Conversations Minutes, 27 March 1941, U.S. Serial 09212–21, U.S. Navy, Naval Archives. See also Bellairs Diary, 27 March 1941, and Slessor, *Central Blue*, pp. 356–59. The Air Vice Marshal comments that some Americans always suspected that they were being "outsmarted by the subtle British" and goes on beguilingly to note that this was "perhaps because we sometimes do such stupid things that they cannot take them at their face value but suspect them of being a part of some dark design" (Slessor, *Central Blue*, p. 358).

44. A copy of the full report can be found in *PHA*, 15:1485–1550.

45. Bellairs Diary, 29 March 1941.

46. US–UK Conversations Minutes, 29 March 1941, U.S. Serial 09212–22, U.S. Navy, Naval Archives.

Chapter 16

1. Memorandum, C.O.S. to Churchill, 15 December 1941, PREM 458 (7). Danckwerts's view is contained in Letter, Danckwerts to Admiral T. S. V. Phillips, 23 June 1941, Cab 122/4, PRO.

2. *PHA*, 15:1494.

3. Memorandum, Clarke, no addressee, 19 May 1941, WPD 4402–10, U.S. Army, National Archives.

4. "History of British Naval Staff Mission, 1941–1946," ADM 205/1236, PRO. This survey deals almost exclusively with technological matters.

5. It was originally planned to base the Support Force at Londonderry, but the president worried about the political repercussions. The Support Force was eventually based on Newfoundland (Patrick Abbazia, *Mr. Roosevelt's Navy*, p. 217). For information on the bases see Morison, *United States Naval Operations*, 1:53–54. Denfeld was accompanied on his surveying tour by, among others, the new U.S. naval attaché in London, Captain Charles Lockwood. Lockwood kept a record of the tour (see Charles Lockwood Diary, 1941, Naval Archives).

6. *PHA*, 15:1441 and 1525–26.

7. Morison, *United States Naval Operations*, 1:51; Abbazia, *Mr. Roosevelt's Navy*, pp. 142–43; Admiral Ernest J. King and Walter M. Whitehill, *Fleet Admiral King*, p. 319.

8. "Administrative History, Commander in Chief, Atlantic Fleet," 2:25, U.S. Navy, Naval Archives.

9. This force had been designated in ABC-1 as the one to escort, cover, and patrol the North Atlantic Zone, which had been assigned to the U.S. Navy (*PHA*, 15:2163).

10. *PHA*, 5:2292 ff.

11. Langer and Gleason, *World Crisis*, 2:428.

12. For 11 April message see Francis Loewenheim, Harold D. Langley, and Manfred Jonas, eds., *Roosevelt and Churchill*, pp. 137–38. For atmosphere within the president's official family during this period see James MacGregor Burns, *Roosevelt* (1970), chap. 3.

13. This was the Tobey Resolution (SJR 62), but then a whole series of similar resolutions were introduced in early April. For public reaction see *Public Opinion Quarterly* 5 (1941): 438, and *New York Times*, 11 May 1941.

14. *PHA*, 15:2292 ff and 16:2163–65. See also Watson, *Chief of Staff*, pp. 390–91. See discussion in Quinlan, "The United States Fleet," pp. 179–80.

15. *PHA*, 1:122 ff; 5:211 ff; 16:2163 ff. See also Abbazia, *Mr. Roosevelt's Navy*, chap. 13; and Langer and Gleason, *World Crisis*, 2:451.

16. As quoted in Morison, *United States Naval Operations*, 1:78

17. Kittredge MS, sec. 5, pt. B, vol. 5, p. 547. Also see Abbazia, *Mr. Roosevelt's Navy*, pp. 214–15.

18. Theodore Wilson, *The First Summit*, pp. 141–44.

19. Letter, Little to Pound, 15 July 1941, ADM 205/14, PRO.

20. Morison, *United States Naval Operations*, 1:82. For Admiral Stark's desire to get a shot at the *Tirpitz* see Abbazia, *Mr. Roosevelt's Navy*, p. 241.

21. For full coverage of the *Greer* incident see Abbazia, *Mr. Roosevelt's Navy*, chap. 20. See also *PHA*, 6:2842.

22. Morison, *United States Naval Operations*, 1:80.

23. Regarding personal associations see Sherwood, *Roosevelt and Hopkins*, p. 358. For reconstructing the conference I have been assisted by published works, most notably Theodore Wilson's excellent *First Summit* and the journalistic, but still useful, *Atlantic Meeting* by H. V. Morton. I have also used the unpublished journal accounts of two British participants, Admiral B. B. Schofield and General Sir Ian Jacob, and that of U.S. General H. H. Arnold. There also is an informal report on the meeting written by Captain (later Admiral) Forrest Sherman in the U.S. Naval Archives. Also helpful were Matloff and Snell, *Strategic Planning*, pp. 52–58, and Abbazia, *Mr. Roosevelt's Navy*, pp. 219–22.

24. Wilson, *First Summit*, pp. 141–44.

25. Copy of Stark's remarks found in the Schofield Memoirs, n.d.

26. Wilson, *First Summit*, p. 147. The British had had high hopes; as one observer said, "What we had all subconsciously hoped for, and not perhaps, entirely subconsciously, was a declaration that America was coming into the battle with us" (H. V. Morton, *Atlantic Meeting*, p. 160).

27. Wilson, *First Summit*, p. 148.

28. Ibid.

29. Ibid.

30. Watson, *Chief of Staff*, pp. 406–10.

31. Letter, Danckwerts to Pound, 17 April 1941, Cab 105/36, PRO.

32. *PHA*, 15:1678.

33. Cable, CNO to Commander in Chief, Asiatic Fleet, 15 February 1941, ABDA–ANZAC Correspondence, WPD:CNO, U.S. Navy, Naval Archives.

34. Cable, Commander in Chief, Asiatic Fleet to OpNav, 3 March 1941, CMD, National Archives.

35. Letter, Brooke-Popham to Ismay, 28 February 1941, V/1/7, Brooke-Popham Papers.

36. *PHA*, 15:1502.

37. Admiral Thomas Hart, "Narrative of Events, Asiatic Fleet, Leading Up to War and from 8 December to 15 February 1942," June 1942, Naval Archives.

38. *PHA*, 15:1564–67.

39. "Hart Narrative," June 1942, Naval Archives.

40. Letter, Hart to Stark, 29 April 1941, US–UK–Dutch, Singapore File, WPD:CNO, Naval Archives.

41. The British were still being cagey on this issue as late as 15 November 1941 (see Letter, Eden to Dutch Minister, PREM 3/326, PRO).

42. Letter, Brooke-Popham to Ismay, 16 May 1941, Brooke-Popham Papers.

43. For a copy of ABD-1 see *PHA*, 15:1551–85.

44. According to Morison ABD-1 was disapproved because the "whole thing pivoted on Singapore" (see Morison, *United States Naval Operations*, 3:55). For the Stark-Marshall letter see *PHA*, 15:1677–79.

45. Dispatch, Stark to Commander in Chief, Asiatic Fleet, 11 November 1941, Asiatic Fleet Dispatches, Naval Archives. ABD-2 was a modification of ABD-1.

Bibliography

MANUSCRIPT SOURCES

Great Britain

LONDON
Beaverbrook Library.
    David Lloyd George Papers, 1940–41.
King's College.
    Air Marshal Sir Robert Brooke-Popham Papers, 1940–41.
    Lord Ismay [Hastings Ismay] Papers, 1940–55.
London School of Economics.
    Hugh Dalton Diary, 1939–41.
National War Museum.
    Sir Henry Tizard Diary, 1940.

MEDMENHAM
B. H. Liddell Hart Library.
    Sir B. H. Liddell Hart Papers, 1936–41.

OXFORD
Nuffield College, Oxford University.
    Lord Cherwell [Frederick Lindeman] Papers, 1932–41.

PRIVATELY HELD PAPERS
    Sir Arthur Balfour Memoirs. London.
    Rear Admiral Roger M. Bellairs Diary, 1940–41. Hascombe, nr. Godalming.
    Captain Arthur W. Clarke Diary, 1940–41. Southsea.
    Captain Arthur W. Clarke. "Historical Sidelight" (1961). MS in possession of the author.
    Diary of a Naval Officer, 1940–41. Oxford.
    Leonard K. Elmhirst Diary, 1939–40 (selected portions). Totnes, Devon.

Lord Halifax [Edward Wood] Diary, 1940–41. York.
General Sir Ian Jacob Diary, July–August 1941. Ipswich.
Sir Charles Peake Diary, 1941. London.
Admiral B. B. Schofield Diary, July–August 1941. Henley.
Admiral B. B. Schofield Memoirs. Shiplake, nr. Henley.

United States

CAMBRIDGE, MASS.
Harvard University Library.
Jay Pierrepont Moffat Diary and Papers, 1939–41.

DURHAM, N.C.
Duke University Library.
General Franz Halder Diaries, 1939–40.

HYDE PARK, N.Y.
Franklin D. Roosevelt Memorial Library.
Harry Hopkins Papers, 1940–41.
Henry Morgenthau, Jr., Diary, 1940–41.
Franklin D. Roosevelt Papers, 1938–41.
Franklin D. Roosevelt Press Conferences, 1940–41. Microfilm.
Henry A. Wallace Papers, 1940–41.

NEW YORK, N.Y.
Columbia University.
Sir Normal Angell Oral History Project, 1951.
Admiral James Fife Oral History Project, 1962.
Admiral Alan G. Kirk Oral History Project, 1961.

PRINCETON, N.J.
Princeton University Library.
Bernard Baruch Papers, 1932–41.

WASHINGTON, D.C.
Library of Congress.
General H. H. Arnold Diary, 1941.
Joseph E. Davies Diary and Papers.
Norman A. Davis Papers.
Felix Frankfurter Papers.
Cordell Hull Papers.
Frank Knox Papers.
Admiral William Leahy Papers and Diary, 1937–41.
Breckinridge Long Diary, 1939–41.
General Carl A. Spaatz Diary and Papers, 1939–40.
Laurence A. Steinhardt Papers.

PRIVATELY HELD PAPERS
Vice Admiral Bernard L. Austin Diary, 1940–41. Washington, D.C.
Adolf A. Berle Diary, 1940–41. New York, N.Y.
Rear Admiral Robert L. Ghormley Diary and Papers, 1940–41. Washington, D.C.
Brigadier General Raymond E. Lee Journal. Washington, D.C.

OFFICIAL ARCHIVES

Great Britain

EDINBURGH
National Library of Scotland.
  Lord Elibank [Arthur Murray] Papers, 1937–40.
Scottish National Archives.
  Lord Lothian [Philip Kerr] Papers, 1939–40.

LONDON
Admiralty Historical Branch.
  Memoirs of Rear Admiral John Godfrey.
Public Record Office.
  Admiralty Records, 1937–41.
  Cabinet Office Papers and Memoranda, 1937–41. (After 2 September 1939 the Cabinet Office became the War Cabinet Office.)
  Foreign Office Papers, 1937–41.
  War Office, 1939–41.

United States

WASHINGTON, D.C.
National Archives.
  U.S. Army. Office of the Chief of Staff Files, 1940–41.
  ————. Operations Division Files, 1940–41.
  ————. War Plans Division Files, 1940–41.
  U.S. Department of State. Diplomatic Files, 1937–41.
  U.S. Navy. Classified Microfilm Dispatches, 1940–41.
Operational Naval Archives, U.S. Navy.
  Asiatic Fleet Dispatches, 1940–41.
  Chief of Naval Operations Files, 1938–41.
  War Plans Divisions Files, 1938–41.
  Commander, Naval Forces Europe Files (ComNavEu), 1939–41.
  Alusna Secret Messages.
  Vice Admiral Robert L. Ghormley [Official] Diary and Papers, 1940–41.
  ————. Conference Data File, 1940.
  ————. Message File, 1940–41.
  ————. Secret File, 1940–41.
  Naval Attaché Files, 1939–41.
  General Board Files, 1939–41.
  Admiral Thomas Hart. "Narrative of Events, Asiatic Fleet, Leading Up to War and from 8 December to 15 February 1942." June 1942.
  The History of U.S. Naval Research and Development in World War II.
  Vice Admiral Alan G. Kirk Papers and Diary, 1938–40.
  Captain Tracy B. Kittredge. "United States–British Naval Cooperation, 1939–42."
  Captain Charles Lockwood Diary, 1941.
  Operations Division Files (OpNav), 1940–41.

U.S. Naval Administration in World War II: Office of CNO:ONI. War Plans Division Files, 1938–41.
> ABDA-ANZAC Correspondence, 1940–41.
> Vice Admiral Royal E. Ingersoll File.
> United States–United Kingdom Staff Conversations Correspondence.
> United States–United Kingdom Staff Conversations Minutes.
> Captain Russell Willson, "Notes on Conversations with Admiralty, 1938."

GOVERNMENT DOCUMENTS

Great Britain
Foreign Office. *Documents on British Foreign Policy, 1919–1939.* 3d Series: 1938–39. Edited by Sir Llewellyn Woodward and Rohan Butler. London, 1950.
Parliament. *Parliamentary Debates*, Commons (1940).

United States
U.S. Congress. House. Naval Affairs Committee. *Hearings on Sundry Legislation Affecting the Naval Establishment, 1940.* 76th Cong., 3d sess., 1940.
U.S. Congress. Senate. Committee on Naval Affairs. *Hearings on Construction of Certain Naval Vessels, 1940.* 76th Cong., 3d sess., 1940.
————. *Congressional Record.* 76th Cong., 3d sess., 1940.
————. *Pearl Harbor Attack: Hearings of the Joint Committee on the Investigation of the Pearl Harbor Attack.* 79th Cong., 1st sess. Pursuant to S. Con. Res. 27. 39 vols. Washington, D.C., 1946.
U.S. Department of State. *Foreign Relations of the United States: Diplomatic Papers. 1937,* 5 vols.; *1938,* 5 vols.; *1939,* 5 vols.; *1940,* 5 vols.; *1941,* 7 vols. Washington, D.C., 1955–63.
————. *Peace and War: United States Foreign Policy, 1931–1941.* Washington, D.C., 1943.

NEWSPAPERS

Christian Science Monitor.
New York Times.
Times (London).
Washington Times Herald.

INTERVIEWS

Agar, Herbert. London, April 1967.
Austin, Admiral Bernard L. Washington, D.C., November and December 1966.
Backer, George. New York, August 1967.

Balfour, Sir John. London, July 1971.

Berle, Adolf A. New York, December 1966 and January 1967.

Berlin, Sir Isaiah. Oxford, England, April and May 1967.

Birkenhead, Lord. Charlton, England, June 1967.

Bowra, Sir Maurice. Oxford, England, April 1967.

Bridges, Lord. London, April 1967.

Butler, Sir J. R. M. Cambridge, England, March 1967.

Butler, Sir Neville. London, April 1967.

Chandos, Lord. London, April and May 1967.

Clarke, Captain A. W. London, April and May 1967.

Cohen, Benjamin V. Washington, D.C., November 1966.

Cornwall-Jones, Brigadier A. T. Waltham St. Lawrence, England, May 1967, and Henley, England, June 1967.

Daniel, Admiral Sir Charles. Sulhamstead, England, June 1967.

Dewing, General Richard Henry. Salisbury, England, May 1967.

Edison, Charles A. New York, December 1966.

Elmhirst, Leonard K. Totnes, England, February 1968.

Farley, James A. New York, December 1966.

Greenfield, Kent Roberts. Baltimore, August 1966.

Hall, Sir Noel. Oxford, England, April and May 1967.

Hickerson, John D. Washington, D.C., August 1966.

Hill, Senator Lister. Washington, D.C., September 1967.

Hitchcock, Captain Norman. Washington, D.C., August, 1967.

Inchyra, Lord. London, May 1967.

Jacob, General Sir Ian. Ipswich and London, April and May 1967.

Kennedy, General Sir John. London, May 1967.

Liddell Hart, Sir Basil H. Medmenham, England, March and June, 1967.

MacDonald-Buchanan, Major Sir Reginald. London, March 1967.

Miller, Colonel Francis P. London, April 1967.

Moran, Lord. London, March 1967.

Mowrer, Edgar Ansel. Washington, D.C., January 1967.

Pogue, Forrest C. Washington, D.C., January 1967.

Portal, Lord [Marshal of the Royal Air Force]. London, April 1967.

Roosevelt, James. New York, N.Y., December 1967.

Roskill, Captain Stephen W. Oxford, England, April 1967.

Schoenfeld, Rudolph E. Washington, D.C., November 1967.

Schofield, Admiral B. B. Henley, England, April and May 1967.

Spaatz, General Carl A. Washington, D.C., December 1967.

Stark, Admiral Harold R. Washington, D.C., December 1966 and January 1967.

Taylor, A. J. P. Oxford, England, May 1967.

Thompson, R. W. Belchamp Walter, England, June 1967.

Wheeler-Bennett, Sir John. Oxford, England, May 1967.

BOOKS AND ARTICLES

Abbazia, Patrick. *Mr. Roosevelt's Navy: The Private War of the U.S. Atlantic Fleet, 1939–1942.* Annapolis: U.S. Naval Institute Press, 1975.

Adler, Selig. *The Uncertain Giant, 1921–1941.* New York: Macmillan Co., 1965.

Amery, Leopold S. *My Political Life.* 3 vols. London: Hutchinson, 1953.

Arnold, Henry H. *Global Mission.* New York: Harper & Brothers, 1949.

Attlee, Clement. *As It Happened.* London: William Heinemann, 1954.

————. "The Churchill I Knew." In *Churchill by His Contemporaries*, edited by Charles Eade. London: Reprint Society, 1953.

Barclay, Glen St. John. "Singapore Strategy: The Role of the United States in Imperial Defense." *Military Affairs* 49 (April 1975): 54–58.

Baxter, James P. *Scientists against Time.* Boston: Little, Brown & Co., 1946.

Beard, Charles A. *President Roosevelt and the Coming of the War, 1941.* New Haven: Yale University Press, 1948.

Berlin, Sir Isaiah. *Mr. Churchill in 1940.* London: John Murray, n.d.

Bevan, Aneurin. "History's Impresario." In *Churchill by His Contemporaries*, edited by Charles Eade. London: Reprint Society, 1953.

Birkenhead, Earl of. *Halifax.* Boston: Houghton Mifflin Co., 1965.

Blum, John Morton. *From the Morgenthau Diaries.* Vol. 1, *Years of Crisis, 1928–1938.* Vol. 2, *Years of Urgency, 1938–1941.* Boston: Houghton Mifflin Co., 1959, 1965.

Bonham-Carter, Violet. *Winston Churchill: An Intimate Portrait.* New York: Harcourt, Brace & World, 1965.

Borg, Dorothy. "Notes on Roosevelt's Quarantine Speech." *Political Science Quarterly* 72 (September 1957): 405–33.

Borg, Dorothy, and Okamota, Shumpei, eds. *Pearl Harbor as History: Japanese-American Relations, 1931–1941.* New York: Columbia University Press, 1973.

Briggs, Herbert W. "Neglected Aspects of the Destroyer Deal." *American Journal of International Law* 34 (1940): 569–87.

Bryant, Sir Arthur. *The Turn of the Tide.* London: Doubleday & Co., 1957.

Burns, James MacGregor. *Roosevelt: The Lion and the Fox.* New York: Harcourt, Brace & World, 1956.

————. *Roosevelt: The Soldier of Freedom.* New York: Harcourt Brace Jovanovich, 1970.

Butler, Sir J. R. M. *Grand Strategy, September 1939–June 1941.* Vol. 2, *History of the Second World War.* United Kingdom Military Series. London: Her Majesty's Stationery Office, 1964.

————. *Lord Lothian.* London: Macmillan & Co., 1960.

Cadogan, Alexander. *The Diaries of Sir Alexander Cadogan.* Edited by David Dilks. New York: G. P. Putnam's Sons, 1972.

Casey, Richard G. C. *Personal Experiences, 1939–1946.* New York: David McKay Co., 1963.

Chadwin, Mark L. *The War Hawks of World War II*. Chapel Hill: University of North Carolina Press, 1968.

Churchill, Randolph. *Winston S. Churchill*. 2 vols. Boston: Houghton Mifflin Co., 1966, 1967.

Churchill, Winston. *Blood, Sweat, and Tears*. New York: G. P. Putnam's Sons, 1941.

————. "Bombs Don't Scare Us Now." *Colliers*, 17 June 1939, pp. 11 et seq.

————. "Can America Keep out of War?" *Colliers*, 2 October 1937, pp. 14–15 et seq.

————. "Defense in the Pacific." *Colliers*, 17 December 1932, pp. 12–13 et seq.

————. "Let the Tyrant Criminals Bomb!" *Colliers*, 14 January 1939, pp. 12–13 et seq.

————. *The Second World War*. 6 vols. Vol. 1, *The Gathering Storm*. Vol. 2, *Their Finest Hour*. Vol. 3, *The Grand Alliance*. Boston: Houghton Mifflin Co., 1948, 1949, 1950.

————. "To End War." *Colliers*, 29 June 1935, pp. 12 et seq.

————. "War, Now or Never." *Colliers*, 3 June 1939, pp. 9–10 et seq.

————. "While the World Watches." *Colliers*, 29 December 1934, pp. 24–25 et seq.

Clarke, Ronald W. *Tizard*. Cambridge, Mass.: MIT Press, 1965.

Cline, Ray S. *Washington Command Post: The Operations Division*. United States Army in World War II. Washington, D.C.: Department of the Army, 1951.

Coit, Margaret. *Mr. Baruch*. Boston: Houghton Mifflin Co., 1957.

Cole, Wayne S. "American Entry into World War II: A Historiographical Appraisal." *Mississippi Valley Historical Review* 43 (March 1957): 595–617.

Conn, Stetson. "Changing Concepts of National Defense in the United States, 1937–1941." *Military Affairs* 28 (Spring 1964): 1–7.

Conn, Stetson, and Fairchild, Byron. *The Framework of Hemisphere Defense*. United States Army in World War II. Washington, D.C.: Department of the Army, 1960.

Cooper, Duff. *Old Men Forget*. London: Rupert Hart-Davis, 1953.

Creel, George. *Rebel at Large*. New York: G. P. Putnam's Sons, 1947.

Dalton, Hugh. *Memoirs*. 2 vols. London: Frederick Muller, 1953, 1957.

Davis, Forest, and Lindley, Ernest K. *How War Came: An American White Paper*. New York: Simon and Schuster, 1942.

Davis, Vincent. *The Admirals Lobby*. Chapel Hill: University of North Carolina Press, 1967.

Divine, Robert A. *The Illusion of Neutrality*. Chicago: Quadrangle Books, 1968.

————. *The Reluctant Belligerent: American Entry into World War II*. New York: John Wiley & Sons, 1965.

Donovan, William, and Mowrer, Frank. *Fifth-Column Lessons for Americans*. Introduction by Frank Knox. Washington, D.C.: American

Council on Public Affairs, 1941.

Dulles, Allen. *The Secret Surrender*. New York: Harper & Row, 1966.

Dulles, Foster R., and Ridinger, Gerald. "The Anti-Colonial Policies of F. D. R." *Political Science Quarterly* 70 (March 1955): 1–18.

Dziuban, Stanley W. *Military Relations between the United States and Canada, 1939–1945*. United States Army in World War II. Washington, D.C.: Department of the Army, 1959.

Eden, Sir Anthony. *The Memoirs of Anthony Eden, Earl of Avon*. 3 vols. Vol. 1, *Full Circle*. Vol. 2, *Facing the Dictators*. Vol. 3, *The Reckoning*. Boston: Houghton Mifflin Co., 1960, 1962, 1965.

Edwards, Cecil. *Bruce of Melbourne*. London: William Heinemann, 1965.

Elibank, Viscount [Arthur C. Murray]. "Franklin Roosevelt: Friend of Britain." *Contemporary Review* 187 (June 1955): 362–68.

Elliot, Charles F. "The Genesis of the Modern U.S. Navy." *United States Naval Institute Proceedings* 92 (March 1966): 62–69.

Emerson, Walter R. *"F.D.R." in the Ultimate Decision*. Edited by Ernest R. May. New York: George Braziller, 1960.

Feiling, Keith. *The Life of Neville Chamberlain*. London: Macmillan & Co., 1946.

Feis, Herbert. *The Road to Pearl Harbor*. New York: Atheneum Publishers, 1964.

Ford, Corey. *Donovan of OSS*. Boston: Little, Brown & Co., 1970.

Forrestal, James. *The Forrestal Diaries*. Edited by Walter Millis and E. S. Duffield. New York: Viking Press, 1951.

Freidel, Frank B. *Franklin D. Roosevelt*. 3 vols. Vol. 1, *The Apprenticeship*. Vol. 2, *The Ordeal*. Vol. 3, *The Triumph*. Boston: Little, Brown & Co., 1952, 1954, 1956.

Furer, Rear Admiral Julius Augustus. *Administration of the Navy Department in World War II*. Washington, D.C.: U.S. Government Printing Office, 1959.

Gerhard, Eugene C. *America's Advocate: Robert H. Jackson*. Indianapolis: Bobbs-Merrill Co., 1958.

Goodhart, Philip. *Fifty Ships That Saved the World*. Garden City, N.Y.: Doubleday & Co., 1965.

Gowing, Margaret M. *Britain and Atomic Energy, 1939–1945*. New York: St. Martin's Press, 1964.

Greenfield, Kent Roberts. *American Strategy in World War II*. Baltimore: Johns Hopkins University Press, 1963.

Grigg, P. J. *Prejudice and Judgment*. London: Jonathan Cape, 1948.

Haight, John McVicker, Jr. "Franklin D. Roosevelt and a Naval Quarantine of Japan." *Pacific Historical Review* 40 (May 1971): 203–26.

Halder, General Franz. *The Private War Journal of General Halder, 1939–1942*. Edited and translated by Arnold Lissance. 9 vols. Washington, D.C.: Library of Congress, 1966.

Halifax, Lord. *Fullness of Days*. New York: Dodd, Mead & Co., 1957.

Hall, H. Duncan. *North American Supply. History of the Second World*

War. United Kingdom Civil Series: War Production Series. London: Her Majesty's Stationery Office, 1955.

Hankey, Maurice. *Diplomacy by Conference.* New York: G. P. Putnam's Sons, 1946.

Heinrichs, Waldo, Jr. "The Role of the United States Navy." In *Pearl Harbor as History: Japanese-American Relations, 1931–1941*, edited by Dorothy Borg and Shumpei Okamota. New York: Columbia University Press, 1973.

Hore-Belisha, Leslie. *The Private Papers of Hore-Belisha.* Edited by R. J. Minney. London: Collins, 1960.

Hull, Cordell. *The Memoirs of Cordell Hull.* 2 vols. New York: Macmillan Co., 1958.

Hyde, Harford Montgomery. *Room 3603.* New York: Farrar, Straus & Giroux, 1963.

Ickes, Harold L. *The Secret Diary of Harold L. Ickes.* Vol. 2, *The Inside Struggle, 1936–1939.* Vol. 3, *The Lowering Clouds, 1939–1941.* New York: Simon and Schuster, 1954.

Ismay, Hastings Lionel. *The Memoirs of General the Lord Ismay.* London: William Heinemann, 1960.

Jacob, General Sir Ian. "Churchill as a War Leader." In *Churchill by His Contemporaries*, edited by Charles Eade. London: Reprint Society, 1953.

Johnson, Ethel M. "The Mr. Winant I Knew." *South Atlantic Quarterly* 48 (January 1949): 24–41.

Johnson, Franklyn. *Defense by Committee.* London: Oxford University Press, 1960.

Johnson, Walter. *William Allen White's America.* New York: Henry Holt & Co., 1947.

Jones, Thomas. *A Diary with Letters.* London: Oxford University Press, 1954.

Jowett, Sir William Allen. *Some Were Spies.* London: Hodder & Stoughton, 1954.

Kennedy, General Sir John. *The Business of War.* London: William Morrow & Co., 1957.

Kimball, Warren. *The Most Unsordid Act: Lend-Lease, 1939–1941.* Baltimore: Johns Hopkins University Press, 1969.

King, Admiral Ernest J., and Whitehill, Walter M. *Fleet Admiral King: A Naval Record.* New York: W. W. Norton & Co., 1952.

Kittredge, Tracy B. "Muddle before Pearl Harbor." *U.S. News and World Report*, 3 December 1954, pp. 52–63 et seq.

———. *Naval Lessons of the Great War.* Garden City, N.Y.: Doubleday, Page and Co., 1921.

Knox, Dudley. *The Eclipse of American Seapower.* New York: Army-Navy Journal, 1922.

Langer, William L., and Gleason, S. Everett. *The World Crisis and American Foreign Policy.* 2 vols. Vol. 1, *The Challenge to Isolation, 1937–1940.* Vol. 2, *The Undeclared War, 1940–1941.* New York: Harper & Brothers, 1952, 1953.

Lee, Bradford A. *Britain and the Sino-Japanese War, 1937–1939.* Stanford, Calif.: Stanford University Press, 1973.

Lee, Raymond E. *The London Journal of General Raymond E. Lee.* Edited by James R. Leutze. Boston: Little, Brown & Co., 1971.

Liddell Hart, Sir Basil H. "Churchill in War." *Encounter* 26 (April 1966): 14–22.

————. *The German Generals Talk.* New York: William Morrow & Co., 1967.

————. *The History of the Second World War.* New York: G. P. Putnam's Sons, 1971.

————. *The Liddell Hart Memoirs.* 2 vols. New York: G. P. Putnam's Sons, 1966.

Loewenheim, Francis; Langley, Harold D.; and Jonas, Manfred, eds. *Roosevelt and Churchill: Their Secret Wartime Correspondence.* New York: Saturday Review Press, 1975.

Long, Breckinridge. *The War Diary of Breckinridge Long.* Edited by Fred L. Israel. Lincoln: University of Nebraska Press, 1966.

Looper, Robert B. "Franklin D. Roosevelt and the British Empire." *Occidente* 12 (July 1956): 348–63; (October 1956): 424–36.

McCormick, Donald. *The Mask of Merlin.* New York: Holt, Rinehart & Winston, 1964.

McIntire, Vice Admiral Ross T. *White House Physician.* New York: G. P. Putnam's Sons, 1949.

McLachlan, Donald. *Room 39: Wherein Took Place the Exciting Story of British Naval Intelligence in World War II.* New York: Atheneum Publishers, 1968.

Macleod, Iain. *Neville Chamberlain.* New York: Atheneum Publishers, 1962.

Matloff, Maurice. "Prewar Military Plans and Preparations, 1939–1941." *United States Naval Institute Proceedings* 79 (July 1953): 741–48.

Matloff, Maurice, and Snell, Edward M. *Strategic Planning for Coalition Warfare, 1941–1942.* United States Army in World War II. Washington, D.C.: Department of the Army, 1953.

May, Ernest. "The Development of Political-Military Consultation in the United States." *Political Science Quarterly* 70 (June 1955): 161–80.

Medlicott, W. N. *The Economic Blockade.* 2 vols. London: Her Majesty's Stationery Office, 1952, 1959.

Moffat, Jay Pierrepont. *The Moffat Papers, 1919–1943.* Edited by Nancy H. Hooker. Cambridge, Mass.: Harvard University Press, 1956.

Monger, George. *The End of Isolation.* London: Thomas Nelson & Sons, 1963.

Mooney, James D. "War or Peace in America." *Saturday Evening Post,* 3 August 1940, pp. 29 et seq.

Moran, Lord. *Churchill: Taken from the Diaries of Lord Moran.* Boston: Houghton Mifflin Co., 1966.

Morgenthau, Henry, Jr. *From the Morgenthau Diaries*. Edited by John M. Blum. Vol. 1, *Years of Crisis, 1928–1938*. Vol. 2, *Years of Urgency, 1938–1941*. Boston: Houghton Mifflin Co., 1959, 1965.

———. "The Story behind Lend-Lease." Part 4, "The Morgenthau Diaries." *Colliers*, 18 October 1947, pp. 16–17 et seq.

Morison, Elting E. *Admiral Sims and the Modern American Navy*. Boston: Houghton Mifflin Co., 1942.

———. *Turmoil and Tradition*. Boston: Houghton Mifflin Co., 1960.

Morison, Samuel Eliot. *The History of United States Naval Operations in World War II*. 15 vols. Vol. 1, *The Battle of the Atlantic, September 1939–May 1943*. Vol. 3, *The Rising Sun in the Pacific, 1931–April 1942*. Boston: Little, Brown & Co., 1947, 1948.

———. *Strategy and Compromise*. Boston: Little, Brown & Co., 1958.

Morton, H. V. *Atlantic Meeting*. New York: Dodd, Mead & Co., 1943.

Morton, Louis B. "Germany First." In *Command Decisions*, edited by Kent Roberts Greenfield. Washington, D.C.: U.S. Government Printing Office, 1960.

———. *The War in the Pacific: Strategy and Command*. United States Army in World War II. Washington, D.C.: Department of the Army, 1962.

———. "War Plan ORANGE: Evolution of a Strategy." *World Politics* 11 (January 1959): 221–50.

Mowrer, Edgar Ansel. *Triumph and Turmoil*. New York: Weybright and Talley, 1968.

Murphy, Robert. *Diplomat among Warriors*. Garden City, N.Y.: Doubleday & Co., 1964.

Neumann, William L. "Franklin Delano Roosevelt: A Disciple of Admiral Mahan." *United States Naval Institute Proceedings* 78 (July 1952): 713–19.

Nicolson, Harold. *Diaries and Letters, 1930–1939*. Edited by Nigel Nicolson. Vol. 2, *The War Years, 1939–45*. New York: Atheneum Publishers, 1967.

O'Connor, Raymond G. *Perilous Equilibrium: The United States and the London Naval Conference of 1930*. Lawrence: University Press of Kansas, 1962.

Palmer, Frederick. *Newton D. Baker: America at War*. 2 vols. New York: Dodd, Mead & Co., 1931.

Pelz, Stephen E. *Race to Pearl Harbor: The Failure of the Second London Naval Conference and the Onset of World War II*. Cambridge, Mass.: Harvard University Press, 1974.

Perkins, Frances. *The Roosevelt I Knew*. New York: Viking Press, 1946.

Phillips, William. *Ventures in Diplomacy*. Boston: Beacon Press, 1953.

Pogue, Forrest C. *George C. Marshall*. Vol. 2, *Ordeal and Hope*. New York: Viking Press, 1966.

Pratt, Lawrence. "Anglo-American Naval Conversations on the Far East of January 1938." *International Affairs* 47 (October 1972): 745–63.

Quinlan, Robert J. "The United States Fleet: Diplomacy, Strategy and the Allocation of Ships (1940–1941)." In *American Civil-Military Decisions: A Book of Case Studies*, edited by Harold Stein. Birmingham: University of Alabama Press, 1963.

Reagan, Michael D. "The Far Eastern Crisis of 1932: Stimson, Hoover and the Armed Services." In *American Civil-Military Decisions: A Book of Case Studies*, edited by Harold Stein. Birmingham: University of Alabama Press, 1963.

Rauch, Basil. *Roosevelt: From Munich to Pearl Harbor*. New York: Creative Age Press, 1950.

Richardson, Admiral James O. *On the Treadmill to Pearl Harbor: The Memoirs of Admiral J. O. Richardson*. Edited by Admiral George C. Dyer. 2 vols. Washington, D.C.: U.S. Government Printing Office, 1973.

Roosevelt, Elliott. *As He Saw It*. New York: Duell, Sloan and Pearce, 1946.

Roosevelt, Franklin Delano. *F. D. R.: His Personal Letters*. Edited by Elliott Roosevelt. 4 vols. New York: Duell, Sloan and Pearce, 1947–50.

————. "Our Foreign Policy." *Foreign Affairs* 6 (July 1928): 373–86.

————. *The Public Papers and Addresses of Franklin D. Roosevelt*. Introduction by President Roosevelt. Edited by Samuel I. Rosenman. 13 vols. Vol. 8, *War—and Neutrality, 1939*, and Vol. 9, *War—and Aid to Democracies, 1940* (New York: Macmillan Co., 1941); Vol. 10, *The Call to Battle Stations, 1941* (New York: Harper & Brothers, 1950).

Roskill, Stephen W. *British Naval Policy between the Wars*. 2 vols. Vol. 1, *The Period of Anglo-American Antagonism, 1919–1929*; Vol. 2, *The Period of Reluctant Rearmament, 1930–1939*. New York: Walker & Co., 1969, 1976.

————. *The War at Sea, 1939–1945*. 3 vols. Vol. 1, *The Defensive*; Vol. 2, *The Period of Balance*; Vol. 3, *The Offensive*. United Kingdom Military Series. London: Her Majesty's Stationery Office, 1954–56.

Schlesinger, Arthur M., Jr. *The Age of Roosevelt*. 3 vols. Vol. 2, *The Coming of the New Deal*. Vol. 3, *The Politics of Upheaval*. Boston: Houghton Mifflin Co., 1959, 1967.

Schroder, Paul W. *The Axis Alliance and Japanese-American Relations, 1941*. Ithaca, N.Y.: Cornell University Press, 1958.

Scott, William E. "Neville Chamberlain and Munich: Two Aspects of Power." In *The Responsibility of Power*, edited by Leonard Krieger and Fritz Stern. Garden City, N.Y.: Doubleday & Co., 1967.

Sherwood, Robert E. *Roosevelt and Hopkins: An Intimate History*. Rev. ed. New York: Harper & Brothers, 1948.

Slessor, Air Marshal Sir John C. *The Central Blue*. New York: Frederick A. Praeger, 1957.

Smith, Janet Adam. *John Buchan*. London: Rupert Hart-Davis, 1965.

Smith, R. Harris. *OSS: The Secret History of America's First Central Intelligence Agency*. Berkeley: University of California Press, 1972.

Snell, John S. *Illusion and Necessity: The Diplomacy of Global War, 1939–45.* Boston: Houghton Mifflin Co., 1963.

Snow, C. P. *Variety of Men.* New York: Charles Scribner's Sons, 1967.

Sprout, Harold, and Sprout, Margaret. *The Rise of American Naval Power.* Princeton, N.J.: Princeton University Press, 1939.

Stein, Harold, ed. *American Civil-Military Decisions: A Book of Case Studies.* Birmingham: University of Alabama Press, 1963.

Stettinius, Edward R., Jr. *Lend-Lease Weapon for Victory.* New York: Macmillan Co., 1944.

Stevenson, William. *A Man Called Intrepid: The Secret War.* New York: Harcourt Brace Jovanovich, 1976.

Stimson, Henry L. *The Far Eastern Crisis.* New York: Harper & Brothers, 1936.

Stimson, Henry L., and Bundy, McGeorge. *On Active Service in Peace and War.* New York: Harper & Brothers, 1947.

Strunk, Mildred. *Public Opinion, 1935–1946.* Edited by Hadley Cantril. Princeton, N.J.: Princeton University Press, 1951.

Sylvester, Albert James. *The Real Lloyd George.* London: Cassell & Co., 1947.

Tansill, Charles C. *Back Door to War: The Roosevelt Foreign Policy, 1933–1941.* Chicago: Henry Regnery Co., 1952.

Taylor, A. J. P. *English History, 1914–1945.* Vol. 15 of *The Oxford History of England*, edited by Sir George Clark. New York: Oxford University Press, 1965.

Templewood, Sir Samuel Hoare. *Nine Troubled Years.* London: Collins, 1954.

Thompson, Reginald William. *The Yankee Marlborough.* London: George Allen & Unwin, 1963.

Tugwell, Rexford. "The Compromising Roosevelt." *Western Political Quarterly* 6 (June 1953): 320–41.

Wallace, William V. "Roosevelt and British Appeasement, 1938." *Bulletin of the British Association for American Studies* 5 (December 1962): 4–30.

Watson, Mark S. *Chief of Staff, Prewar Plans and Preparations.* United States Army in World War II. Washington, D.C.: Department of the Army, 1950.

Watt, Donald C. *Personalities and Policies.* Notre Dame, Ind.: University of Notre Dame Press, 1965.

Wedemeyer, Albert C. *Wedemeyer Reports.* New York: Henry Holt & Co., 1958.

Welles, Sumner. *Seven Decisions That Shaped History.* New York: Harper & Brothers, 1951.

———. *The Time for Decision.* London: Hamish Hamilton, 1944.

Whalen, Richard J. *The Founding Father.* New York: New American Library, 1964.

Wheeler, Gerald E. *Admiral William Veazie Pratt, U.S. Navy: A Sailor's Life.* Washington, D.C.: U.S. Government Printing Office, 1974.

Wheeler-Bennett, Sir John. *King George VI.* London: St. Martin's Press, 1958.

Williamson, Samuel R., Jr. *The Politics of Grand Strategy: Britain and France Prepare for War, 1904–1914.* Cambridge, Mass.: Harvard University Press, 1969.

Wilson, Theodore. *The First Summit.* Boston: Houghton Mifflin Co., 1969.

Winant, John G. *Letter from Grosvenor Square.* London: Hodder & Stoughton, 1947.

Woodward, Sir E. L. *British Foreign Policy in the Second World War.* London: Her Majesty's Stationery Office, 1962.

————. *British Foreign Policy in the Second World War.* 3 vols. London: Her Majesty's Stationery Office, 1970.

Woodward, Sir E. L., and Butler, Rohan, eds. *Documents on British Foreign Policy, 1919–1939.* London: Her Majesty's Stationery Office, 1946– .

Young, Kenneth. *Churchill and Beaverbrook.* New York: William Heinemann, 1966.

Index

British strategy in the Far East, 189–90, 212–13, 217; and preparations for ABC Conference, 211–12

Pratt, Captain W. V., 20

Prince of Wales, 262

Prinz Eugen, 258

Purnell, Captain W. R., 172, 263–65

Fleet transfer, 89, 99, 107, 108–9, 115–16, 118–19, 120, 123, 126; Roosevelt's attempts to circumvent or deceive, 108–9, 115–16, 120, 239–40, 249; attitude toward staff conversations, 147; and possible declaration of war, 190, 263; and Lend-Lease Bill, 217–18, 240, 247

United States Fleet, 77, 255; based at Pearl Harbor, 82, 180–82, 219; British desire to have based at Singapore, 156, 202, 234–35; activities of, 226, 227; Atlantic Fleet to be buttressed by units from, 229

United States Marines, 135

United States Navy: assumes increasing responsibility in Atlantic, 4, 43, 52, 199, 238, 239–40, 255–58, 262; Scouting Force transferred to Pacific, 5; expansion of, 6, 14, 30, 118; decentralized administrative structure of, 6, 13, 184; favors offensive strategy in Pacific, 11–12, 17, 29–30, 87; Roosevelt proposes to blockade Japan with, 24; and security of Australia and New Zealand, 35–36; major fleet units moved to West Coast, 36; effect of Leahy-Hampton conversations on, 40; and RAINBOW, 40–41; rivalry with U.S. Army, 41; and Atlantic neutrality patrol, 43, 52; and *Admiral Graf Spee* incident, 52; observers with Royal Navy, 64; and radar development, 65; Roosevelt's view of Atlantic role of, 84; and Singapore, 130, 189–90, 206, 234–35, 241–42; Bailey Committee's ideas about, 134–35; Ghormley's problem in representing the views of, 175; assumes leadership on national security planning, 179; and Plan D, 193, 195–96; and ABC Conference, 223, 229–30, 231–32, 238, 239–40, 245; wanted no responsibility for Far

East, 246; and escort of convoys in Atlantic, 255–59. *See also* Asiatic Fleet, U.S.; Atlantic Fleet, U.S.; Navy Department, U.S.; Pacific Fleet, U.S.; United States Fleet

United States Task Force, 257

U.S.-U.K.-Dutch Technical Conversations, 172

V
Vansittart, Sir Robert, 104, 165
Vinson Act, 30
Vinson-Trammel Act, 5

W
Walsh, Senator David I., 121
War Cabinet, British, 79–80, 105, 106, 116–17, 124, 170, 223
War Department, U.S., 77
War Office, British, 96, 254
War Plans Division, U.S. Army, 202, 209
War Plans Division, U.S. Navy, 130, 183, 186
Washington Conference, 4
Wasp, 157
Watson-Watt, Sir Robert, 68–69
Wehrmacht, 154
Welles, Sumner, 26, 28, 34–35, 78, 180–81; and staff conversations, 16, 17, 18, 165; and Japanese actions in China, 24–25; and neutrality patrol, 44; and Donovan mission, 102; and Destroyer-Bases-Fleet transfer, 109, 112, 116, 119, 121; excluded from ABC Conference, 221
West Indies, 95
Wheeler, Senator Burton K., 257, 258
White, William Allen, 108–9, 115–16
Willkie, Wendell, 108–9, 115–16, 117, 164
Willson, Captain Russell, 31–32, 33
Wilson, Woodrow, 17